PHYLLIDA BARLOW

PHYLLIDA BARLOW

COLLECTED LECTURES WRITINGS AND INTERVIEWS

EDITED BY
SARA HARRISON

Hauser & Wirth Publishers

CONTENTS

FOREWORD

PROLOGUE

LECTURES AND WRITINGS

CONVERSATIONS AND INTERVIEWS

ON DRAWING

ON TEACHING

ON OTHER ARTISTS

POSTSCRIPT

FOREWORD

Foreword

Sara Harrison, Editor

In 2019 Phyllida Barlow was invited to be a provocateur for the inaugural Yorkshire Sculpture Triennial, for which she provided a series of statements about sculpture, without indicating if they were aligned or at odds with her own thinking. With each assertion, counter-assertion, and query, the text reads like a manifesto simultaneously writing and unwriting itself as it evolves, suggesting an author buffeted by the constant noise and ever-shifting arguments that circle around her discipline. The assertions Barlow makes and questions she raises cover many of the topics addressed in both her work and her conversations and writings from throughout her career; for this reason this text, published here for the first time, has been chosen as the prologue to this book.

The guiding principle in selecting texts for this publication has been to honour the breadth of Barlow's interests and bring together her different voices, as lecturer, interviewee, and writer. Aiming to be comprehensive in scope, material published in disparate sources is collated alongside numerous recordings transcribed for the first time and previously unpublished material from Barlow's own archive. The content is divided into chapters, which group 'Lectures and Writings', 'Conversations and Interviews', and texts 'On Drawing', 'On Teaching', and 'On Other Artists'. There is some overlap (interviews about drawing and other artists, for example), but overall, these groupings emerged naturally to create a coherent and navigable whole.

The 'Lectures and Writings' are far ranging in their subject matter, from a talk on the impact of the New Generation and the influences of the 1960s, *Hearsay, Rumours, Bedsit Dreamers, and Art Begins Today* (2002), to an account of Barlow's first studio visit, at the age of six, in *Fragmented Memories* (2016). Many of the 'Conversations and Interviews' shed light on the thinking behind some of her major exhibitions of recent years while 'On Drawing' focuses on an activity that lies at the very core of her practice. Before the international recognition her work attained in the last decade, Barlow was well known and highly regarded as a teacher within the UK, and the chapter 'On Teaching' pays attention to her career in education, through two interviews and her account of a workshop in Pakistan in 1997. 'On Other Artists' covers writings about those she has known personally, as friend, colleague, student, or teacher, and those she has known solely through their work; Louise Bourgeois, a formative influence and figure of enduring interest is the topic of three different texts. Fascinating as interpretations of fellow artists' work, they are doubly interesting for the less explicit route they provide into understanding Barlow's own practice. The 'Postscript' is a recent account by Barlow of a childhood experience, which has fed into a new sculpture for an exhibition at Hauser & Wirth Los Angeles.

While Barlow's activity as an artist spans sixty years, except for one brief text about drawing from 1974, this collection covers the period from the mid-1990s onwards, with a heavy weighting towards the last decade. This time span reflects what has been preserved and archived but also the far greater opportunities and standing Barlow has enjoyed in later years.

Within each section the texts appear chronologically. The only exception is the very first entry in the first chapter, *For No Reason* (2019), which is the most recent. This is Barlow's most comprehensive lecture, transcribed and published here for the first time. In it she offers an overview of her interests, influences, and key projects and for this motive it has been pulled to the fore. As an extensively illustrated slide lecture, the images have necessarily been edited down, but the aim has been to adhere as closely as possible to its original content and structure.

Each text is preceded by a brief introduction that summarises its content, allowing readers to dip in and out and focus on their particular areas of interest. For entries that have been previously published or are available as an audio source, the information is given at the end of each piece; many of the texts are in print for the first time.

In the conversations and interviews there was a certain amount of conversational verbiage to be tidied up to enhance their smooth flow, but overall the informality of the original spoken format has been respected. Some texts have been edited to create a particular focus and others have been cut to avoid excessive repetition across the book as a whole. In selecting material for inclusion, the biggest challenge was deciding what to cull, and the deciding factor was by and large that the subject matter was covered adequately elsewhere. Some repetition has been permitted. Interviewers pose similar questions, eliciting similar answers. But more significantly the repetition acknowledges and allows us to understand Barlow's primary concerns and the consistency of her thinking and, more often than not, new angles and insights surface when a topic is revisited.

That much, even most, of Barlow's sculpture from throughout her career that was made prior to the last decade no longer exists is something she views with a notable lack of sentimentality. This absence does however render the need to preserve and collect her words and her thoughts all the more compelling. Whether a discussion of her own work or her life as a practising artist, a consideration of an art-historical moment or idea, a personal account of a formative experience or a study of a fellow artist, all the conversations and writings collected here add another layer: a snapshot of an artist's life and career, a context, a moment in time. These words greatly enrich our understanding and enjoyment of Barlow's work and are a testament to the passion to both make and debate sculpture that has driven her throughout her life.

When Barlow joined Hauser & Wirth in 2010, I was a senior director at the gallery in London, and we began working very closely together and continued to do so until I left at the end of 2018. Alongside my colleagues I supported her through many ambitious and exciting projects including the Tate Britain Commission (2014) and the British Pavilion at the Venice Biennale (2017). Passionate about her drawing archive, we collaborated on the exhibition *Phyllida Barlow: Fifty Years of Drawings* at Hauser & Wirth London (2014), and I edited the eponymous publication. I thoroughly enjoyed the close working relationship that developed during these years, the knowledge of her work and thinking that I acquired, and our enduring friendship.

First and foremost I wish to thank Phyllida for her trust and enthusiasm. It has been a real pleasure to research and compile this publication and to have the opportunity to study in depth her brilliant work and words. As with all my experiences of working together, the intelligence, good humour, and generosity Phyllida brings makes any collaboration deeply rewarding and thoroughly enjoyable. On numerous occasions Michaela Unterdörfer and I spoke of the 'need' to make this book, and I would like to thank Michaela for her commitment to this project. I thank Jennifer Magee and Stefan Zebrowski-Rubin for all their hard work, expertise, and encouragement in realising it, with further thanks to Rosa Bacile, Elly Hawley, Mélanie Letoré, Sophie Treharne Nurse, and Madeline Warren. Thank you to Tas Skorupa for his guidance and copy-editing, and to Elizabeth McLean for her flexibility and creativity in designing this book. I am grateful to Manuela and Iwan Wirth and Marc Payot for supporting this publication, and I wish to thank all those who have granted permission for their work to be reproduced here, as text or image. Lastly, I would like to thank Joel Croxson for all his invaluable advice, encouragement, and support.

PROLOGUE

Invited to be a provocateur for the first Yorkshire Sculpture International in 2019, Barlow wrote a series of statements about sculpture, without indicating whether they were aligned with her own views or not. For its overarching theme, the festival chose 'Sculpture is the most anthropological of the art forms'.

Provocations for the Yorkshire Sculpture Triennial

2018

The statements below have emerged from the two meetings I attended with all those involved in the Triennial.

The statements reflect my own concerns as well as addressing issues which arose from the meetings.

There are two sets of statements; I have not indicated whether I agree with the statements or not.

1

- It is pointless to define what sculpture is.
- Anything can be sculptural – weather, speech, smell, temperature, darkness, light, invisibility, reflections, movement, stillness, silence, noise, chaos, order …
- All these qualities have become art and have been used as art.
- There are no surprises.
- Rothko paintings are sculptural.
- Nauman walking around his studio (video) is sculptural.
- Bernini's *Ecstasy of Saint Teresa* is film and not sculpture.
- What is 'work', 'labour', 'effort' in relationship to 'making'?
- Do moral attitudes to the above, and to the handmade, impede?
- All ways of making involve the handmade.
- There is no difference between the handmade and the fabricated/manufactured.
- Everything is appropriated.
- It is not interesting to be obsessed by invented form.
- What is invented form?
- Sculpture's silent and motionless character does not reflect the times we live in – politically, environmentally, economically, socially.

- Subject, Form, and Content dominate all creative processes.
- 'Subject' has been the dominant concern for the past three decades.
- 'Subject' has itself become dominated by 'issues' – gender, sexuality, abuse, ethnicity, race, class, economics.
- Issues of war, migration, immigration, refugees are too important not to be major concerns for artists today.
- It is not viable to make art where 'content' and 'form' are more important than 'subject'.
- The beauty of sculpture is its relationship to failure.
- The failure of sculpture is rooted in its obduracy.
- Sculpture changes the spaces it inhabits.
- Everything changes the space it inhabits.
- Sculpture must be more concerned with time than image.
- Image destroys sculpture.
- Sculpture fails because it will always be an image.
- Truth is a fallacy in art.
- In particular, truth is a fallacy in sculpture.
- Lies, and how to lie, are a powerful imaginative force for both artist and viewer.

2

- 'Documentary' is an art genre that goes back to prehistory.
- 'Documentary' as an art genre includes history painting, portraits, memorials, commemorations, performance, film/video, cave drawings.
- 'Modernism' is dominated by moral attitudes of good/bad, right/wrong.
- 'Authenticity' is the new morality.
- Sculpture is inherently inauthentic.
- Making is making a comeback!
- Making is not sculpture.
- Who cares if 'making' is sculpture or not?
- Art is evidence.
- Art is anthropological.
- Sculpture is the most anthropological of all the arts.
- Sculpture is as simple as digging a hole or cutting a slice of bread.
- Sculpture must not show, or tell, its labour.
- Sculpture must be effortless.

- Arte Povera changed attitudes to making more than Minimalism did.
- Arte Povera was European; Minimalism was American.
- Minimalism has edges; Arte Povera has no edges.
- Adorno refers to the shifting borders of Europe and how this influenced European culture.
- What is Yorkshire art?
- Themed exhibitions are a curse.
- Themed exhibitions are PhD-heavy.
- Themed exhibitions are more about the curators than the artists.
- Artists crave freedom.
- No, they don't.
- The word 'sculptor' no longer applies.
- Sculpture will not survive as a studio activity.
- Sculpture is too expensive and requires too much space for experimentation.
- Sculpture has become design.
- Sculpture will eventually always be made by fabricators.
- Sculpture is an old-fashioned medium entrenched in convention and orthodoxy.
- Challenge is always good.
- Belief is always dangerous.
- Is everyone an artist?
- Therefore, is everyone a sculptor?
- Many people have access to a pencil and a piece of paper.
- Many people have access to phones with photography and video applications.
- Not many people have access to a lump of clay.
- Everyone has imagination.

LECTURES AND WRITINGS

This lecture was given as the Townsend Memorial Lecture at the Slade School of Fine Art, London, on 5 November 2014 and then again as the Dasha Shenkman Lecture in Contemporary Art at the University of Guelph in Ontario, Canada, on 20 March 2019. A transcript of the second version is included here.

Structured in three parts, this lecture gives a succinct overview of the interests, concerns, and influences that have defined Barlow's career as a sculptor. She opens with some 'non-art' images, explaining their appeal, then moves through examples of her own work, connecting them to the verbs that inform or define her sculptural activity. In the second part she presents works by other artists who have been significant for her during the course of her career: Louise Bourgeois, Étienne Martin, Gilbert & George, Franz West, Michelangelo Pistoletto, Gian Lorenzo Bernini, Bruce Nauman, Walter De Maria, Jackie Winsor, Lucio Fontana, Barbara Hepworth, Jean Fautrier, Germaine Richier, David Smith, Claes Oldenburg, Marcel Duchamp, Alberto Giacometti, Lynda Benglis, and Robert Morris. She hones in on five works that are key for her by an unknown artist from around 20,000 BC, Eva Hesse, Pablo Picasso, Gordon Matta-Clark, and Louise Bourgeois. In the third part of the lecture she returns to her own work and outlines the thinking behind her exhibitions from the last decade and discusses how she was prompted to reassess her work after representing Britain at the Venice Biennale in 2017.

For No Reason

2019

I want to begin by, in a way, asking the question, What do I want this talk to be? And will it be of any interest when I do find out what I want it to be? Of any interest to you, because it's important that the lecture, the talk I'm about to give, is given to you. I have decades of work to show, and therefore making a choice of what to show was a challenge in itself. So this talk is a kind of investigation for me to perhaps learn something about myself in this very exposed situation. Therefore, in a way, it's going to be quite a private journey and quite a personal journey that I hope you will join me on.

So, I will begin with a few slides from thirty years ago – thirty, or even more than that – when I first started giving talks. I thought I would begin with that because, in a way, I think I'm an artist with quite a limited repertoire of things that I enjoy investigating, including materials.

I'll begin with these four images. This one is looking at the rubbish, the waste disposal unit in North London, places where all the domestic rubbish is tipped (fig. 1). It's about twice the size of this room. I went there in about 1988, and this image is from that. I was just intrigued by this huge ebb and flow of debris that's everywhere and what happens to it. How it's constantly being remodelled and reworked in some way. The whole process of how to deal with it intrigued me. Then the other image is taken up in Scotland of a cormorant caught in a slick of oil (fig. 2). And that, in a way, showed my fascination in spillage and where the edges of things are. Then, this is for me the opposite (fig. 3). This is a kind of ruined modernist building that I find intensely beautiful. It's really quite a recent structure, but its sense of dilapidation carries with it something that's very new as well. It's not an ancient thing. It's a new thing that's gradually falling into a state of disrepair. Yet, it's got this very, very sort of systematic way of being built that's very exposed, very structural. Then, the netting, which was a temporary structure down again in London, in King's Cross (fig. 4). That was when they were beginning to clear the King's Cross area into what is now a very sort of pseudo-glamorous, hideous, built-up area, with masses of apartments for sale, most of which are empty, which seems to be the way cities are going. They had all these temporary areas there. This was a golf course, so the nets were to stop the golf balls going over, but I thought it was a fantastic structure. So this play between things that have inherent structure compared with the idea of spillage and formlessness are qualities that have been fascinating me for years, and how sculpture can absorb those qualities.

Then the next set of slides have these **words at the bottom of them**, which is really, I suppose, where my fascination for sculpture lies, how it occupies those words. I think the kind of work I make is very non-verbal. And therefore, I talk a lot about it in contrast to it. It is a kind of way of trying to pursue something, trying to find how language can fit the acts of making, that in a way don't have an idea and don't have a thought, and certainly don't have a verbal language attached to them. But then finding these words that somehow associate themselves with how the work gets built is what these words at the bottom are about.

[**Floor, ground, store, place**.] I just used two examples here of where the floor and the ground are ... then how that relates to place and in a way it relates to something about the way things are stored. Those qualities: what happens to the underneath of the sculpture? What is its contact with the ground (figs. 5–6).

Then the acts of making and building the **upright**, the **stack**, the **heap** (fig. 7), and also the **spineless** object (fig. 8), the object that is just so amassed with stuff that it needs something else, like a skin thrown over it to hold it in place.

Next is **collapse, break, mend, wrong**. This work (fig. 9) is a whole heap of offcuts that were in my studio that I took to a quarry. I wove into the quarry these materials, in a way, mending the huge hole that was excavated out of the quarry, a kind of repair. Also the idea that the thing kept on collapsing into the hole and using that as a way of making. The small work I made at night (fig. 10), when the children were very young. I would go into the studio very late and collect materials around me, and turn the studio lights off and just produce these works really through the tactile experience. And in a way, the idea of something being wrong started to fascinate me, and I began to enjoy a kind of pleasure, anarchic pleasure. Maybe a work doesn't have to be either right or wrong – it can just be what it is.

[**Measure, organise, enclose**.] Then these are more about having a very particular need to make something have some kind of accuracy about it (figs. 11–12). So, where measurement comes in and organising comes in. Also the idea of things becoming enclosed through structures and through the use of measurement. So, the contrast between needing to be organised and measuring, versus things that have a certain inherent chaos about them, are still things that even today I enjoy very much playing one off against the other.

Next is **doing, quick, undoing, stretching**. Doing for me is essential. There's always the urgency to do. And that's really in a way what the title of this talk is: 'For No Reason'. Again, I think I'm an artist who doesn't have an

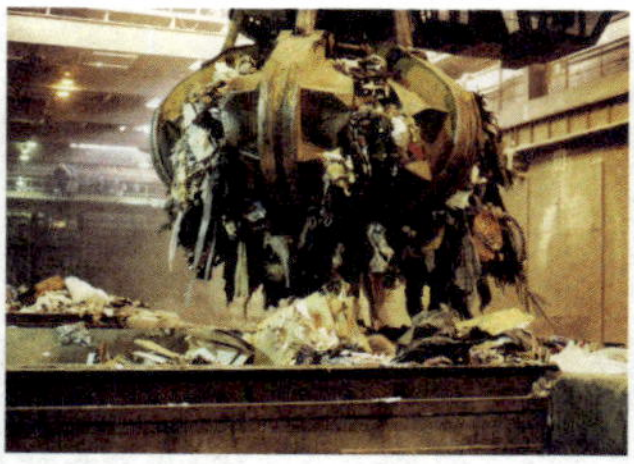

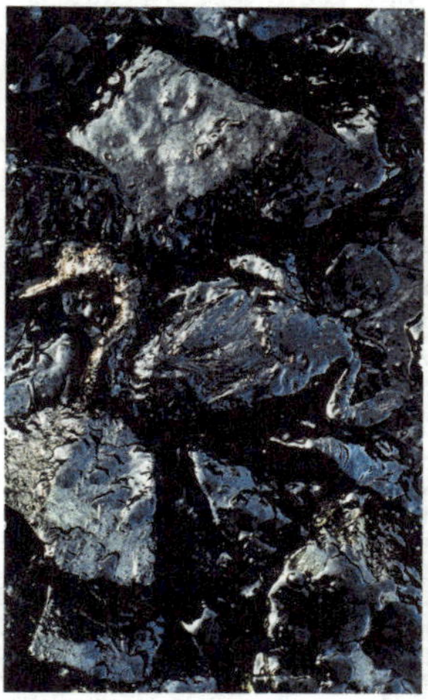

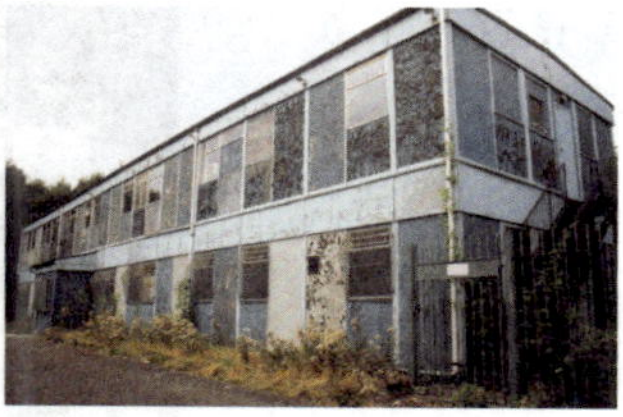

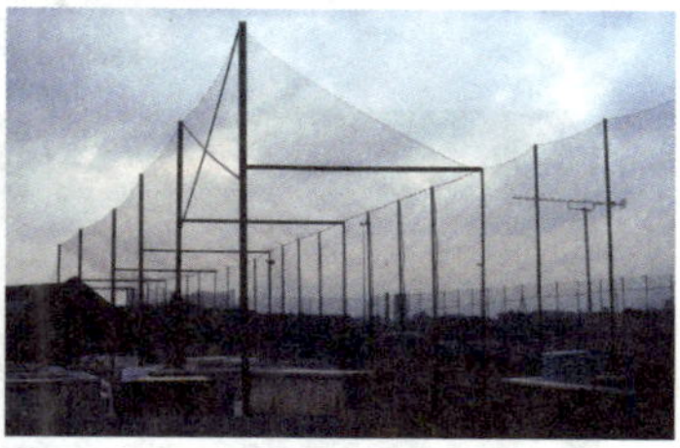

CLOCKWISE FROM ABOVE:
fig. 1 Waste disposal centre, North London
fig. 2 Cormorant in oil slick, Scotland
fig. 3 Ruined modernist building
fig. 4 Netting, King's Cross, London

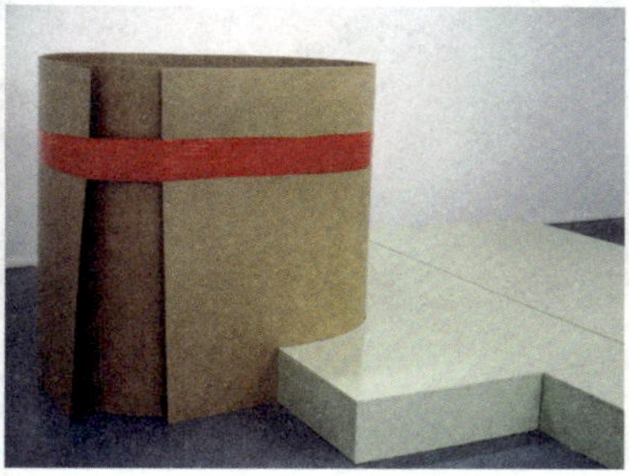

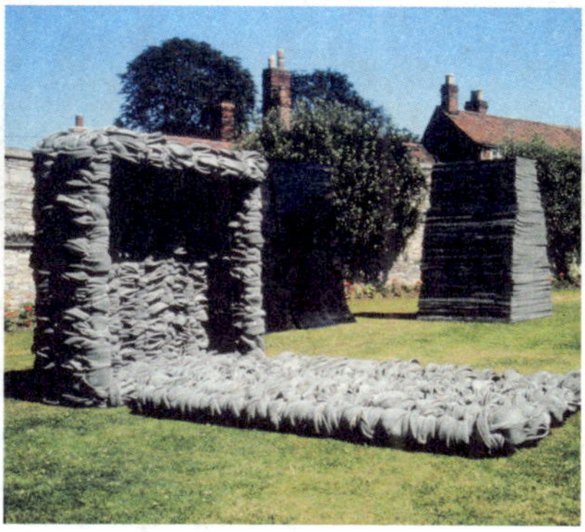

LEFT TO RIGHT:
fig. 5 Installation view, *Depot*, Museum of Installation, London, 1995
fig. 6 *untitled (four)* (detail), 1977

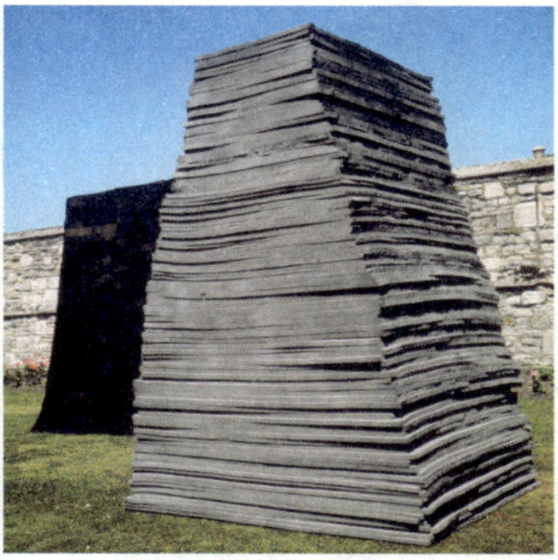

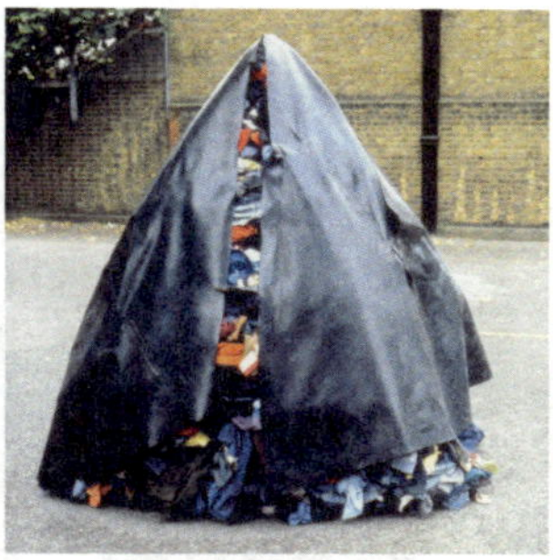

LEFT TO RIGHT:
fig. 7 *untitled (four)* (detail), 1977
fig. 8 *Strangers* (detail), 1985

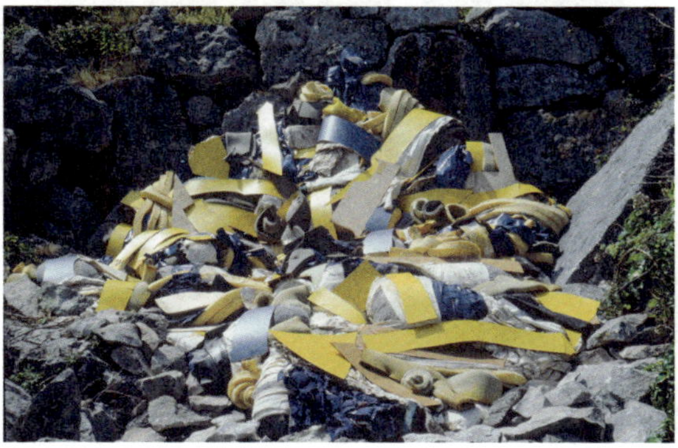

LEFT TO RIGHT:
fig. 9 *Fill* (detail), 1983
fig. 10 *Touchpiece III*, 1982

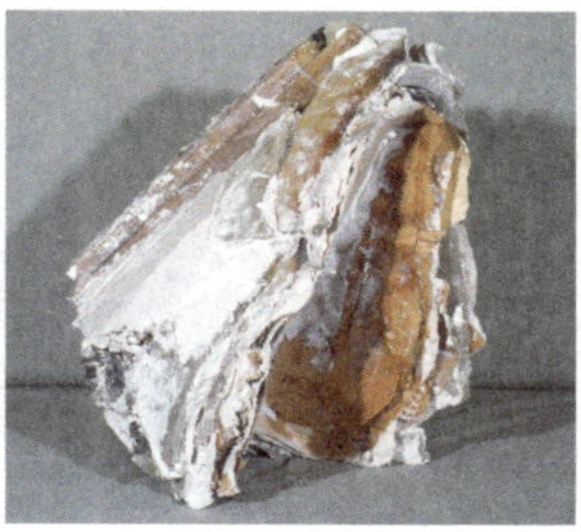

LEFT TO RIGHT:
fig. 11 *Landscape*, 1968
fig. 12 *Truce* (detail), 1997

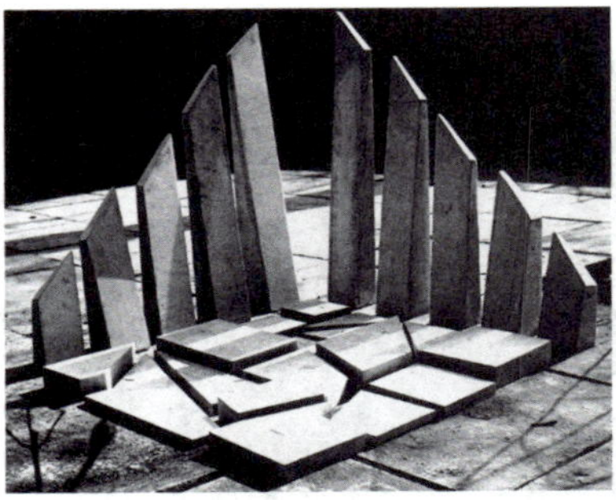

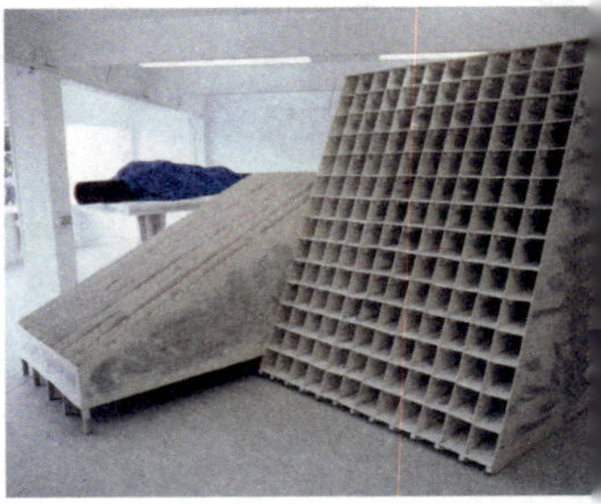

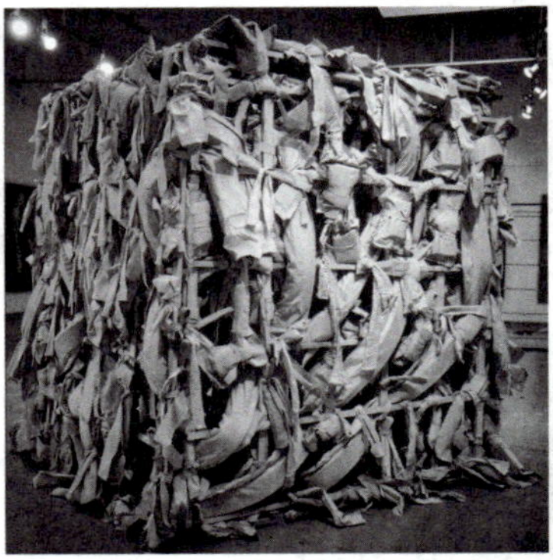

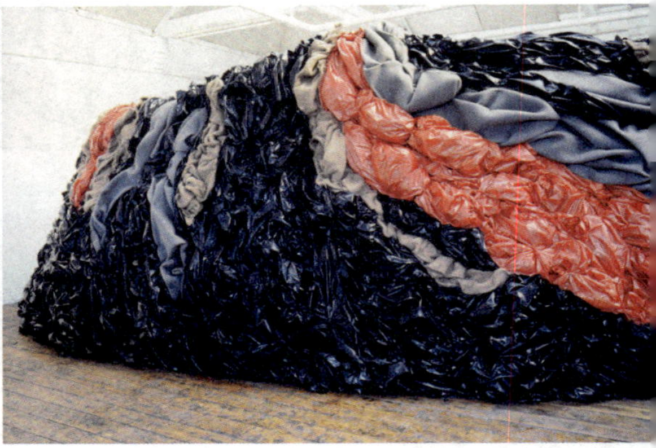

ABOVE LEFT TO RIGHT:
fig. 13 *Shedmesh*, 1975
fig. 14 *Expanse* (detail), 1987

BELOW:
fig. 15 *Truce* (detail), 1997
RIGHT:
fig. 16 *untitled: metropole* (detail), 2003

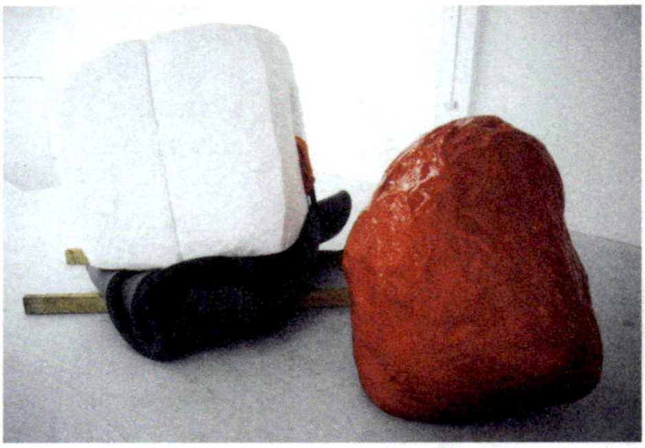

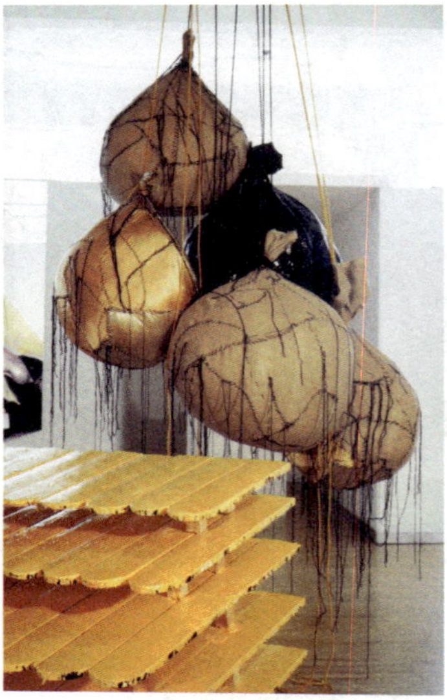

LEFT TO RIGHT:
fig. 17 *HOST I*, 1986–9
fig. 18 *smallwallwork: 3*, 2010

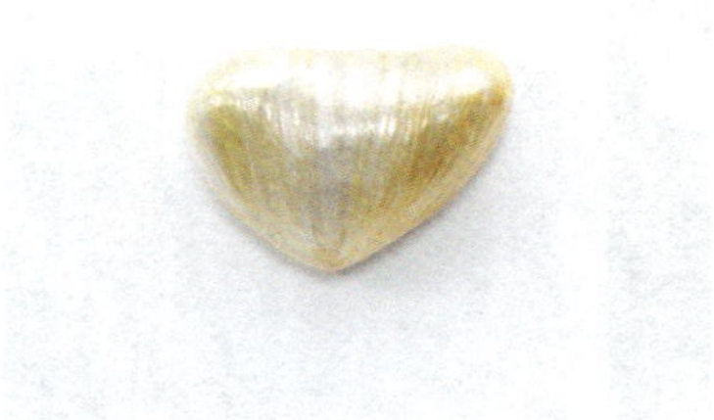

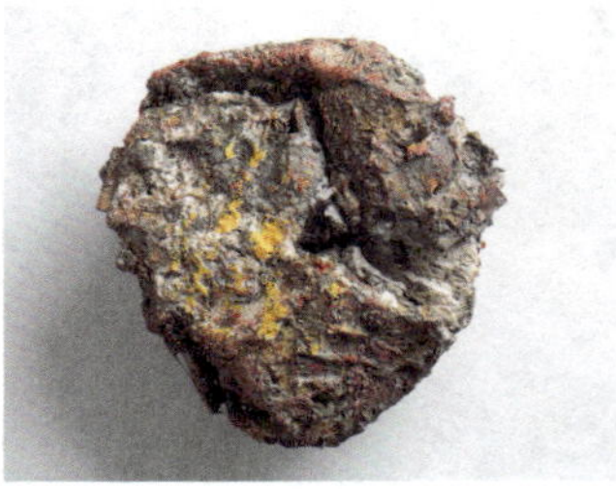

idea at the outset. A lot of the work doesn't have an idea. It has thoughts and it has a sort of speculative drive about it. But the actual idea that I know what the outcome will be, is very, very rare in my work. Therefore, the act of doing is the way that leads me to what the idea might be, and also a great pleasure in working quickly. I like the results to be there at the end of the day. I think that also comes from anyone who's got children. You've got those opportunities of a few hours to do something. My rule was that when I had those few hours I had to actually have a result at the end of that time. The tying work was made from something like a hundred discarded stretchers that were being chucked out of where I was teaching at Chelsea School of Art (fig. 13). I collected them and bound them all together with offcuts of canvas and upholstery foam to make this work. So, the actual way of making it and what it became were all very much feeding one into the other. The same with the next work – it was all materials I'd used before (fig. 14). I took them to the space, and they were filthy, so I started cleaning them. And as I was cleaning them, the stretching and pulling them out began to make the work take shape.

Drop, weigh, lazy, casual. I very much like the lazy gesture. And actually, the lazy gesture requires an enormous amount of organisation and exact precision to get it right. So, the lazy gesture might be something that's thrown over or something that's just rolled into place, or something placed on top of folded materials (fig. 15). But in order to get that kind of sense of informality, there is a precision involved. Weight I find intriguing. I like the fact that gravity is a material in sculpture just as much as spaces. That the way gravity has to be worked with and against means it's a very powerful companion alongside everything that one is doing with this kind of sculptural work. And it never goes away. It's always there pushing things over, making things sit in a peculiar way. Working with it and against it becomes a real force for the making of the work. Then, along with gravity, there comes a way of using it through dropping and letting things fall (fig. 16). And I think that's also part of a kind of a lazy gesture, which intrigues me.

These are small works. Alongside the large works, I do a lot of small works, and they're in a way the kind of kernel of how I work. They're the sort of very private encounter with making. These are **hold, pull, push, cover**. So, one of them is made of solid Sellotape wrapped round my left hand (fig. 17). And the other one was made out of plaster and scrim and all sorts of liquid-to-solid materials, which I love, that was wrapped around my right hand, so that there was this sense of making the act of making quite difficult in a way, and just seeing what that result was (fig. 18).

[**Approximate, not quite, could be**.] I think the idea of something being approximately right intrigues me (figs. 19–20). What is the exact way an object can be? Do I know? And the answer is no, I don't. Something can be not quite right or not quite there. But what that does for me is that it stimulates me to get on and make another one. I think it's a great driving energy for how I make work. So, all these objects here may be and could be adjusted in some way or changed in some way. And that idea of approximation, not only in how the object is made, but maybe what its origins are as well. What is it, where does it come from? That intrigues me.

Where, which is what this one is, was something that I became very, very involved with in the early 1990s, when I wasn't having any shows or exhibitions. I think that's always a very interesting time for an artist, and probably a time where an artist can really actually experience great freedom, if they have the financial resources to do so. To be non-visible, to be invisible and not showing, it leaves this enormous space to sort of wander wherever you like (fig. 21). And I began to think of where sculpture ends up, where artworks end up, and how they end up in people's homes, and what happens if the object is an uninvited guest, a kind of parasite to the domestic space and overwhelms that space (fig. 22). Is there also a way in which artworks can be very well behaved? And what happens if they're not? I like that idea of them, in a way, taking over the domestic space that they've been invited to, or maybe not invited to inhabit.

[**Now remember, forget again**.] Drawing is constant for me and very much about this idea of approximation (fig. 23). I like the way in which I can notice things very quickly and that becomes about remembering. So, drawings are about how I remember and what I remember and not about an exact replica of the world I live in. The way that remembering becomes erased gradually, and the drawings begin to take on their own autonomy. They begin to take on objects or images of objects that are things in their own right, and not just copies of things I've noticed in the world around. I think the speed at which I can, and any of us, can notice things intrigues me. That you can catch a glimpse of something and it becomes a very powerful image, or very powerful memory. And it may not be an image, and I think that's just as fascinating. It may be intense heat or intense cold, or smell, or touch, something that's utterly sentient. How does one draw that? And then, the way we can forget things as well, I think that becomes a very important part for me of drawing. What is the thing that remains? [...]

This is probably another kind of heart of this talk. Which is to talk about the artists that I've felt passionate about, and the kind of complexity of issues they've raised for me. First is the Louise Bourgeois, a wonderful piece (fig. 24). This is the plaster version of it made in 1968–9, and then repeated over and over again throughout her career. Often, just the top section of the work would be cast and then reused in all sorts of ways. And I like this idea that, in a way, it's a kind of monstrous form. It has maybe a sort of ugliness

LEFT TO RIGHT:
fig. 19 *Truce* (detail), 1997
fig.20 *Dawn till Dusk* (detail), 1999

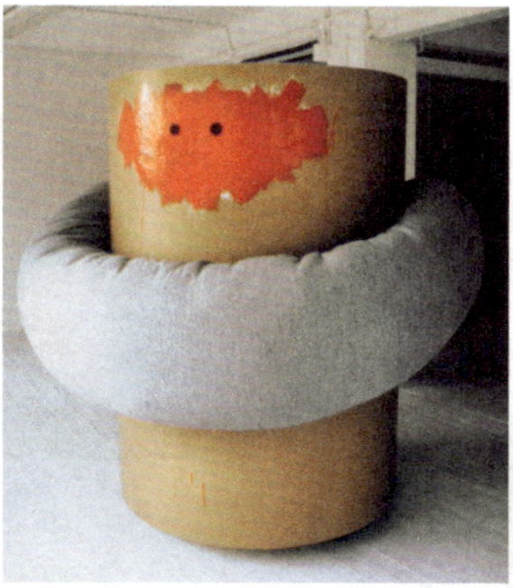

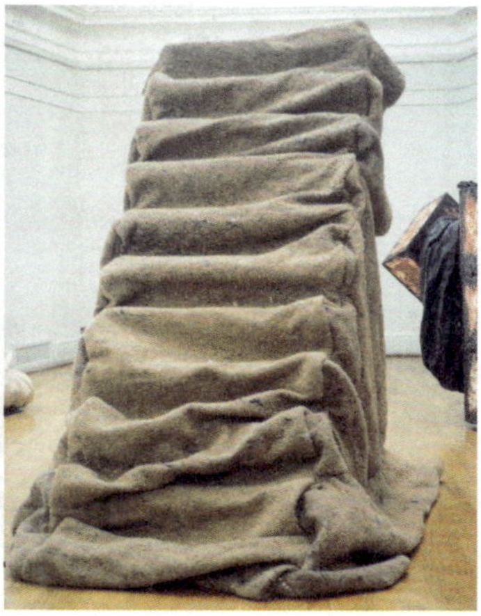

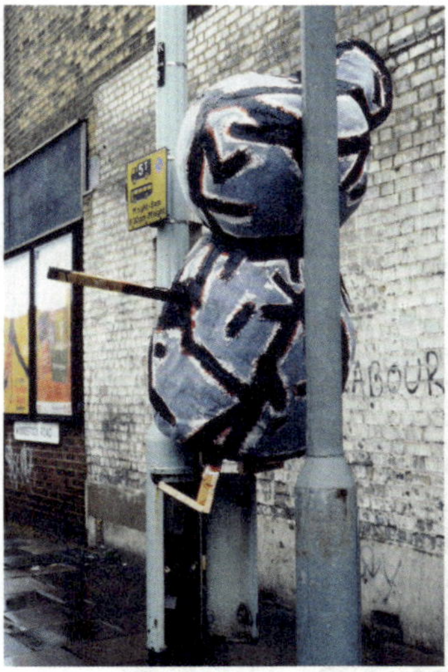

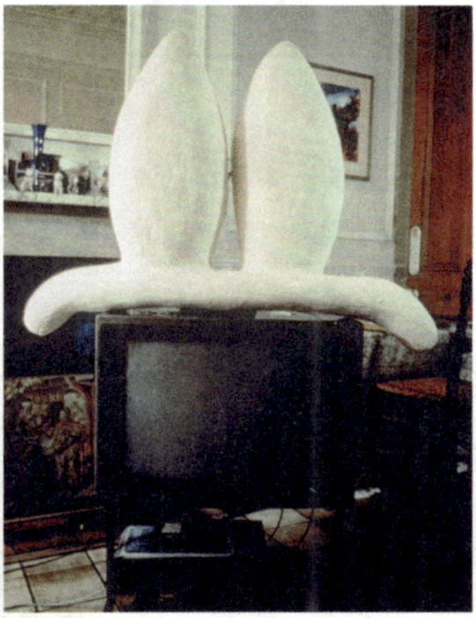

LEFT TO RIGHT:
fig. 21 *Object for a lamp post*, 1999
fig. 22 *Object for the television*, 1994

BELOW:
fig. 23 Installation view, *Phyllida Barlow: Bad Copies*, Henry Moore Institute, Leeds, 2012

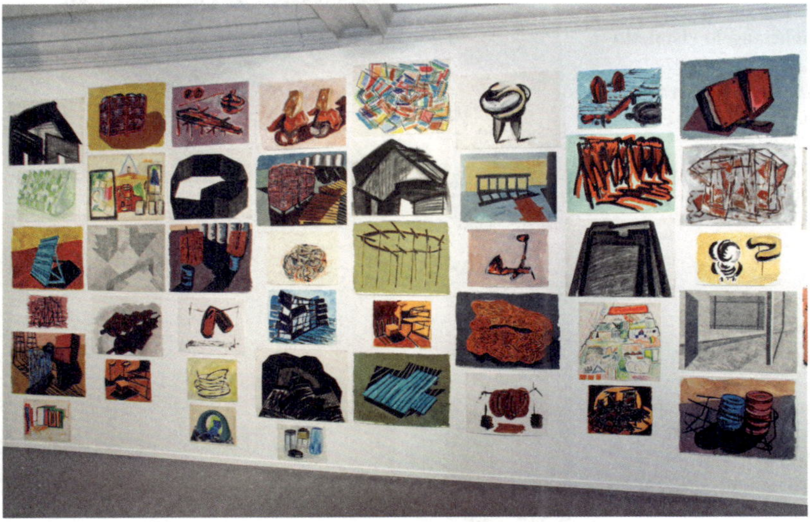

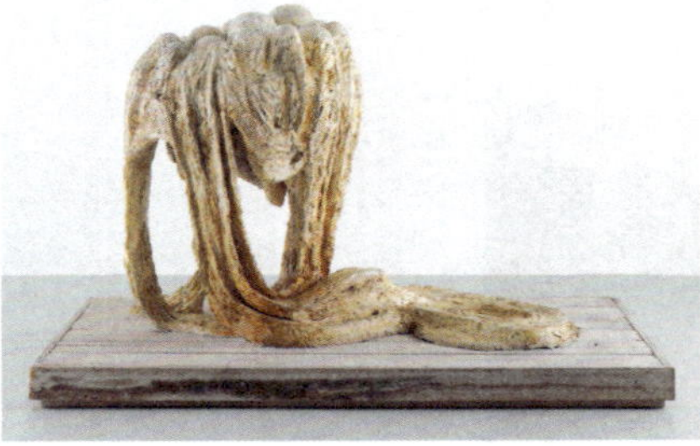

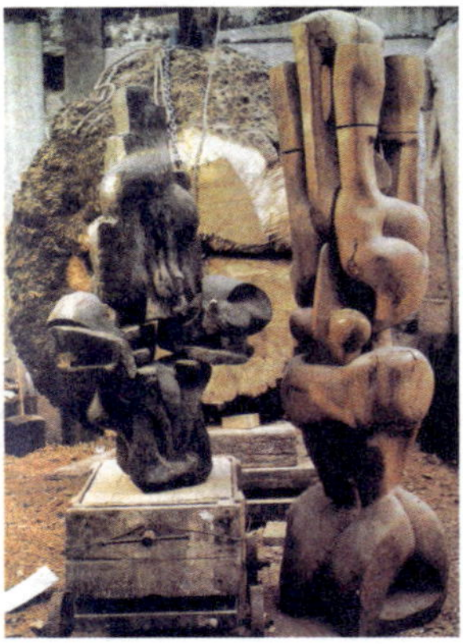

ABOVE LEFT TO RIGHT:
fig. 24 **Louise Bourgeois**
Avenza Revisited II, 1968–9
fig. 25 **Étienne Martin**
The Nina Night, 1950,
and *Large Couple*, 1946

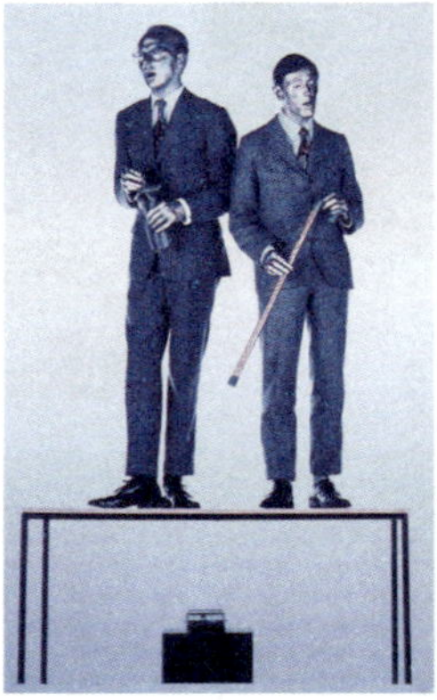

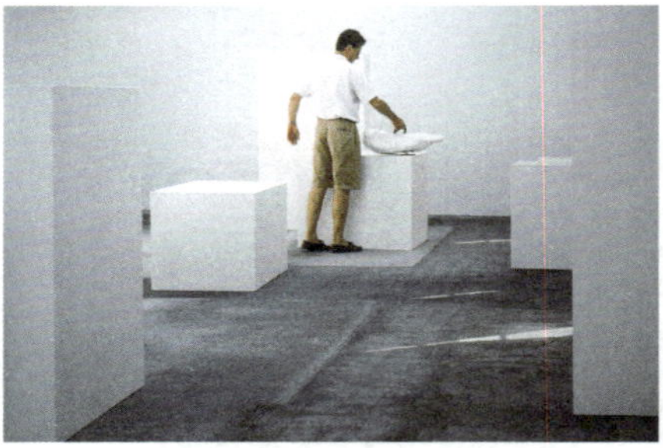

LEFT TO RIGHT:
fig. 26 **Gilbert & George**
Singing Sculpture, 1970
fig. 27 **Franz West**
3 or 17, 1992–3

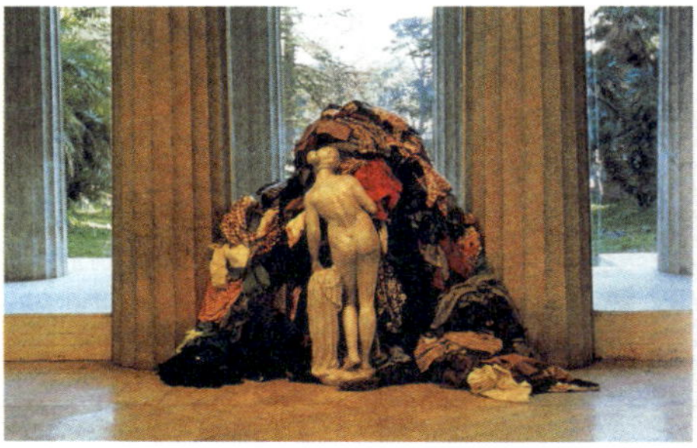

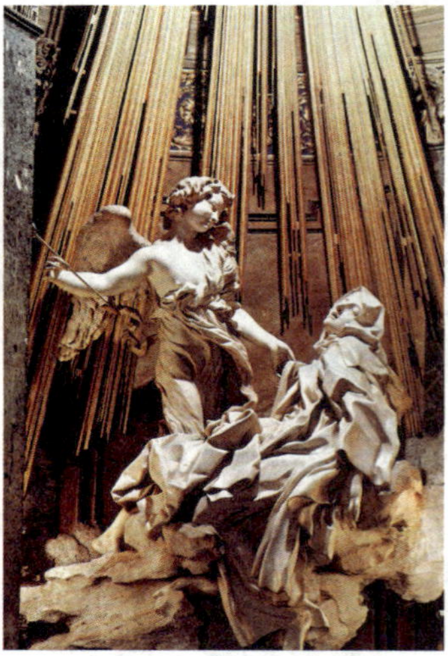

ABOVE LEFT TO RIGHT:
fig. 28 **Michelangelo Pistoletto**
Venus of the Rags, 1967/1974
fig. 29 **Gian Lorenzo Bernini**
Ecstasy of Saint Teresa, 1647–52

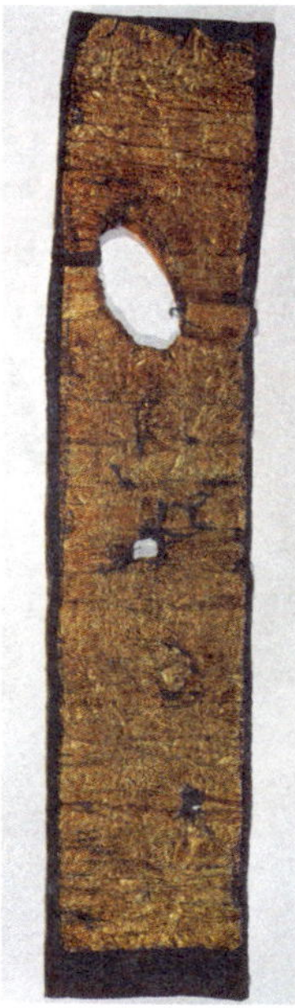

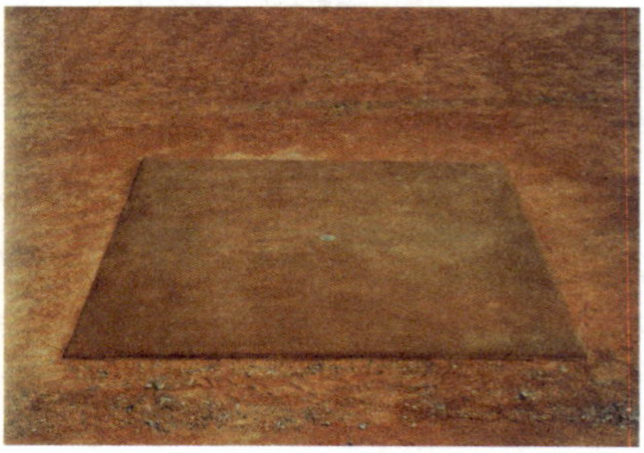

LEFT TO RIGHT:
fig. 30 **Bruce Nauman**
Collection of Various Flexible Materials Separated by Layers of Grease with Holes the Size of My Waist and Wrists, 1966
fig. 31 **Walter De Maria**
The Vertical Earth Kilometer, 1977

about it that she has made extremely beautiful. And then, the Étienne Martin, who was a French artist working during the 1930s, 1940s, and 1950s (fig. 25). His work, like a few others, represents the very resilient kind of sculpture that was being produced in Europe during that time and where, in a way, there was a tremendous belief system in what sculpture was and should be, its formal qualities, and also, in his case, extremely ugly shapes. I'd love to know who loves that work in this audience. If anyone is attracted to it. It was the kind of work that I turned against when I was a student in the 1960s, and I would not look at anything like this at all. Because what was beginning to happen was that sculpture was beginning to be taken apart in all sorts of ways and reinvented through a whole series of very fast movements that came in one after another. Sort of culminating, for me, in Arte Povera. This work represents the kind of antithesis of that, where it's still very rooted in craft and skill and technique.

Gilbert & George here, the Living Sculptures they called themselves, performing *Singing Sculpture* in 1970 (fig. 26), I think where the artist sits in the work … what is the work? That began to interest me as a sort of anarchic gesture that maybe sculpture was on the rocks and was being challenged in terms of what its actual role was. If you removed the skill and the technical aspects of sculpture, what were you left with and what would happen if the human being, the artist, took over that space and became the work itself? With Franz West's work, inviting the audience to actually take possession of the work (fig. 27). So this sort of challenging of sculpture as a fixed object intrigued me. […]

This is Michelangelo Pistoletto, his *Venus of the Rags* (fig. 28), and I think the comparison to Gian Lorenzo Bernini's *Ecstasy of Saint Teresa* (fig. 29) I find quite intriguing. The kind of culmination and, in a way, Pistoletto's sort of ironic take on great art. In fact all Arte Povera's undermining of the idea of great art was for me incredibly inspirational. That things could be gestural and direct and that the act of making was enough. It didn't need to be heroic in any way. That was removed. But I think despite that, I think the Bernini is just quite incredible. I'm not sure for me that it's sculpture. I think it's film and I think it's painting. There's something so extraordinarily ecstatic as its title infers about the moment that these two are caught. And certainly, Pistoletto's has no sense of that capture, but it has a great sense of gesture about it.

Bruce Nauman's piece for his waist and his wrists (fig. 30), again, I think is taking the idea of the object into the body and making it become this fragile skin. Walter De Maria's kilometre rod, where there's just the top of the rod showing through the earth, and yet it goes down one kilometre (fig. 31). These are sort of exploratory questions about sculpture, both as a sort of intimate, highly personal experience, and then inverting the monument into something that's hidden and invisible.

Nauman again (fig. 32), his enclosing of space through the unfinished and the incomplete, and a precarious sense of things in a state of balance and flux, but charging that interior space with such a dynamic invitation to enter them, while at the same time, keeping you out. That became a great influence on me of the occupation of space by sculpture. Jackie Winsor's bound shapes, in a way, the opposite to the Nauman. Tightly enclosing space, trapping it by these four objects.

Lucio Fontana's amazing sliced object (fig. 33). Sort of vicious in a way, in letting you ... There's something explosive about it. And Barbara Hepworth, the opposite, something very calm and still (fig. 34). But that sense of entering the form, penetrating the form to get within it, and in Hepworth's case then looking at the other side. Hepworth who, again, I took hugely against during the early 1960s, seeing her work as just pure craft and feeling that I really wanted to rebel against that. I think that's a certain kind of art-school training I had, not necessarily at Chelsea, which was a tremendously vibrant place in the early 1960s. But the Slade was a dark, gloomy place, and it didn't fulfil me really. On the second day of being at the Slade, Reg Butler, who was the distinguished Head of Sculpture, came up to me and said, 'I won't be talking to you very much, because by the time you're thirty, you'll be having babies and making jam.' And I had the good sense to say, 'What's wrong with that?' He didn't have much to say to that. But I think that atmosphere was still incredibly prevalent at that time, and something that needed to be overcome.

Although I took against British art, violently, seeing it as moral and corrective, during that same era, I was looking very much at European art. And artists like Jean Fautrier (fig. 35) and Germaine Richier (fig. 36) I've continued to love the whole time, because they seem to be doing something with materials that gave the materials a different kind of voice. They weren't just rooted in skill and craft. There were things going on in the surface that were absolutely alive. Richier always said about clay, 'You mustn't touch it too much. It knows what it wants to do. It is a hysterical medium.' I love that idea.

David Smith, I think, talking about structural things, I love the way the wheels were added so that he could wheel these things around his studio, and the simplicity about it (fig. 37). I think it's one of these things where, again, with sculpture, not quite knowing how to name an object. What is it? How would one name it? I don't think one can. Yes, you can name the wheels, but I don't know anything beyond that. And that uncertainty of what it is, I think, is so compelling. It's just a futile, useless object in its own right, but utterly commanding in every possible way. I mean, monumental, as is Claes Oldenburg's plug (fig. 38).

Marcel Duchamp, my enemy! He is an extraordinary artist. There's no doubt about it. But I think he occupies art historically the intellectual high ground. I certainly don't think like that in any way, where I know what the

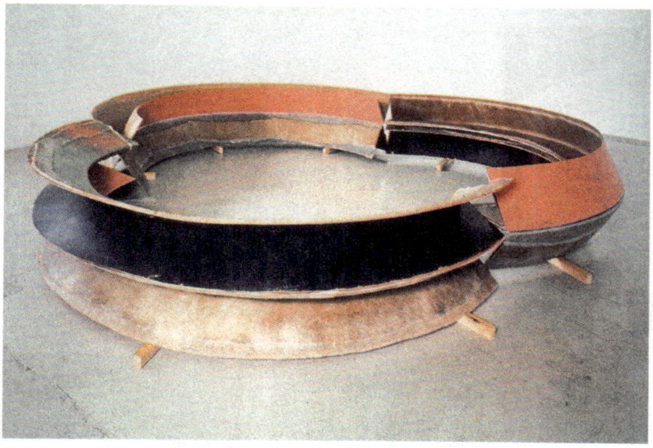

LEFT:
fig. 32 **Bruce Nauman**
Model for Tunnel, 1978

LEFT TO RIGHT:
fig. 33 **Lucio Fontana**
Nature, 1959–60
fig. 34 **Barbara Hepworth**
Pelagos, 1946

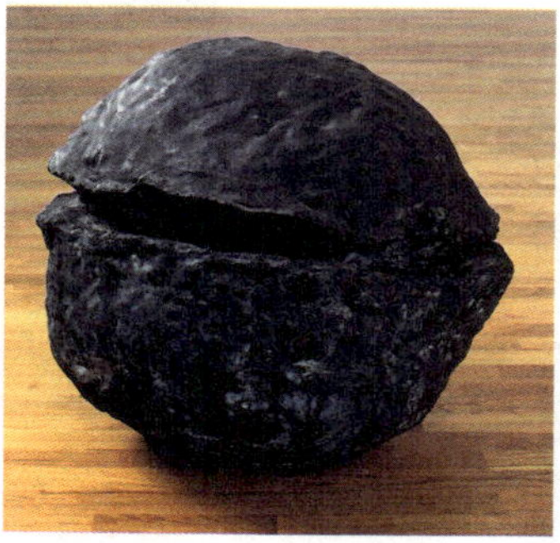

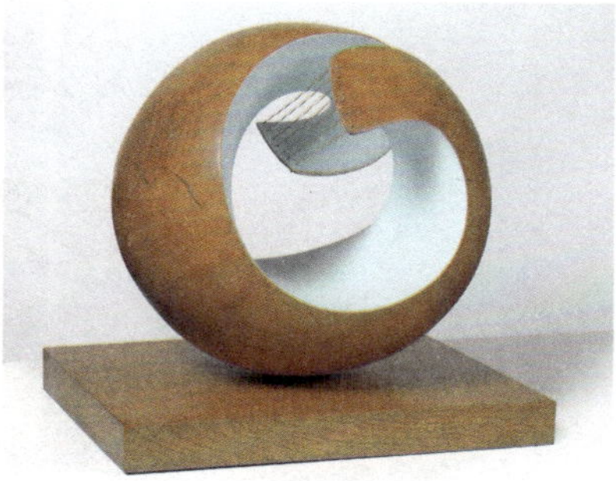

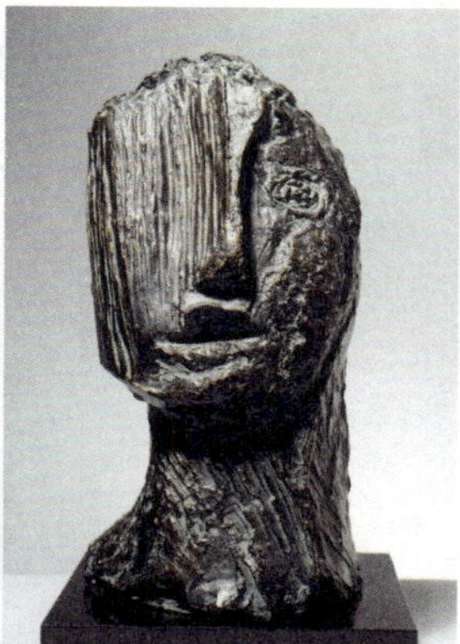

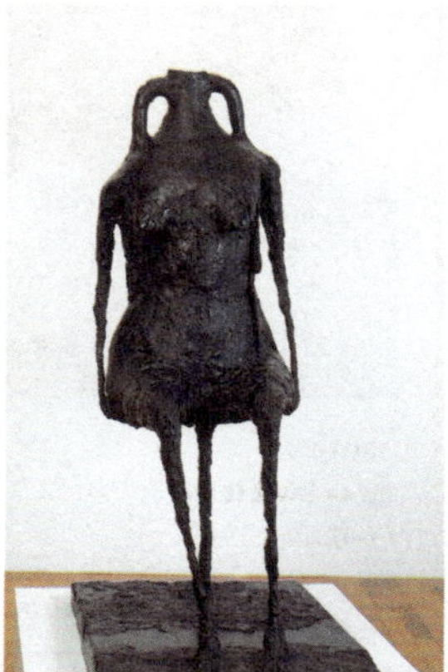

LEFT TO RIGHT:
fig. 35 **Jean Fautrier**
Large Tragic Head, 1942
fig. 36 **Germaine Richier**
Water, 1953–4

BELOW LEFT TO RIGHT:
fig. 37 **David Smith**
Wagon II, 1964
fig. 38 **Claes Oldenburg**
Model for a Mahogany Plug, Scale B, 1969

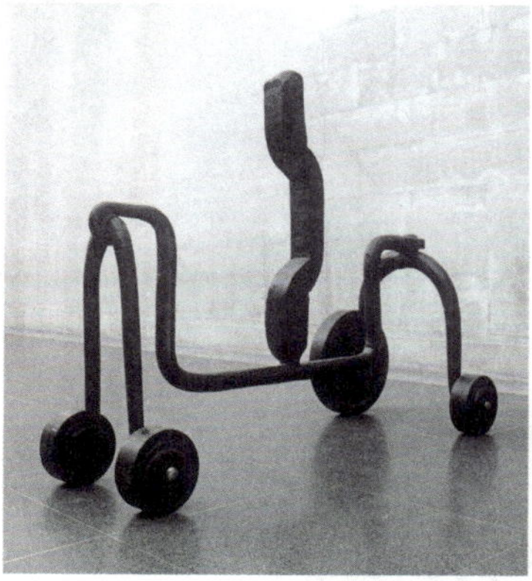

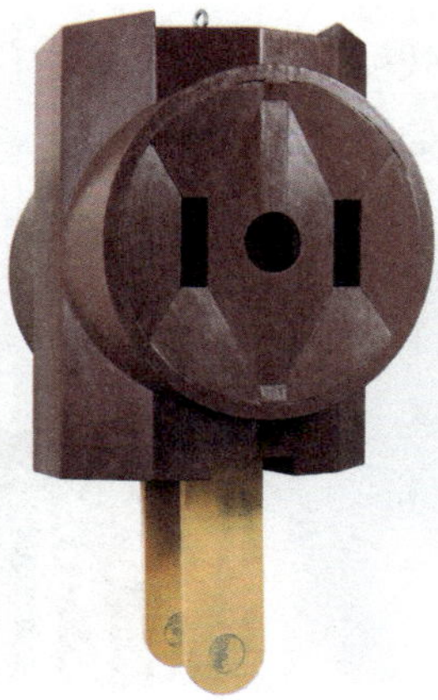

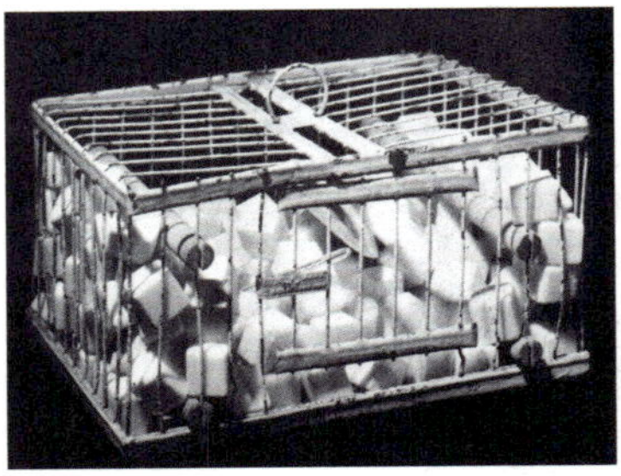

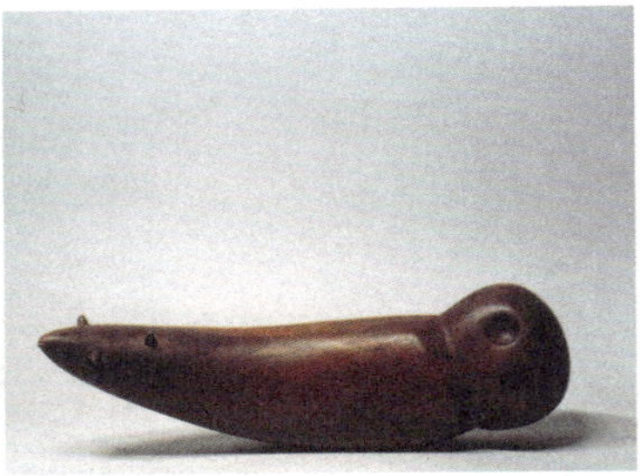

LEFT TO RIGHT:
fig. 39 **Marcel Ducham**
Why Not Sneeze, Rose Sélav
1921
fig. 40 **Alberto Giacom**
Disagreeable Object, 1931

LEFT TO RIGHT:
fig. 41 **Lynda Benglis**
Quartered Meteor, 1969
fig. 42 **Robert Morris**
Untitled (Steam Work for Bellingham), 1974

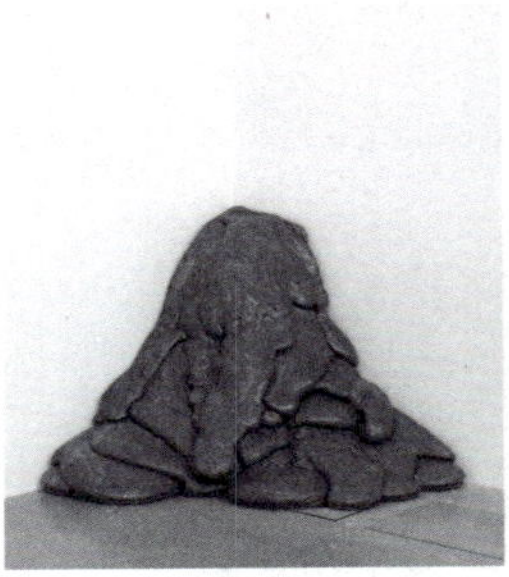

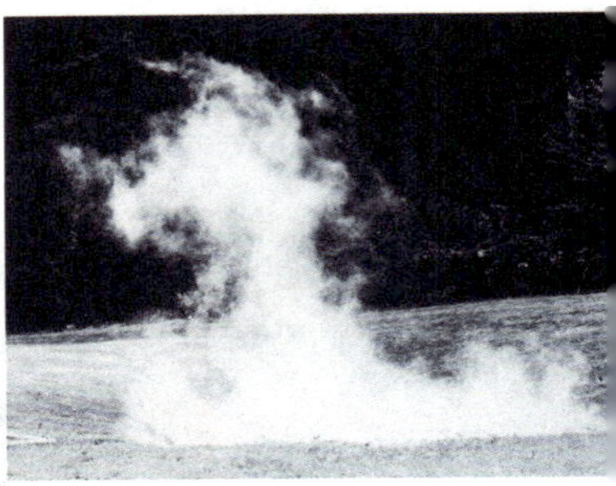

BELOW:
fig. 43 Stencilled hand

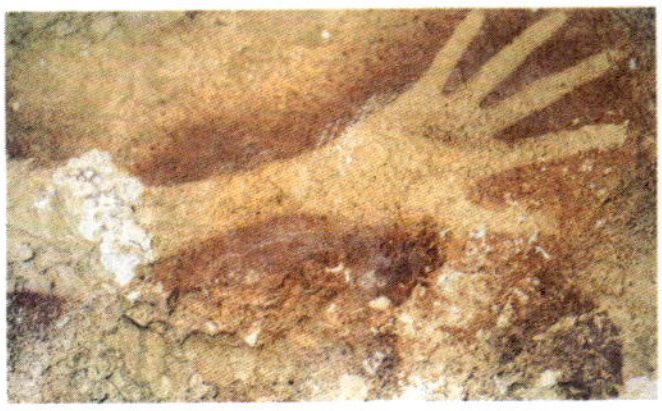

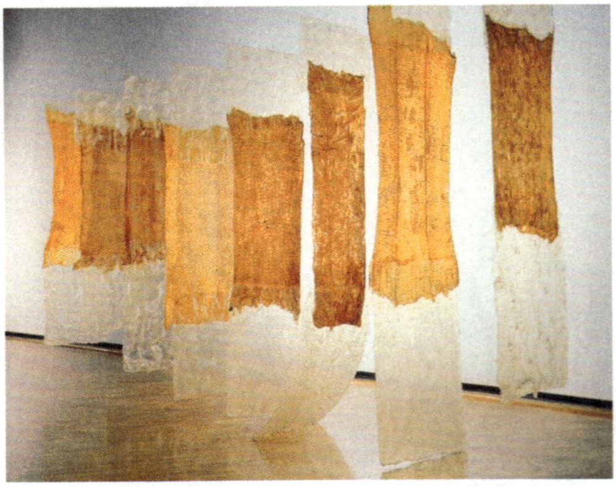

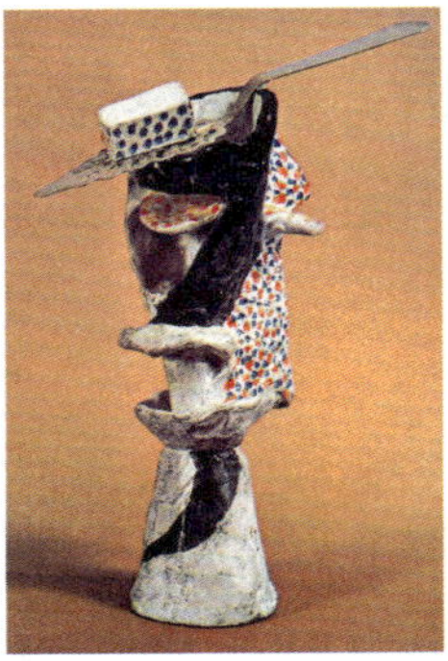

ABOVE:
fig. 44 **Eva Hesse**
Contingent, 1969
LEFT:
fig. 45 **Pablo Picasso**
Glass of Absinthe, 1914

LEFT TO RIGHT:
fig. 46 **Gordon Matta-Clark**
Day's End (Pier 52), 1975
fig. 47 **Louise Bourgeois**
The Blind Leading the Blind, 1947–9

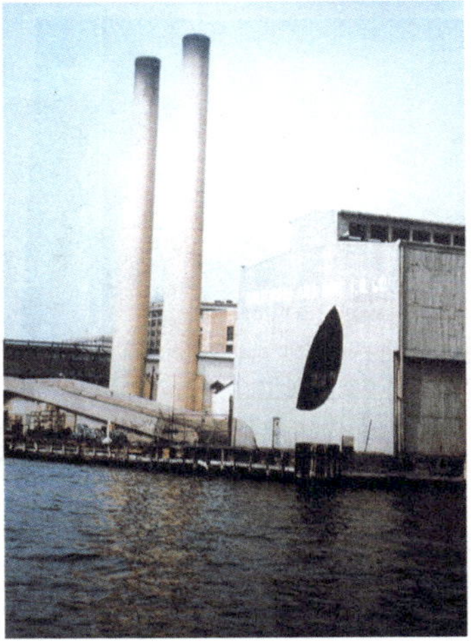

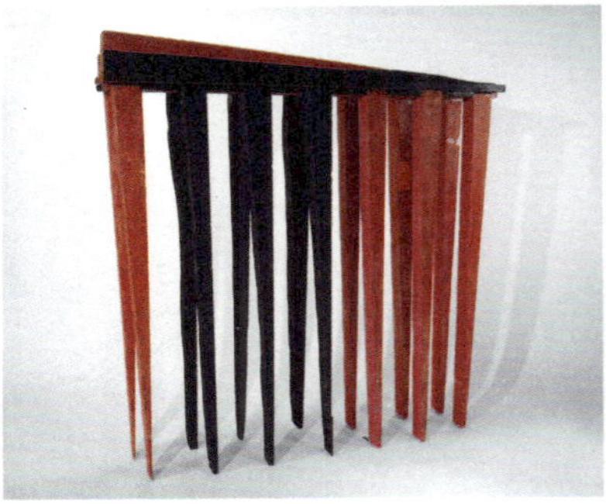

pun with the materials is, and I know the sort of semiotic trail of how you unravel the work. I think he's become hugely the possession of the academics. He's become a kind of academic artist, which is quite extraordinary, considering that that's really what he was, in a way, fighting against. But I think this is a remarkable work, a very sexually charged work called *Why Not Sneeze, Rose Sélavy?* (fig. 39). It's filled with these marble cubes that look just like sugar cubes and it has this cuttlefish bone in it, and a thermometer. It's just got this sense of waiting. And the sneeze as a sort of idea of sexual thrill is obviously something that I think Duchamp played around with a lot. I think it's an extraordinary work, as is Alberto Giacometti's *Disagreeable Object* (fig. 40). They both seem very, very charged works and very, very complete in that way. Certainly, the Giacometti is violent and phallic, and all those things that make it, in some ways, again, a kind of nameless object.

Lynda Benglis pouring things: I always think with her, when did she know where to stop (fig. 41)? Again, the gesture just being kept in check. And Robert Morris's steam pieces, where a sort of sculptural form is constantly changing, but still in a way a very classical work (fig. 42).

I was asked, in a talk I had to give, to name the five works that have most influenced me. So, I chose these five works. One is the hand, a stencilled hand from 20,000 years BC, where the hand was placed on the wall and, they think, then sprayed around with plant dye (fig. 43). An extraordinary sense of it being in the present tense.

Then Eva Hesse's *Contingent* (fig. 44). A wonderful work, where half of it is dipped in latex, and the other half in resin. I just think that way of claiming space, again, through something … is it finished? Could it have been ten more? So many, I think, very, very poetic questions that can be asked about it. The fact that one's just tipping on the floor, and yet they're these incredibly delicate objects. Yet, again, nameless, but utterly compelling and completely mesmerising in how they hover there in space, and the simplicity of them. Hesse fascinates me because she's always considered to be this very tactile artist, but I think it's one of those paradoxes where, in fact, she hardly touched these works at all. She invented these wooden tools for handling these lethal materials. So, there's always this paradox that things that look as if they're incredibly touched might be barely handled, like a Jeff Koons which looks so untouched, every inch is polished. So it's completely touched all over.

Then Pablo Picasso's *Glass of Absinthe*, which for me shows this interior, this exterior space (fig. 45). It does everything. It has a readymade in it. It confuses you. Shadows become solid things. Interior space becomes exterior space. It's a sculpture for all time. I think it heralded the twentieth century as the century that was going to mess with sculpture in some way.

Gordon Matta-Clark's extraordinary slice in the warehouse buildings on the Hudson (fig. 46). Just that adventuring to take possession of a building through such a simple incision but requiring such enormous physical adventure to do so.

And then, Louise Bourgeois's *The Blind Leading the Blind* (fig. 47). I think these are all works that I see as my sort of travelling companions and are hugely important to me in that respect.

I'm just going to go through my work quite quickly. [...] This is at the Serpentine (fig. 48). And what I want to do now is try and explore what I'm trying to do with exhibitions and making the work. From using the exhibition space in this kind of way, which is quite conventional, objects play off against each other. The structural ones that I was talking about earlier play off against the unstructural ones.

My love of enclosing space or taking space over so that there's very much an exterior form, and then the interior space can't be accessed (fig. 49). So, there's this need to walk around it. What really fascinates me about sculpture is the idea that holding on to the information that you experience with a work where you're seeing one side, but there's still the other side, and the process of forgetting that as you walk around it.

Colour and the whole idea of taking familiar things like banners, and them becoming sedentary objects (fig. 50). Even though the banner is often a thing that's on the move. It's in streets or part of protests or celebrations, but making it become a still object is like a kind of contradiction. The stillness of sculpture makes me anxious in a way. I don't know why. But I think, is it inherently dull, its stillness? Or is it its great strength? And that's up to the artist to battle that one out.

The idea of the lazy object or the casual object is very much for me in these piles of stuff that accumulate (fig. 51).

Then I began to see the exhibition as an exploratory space where the aim was to use the full height and breadth of the space and enable the viewer to get in amongst that. So that with this show (fig. 52), which was in 2011 or 2012, it was really to begin to engage with the idea of protagonists, that the space was a protagonist, the sculpture would be a protagonist, and then the viewers would be the final protagonist, and that somehow the three would work together.

This is another space where, again, the height is used (fig. 53). So, the act of looking up becomes, for me, very performative. [...] This was a space where the work had two very distinct viewing places, one when you came in and were confronted almost like a barrier that prevented access and the other was from the top of it where you saw it as a very different form (fig. 54).

Then these other objects in this show that were very much about using the entire space of the building. Where surprise would be the main objective

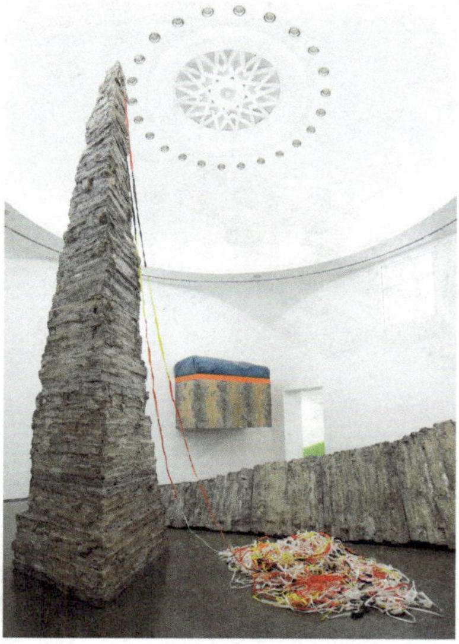

LEFT:

fig. 48 Installation view, *Nairy Baghramian and Phyllida Barlow*, Serpentine Gallery, London, 2010

BELOW:

fig. 49 *SWAMP; untitled: barrier*, 2010, installation view, *Displaced Fractures*, Migros Museum für Gegenwartskunst, Zurich, 2010

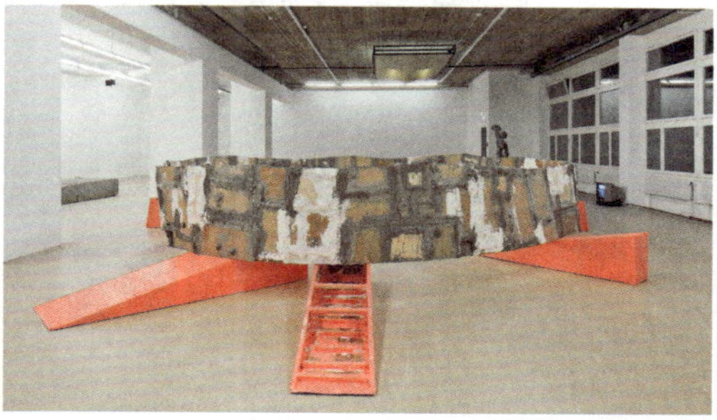

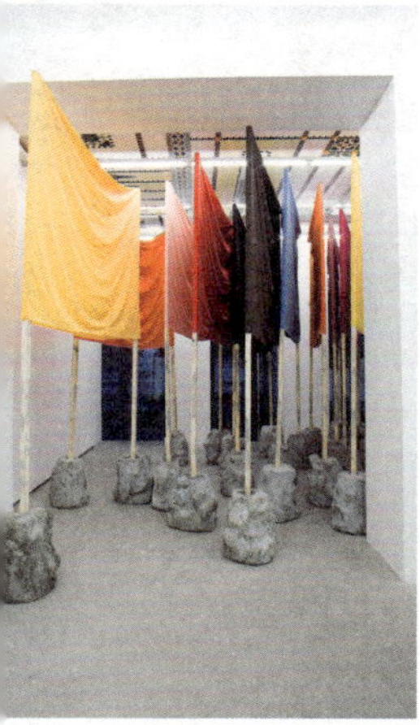

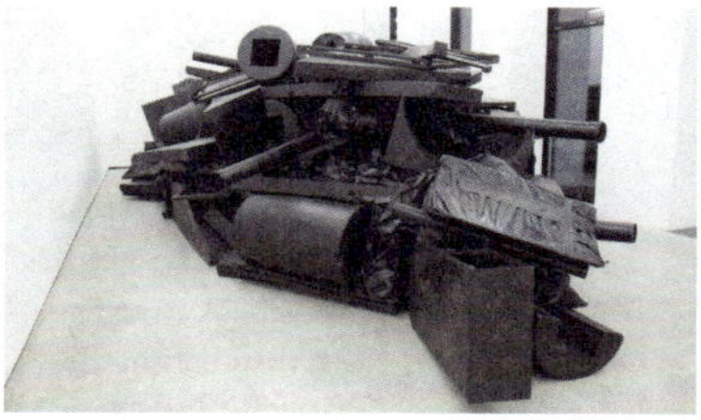

LEFT TO RIGHT:

fig. 50 *STREET untitled: banners*, 2010

fig. 51 *STREET untitled: heap 4*, 2010

Both installation views, *Phyllida Barlow: STREET*, BAWAG P.S.K. Contemporary, Vienna, 2010

fig. 52 *untitled: structure*, 2011, installation view, *Phyllida Barlow: Cast*, Kunstverein Nürnberg, Nuremberg, 2011

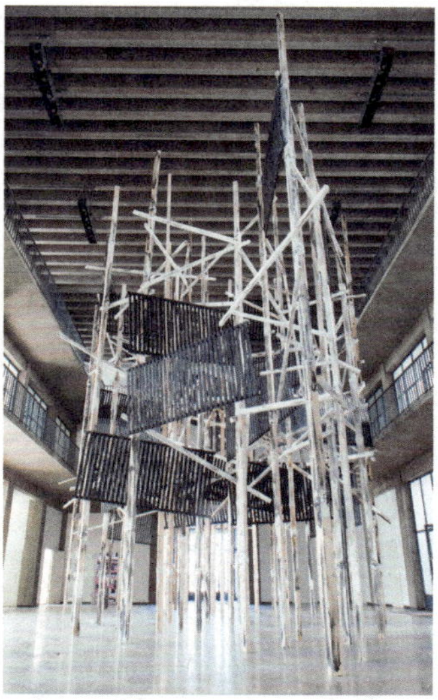

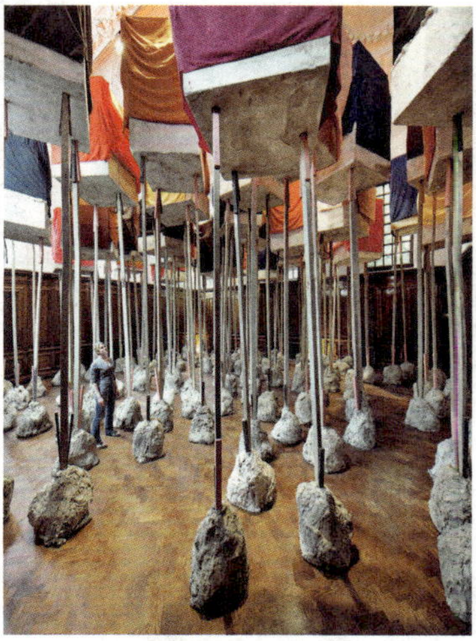

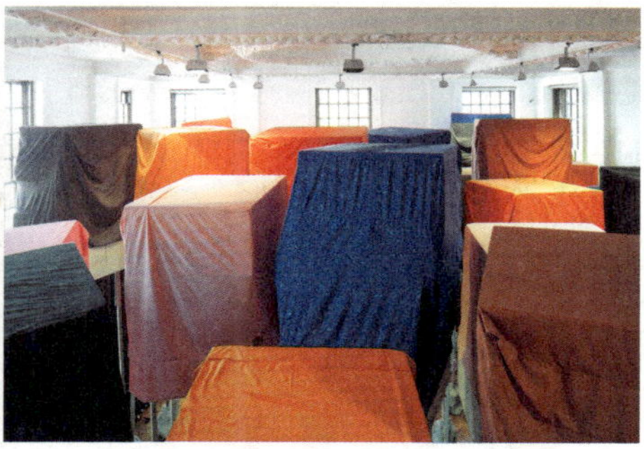

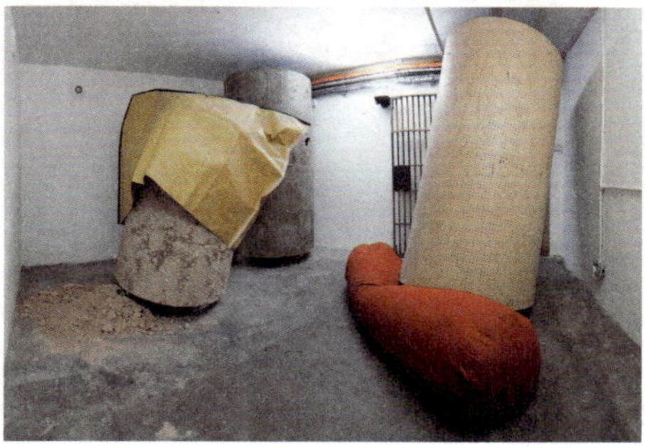

CLOCKWISE FROM ABOVE:

figs. 53–4 *RIG: untitled; blocks* (detail), 2011

fig. 55 *RIG: untitled; containers; leaningcoveredholed*, 2011.

All installation views, *Phyllida Barlow: RIG*, Hauser & Wirth Piccadilly, London, 2011

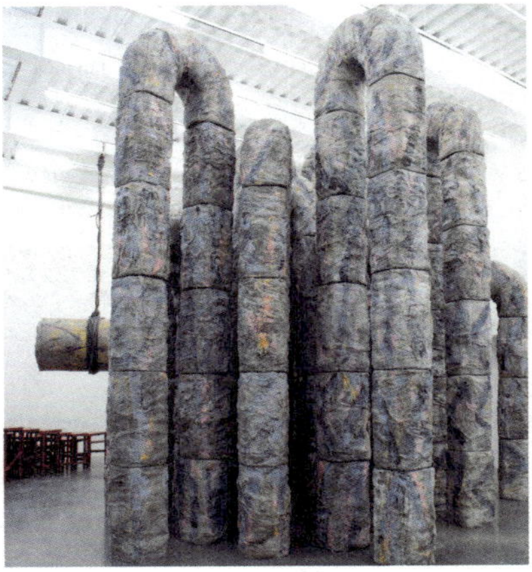

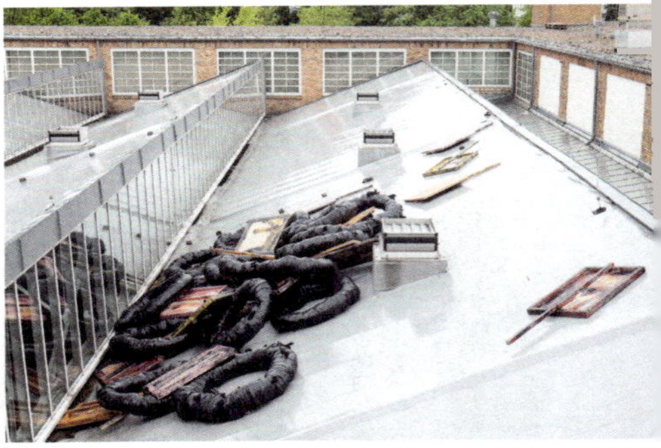

ABOVE:
fig. 56 untitled: *21 arches*, 2012, installation view, *Phyllida Barlow: siege*, New Museum, New York, 2012

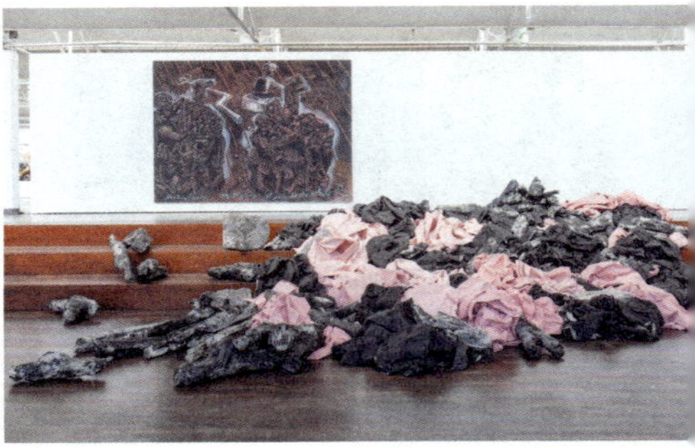

ABOVE TOP TO BOTTOM:
fig. 57 untitled: *tyresplacards*, 2012
fig. 58 untitled: *tarpaulinsrockssticks*, 2012
Both installation views, *Phyllida Barlow: BRINK*, Ludwig Forum für Internationale Kunst, Aachen, Germany, 2012

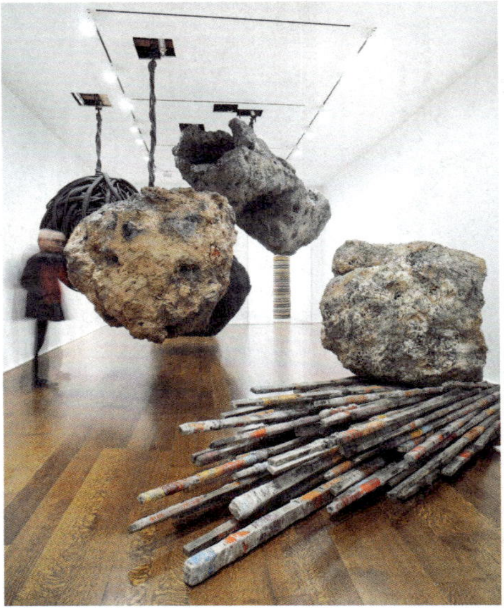

ABOVE, BELOW, AND RIGHT:
figs. 59–61 Installation views, *Phyllida Barlow: … later*, Hauser & Wirth New York, 2012

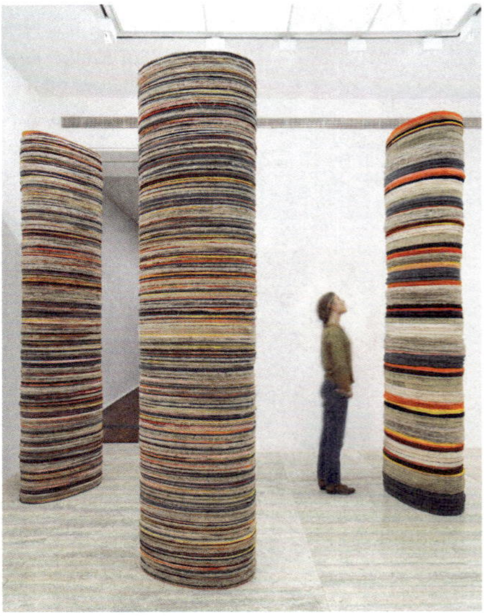

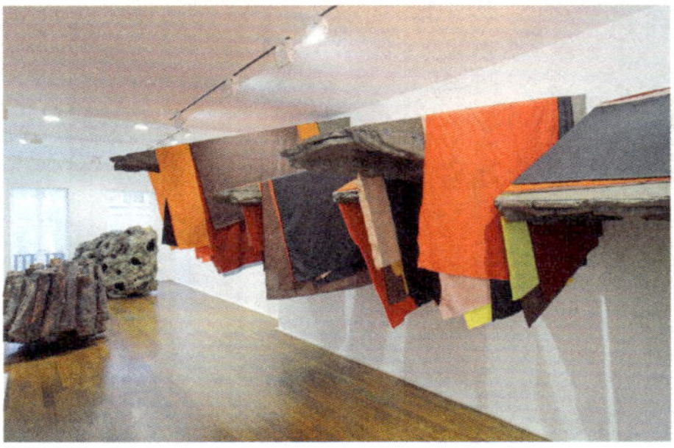

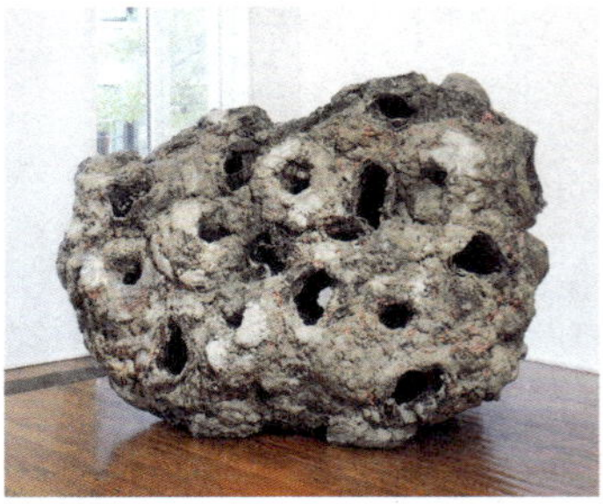

LEFT:
fig. 62 untitled: *holedwall*, 2012

of the way of using that space. So, I was beginning to see whether objects and sculptures could do more than just be a conventional arrangement (fig. 55).

This is at the New Museum in New York, on the top floor, which was a very difficult space because you come straight out of the lift, straight into the space (fig. 56). So you're confronted by the space. There are no hidden areas. So I blocked the entrance off with the columns, and that meant that there would be a reveal as you walked round the space. That has become an increasingly important issue about how a viewer encounters the work. Not just in one go, but how that can be broken up or staggered. I think this is all for me very much about the theatre of sculpture, and leaving things to have some kind of narrative, not a literal narrative, but a spatial narrative about how things unfold. And the opposition between very structured forms and things that are in a state of flux, either coming or going, I'm not sure which.

This was in Aachen, where I also worked with their wonderful collection. I like the idea of taking the work outside the space, so I took these heaps of things that I do. This one went on the roof of the Ludwig Forum in Aachen (fig. 57). And then these spillages where there is this kind of casual arrangement that spills into the space, but actually they always take the longest time to make, because getting something to look informal and unarranged is just tricky (fig. 58). In the end, it will always look quite formal and arranged. And that was in contrast to something that again has this very structural component about it.

Hanging shapes intrigue me because I think they carry for me a kind of unsettledness (fig. 59). And again, the stillness of a hanging form, there's something predatory about it. I like the fact that the whole shape can be investigated. It doesn't have the floor interrupting it. These columns, in terms of materials, which I haven't talked much about because I don't think I'm that interested in materials, I think I enjoy materials as far as they can do what I want them to do, rather than them being just a thing in themselves. But these columns were made out of all the offcuts in my studio of fabric and plywood and felt (fig. 60). I think the contrast of materials, like cement and fabric, as with these awnings, is very important (fig. 61). A kind of oddness about the way surfaces meet each other. Then, during this time, I began to relook at the sculpture that I had abandoned so vigorously in the 1960s. And relooking at this, a lot of French sculpture from that time and seeing it in a completely new light as a very brave, in a way quite violent, time for making sculpture where the work reflected maybe the post-war years very potently. And a lot of work needing that kind of penetration into it, getting into the centre of it, finding the interior space (fig. 62). [...]

The idea of a spreading work, this fascination for where the edges are with things, the edges of sculpture. I make these platforms, which are very much about the kind of spillage, and the spillage being just kept in check by the structure underneath it. With this one (fig. 63), it was originally in Munich and then it moved to Basel, where it became a much more organised work. But what intrigued me was that it's a work where you can see the two sides of it. So, you can walk into it from one end of it, where it's about ten, twelve feet tall. And as you walk round it, the top surface then reveals itself. So, it's got an inside and an outside, but in a very, very flat stage-like way.

This is another version of this idea of the stage, the platform, where getting into the underneath of it is one aspect of it, and then coming round the front, it becomes a very different object (figs. 64–5). And the scatter of painted surfaces, making it have this instability. Again, this was a new set of awnings with these fabrics draped over the cement (fig. 66). I think it's interesting to repeat works, just to see where the repetition of doing the same work again takes me. Whether it leads to a different kind of approach to that work.

This is a Richard Serra, and the other work is mine (fig. 67). And yes, I don't know! What can I say?! Anyway, this was a show curated by Daniel Baumann. He said he wanted me to do the work outside. And really, what with the front of the museum – this is the Carnegie in Pittsburgh – being very, very busy, just squeezing in between the Serra and the fountains, was the only opportunity. Then, as we were making this work, it sort of grew and grew and grew until I was just about twelve inches away from the Serra, and it felt so dangerous. I don't know. And somehow it took on the kind of, I don't know, slightly facetious comment on the Serra, which it wasn't really intended to do.

These upturned houses, I made three of them (fig. 68). And the idea was really based on the fact that after Hurricane Katrina, there was a radio programme, and I heard this man who left the sports centre where people had gone for some sort of refuge, and he decided to try and go and find his house as the waters were receding. And he walked and walked and walked in the direction, saw this road ahead of him with a tree that he knew was the tree, and then he walked down the road. And what moved me so intensely was that he said, 'And then I saw my home.' He didn't say, 'I saw my house.' He said, 'I saw my home because I recognised the colour of the walls on the inside.' He then described this home of his and the state it was in. It was such an incredible, vivid description. Again, to do with language, he didn't name it as a house, so what emerged through his verbal description was an incredibly powerful object that was resonant with all the memories, and incredibly tragic. And in a way these three upturned houses of which this is one, were very much based on that, of the kind of abstracting of certain qualities. This has nothing to do with that story, but I just liked the idea that he had said his house had been completely upturned. And I took that and

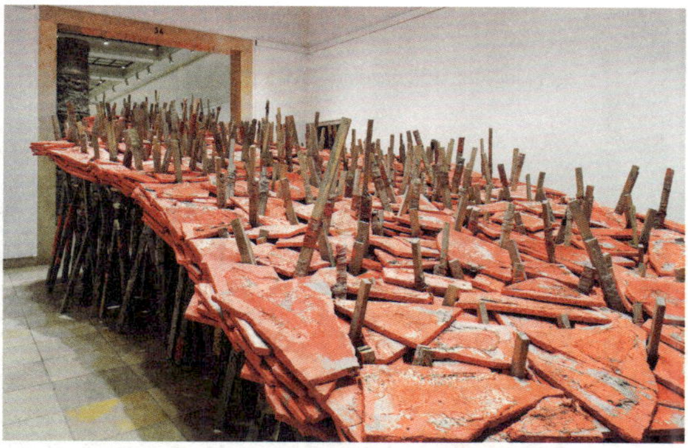

LEFT:
fig. 63 untitled: *stage*, 2011, installation view, *Sculptural Acts*, Haus der Kunst, Munich, 2011–12

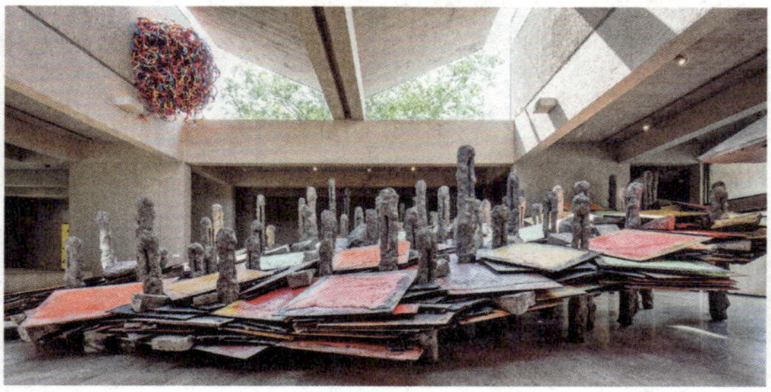

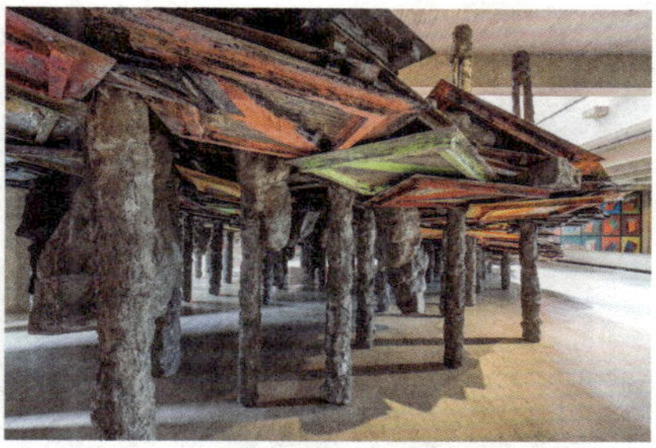

CLOCKWISE FROM ABOVE:
figs. 64–6 Installation views, *Phyllida Barlow: scree*, Des Moines Art Center, Des Moines, US, 2013

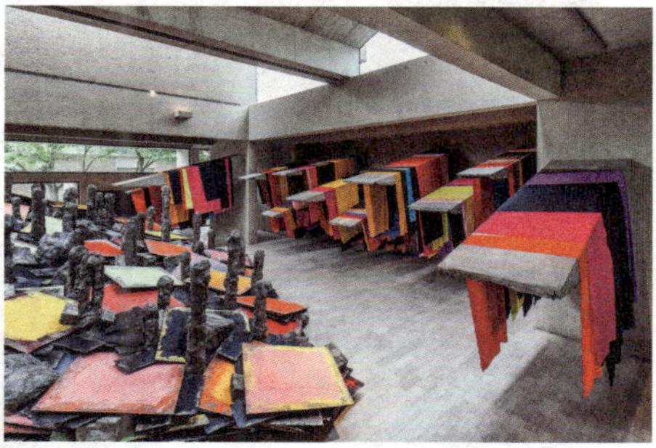

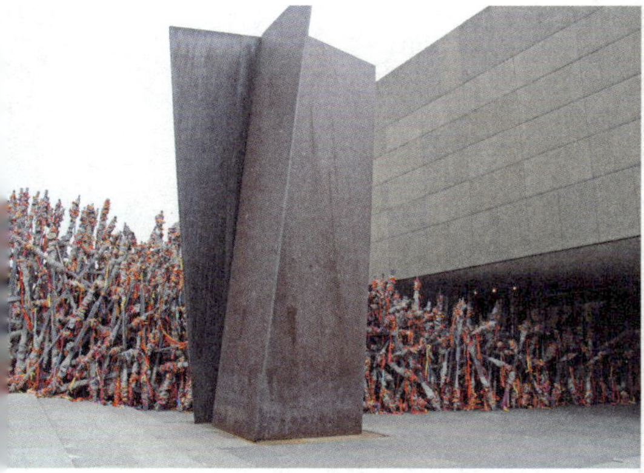

VE:
7 Phyllida Barlow
2013, and
hard Serra
egie, 1985, installation view,
3 Carnegie International,
negie Museum of Art,
sburgh, US, 2013–14

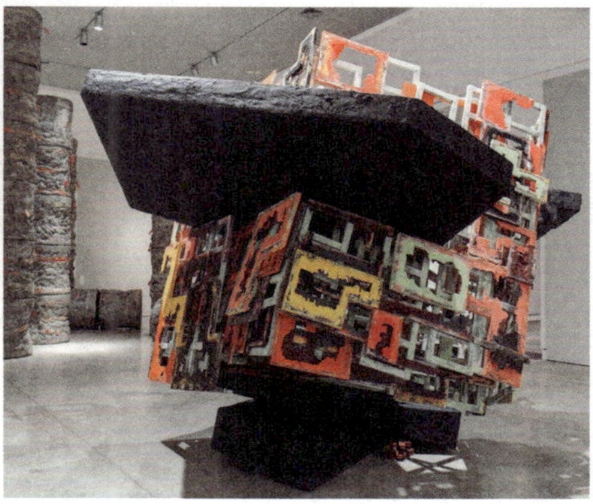

ABOVE:
fig. 68 untitled: *brokenupturnedhouse*, 2013, installation view, *Phyllida Barlow: HOARD*, Norton Museum of Art, West Palm Beach, US, 2013–14

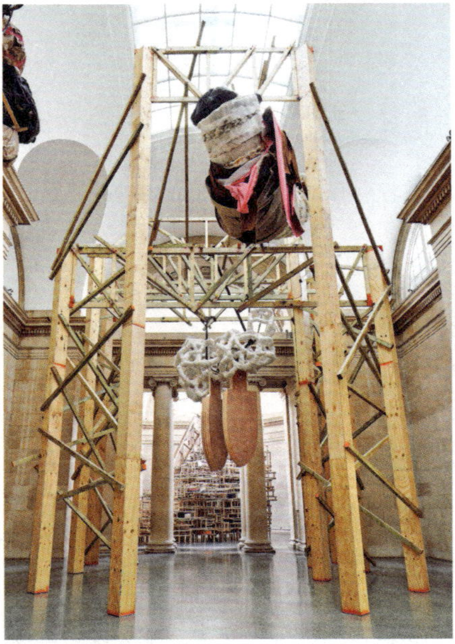

LEFT:
fig. 69 Installation view, *Phyllida Barlow: dock*, Tate Britain Commission, London, 2014

BELOW:
fig. 70 *untitled: 100 drawings*, 2013

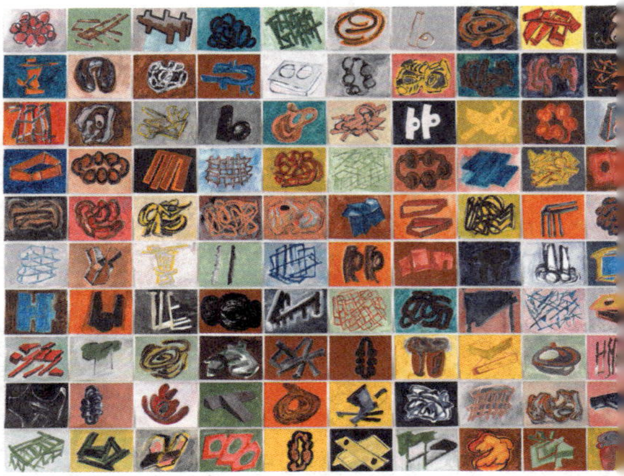

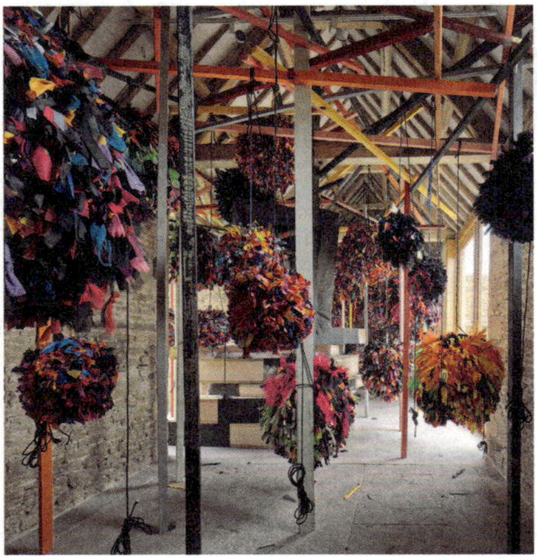

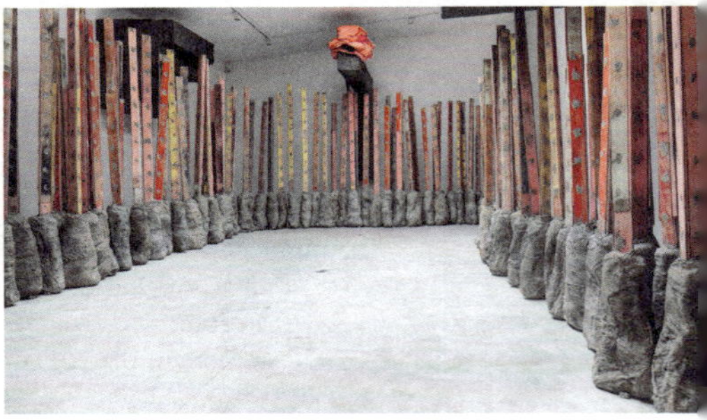

LEFT TO RIGHT:
fig. 71 *untitled: GIG*, 2014
fig. 72 *untitled: postscorral*, 2014
Both installation views, *Phyllida Barlow: GIG*, Hauser & Wirth Somerset, 2014

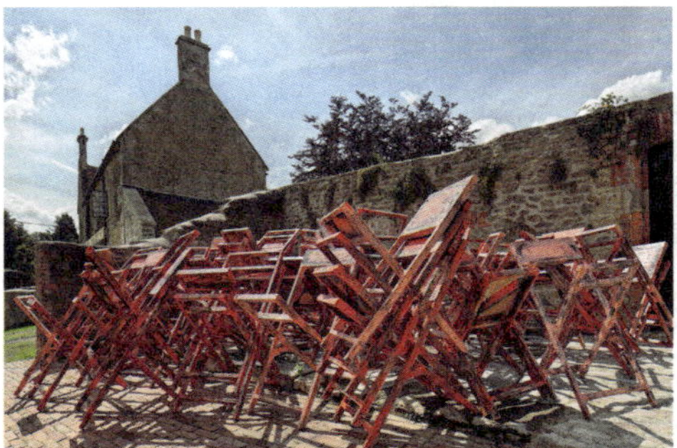

ABOVE:
fig. 73 *untitled: stackedchairs*, 2014, installation view, *Phyllida Barlow: GIG*, Hauser & Wirth Somerset, 2014

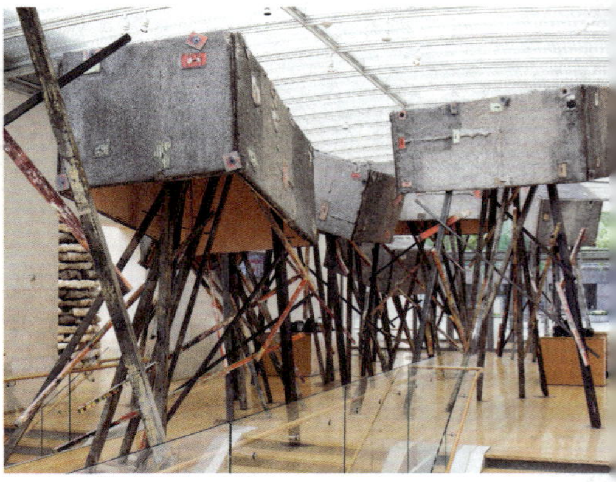

ABOVE:
fig. 74 Installation view, *Phyllida Barlow: tryst*, Nasher Sculpture Center, Dallas, 2015

decided to make these upturned objects that were constructed out of these brightly coloured panels, so that in a way it was using an idea of painting as well.

The hanging objects became very important in this show at the Tate, where I wanted to make the work so that nothing touched the ground (fig. 69). And just the floor space became the space for the audience. Again, making in the studio, it's very intense, working with assistants, directing them the whole time. I have no consideration for the audience whatsoever. Often, the work can't be seen because it's too big to be put together, and that certainly was the case with this Tate work. So, going there, a lot of the work, the first time I could see it was when it was assembled in this space. Most of the works were suspended above eye level, making the space like, I suppose, a kind of stage space for the audience. And with this work, it really became very much a conscious idea that everything had a performative role: the sculptures, the viewer, and the space itself. The idea of overwhelming the space became very much a conscious decision.

These are one hundred drawings that were all done from this book of sculpture I had, which I got in about 1959, which shows all this work (fig. 70). It's called *Contemporary Sculpture*, but it's from the 1950s. And it just is packed with all these sculptures from France, from Europe mainly, and America, that shows so clearly this incredible belief in sculpture that I think the 1960s then completely took apart. But relooking at that work, I found very inspirational. So, I made my own archive of it.

Then spaces that can be charged with sort of celebration in a way (fig. 71). And then change that mood into something else, I think that's important. This is a very enclosed space in the same exhibition (fig. 72). Again, using the idea of the space that gets enclosed, becoming, in a way very dynamic, but somehow utterly silenced by not being able to enter it. Sometimes things are literally what they are, like these are, I think, eighty chairs and they look like chairs, but they're not chairs (fig. 73). I think that confusion of naming is very important to how the work comes into existence. Can a named thing then become unnamed? I like to think it can.

This space in Dallas, the Nasher Sculpture Center, designed by Renzo Piano, where you couldn't touch the floor, walls, or ceiling (fig. 74). [...] So, everything had to have these special silicone mats. It's an incredible space to show in, but it's so architecturally designed that it becomes ... well, it doesn't become unusable, but it's only usable in certain ways, which I think I wanted to take that over in a very bold way to really make the space be resilient with sculptural language.

Then this is in a place called the Fruitmarket up in Edinburgh, where I crammed it full, a bit after the Dallas show, deciding to make sculpture take on an atmosphere of being stored, being in waiting. As though it was backstage (fig. 75). Going back to this idea of place and the first slides I've shown, of how objects are stored when they're not arranged, when they're not given a precise place to be, and in a way, trying to explore that with sculpture. So, the spaces were jumbled and crowded. Then up above I enclosed the entire upstairs space with these walls that went round the whole room up there (fig. 76). So, it's as though the two spaces, one on top of the other, contrasted as if the upstairs space has tipped all its goods into the ground-floor space.

And that, again, was coincidentally what happened in the Zurich show where the upstairs galleries were being rebuilt. So, downstairs I made this space, where my rule was that everything was half finished (fig. 77). So, all these objects that went in here were in a state of incompletion. Then upstairs, I built this huge stage where the viewers could look through into the spaces, holes were bored where the new building was being built (fig. 78). And for me, it was a kind of comment on the ebb and flow of how things are in the world. There's some sort of uncertainty about things where they are in a kind of state of completion or incompletion.

This is Venice (fig. 79). This was quite a challenging and interesting idea of representing one's country that at that time was quite, well, ongoingly problematic politically because of Brexit, and a kind of feeling that the whole enterprise of Brexit, and how it came into being, was a folly. So, this work was titled *folly*. And what was so wonderful about this space is that you could enter it from the front. The main gallery you came into had smaller galleries going off it (fig. 80). So, it was a completely 360-degree experience of walking round it. And I decided to use that very much as the point of the show, but also in a way to overfill the gallery like a space that was bursting out, which I think was a kind of metaphor for how I felt the political predicament to be. When I came away from Venice, I had a sort of, not exactly a crisis, but a kind of rethink about what I wanted to do with sculpture. There was this incredible pavilion, the German pavilion with a very young performance artist who put these glass tables in and had performers underneath and extraordinary symbolic objects. Watching the audience in that show taught me a lot. The audience came in and were just completely awestruck, and then just stood absolutely still watching this performance or waiting for the performance to begin. Then Geoffrey Farmer, the Canadian artist, had these extraordinary waterspouts and fountains, where you trod on the ground, and it sort of set them off. So, that was performative as well. Then there was the British pavilion with this work in it. Then there was the French pavilion, where it was a recording studio. And I began to think about sculpture as this very … it really came home, that it was this still, silent work. And what was the audience's role in that? I became intrigued by the idea that a

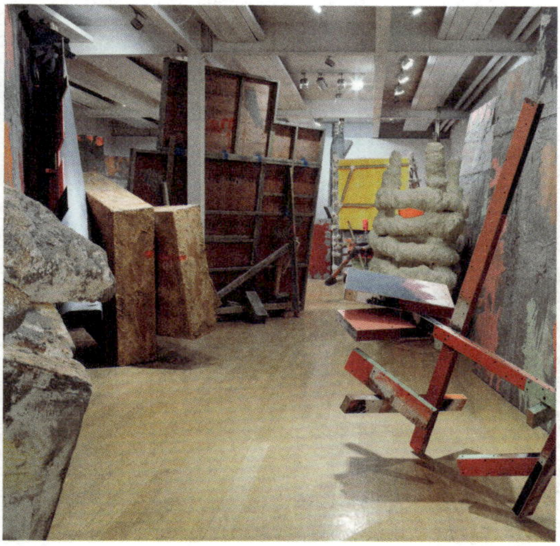

LEFT TO RIGHT:
figs. 75–6 Installation views, *Phyllida Barlow: set*, The Fruitmarket Gallery, Edinburgh, 2015

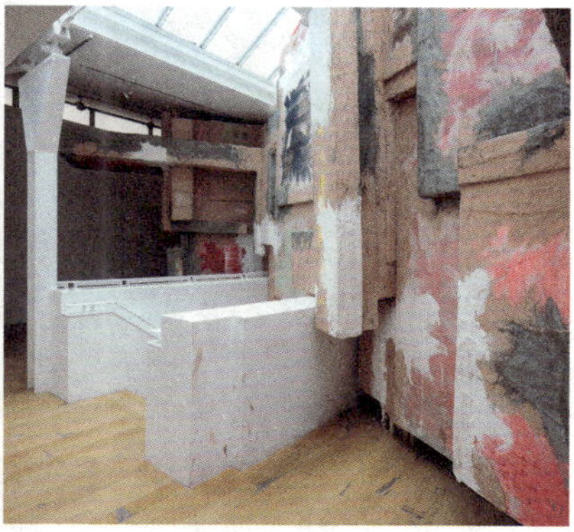

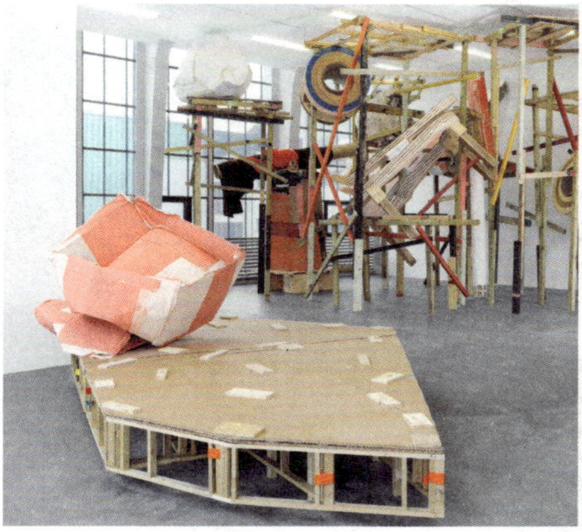

LEFT TO RIGHT:
figs. 77–8 Installation views, *Phyllida Barlow: demo*, Kunsthalle Zürich, 2016

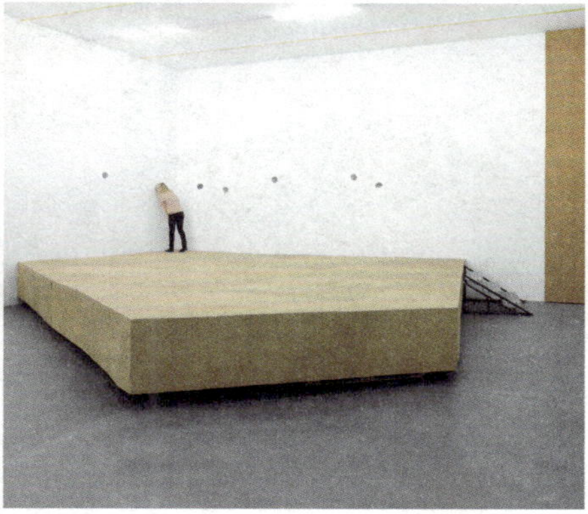

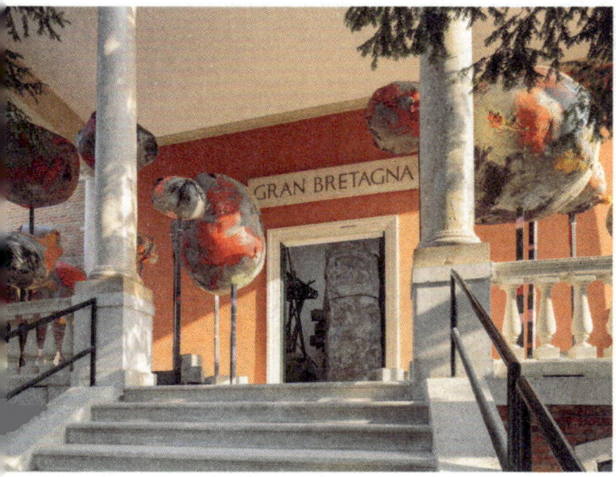

ABOVE AND RIGHT:
figs. 79–80 Installation views, *Phyllida Barlow: folly*, British Pavilion, 57th Venice Biennale, 2017

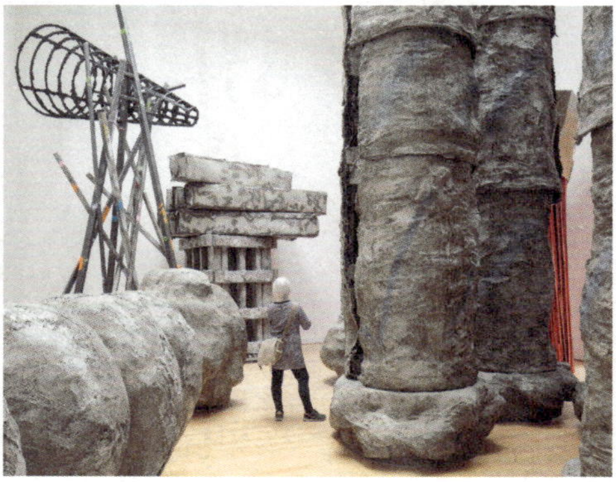

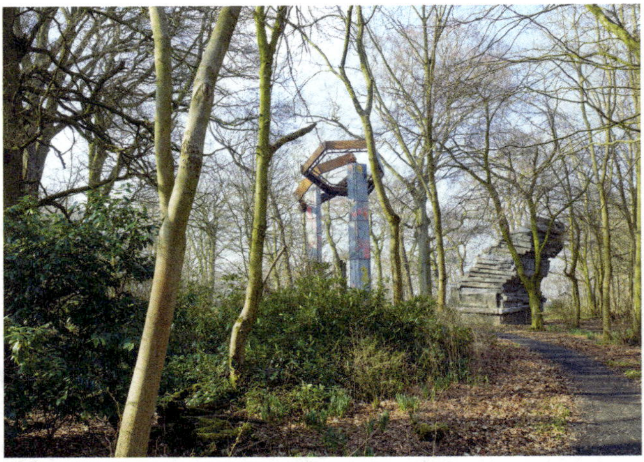

LEFT:
fig. 81 *quarry*, 2018

BELOW:
fig. 82 *prop*, 2018, installation view, High Line, New York, 2018–19

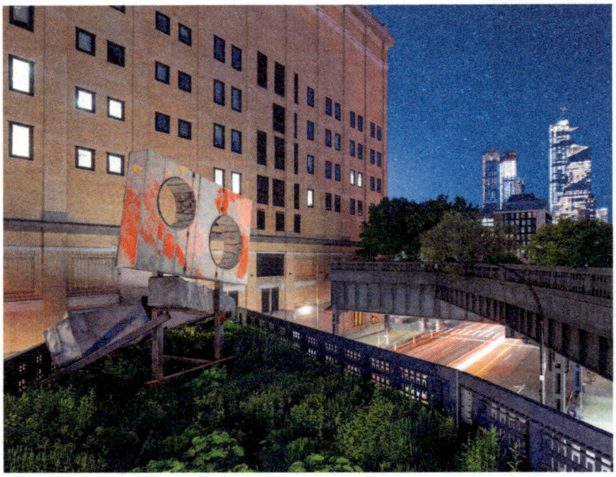

BELOW:
fig. 83 Installation view, *Phyllida Barlow: tilt*, Hauser & Wirth New York, 2018

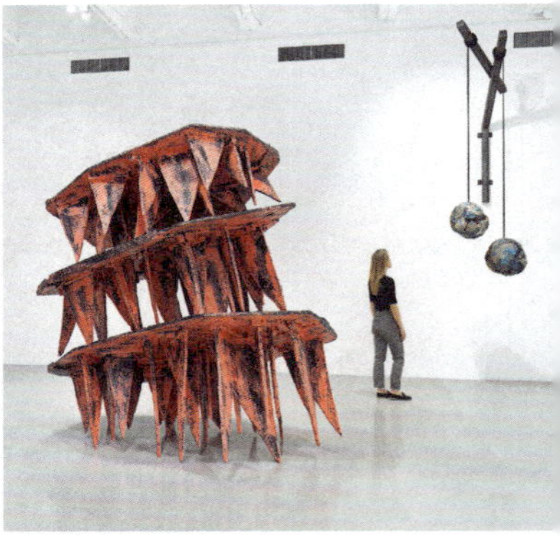

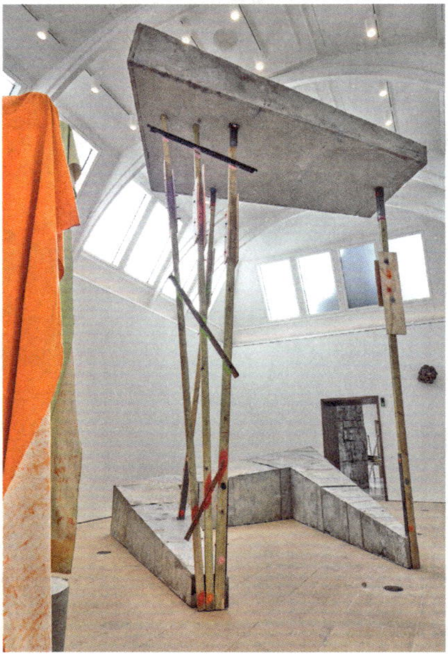

LEFT TO RIGHT:
figs. 84–5 Installation views, *cul-de-sac*, Royal Academy of Arts, London, 2019

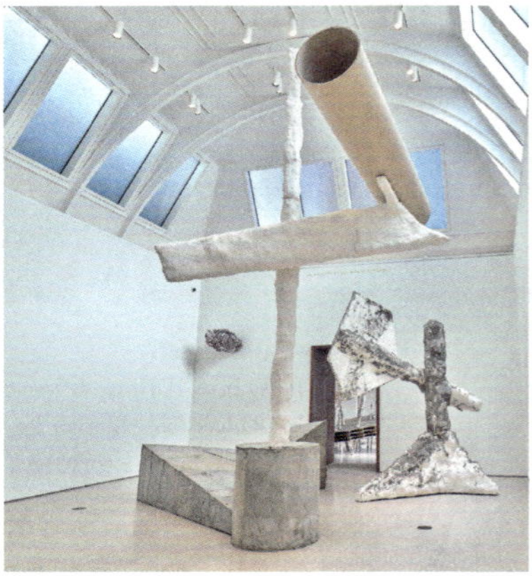

passive audience that could watch the – this isn't a judgemental thing, it's a compliment – the work would come to the audience, and that that was what was happening. The three pavilions that I was surrounded by, in a way, was what that was happening with all the work. But in the British pavilion, nothing happened. The only way it could be made to happen was for the audience to become very active and become the moving part around the work. And I became very critical of that or, in a way, stymied by that. The fact that I had filled the pavilion to the full meant that that movement was very, very controlled, and I just began to really think about these things but began to see this idea of the active audience as a very important part of how sculpture is.

This was an outside commission, which was a new experience, working with nature and trying to make the natural environment of these trees have equal command as the objects I put in there (fig. 81). One is twelve metres, going up to fourteen metres, and the other is ten metres. So they were a great height. That was really all about looking up and making that role of the audience somehow … again, this idea of being very active, of being able to engage with the act of looking up, as it is under the trees.

Then the High Line, a kind of memorial in a way to something that was there (fig. 82). But a sort of riposte to the buildings behind. A work I felt that was very conscious of its environment, and a work that was sort of staring at the High Line, and the way the High Line is used.

Then this post-Venice time meant that I was very much interested in reducing the work to just its essential parts. And that led very much to the show in New York, where the space in a way wins (fig. 83). Rather than me aggressively subduing the space, I was allowing the space to take over and become the vibrant part of it with these solitary objects, autonomous objects in it. And fascination in the stand-alone sculpture. So instead, I think of putting two other works with this, I just became very much about seeing these works as performing on their own.

[…] This is at the Royal Academy now (fig. 84). The idea was that, coming into this space, what happens is you look straight at the wall at the back. And I thought that was very interesting, because there's only two ways to go, left or right. Then it's three galleries in a row, and then you come back the same way. So, it seemed like an ideal opportunity, as with Venice, of being able to give this very active way of looking at the work twice – once when you went through it and then when you came back again. Because the space is very processional, and in a way very linear. It seemed interesting to try and take advantage of that. […] It was like walking to the end of this space here with these blocks, and then turning round and coming back again, with these punctuation marks of the wall works (fig. 85). The large, flat cement shapes are the shadows to the works that they're attached to. The idea of a shadow becoming a very solid object, again, to me is a kind of paradox that I want to play with a lot more. Then putting very, very heavily built structures in contrast with something that appears to have a much greater informality.

So, in a way, I'm ending the talk none the wiser. Other than I know I'm at a very different point with having to face the work being much more on its own, much more simplified, and having to stand up for itself much more than maybe some of the previous works. And that seems like a new adventure.

A video of this talk is available on the University of Guelph College of Arts' YouTube channel.

This text was first presented as a paper at the 'Sculpture, Method, Research' conference at Central Saint Martins, London, held on 14 and 15 September 1995. Barlow deploys the fiction of 'the hatred of the object' to examine arguments around making sculpture. She identifies the models of the 'enlightened' and 'grim' studios, anchoring her experience of the grim studio to her education at Chelsea College of Arts, London, and the Slade School of Fine Art, London, and she observes a moralistic reverence for craft and struggle. She discusses the hands-off approach to making and the use of the vitrine as exemplifying a shift towards the pictorial rather than sculptural and notes its taming and sanitising function. She considers the work of Louise Bourgeois and if its popularity signals the demise of the hatred of the object.

The Hatred of the Object

1995

In this thirty-minute talk I want to put forward and unravel a disparate collection of thoughts based on what I diagnose as 'the hatred of the object'.

I believe that the studio, and in particular the sculptor's studio, is somehow at the centre of this hatred, and to some extent the victim of it. My argument focuses on two kinds of traditional studios: the enlightened studio and the grim studio.

In the enlightened studio, curiosity is fundamental to how ideas are explored, manifested through the physical manipulation of material, privately and intimately, where there is a slow evolution of processes, intellectual and practical, involving experimental approaches to concepts, techniques, forms, and aesthetics. My experience of such a studio is that the artist is at the centre of this self-created world, independently selecting and discarding, and in control of the development and eventual showing to the outside world of their individual expression.

However, parallel to this ideal vision of the enlightened studio there is also a darker, predatory vision of the traditional studio, one which, I believe, stands in direct contention to the experimental needs and economic restrictions experienced by today's artists, and this is the grim studio.

My understanding of this kind of studio is based directly on my art-school experience at Chelsea School of Art and then the Slade, in the early 1960s. I was given a traditional education in sculpture where I was taught a repertory of sculpture techniques. It was accepted that these techniques provided the young sculptor with all they needed to know in order to physically produce sculpture. And from my own experience, they constituted a somewhat grim ritual by which the student was initiated into the highly specialised and selective, even elitist, world of sculpture.

Therefore my education involved clay modelling, casting, plaster modelling, armature construction, and assemblage with metal and wood. The emphasis was on self-sufficiency through hard work, preferably involving a great input of labour. Tutorials and seminars did not exist as such, but at the end of a long and compulsorily hard day's work everyone met up in the pub where there was avid talk but little discussion about the day's events in the studio. Existentialism was the religion and hard drinking and hard working were the rules of the game.

However much I may have departed from this training, it is in fact deeply ingrained within me. The root of all my working methods seems to be somehow related to my early experiences with clay, which was very much my preferred medium because it involved the least amount of technical equipment and kept processes close to the hand.

But more than anything else, this training provided me with the independence to make simply and expediently, enabling me to do so almost anywhere with the minimum of financial and physical resources. The emphasis which such an education placed on self-sufficiency had, despite its exclusivity and its all-male domination, given me the confidence to set up my own studio in the simplest way and to begin to make work cheaply and conveniently. The privacy and the autonomy quickly lent itself to experimentation and to a drastic distancing from the more restrictive aspects of such an education.

I am grateful for my sculpture training because of the independence it instilled in me and, for better or worse, a certain kind of confidence in the most basic of making. Perhaps more important than anything else has been an appreciation of time: quite simply the time it takes to make something oneself. Sculpture can reflect this element of time, either in how one must move around it, that is, literally walk around it – a kind of stalking – or in what species of physical and material object it is, or in the processes involved in making it what it is and the time it has taken to achieve this. It is the fusion of these characteristics which makes sculpture, whether it be object or installation, project its own particular, inherent sense of time.

I am aware that what I experienced educationally was representative of the traditional studio in its grim and restrictive guise. As such, this kind of studio comes down to us loaded with cumbersome luggage – historical, aesthetic, and moral. The grim studio like this is full of crap which necessarily and understandably has been purged by generation after generation. Especially now that increasing numbers of young artists are rejecting the financial burden of the studio and relying more and more on having their work produced via the desk and telephone, to be organised, managed, and manufactured elsewhere. Reciprocally, ideas are submitted in proposal form or as scale models, thus short-circuiting the necessity for the experimental, time-consuming, trial-and-error processes that are so much part of studio culture. Instead, the emphasis is on a need for designed objects, the making of which can be delegated elsewhere – anywhere, that is, other than the studio.

In comparison to this way of producing a work, the studio in either its enlightened or its grim guise can seem to force a moral attitude to work – passing on an inheritance of a kind of Protestant work ethic in which is entrenched a strong sense of struggle out of which good must surely come. Attached to this disagreeable identity there can also be a resistance to and suspicion of experimentation which is understood as breaking rank with sculpture and which should therefore be expelled from the discipline of sculpture into a kind of purgatory. Such attitudes are backward looking, suggesting a grumbling, discontented relationship with the present and a denial of the fantastic, if difficult, choice of materials and techniques available to the sculptor, all potential for plundering in whatever way possible. To deny this potential further enforces the studio as the grim abode of the punitive, the repressive, and the backward-looking.

For me, the studio is deeply important: emotionally and practically. But it speaks trouble, and although I would not, could not, have it any other way, it can seem to be a shaming thing to be lumbered with, as if the party is going on elsewhere. The grim, traditional studio, rigidly rooted in the past, can now not only be expensive, but boring as well. Rent and amenities, along with the specialist traditional materials such as stone and bronze, cost a fortune, and the desire to limit mistakes in order to keep costs down demands a prescriptive attitude to working methods – paradoxically, not unlike those of artists who have rejected the studio.

Of course, there are many superb artists who use the studio, or not, in whatever way they like, enlightened or otherwise, and their work speaks for itself, being of imagination, originality, and relevance.

But my proposition of the hatred of the object hinges on the perception of the traditional studio as an inheritance loaded with morality and stringent work ethics enforced for no good reason. Furthermore, where such a domain is thought to abide by rigid hierarchies of good and bad, right and wrong, these judgements seem to be passed according to the extent to which the artist can deposit evidence of struggle on their sculpture-object through the act of making.

Craft, and the hands-on/hands-off debate emerges. Again, the spectre of the grim studio rises, claiming the high moral ground with its demand for the handmade, with the added insistence that maximum evidence of the mark of the artist be left on the work. Thus the essential need for the studio is justified – as the place where the object is processed through private and personal rituals of making. In this blinkered environment Duchamp has never existed, nor any attempt to acknowledge the wealth of iconoclastic gestures erupting out of twentieth-century art which have kept the processes of sculpture awake and contentious.

Understandably a revulsion can set in. The object – the hot object – that is, the object loaded with the all-too-visible signs of the act of making, can repulse through its somewhat desperate need to attract. It becomes an object of emotional blackmail, persuading us to feel for it because it shows us so clearly the marks, wounds perhaps, caused through its struggle to come into existence. For those who are questioning the necessity for such agonised creativity, these objects arouse suspicion and eventually a kind of loathing because they rely on predictable mannerisms with which to generate a reaction.

Similarly, our culture abounds with objects demanding to be loved – but produced in a totally different way – that is, industrially designed and manufactured products. These are cool objects, hands-off maybe, but objects which impose a similar emotional blackmail to their opposite numbers, demanding to be bought, to be owned. These product-objects which saturate our daily lives infiltrate our emotions, often seductively and pleasurably. But on closer analysis they can also generate loathing as their true destructive or pollutant identities are revealed behind their fabulous disguise of, for example, rounded forms and glossy surface. The car is, of course, the supreme example.

Therefore my notion of the hatred of the object is born out of what I perceive to be a conflict between opposing species of sculptures: one hot and the other cold. However, their supposed differences can, paradoxically, produce similar responses: both demand to be loved and needed, albeit in different ways, and yet both are infinitely capable of invoking the opposite response to the one intended – instead of love, hatred.

Not surprisingly, finding a way out of this conflict can not only be an attractive proposition but a necessary one. So abandon the studio with its dogged, backward-looking, moral messages and abandon the product with its corrupt disguises and its economic dependency. Where else to move other than to take on production through delegation? Without a studio there can be liberation to explore and exploit diverse media through the specialist agencies, suppliers, and manufacturers. The technology does not necessarily have to be learnt or directly experienced in order for the idea to be manifested: the work can be produced through delegation via desk and telephone or fax machine.

This position makes the technologies of computer and industrial design production available for artists to plunder without the burden of having to own or even learn how to use them.

There can be no need to engage physically or in tactile ways with the stuff with which the proposed work is to be made: it can all happen elsewhere. Again, anywhere but a studio. Such a distance from the manipulative production of the object seems to me to generate a genre of object-sculpture that is more pictorial than sculptural. Nothing exemplifies this more than the on-going use of the vitrine – a compelling, often mesmeric object in its own right – and when deployed as a device for framing and containing, one that becomes an art object with infinite possibilities, all dependent on the choice of thing to be placed within.

The vitrine is, at its most banal, not only a substitute for the plinth but the symbolic equivalent of the screen – that of television, film, computer, video, x-ray, radar, and a host of others. It so conveniently and, funds permitting, so beautifully offers the real as the anti-real within a space that is pretence.

For me, the vitrine tidies up, cleans up. It makes safe the horrific so that objects of danger, disease, terror, and violence can be shown as easily as objects of desire and seduction. Anything and everything can be tamed into submission once framed within and behind the glass defence.

It must be the vitrine's ability to accommodate anything and everything that makes it so compelling but, at the same time, it does more than this. It removes both viewer and artist from the work, it tames and sanitises and although it makes possible an astonishing choice of content, materially and technically, to be acted upon, in the end my response has been that, as a device, it deadens opinion, rendering the status of the object as a wild, messy, unpredictable, ugly, difficult thing to being cleansed, tamed, glamorised, polite. A shift from raw experience to managed spectacle.

Therefore the confrontation with raw experience and the unpredictable must be through the uncontained object, the wild object – one which can be approached close up, which can be walked around, experienced in real time. I believe this kind of object to be inherently difficult and more likely to be experienced as so, even as uncomfortable and confusing. And even more problematic, such an exposed object might fail to arouse any response whatever, because when so blatantly displayed it is not glamorous, and must stand up to close, uncompromising scrutiny through which all is revealed. This is very different from the vitrined object which can cunningly both mask and hide parts of itself, if so wished. The naked object, raw and exposed, does at least offer itself for opinion, showing that a risk has been taken even if it has perhaps failed.

Not so with the vitrined object. It can never fail. The object is repressed and once removed. It becomes pictorial, framed and glazed – quite literally glossed by the shiny reflective glass. It seems almost more akin to photography than to the confrontationally presented object. It therefore becomes a made-easy experience.

Consequently, the vitrine, for me, induces disappointment: like the wild animal in captivity, the object is emasculated, the potential of its physicality reduced to a mere virtual identity. Vitrines are an invitation to remove the potency of an object, its repulsiveness, its seductiveness, its beauty, or its ugliness – all hugely powerful characteristics in their emotional effect. These characteristics potentially invoke hatred because they perhaps remind us of the uncontrollable sides of ourselves and could be too strong to deal with. Therefore the vehicle of these emotions, that is the object, must, quite literally, be removed, put away, to be scrutinised from a safe distance and to function only as a reminder of possible threat.

The vitrine can reduce the material physicality of objects to a pictorial status. But the contention of the sculpture-object is to oppose the pictorial and to offer experience in real time – the time required by the object and its space to be walked around, through, across, using memory – to remember this part whilst you are experiencing that part – so that the work unfolds through the senses and is the antithesis of the pictorial.

The sensory aspect of sculpture is more than just the state of appearance. It is a whole relationship with the process of making and can engage with the non-visual as much as with the visual. The vitrine exemplifies how an object can be produced through delegation where there is no need for a studio: the work can be produced, through design and specification, by specialists. The contents, likewise, can be brought together through the appropriate research and, if necessary, sponsorship. Without doubt there is considerable work involved, but little that demands the physical and tactile involvement with materials where processes of trial and error inevitably create sensory and sensual relationships with the emerging object. Because of this the vitrine triumphs. It is as free of historical luggage as a studio-produced object might be. In this way the vitrine, yet again, proves itself to be an enviable device.

Those artists who desire to make sculpture have chosen an increasingly difficult art form. When there are already so many objects in the world and so much manufactured stuff in production the sculptor is challenged from every side. Because of this, I consider sculpture to be a minority art form – preferably highly elitist – and in constant need of critical reassessment.

The burgeoning number of students taken on to sculpture courses indicates that only a few will pursue sculpture as rooted in the traditions I have described, both in how they will use a studio, an enlightened one I hope, and how they relate to making processes. For me, this is a healthy state of affairs.

Traditionally sculpture courses have offered only a few places, for practical reasons as well as those of demand. Since the idea of what sculpture can be has diversified, so have the numbers wishing to enter sculpture courses increased. The traditional object-maker, using hands-on processes and workshop techniques, is surrounded by performers, film-makers, and object-designers in an environment where proposals for sponsorship abound and the act of physical making is kept to a minimum. A rich symbiosis is generated in which the independence and close involvement of the maker is in contention with their opposite number – the delegator – and a tough coexistence is established between the two.

The delegated object, also the designed object, produced by specially chosen manufacturers or craftspeople, combined with the significant role of the vitrine, signal the importance of the written proposal in seeking out and achieving the artist's intended objective. This represents the reality of being an artist today, whereas crass economics can determine so much. The vitrine could be understood as being economically accommodating. Once made, admittedly probably at some considerable expense, anything can be placed within it, probably at less expense. If there are no studio overheads (the vitrine would be factory-produced), there would be little or no experimental making, no trial-and-error processes, therefore no outlay on materials, etc. The written proposal would determine how and by whom and with what this object would be realised, and it could be no more expensive, probably less so, than the cost of maintaining a studio and all that goes on in it.

Without doubt, the vitrine is endlessly fascinating, but now familiarity is beginning to breed contempt – it has become an overused and therefore abused device. Aesthetically stunning, capable of beautifying anything from shit to sheep, and portraying the already desirable as unreachable and untouchable, the vitrine seems to have captured the imagination of artists and viewers alike, perfectly symbolising how we are now forced to experience aspects of contemporary life. Its glory is becoming muted, its message repetitive.

The vitrine clearly demonstrates the endless possibilities of making without making, signalling how the artist can be emotive whilst keeping their distance from their work, delegating its production, and thus rendering the studio unnecessary.

Therefore the hatred of the object is manifested through the mistrust and abdication of the studio. The demise of the studio equates with a shunning of and a hatred of the object.

In researching the sculpture of Louise Bourgeois I came face to face with my contention of the hatred of the object. Her sculpture has received unanimous appreciation in recent years, even more so since the *Rites of Passage* exhibition at the Tate and the Paris retrospective, both showing the rich extremes typical of her work, which refutes typecasting and stylistic formulae. Her sculpture emerges without self-conscious strategies for making and unashamedly identifies itself with its roots in traditional sculpture processes of carving, construction, modelling, and casting, so prevalent in the middle years, the 1930s and 1940s, of the twentieth century in Europe when Bourgeois was just beginning as an artist. These processes are exemplified by the brooding, cumbersome sculpture of artists such as Étienne Martin, François Stahly, Ossip Zadkine, and to some extent Jean Arp, who were her influential contemporaries. Because of its traditional roots, the sculpture of Louise Bourgeois is the antithesis of the hatred of the object, and from this point of view I am perplexed as to its popularity when it stands for everything which has been so drastically repudiated in the way I have described.

Perhaps it is because her work transcends the grim spectre of traditional practice and is unpredictable and diverse enough to refute classification. Also, her art absorbs contemporary debate. There seem to be shrewd calculations made as to where she positions herself in the work: sometimes every trace of making is left evident and exposed on the surface of the object and at other times the surface is stretched and cleansed of all such marks, indicating an impeccable craft process. Similarly, appropriated objects, *objets trouvés*, and designed factory-produced objects coexist in harmonious abandon with the overtly handmade.

This work stands unprotected, open and exposed, offering itself for the closest of scrutiny, strategically involving the viewer in very specific acts of looking, and all the while there is the sense of the work looking back, at times insolently answering back the viewer's gaze. This is sculpture which operates in total antithesis to the vitrine: the objects celebrate, reveal, and confront the desirable and the repulsive, the beautiful and the ugly, the seductive and the repellent. The sculpture, whether it is autonomous object or installation, contrives to meet the viewer with the demand to be investigated, to be walked around, pried into, stalked, looked under and over. These are object experiences that jolt us into seeking out comparisons, to find equivalents, emotional and physical, which stir our imagination to question what we are looking at and what it is saying to us. There are no quick answers and no conclusions, just stark, undiluted confrontation with raw emotions.

Perhaps in the end the hatred of the object has had its day, and maybe the tremendous acclaim awarded to Bourgeois's sculpture is part of the hated object's demise. Perhaps the *tabula rasa* of traditional sculpture processes has been fulfilled and these processes can now be reclaimed and reinvested and their potential can be rediscovered. I would certainly welcome this as I do consider that these ancient processes are not necessarily an end in themselves but a means to an end. They provide independence and an appropriate, expedient, and human antidote to the worlds of the virtual and the removed, the sanitised and the hands-off.

The hatred of the object is a fiction I have invented in order to understand and contextualise some of the issues emerging from contemporary art. Within my arguments are, possibly, some truths, but there is also a good deal of conjecture, some of it all too familiar. However, for me, the idea of the hatred of the object is important because it enables me to examine and make clear to myself the importance of the studio and its harbouring of those private acts of making which, however removed they may be, are in my case deeply rooted in the traditional sculpture processes of modelling, casting, and construction. And I value them all the more because they are vulnerable to misinterpretation and abuse, and therefore easily dismissed and overlooked. Their coexistence with the productions of the delegators and the non-studio makers forces debate and a continuing critical exchange, ensuring that all acts of making are infinitely possible and necessary for a rich and challenging diversity of sculpture to be produced.

First published in Stuart Evans, Joanna Greenhill, and Ingrid Swenson, eds., *Matrix 3D: Sculpture, Method, Research* (London: Lethaby Press, 1997), 22–33. Also published in *Phyllida Barlow: Objects for … and Other Things* (London: Black Dog Publishing, 2004), 180–8, and Tanya Harrod, ed., *CRAFT* (London: Whitechapel Gallery; Cambridge, Mass.: MIT Press, 2018), 156–60.

This paper was given as part of the symposium 'Artistic Judgements: A Discussion about Quality in the Visual Arts', organised by the Southern Arts Board and held at St Catherine's College, Oxford, on 8 September 2000. Taking the idea of judgement in art as her starting point, Barlow outlines her interest in and the importance for her of the territory between the two poles of success and failure. She considers the commodification of art, the role of the exhibition, and judgement in relation to art education. Within this framework, she describes some recent visits to exhibitions and her encounters with works by Susan Hiller, Mirosław Bałka, Carl Andre, and Lee Hassall.

On Being Judged

2000

I want to give a brief introduction to my talk.

'On Being Judged', as a title, seems more appropriate as a subject for the Radio 4 panel game *Just a Minute*: to talk about 'on being judged' for sixty seconds, without repetition, hesitation, or deviation. Unfortunately, this is not such a panel game, and I regret that my talk will not be witty or entertaining. In fact, I found this subject incredibly slippery. Everybody judges and is judged, with all the pleasure and pain which accompanies such a process. It is no different for artists and their work. Therefore, to avoid losing control by accommodating the many different positions which impinge on this subject, I have opted for pursuing a single train of thought. I have concentrated on where I believe the process of judgement might be situated within the visual arts, particularly with relationship to the creative process and exhibitions. I am aware of the flaws in having narrowed down my point of view, and which I have not been able to resolve within the allocated twenty minutes. I hope you can unravel some of the content and, of course, be the judge of it!

Judgement is personal when it comes to the visual arts – and with choosing a detergent. But choices are restricted by what is available, at what cost, where from, what for, and its supposed and acclaimed reliability. Our preferences are rooted in expedience and expectation.

Consequently, expedience controls judgement through what is available and accessible. Better the devil you know than risk an as-yet unproven and possibly unreliable newcomer, or unknown old-timer. Therefore newcomers and old-timers must prove themselves through applications to whatever might still be prepared to take a risk.

I have switched from detergent to art, and it hardly seems to matter because, of course, artists make products and products cost money and money is time, space, accountability, and much else besides, on to which judgements can be pinned, and which then determine the two great choices: success or failure. Nothing more, nothing less.

My contention is that the territory between these two ultimates, success and failure, is unmapped, and cannot be mapped in the way that the territory occupied by works pronounced as either successes or failures will have been mapped. Both positions, success and failure, lead to a kind of condemnation because they limit how work is experienced. Both are the results of judgements, with opinions and decisions explained and keyed, locked into position: ultimatums which could take a lifetime to alter.

But the unmapped territory between success and failure generates doubt, time, and indifference. Indifference to an audience, indifference to a final outcome, and indifference to being sensible, particularly financially. Who else, other than an artist, or maybe an obsessive hobbyist (but that's another story) is prepared to use large parts of their, usually meagre, incomes on producing work, a product borne out of doubt, for which there is no guaranteeable future, and for which no particular future has yet been planned? So very different from the life cycle of the detergent.

Must the guaranteed successful product, as identified through consumerism, be the only model for a successful artwork? And if so, why? An answer could lie in a lethal cocktail of fundamentalist beliefs in the bums-on-seats style of consumerism, the overuse of dated, ill-researched, French-influenced art theories, and squeaky-clean curating, all of which I relate back to Thatcherism. This is something which began to bite deep into art later than the Mrs Thatcher reign itself, and which, for some reason, has had an enduring influence on contemporary art as we know it, and the administrative machines which embrace that art.

Having got this far, am I missing the point? The commodification of art is a concern at the periphery of my day-to-day experience as an artist, and on that day-to-day basis I do not give a toss about it. In fact, it gives and has given me a lot of pleasure, and has generated a lot of ammunition with which I have tried to galvanise my own creative identity and position, and enhance and develop my relationship with young artists and their work in my job of running a sculpture course.

What I do want to emphasise is the importance of that in-between territory. I identify this territory as the creative and emotional place where there are no ultimatums, no predatory and judgemental viewers, critics, curators. This place has no rules or laws for how, what, and why an artwork should be, and its most powerful protagonist is the imagination. Guesswork, time, doubt, passion, all coexist in a potentially chaotic and irrational society out of which and with which anything is possible. Beliefs, trust, and confidence emerge from this *mêlée*, free from any scrutinising gaze other than that of the artist.

It sounds easy enough, and luxurious, and self-indulgent. And it may well be these but, of course, it is more than likely not to be. Financial constraints, lack of time, loneliness and isolation, loss of confidence, lack of trust in a creative identity, and the ruthless criticisms from artists themselves are spectres which haunt this territory, and which have to be met and confronted. It is the land of struggle, survival, and also delight. But most of all, the pressures from the two hostile countries, success and failure, which border and surround the in-between, are persistent reminders of the destinies awaiting what emerges from the in-between. All the more reason, then, for the in-between to make itself known, to assemble its forces of guesswork, doubt, time, and passion and incite its leader, imagination, to be uncompromising, brave, and assertive.

There has to be the time for artists to immerse themselves completely in their relationship with their work, without the compromise of having to justify what they are doing. There has to be that risk. For myself, time has been hugely important. I am aware that I have had the benefits of constant art-school employment, from its earlier incarnation as liberal patron to artists, when there was no need to account for your work other than through the contributions of your experience as an artist, through to the aggressive educational imperatives of today, when everything is measured, quantified, assessed, and, of course, judged. No time, now, for time to let work grow and change. Instead that struggle is deemed unproductive until it can be justified as an outcome of research. The in-between territory is being squeezed from every side and the enemies are insisting on compulsory uniforms for all: 'research and practice' replace creative activity; 'outcomes' replace the fine-art disciplines of sculpture, painting, film, photography, video etc.; 'aims, objectives, learning results' replace the time-honoured processes of thinking, experimenting, making, and talking; 'skill facilities' replace studio and workshop. Semantics rule, but why, for what, and for whom?

My rant stops me from going any further with this line of enquiry. Instead, I'm drawn back to the way in which imagination embraces and encourages guesswork, doubt, time, and passion in order to contend judgement, and that these are potential antidotes to judgement which, if rigorously engaged, outwit those orthodoxies and conventions used to determine how judgements are exercised within the visual arts. The slogan 'nothing succeeds like success' is writ large over many a contemporary exhibition, and why not? No one wants to look at failures, do they? But perhaps it is a bit like the 'where are all the bad Rembrandt drawings?' argument, which makes me curious.

The pressure is that an exhibition, the work, has to be good, and the process of selection, the choice, for exhibitions has to be viable from every point of view: financial, theoretical, audience-friendly, political, critical. And even when the work in an exhibition is not that good, the pressure that it should and must be inhibits imaginative decision-making and the taking-on-board of guesswork, doubt, time, and passion.

But what I am trying to unravel is how can orthodoxies be contended, and how can risks be taken? And that I believe the in-between territory is the rich resource which can inform and inspire those risks. Clearly, curators, critics, even viewers and the public need artists more than the artists need them, which indicates, for me, that depending on proven success is an unreliable resource because to every artist who is showing, there are a hundred who are not, but could be. Choices, and their accompanying opinions, can become too predictable and dependable, and the means by which other participants can be sought becomes considered too difficult, too risky, too unpredictable, potentially too disruptive of the status quo.

I have identified the exhibition as a particularly significant player within this talk on judgement. I understand the exhibition as a bringing together of all aspects of judgement, and a fusion of choice and opinion. These qualities imply risk, bravery, originality, and innovation, and, above all, knowledge. However, disappointment can be the experience, not for any other reason than what is being held up as risky, brave, original, innovative, and knowledgeable fails to meet that mark, mainly because the expectation of these claims outdoes the reality. The qualities of risk, bravery, originality, innovation can be merely words attached to the work in order, perhaps, to protect it.

I have slipped up and resorted to the very language I am trying to challenge. 'Fails to meet that mark', I said, when what I am trying to describe is the disappointment when orthodoxies remain unchanged and unchallenged. I believe these orthodoxies do remain in place until the in-between is recognised as the repository of risk, bravery, originality, innovation, and knowledge, and that the awkward, unpredictable, and sometimes hostile companions to these are doubt, indifference, and time. These are not good promotional material for exhibitions and therefore are vulnerable to being ignored.

I also see embedded within this in-between, dystopic utopia, the work whose outcome is not known, not stitched up, which requires more than being judged good or bad, but a recognition that it is on its way somewhere, destination as yet unknown, and that it is an exploration beyond the superficial clutches of good or bad, success or failure. Work which is difficult to pin down.

And, for me, difficult work raises the equally difficult bogeyman (or bogeywoman) of elitism. Not exclusivity, that is another world that I am aware of, but have no interest in. By elitism I mean the right for the artwork to exist on its terms, for it to have its demands met and fulfilled, however obscure, user-unfriendly, and expensive these may be. Elitism exists in all disciplines without damaging how the public receives that discipline. Without doubt, there are wonderful and brave examples of how organisations have fulfilled an artwork's intentions in specific and breathtaking ways, elitist ways, but not exclusive ways, and I hope my descriptions towards the end will support this.

Referring back to art education where the 'stack 'em high, sell 'em cheap' educational philosophy is biting deep in the guise of democratisation, there is the threat that BA fine-art degree exhibitions will be reduced to art-fair-styled displays, not much different from A level, in order to accommodate the increased number of students. The effect of this is the editing-out of the curriculum serious discussion about and experimentation with what the destination for an artwork can be and how the possibilities can be encouraged which challenge orthodox and conventional presentation methods. Young artists are being denied the opportunity to test out their wildest dreams in the protected environment of the art school, which itself is in danger of becoming nothing more than an obedient and submissive cog in an oversimplified, art-for-all machine. Creative ambition is being replaced by expedience and conformity.

The judgements on what art education should be and for whom will, I believe, have a profound influence on an understanding of and an ability to take on the complex and difficult experiences of guesswork, doubt, time, and passion. These could be threatened with extinction because they will be deemed too costly, too unreliable, too elitist for the dreaded bums-on-seats prerogatives.

Before I end, I want to reveal my passion for contemporary art. Two exhibitions I have been to this summer stay in my mind. First, Susan Hiller's *Witness*: the Artangel version in the semi-derelict chapel on Golborne Road, Notting Hill, not the diminished version in *Intelligence* at Tate Britain (fig. 86).

Witness lingered cryptically in the darkened upper storey of its protective shelter, stunning in its ghostly simplicity of glinting, dangling wires and muttering mini-speakers, approached by a narrow, spiral staircase, hidden at the back of the downstairs entrance. As intended, I was drawn into the work's centre to become immersed in the cacophony of descriptions offered by the mini-speakers. The sounds grew and subsided, like the ebb and flow of a tide. Eventually I felt no necessity to listen to the individual descriptions, which became a fiddly, overresolved intrusion on my relationship to the physicality of the work: its secret sense of place, its eerily illuminated theatricality, its fragmented linear and circular formality, its celestial hum of voices, all of which gave me as much and more than the labour of listening to the individual descriptions of UFO sightings relayed through each mini-speaker. My response was that the heart of the work lay in its physicality, not its literality. More importantly, I was able to have this response with the work delivered on its terms, uncompromised and particular, dignified in its occupation of place and space.

Mirosław Bałka's work on show at Tate Modern, in the exhibition *Between Cinema and a Hard Place*, inhabits a superb gallery within this new and sensational museum but, unlike *Witness*, this work seems independent of its environment, as if it brings its world with it (fig. 87). Initially, the elegant, structural formality of uprightness, squareness, leaningness belied, for me, the depth of emotions harboured within such simple forms. It took time, walking around and waiting, and at first nothing happened, but I was attracted to these hermetic objects, forbidding in their lack of give. I began to feel more of a voyeur and more of a witness than with Susan Hiller's work. I was in the presence of something horribly cruel, but which had been caught and trapped for scrutiny. The severe beauty of the rusted steel captured an association I could make with that sense of ending, a slow death, the leftover ruins, but of what? These sculptures affect an industrial decay and impart an emotional weight: the tragedy of collapse, so reminiscent of the great Andrzej Wajda film trilogy *A Generation*, *Kanal*, and *Ashes and Diamonds*. Sculptures which seemed to arrest time, like a photograph but, also, not like a photograph because of that overpowering sense of being in the presence of something tangible, having its own existence, alarmed, alive, ever awake, tortuously so, whilst sustaining total stillness and silence. That is the fascination of sculpture for me.

The simplistic language of judgement, in fact, denies absolutely the slow, utterly private, sensual, intimate, solitary, often dark engagement experienced with the making of art and with the viewing of it, which I have tried to communicate with my descriptions of the two exhibitions. It has always been the treacherous territory in-between, out of which has emerged a stumbling and hesitant translation into a language, whether that be verbal, visual, tactile, or of sound, or smell, or of time.

Judge, judged, judgement. Each one is like a blunt instrument; onomatopoeic, similar to cudgel and bludgeon and even dungeon. Words which have a finality about them, rooting an event in time and place. Powerful, ancient, old English words conjuring up the necessity for simplicity in law and action and the driving ambition to survive at any price. Words which are as resonant as the things they symbolise. So why is it necessary to resort to such a word when it comes to the arts? Who needs to be equipped with this weaponry?

In stark contrast, Carl Andre's *Karlsplatz* at the Whitechapel is silent, still and solitary (fig. 88). I experienced it as a finality: arrived, complete, defiant of being named, without ownership, and the nearest analogy I found myself making was like being near to something animal, crouched, and squat, almost about to heave with breath, which its solidity contradicted. As I walked round it, straining to see as much of it as possible, to get to its centre, the massiveness and simplicity of the cedar began to change from solid, dumb, repeated structure to warm, fleshiness. I was being given the close-up presence of something usually removed, only to be seen or glimpsed from a distance, like the structures deep beneath a pier, or harbour, or bridge, phenomena and wonders of engineering, to be washed and submerged by heaving tons of water. It generated an extraordinary fluctuating frisson

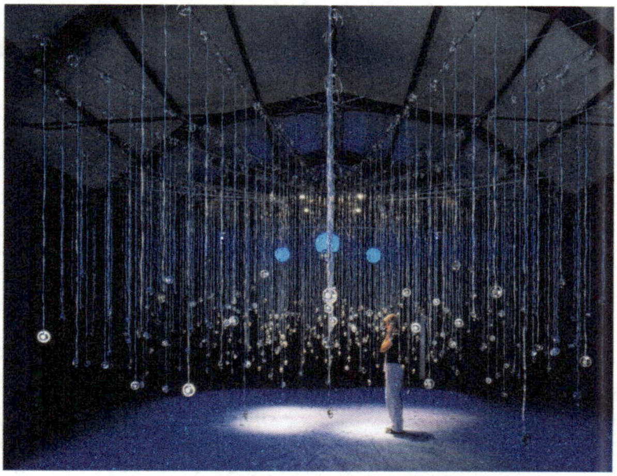

LEFT:
fig. 86 **Susan Hiller**
Witness, 2000,
installation view,
Artangel commission,
The Chapel on Golborne
Road, London, 2000

RIGHT:
fig. 87 **Mirosław Bałka**
Dawn, 1995,
installation view,
Between Cinema and a Hard Place, Tate Modern,
London, 2000

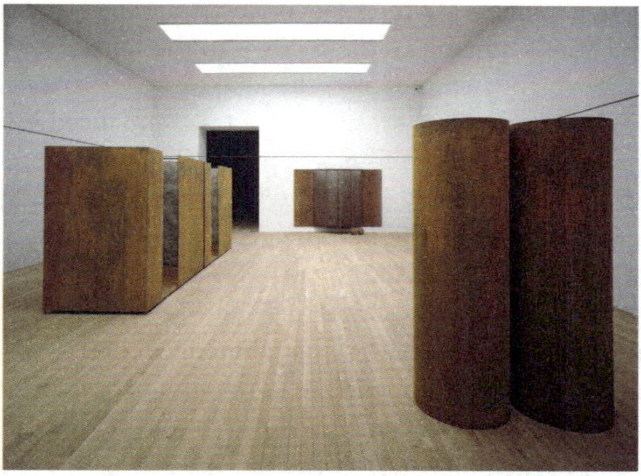

BELOW:
fig. 88 **Carl Andre**
Karlsplatz, 1992,
installation view,
Whitechapel Gallery,
London, 2000

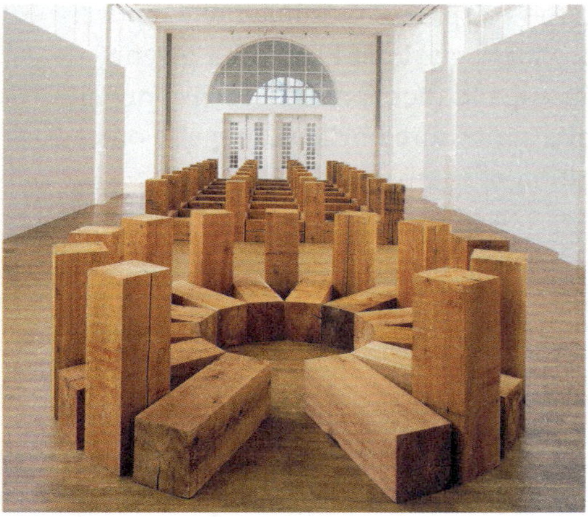

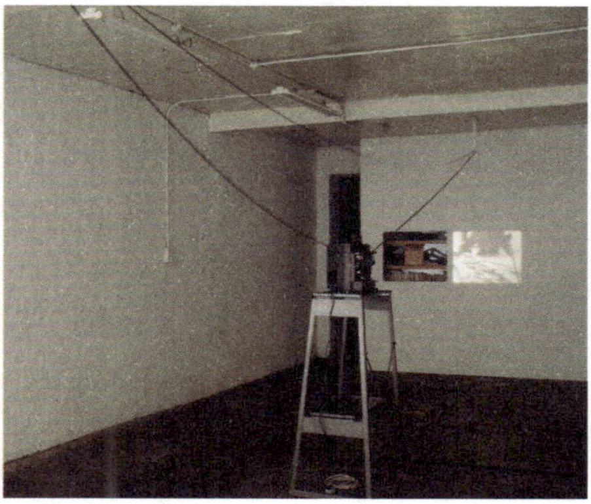

ABOVE:
fig. 89 **Lee Hassall**
Installation view, *Skylark Fashions*,
Fordham Gallery, London, 2000

between art-historical monument and warm-blooded presence, embracing all the senses: the sounds or sea, the smell of warm hide, the touch of rough skin, the sight of something remote, awesomely structural and heavy, the taste of metal. And yet, paradoxically for me, it remains unnameable, despite its tangibility, defiant in its autonomy, supreme in its identity as an art object.

But whether that work was or is that good, or not, is only part of the story. Because it has been selected, it is as if it has no other choice than to be good. It has to succeed. It is as if the process of selection, and the choice of the selection, has to be successful and viable from every point of view: financial, theoretical, critical, audience-friendly. Is this really the case, or is this a flight of an artist's suspicious nature? A bit of both, perhaps.

The second exhibition was at Fordham, an artist-run space off Bethnal Green Road. Here Lee Hassall, recently graduated from Chelsea and before that from the Slade, projected a 16mm looped film showing two Asian pattern-cutters operating their lethal electrical fabric-cutter machine (fig. 89). Filmed in black and white, edited down to the repetitive slicing of the cutter through the thick stash of fabric, the loop's careful scrutiny confronted me with the claustrophobic intensity of the task, enhanced by the impoverished environment in which the film was projected, and the other addition to the installation, a small window cut into the partition at the back of the space, which showed the office behind the gallery, with all the mundaneness of such a work place. The resulting narrative and form inherent to this work were a powerful mix of nostalgia and sentimentality with raw technical and material intervention which grounded me in a contrived metaphor that the fabric-cutters' task was comparable to the film process itself, one a reflection of the other. But I was relieved by a further and, in my opinion, more poetic comparison of the poignancy of the art space reflecting the oppressive and cramped working space of the cutters: the art space is presumed redemptive, and the other oppressed, or could it be vice versa? I felt I had been given something particular and uncompromised, and therefore I could give myself to the work, uninhibitedly, on its terms, unpressured by anything else other than the work and its dignified occupation of its place and space.

First published in *Artistic Judgements: A Discussion about Quality in the Visual Arts: Report on a Symposium Held by Southern Arts Board at St Catherine's College, Oxford* (Winchester: Southern Arts, 2001), 3–10.

This was first given as a paper at the seminar 'Next Generations: Current Sculptural Practice in the UK and Beyond' at the Whitechapel Art Gallery, London, on 20 July 2002, on the occasion of their exhibition *Early One Morning*. Barlow addresses the impact, both immediate and longer term, of the exhibition *The New Generation*, 1965, also held at the Whitechapel. She discusses the influence of the innovations in art taking place in the United States and elsewhere in Europe at this time and witnessing the opening up of the possibilities for what sculpture could be.

Hearsay, Rumours, Bedsit Dreamers, and Art Begins Today

2002

I am having difficulty in pinning down what the significance of *The New Generation, 1965* sculpture exhibition could be. I have resorted to compiling lists, lots of them, and each one with a different inflection. But the crucial thing has to be how to edit these lists into something relevant for this conference. And I keep on going back to the subject of the conference – is it, what is the future *for* sculpture, or the future *of* sculpture, or, maybe, does sculpture have a future? And who cares anyway?

The 1965 *New Generation* exhibition has stuck in my memory, but not because it was an exceptional artistic experience. The opposite is more the case. As Mary Horlock cites in her catalogue essay for this exhibition, 'Early One Morning', Bruce McLean referred to the 1965 exhibition as more of the same: New Generation sculpture was nothing more than Henry Moore with stripes. The exhibition was more relevant to its immediate past than to anything new. New Generation was a kind of mutton dressed as lamb.

Dominating my lists has been the word 'new'. 'New' does signify 'clean', 'fresh', 'bright', 'unused', 'unopened', 'spotless', even 'pure'. Certainly not 'second-hand', 'nearly new', 'borrowed'. And when the new is spoilt, even in the slightest way, a tiny scratch on the new car body, or a spot of grease on new clothes, the entire effect is ruined, and the new becomes a ruin. To have removed the word 'new' from the title of the *New Generation* exhibitions would have lost everything: to have called them the 'Next Generation' would have meant nothing, but would have been, in fact, nearer the truth.

And 'new' does also mean 'young'. Importantly, the *New Generation* exhibitions did herald the importance and excitement of showing new, young artists' work when previously there were few such exhibitions.

But despite the brightness and so-called newness of the *New Generation* exhibition, there was an inherent familiarity about it. A dullness took over: the stillness of the sculpture was bland, not atmospheric; its weight was leaden rather than illusionary; its colour, although its greatest asset, too reminiscent of what had been shown in the previous year's *New Generation* painting exhibition. The 1965 exhibition was destined to be short-lived, and all too quickly it became consumed by institutionalism, its fate sealed into academicism.

The exhibition became a demonstration for how sculpture could be learnt. As an all-male preserve, the *New Generation* exhibition offered a collection of workshop practices, born out of essentially male-based activities: welding, fibreglass and resin casting and construction, and semi-industrial assemblage. Sculpture as such provided an ideal for a 'school of sculpture' to be established, based on sheet metal assemblage and fibreglass and resin techniques, and exercises accompanying these would reveal all.

Also, there was this all-pervading suspicion, through rumour and hearsay of course, that all that was going on in New Generation sculpture, UK, had its origins in the US, and those who had an inkling of this were disappointed in the claims bestowed upon the exhibition. Dominating the experience was not a sense of newness but more of an eclecticism culled from various of-the-moment, American styles. American art was what was craved: stripes, colour fields abounded within and without art schools making the exhibition several years overdue, and out of date quicker than it could have expected.

Therefore, going to see the current Tate Britain collection of 1960s New Generation sculpture restated exactly that sense of dull academicism, where crucial missing ingredients deny the possibility of a more enchanted experience. The emotional denial inherent to the work brought back how easily the New Generation sculpture had become fodder for designers who had plundered its bright, toylike style for their own ends, making the work indistinguishable from the burgeoning Habitat domestic commodities, Galt's faddish, pseudo-crafted toys, as well as packaging, textiles, and new innovations with easy-to-assemble furniture and DIY, also a burgeoning, new industry.

The increasingly tedious debates about sculpture then: to plinth or not to plinth, the value of the laborious grind of making, truth to materials, etc., etc., paled into more art-school academicism as new rumours and hearsay of what was going on elsewhere began to filter through. And what was it that was being talked about and rumoured? Stories of works in deserts and excavations in derelict warehouses employing a different kind of labour: straight manual labour as seen on the street and building site, diggers and excavators, were being appropriated to make sculpture, whilst at the opposite end of the scale, resin and a new material, latex, were being used like paint, not as a substitute for bronze, but as stuff in its own right, to be dunked into, painted on cloth to make it rigid, moulded off rigid forms to make them soft, poured, spilt, and thrown. Weight, mass, scale, and size were all being usurped by gesture, touch, and the here and now. And artists were taking to the streets, like so many others at that time, and foregoing the studio; anywhere and everywhere was a site, and anything and everything could be made into art. Excitement and imagination had arrived. By 1968, the New Generation exhibitions were dead history.

So, what is newness? Interestingly the current exhibition, *Early One Morning*, does not make such a claim, but, as the title suggests, offers energy, vitality, and an anything-goes exuberance. It clearly does delight, and, because it does not offer any definitions for sculpture – which the 1965 show became associated with – there is a free spirit about this exhibition. Whether this free spirit is new or not is another matter, but certainly the 1965 exhibition could make no such claim. All the old rules were firmly in place: craft, weight, formal autonomy, symmetry, asymmetry. The 'new' could be learnt, and art schools were where you went to learn it. A new academicism had been born, and an all-male one at that! Freeness, imagination, and surprise did seem to be missing from the 1965 exhibition. And as the hearsay and rumours increased from the US and Europe, the more academic and institutionalised the British art scene seemed to become. The hearsay and rumours offered an entirely different experience, an experience rooted in the forbidden and despised notion of theatricality. No more the need for permanency, weightiness, handicraft, the learnt, and to be taught restraints of what was and what was not sculpture. Instead, in with impermanency, temporariness, dematerialisation, the fugitive, the ephemeral, the here and now. Out with the welding shop and the learnable techniques and in with experimentation with anything and everything: materials and physicality were opened up for anything, everything, everywhere. And the artist him or herself could be anyone, and as such they could be subject and object of the work.

The beauty of the theatrical lay in its potential to take on anything, anywhere: the stage became container and protagonist for the work and could be anything and everything. Absolutely anywhere could be appropriated as an art space.

Sculpture became the activity incarcerated within an art school, to be taught and learnt. The street and anywhere else became the time and the place. Creative freedom was reciprocal to the political activities raging around Europe and the US. The incident, the act itself was the work, and how it would have permanency would be through its potential for rumour and hearsay, all of which could be endorsed by the most significant of reporters, the camera: the Super 8 movie camera and the 35mm SR, and their rolls of black-and-white film. These were to become the most important travelling companions and accomplices to this ephemeral work.

So for me the legacy of the 1965 exhibition was not in the show itself but in what it spawned as an opposition to it. Sculpture continued to be made in studios but there was a burgeoning feminising of the processes, and a different take on labour intensivity was beginning to emerge. The studio could look beyond itself for inspiration. The kitchen, the dressmaker's, the garage, agriculture, roadworks, building sites, and, of course, the bedsit, the home of most art students, could all provide processes to be plundered and appropriated as means to an end. Speculation was the game and time was of the essence. Why try to compete with the superartists, and their corporate support: the former rebels, who had become the then established global exhibitors: the Smiths, Caros, Kings, Tuckers, yesterday's equivalents to today's Turrells, Violas, Christos, Pistolettos. Why devote hours to labour-intensive activities when results could be produced immediately, as was beginning to be seen through the work of Hesse and Bourgeois. Why go to the macho means of production when twiddling your thumbs and putting things together from your immediate environment was all you could afford to do. What about staring at the bedsit ceiling and dreaming up the wild, the wonderful, and the way beyond from the patterns on the ceiling and making it become reality by any means possible? The smoothed-out surfaces of the fibreglass and resin aficionados were becoming clichéd, let alone the fact that resin was carcinogenic, and therefore an unsuitable material to spend too much time with. All the more reason for speedy, direct application; all the more reason for hit-and-run techniques.

Theatricality and time became absorbed into all aspects of sculpture. Issues about the plinth blurred into comparative obscurity and irrelevance. Space became location and place, a material in its own right and the object could both occupy and disown that space: the object could be dematerialised. Its presence could, and can, for that matter, be manifested through its absence, and again the hearsay and rumours of such work were as important as the work itself. Again, it was and is the camera in all its guises which provided the evidence, and it is only evidence, of such work. Therefore, I believe, sculpture as a fundamentalist activity which could only tell the truth, the whole truth, and nothing but the truth became tedious and irrelevant. Released from its history of permanency and absolute materiality, sculpture could fragment space, could be cinematic in its relationship to how to occupy space, and could fib and lie itself into its own reality. Objects could connect and interrelate over spaces that they would charge with atmospheric and moody resonances, and time had to be taken to experience the whole encounter: objects, space, time.

And so hearsay, rumours, bedsit dreams, and 'art-begins-today' attitudes came to stay and have stayed. Sculpture, for myself, still resides in the experience of unreality: the walking around of things that have no use in the world and which defy absolute categorisation and definition. I do not want to be told about things which I already know about, unless of course it is to be surprised, to be offered a glimpse of something which I could never conceive of being what it is. The fugitive and the ephemeral are still exciting; the place of where something might be and could be, whether that is brought into an official art space, or whether that is claiming somewhere else, is still exciting. And the here and now, which has to be the most exciting and enduring of sculptural experience, where once you have gone away from the object it somehow cannot quite be retrieved. It demands that you have to be there with it, to experience it, to know it.

Even though Conceptual Art raged like wildfire and tried its hardest to establish its own domination, it could not override the enthusiasm for making and doing in its revitalised, theatrical form. It did have an influence, undoubtedly so, causing a wave of doubt and reconsideration of who art was for, where it should and could be seen, with what, how, and why. Again, the dominant tool was the camera, and so a crossover between the mental and physical approaches to making became inextricably bound, and the rest is history.

Likewise with commodification: it may come and go, with its boxed, based, and vitrined symptoms of conventionalism and conservatism; they may have abounded, and still do abound, incarcerating and taming aesthetics, and emasculating and caging form, as they do, where the wild, untamed, and visceral is brought to heel under the whip of consumerist, product-led, and commercially driven incentives. Importantly as well, hearsay and rumour have now found perfect accommodation within the catalogue, which has undoubtedly become the most important record, souvenir, and take-away memorandum of what is shown: no catalogue, no exhibition? So what becomes of rumour and hearsay under these circumstances? Time will tell.

But the most significant influences on sculpture for the present and for its future do still remain beyond the institutions, firmly residing in the sphere of the artist him or herself. Where, with what, how, why, when can still surprise, be momentary, difficult to access, or even be known about, but because of these difficulties and awkwardnesses, not despite them, hearsay, rumour, bedsit dreamers, and art-begins-today attitudes will prevail and will be initiated and stimulated by the favoured art of the time, even by default, even for the sake of contrariness, even to stake out an opposition, all of which provides the resource and incentive for what will happen next.

The 1965 New Generation sculpture galvanised something: whether, through opposition, it was an anti-historicism and anti-institutionalism on one hand, which has not endured. Or whether it is the spirit of adventure centred on the individual and how he or she releases that, whatever their life experience, bedsits or otherwise, which has endured. Whatever the influences from 1965 might be, if any, the future of sculpture always lies in the unexpected. Therefore, this most awkward, recalcitrant, and unmanageable of art forms can be relied upon to make believable the imagination. Imagination has to be what is inherently new and surprising, and essential to sculpture, its past, its present, and its future.

Published in *Phyllida Barlow: Objects for ... and Other Things* (London: Black Dog Publishing, 2004), 210–13.

This lecture was given on 20 February 2004 at the conference 'The Treason of Images: Teaching Modern Art' at Tate Modern, London. Barlow begins by offering two unidentified descriptions. From here she moves on to discuss installation art. She examines the role of the viewer, the idea of watching rather than looking, the creation of a spectator, and theatricality. She considers the installation as object, the economics of such work, the status of ephemerality, and discusses installation art in relation to art education.

Throwing Away the Maps

2004

The title of my talk is 'Throwing Away the Maps'. I'll be showing some slides. They're actually not necessarily works that I particularly like, but they're trying to be samples or illustrations of the comments I am making. I am beginning with two descriptions, and this is the first description:

The street is crowded with Christmas shoppers. It is difficult to get to the large wooden doors cutting across the path of so many people. They are heavy double doors that are practically flush with the street. The struggle to open them is self-conscious and the shoppers glance at what is happening as if it is a break-in. Once inside, the world is turned upside down. Despite the heavily wood-panelled walls remaining intact, the space is in the process of being dismantled, screens and boards are stacked and leant whilst large pieces of cumbersome office furniture provide storage spaces for disparate things including rolls of carpet, broken chairs, piles of telephone directories, tipped-over paint cans, scrumpled-up paper, everything jammed together. The place is in turmoil. The lighting is dimmed but brightened by the flickering of videos projected on to the top of a high wall in such a way that one video overlaps the next and it is initially difficult to decipher them. They are showing some kind of nightmarish children's party where the dress code is huge Spitting-Image-style heads of notorious political leaders. Who are they? Margaret Thatcher, George Bush, Ronald Reagan, the Queen. And the games being played stray into eroticism. It seems dangerous. Something is going wrong, but what? And who is going to help prevent catastrophe? The whole vista is chaotic, compounded by a balcony overlooking the space on which are standing a small group of people all gazing, fixedly, at the scene in front of them and below them. They are like spectators watching a disaster. But having negotiated this initial carnage, there are other spaces to investigate, up and down cramped staircases, offices complete with secretaries and further stashes of furniture are revealed. Deep in the basement a video reveals some kind of obscene struggle between an aging male protagonist and a younger female. A bucket of glutinous, shit-like substance is clumsily tipped from a perilously built structure, whilst he awkwardly reveals his bare arse in all its glory, no detail spared. This excruciating drama is unrelenting and drags on and on. The fake excrement is spreading everywhere and the past, whatever that might be, does not seem to have any means of being resolved. In the space in which the video is being projected, a crowd has gathered to watch, and there is a tense hush. There is an atmosphere of dread mingled with repressed humour. The dark underground location is extremely cramped and hot. There is the odd muffled snigger as the abject male bum heaves in and out of view and the ministrations of the younger female seem of no avail. The surrogate shit-pouring apparatus is erratic and the two protagonists have trouble controlling it. They are smeared and spattered with the stuff. It has been going on for fifteen minutes and there seems to be no end. Time to go. Back into the packed street of busy shoppers. And now each reality, the ceaseless flow of shoppers and the tumultuous scenes behind the heavy wooden doors, seem to reciprocate each other, but obliviously so.

And this is the second description:

It is bitterly cold on a dark day with huge clouds building up, swooping in off the North Sea. Across the expanse of concrete is the vast shed with its gaping entrance, protected by thick rubber flaps hanging from the top some six metres up. Everything is on an enormous scale; human size is miniaturised. But through the thick rubber door flaps, a wonderland is revealed. As far as the eye can see there is a white haze which has attached itself to every available surface. The furthest wall at the far end of the space is at least 150 metres away. And the white is like a blizzard, almost obliterating the fabric of the shed's structure, making it pictorial, like a white painting which has been stepped into. Throughout the entire space hundreds of separate horizontal structures are placed, all at waist height, supported on steel trestle legs. Lying on them are various lengths of steel arranged haphazardly creating an abstract pattern, which is carried to the furthest point in a fractured array of perspectival edges like an assault of arrows shot towards an advancing army disappearing into a white fog. But in strong contrast to this implied violence is the ever-present softness of the white haze. On closer inspection the white also evidences itself as lumpy swellings on the ends of each of the trestles, rounding off the rigidity of these multiple structures. In fact, these bulbous growths are everywhere: on the floor, at regular intervals like latent stalactites, and on the walls, and now all around the edge of the entire space. And the white is covering other colours: reds, yellows, greens, browns, blues; have all been frosted, chilled with the all-obscuring layer of white. The faint glow of other colours evidences other lives. Something that has been here before that has been incarcerated in permafrost. This is an interior landscape, frozen in time, completely still without a flicker of light. Shockingly, and terrifyingly, it is awoken from its stasis by a sudden and violent sound. It is a metallic roar, three times, and it heralds a flurry of activity, which happens with apparently no human prompting. Hissings and clankings spring into life, numerous arm-like cranes begin to judder high up in the steel rafters of the shed. And other tubes, half-concealed by a veil of white, begin to unwind nearby. Something is going to happen, and it is time to go and get out fast.

My first description was of Paul McCarthy's recent exhibition at Hauser & Wirth's new space on Piccadilly [*Paul McCarthy: Piccadilly Circus*, Hauser & Wirth London, 2003]. The building this gallery had acquired was formerly a bank, or some such place, which McCarthy took on as the starting point for what was in fact a highly contrived chaos. A staged state of anarchy in direct contrast to the officially formal status of the building. The exhibition was a study in mannerism, where every action and arrangement was precisely intended. The viewer was manipulated and theatrically drawn into each carefully staged drama. The use McCarthy made of the entire building gave the exhibition a theme-park quality. And like all theme parks, every opportunity is exploited to the maximum to make the visitors, or in this case the viewers, respond. And the response that was initiated was that of spectators. The viewers, like the people on the balcony overlooking McCarthy's installation, *were* spectators. And as spectators, they were watching the work perhaps more than looking at it.

Meanwhile my second description was not of an installation nor of an artwork at all. It was a description of the paint shop at the Swan Hunter shipyard at Wallsend on Tyneside which I visited this January. In terms of describing such a place, it could have been an installation in all but what it actually was: a functional place fulfilling functional tasks in as expedient a way as possible. There was no emotional manipulation of the viewer or visitor. All responses were mere interpretations, taking what was purely factual stuff and transforming it into something which it was like, using the simile and the metaphor to raise the pragmatic practicalities of this place and give it an artwork status. Of course, such a remarkable place does not need to have its poetic qualities raised. It is wonderful as it is. And its wonder is brought about by the job of work in hand: the spray-painting of various components required for ship construction. The fact that it reminded me of a snowy landscape is inevitable and if it had been the day that yellow paint was being used it would have no doubt been a very hot, deserty kind of experience.

And this is the competition with which installation has to contend. Therefore it is interesting to attempt to analyse what installation might be in the face of such remarkable competition from the world around, natural and unnatural.

In both my descriptions the physical role of the viewer was essential to understanding the extent of what was going on. This is perhaps the key to installation and also its most vulnerable demand. There is no one viewing point. The viewer becomes a protagonist, walking in amongst the work.

They become like someone who is behind the scenes, watching the performance from the wings, and witnessing the requisite things for the performance close up, warts and all. The action of the viewer references both the sculptural and the pictorial. It is a walking around experience and a looking at experience. The mishmash of possibilities that such viewing offers seems exciting, and it can be. But it can also lend itself to borrowing the spectator style of looking where the gasp of admiration is the highpoint of the experience. This is where installation is so akin to theatricality, that it can be little more than that, a very staged experience, where the viewer's emotions are milked for all they're worth and the exchange between what the viewer is being milked for and what is given becomes a kind of emotional blackmail.

The behind-the-scenes experience can also be subtle, the fact that there is no one viewing point prompts the viewer to make choices about how and where to look at the work. This does make the space itself become a physical material in its own right. All aspects of the space become contingent to the installation, making the physicality of the viewer as important as the work itself. I'm thinking of James Turrell's sky works, and I personally have a lot of problems with Turrell, but I think he is an example of this, where the physical actions of sitting down and looking upwards are as important as the square of sky itself.

Being behind the scenes suggests a viewpoint which is oblique to the conventional viewpoint, where another viewpoint is offered, where a glimpse can be held for longer and something which is usually over in a second can be suspended and protracted. Such is the case with Turrell's sky works and with Louise Bourgeois's *Red Rooms* where the interior space is spied through the chinks and cracks between doors and windows. Such installations alter the viewer's expectations of how something can be looked at where the role of spectatorship is slowed down and shifts to that of intimate scrutiny.

But what of the role of installation as object? Or rather, what kind of object is an installation? Attached to this question come others: how does an installation function in the art market? How does an installation operate in relationship to documentation? And in relationship to memory?

In 1987 Michael Craig-Martin was the external examiner for the postgraduate sculpture course at the Slade. One particular installation was compelling. A group of metal lockers weeping water on to raw concrete. All who saw it, including Craig-Martin, unanimously agreed the opinion that this was an outstanding work. However, he made the following statement – Michael Craig-Martin did – that any fine-art course which continued, in the then economic and political climate, to encourage installation art was acting irresponsibly. Further discussion did make more sense of this drastic statement in so much that what was meant was that art schools should take on the issue of how young artists, fresh out of art school, could survive economically. The non-economic viability of installation art could be seen as a liability, and young artists could be being led into a no man's land of hopeless economic prospects if encouraged to pursue this kind of activity.

However there are numerous examples where installation has proved anything but an economic disaster, beginning, for example, with the sale of Richard Wilson's 20:50 to Saatchi in 1988. This sale was finalised through a specification being proffered from which the work could be reconstructed. This clearly paved the way for sale by specification, releasing installation art from its economic purgatory and in some ways this has also diminished installation's position as a radical art form. Having the potential to be economically viable has lessened its opportunities to reside solely in the realm of the ephemeral. No longer can installation art claim to exist in the moment of its showing but once the exhibition or event or happening is over, then so is the installation of the work. And that the only way it could be recalled would be through documentation or the memories of those who had been there to witness it. Rachel Whiteread's *House* is such a work amongst many.

My idealised notion of installation resides in the sculptural. I understand *this* as the physical interaction between the space and the things within that space. Paradoxically, the most exciting exploitation of installation in this way is ephemeral, or non-permanent. Where the physicality of the work is not necessarily built for perpetuity. For me such work embraces time as well as place. And movement, smell, temperature, light, dark. But above all the sentient experience of moving around the work and being there with it. Ephemerality and non-permanence are also political. The politics of temporary ownership does not seem to require commercial success and commodification. I regard Robert Morris's *Steam Works* as fulfilling all of these qualities, as does Robert Smithson's *Asphalt Rundown*.

But then there are Jessica Stockholder's works which are more permanent and resonant with spontaneity. Or Mike Kelley's installations which hold the viewer in tense anticipation where only a part of a narrative is offered. Similarly so with Robert Gober's work. Compare his political stance with that of Hans Haacke, whose *Standort Merry-Go-Round* challenges the convention of how public monuments unquestioningly take permanent ownership of public spaces. And what of Bruce Nauman's works, the suspended chairs threatening the space beneath them with such authority that no one dares to enter? Such is the poetic and emotive power of these works that the relationship with the viewer and the occupied space is that of the manipulator and the manipulated but where there is a symbiosis between the two and it is interchangeable. The work, the space, and the viewer do both to each other and wilfully so. There is a political challenge posited through these works' use of space, despite their obvious commercial and commodifiable success.

The qualities of time and place and the absolute moment of the work, its moment, are infinitely possible as creative expressions to be encouraged within art schools and very much part of what should be discussed and proposed for critical debate. Installation, as with all the fine-art forms, does not have special treatment when it comes to diagnosing what works or not. Installation is a much-used form within every art school I have worked in and beyond because it does resist certain conventions while sustaining others. It is not radical but it can embrace qualities beyond the status quo of painting and sculpture, letting in those other sentient qualities of sound, smell, movement, temperature. And so much so that I, for one, begin to long for that particular relationship which the status quo of painting and sculpture offers where hybridity is not an issue to be contended with. Issues of the spectator, the spectacular, the behind-the-scenes, the protracted glimpse, the space as material, the ephemeral, the politics of place, the remembered, the sculptural, the sentient, are all as applicable to any artwork which a viewer is prepared to give themselves up to, where they throw themselves into the work without prejudice, whether this be installation or not.

Installation has become ubiquitous, where painters are just as likely to make an installation – as did Chris Ofili for his Venice Biennale exhibition – as video artists and photographers, as sculptors and film-makers and performance artists. It has become an orthodoxy just as much as the readymade is as inherited from Marcel Duchamp and industrially produced sculpture as inherited from the likes of Donald Judd and Jeff Koons. In the end, it is best to throw away the maps and go it alone.

The audio cassettes of this lecture are held by Tate Library, London.

In 2007 Barlow received funding from Arts Council England for a project titled 'What Do Artists Do?'. She invited a group of artists and curators to use a space she had found in order to develop work with no particular outcome in mind, with the aim of questioning the role of experimentation in the production of art and the role of the institution in relation to art. Included here are extracts from her extensive application proposal, which sets out both the thinking behind and practicalities of the project. In the introduction Barlow reflects on working invisibly for the best part of her then forty-year career and questions if this continues to be a viable option for artists. In the first appendix she attempts to define experimentation in relation to the visual arts and sets out two propositions: 'visual artists do not experiment' and 'experimentation is inherent to the visual artist'. The second appendix covers the role of the institution in relation to art and the final section returns to a consideration of invisibility and explores the idea of the non-exhibition.

Arts Council Application: What Do Artists Do?

2007

SECTION 1: INTRODUCTION

With forty years of experience of being an artist, I have the opportunity to look back at how I have got to where I am now. Increasingly, I am critical of the positions I have adopted. In particular, I need to reconsider my persistent repudiation of commercially driven art and its relationship to the art industry as a whole. I now question where my challenge to exhibiting, selling, professionalism, and the art industry have led me.

For many years, this challenge gave me the confidence to accept working invisibly, and I have worked for a major part of my artistic life as such. I have justified such an existence through what I considered to be patronage from art-school teaching, borne out through a passionately held belief in my studio activity, and not only mine, but the studio and its attendant processes and working methods per se, for whomever, whatever, or wherever that might be.

My experiences can seem to be more than ever in direct opposition to the prevailing demands on artists, and unrealistic if not irresponsible in my relationship to teaching and my contact with future artists. But I am intrigued to know just how opposite these experiences are, or whether I can offer myself and others the opportunity to scrutinise, address, challenge, and take on what the realities can be, now, for established artists, for those just setting out, and for those somewhere in between: How do artists make work? What influences their intentions and ambitions for making work, getting it seen, by whom, for what, and where, and how do these relate to economic stability and financial gain? Can artists make work without an audience, money, forthcoming opportunities, space, and without acknowledgement other than through their own self-belief? What is it like to be invisible now with such an emphasis on visibility? How do those in education – both students and teachers – perceive invisibility? How is the creative activity of an artist disseminated when there is no exhibition, catalogue, or other forms of publicity? And how are all these challenging, creative issues addressed by students and teachers, by the public, possible audiences, critics, writers, curators, gallerists, the artists themselves, and those wishing to become artists?

My position, which so confidently accepted invisibility, seems untenable today. However, most art produced today remains unseen. Invisibility, and obscurity, are as prevalent and as inherent to being an artist as they ever were. Therefore, for myself, there is a need to examine the choices we make as artists, the way we operate, what we repudiate and what we desire, what is our worst-case scenario and what is tolerable, what is our responsibility and what is just bad luck, or, for that matter, good luck? Can we continue to make work against all the odds? What is failure and what is success? Why should we even consider these judgements, and to whom do we give the authority to make such judgements other than ourselves?

This questioning is fundamental to my current position as an artist. It forms the central theme to my Arts Council proposal in which I am determined to make my reconsiderations of my forty-year experience as an artist be a starting point for an interrogation into my own work and its potential for change. Also in my proposal, I want to offer artists the opportunity to participate in producing work, more as a process than as the means to a final realisation, and to question their concerns about visibility and invisibility, and whether they consider themselves and their work to be visible or invisible and why, and how this affects their studio activity and working methods and processes. My curiosity favours invisibility as the potentially more challenging position – it is where the artist has to confront their rationale for being an artist, which is ultimately what I want to examine.

[...]

SECTION 10: APPENDICES: APPENDIX TO PART 1

1. An Investigation into Experimentation and Its Relation to the Production of Art

Artists use verbal language as a tool. It is a complex tool with layers of interpretable manifestations. There are no guarantees that the words, and the syntax which accompanies them, which make up the language for discussing, describing, and critiquing art, have single definitions as to their meanings. Consequently, every account of a work is open to examination and scrutiny of the language used to analyse – discuss, describe, critique – the work.

When words are used as if there is a shared understanding that there are definitions which are agreed upon, and when there is an assumption that the words associated with visual art are all understood in the same way, confusions can ensue because this will not be the case.

What are these words?

There are many. Just for starters there are those words which underpin the language of the visual arts: 'aesthetics', 'form', 'subject', 'content', 'dynamic', 'scale', 'size', 'pictorial', 'representation', 'illusion', 'space', 'colour', 'materiality', 'physicality', 'time', 'three-dimensionality', 'two-dimensionality', and 'hyperreality', to name but a few.

However, one word in particular – and especially within the contemporary art context – carries with it a sense of idealism, high intellectual speculation, and integrity. It relates itself to the canons of twentieth-century art which have become identified with radicalism, groundbreaking gestures, and challenges to conventions and orthodoxies. It is deemed anti-institutional and defiant of academicism. It is a word used to defend and uphold the artist's right to work without any particular framework, unanswerable to anyone or anything. It suggests freedom, independence, and an openness (and, yes, what exactly do these words mean as well!) so beloved of the ideologies surrounding contemporary art.

The word up for interrogation is 'experimentation'.

So, what is experimentation as related to the visual arts? And how can experimentation be defined?

For myself, there are two conflicting models of how experimentation and the artist can be considered for investigation.

My first proposition is the following:
'Visual artists do not experiment.'

The premeditated use of media required by the creative process mitigates against experimentation. For example, to bring a work to realisation, there has to be some kind of relationship to process and what will be required for that process to be initiated. Any 'experiment' is therefore dictated and controlled by the practicalities of the materials required for the process however extreme the treatment of those materials might be. Furthermore, to provoke change, and to challenge familiar working processes which are no longer creatively productive, the artist is compelled to investigate different processes of thinking, imagination, techniques, materials, forms – but does this automatically mean 'experimentation'? For the sake of the argument 'Artists do not experiment', the need to change creative direction is not an experimental process. It is one which is dependent on the artist's inherent repertoire of capabilities. Perhaps at some point in the development of the artist, new processes and materials and media opened up possibilities as yet unencountered and therefore stimulating to creative development. But artists are limited by their own creativity. It is not boundless but highly controlled, contrived, and regulated by a host of prescriptions. To remove these prescriptions might be an ambition, and the sweeping changes of the twentieth century seem to have been prompted by such ambitions, but the artist, even though driven to provoke those upheavals, was not experimenting.

Before considering the second model of experimentation and the artist, I want to attempt to define what I think is meant by experimentation within the context of art.

A Definition of 'Experimentation' in the Visual Arts

I am not going to resort to looking up the word in the dictionary because I do not want to be limited in my speculations by such exactness. My conjectures are approximate and have many contingencies which the art context embraces. The word as used within this art context goes beyond the kinds of definitions which will undoubtedly relate to science as a model. I want to avoid that as it will introduce arguments which will provide too many variables to the ones I want to pursue. I do not want to get involved in a science and art debate.

In pursuit of what experimentation means in relationship to art, one aspect is clear: technical investigations and investigations with processes are a territory in which authentic experimentation occurs. Trying out this with that, using materials and processes usually invented for specifications other than the production of art, adopting and adapting these for the purposes of producing art, reinventing tried and trusted processes in different ways, etc., this is experimentation of an important but everyday occurrence for the artist. And this is not what I have in mind when using this word.

Experimentation indicates not knowing what the outcome will be. I also propose that a riskier form of experimentation – and pertinent to this discussion relating to visual art – is how to experiment when you do not know how to start: when creativity and all its intellectual and physical processes have disappeared. This is when experimentation takes place at the limit of creativity, demanding a commitment to creativity at a time when it seems not to exist. Under these conditions, the courage required to make a start is in itself an experiment, even if it means using processes or methods well within the individual artist's repertoire. And there is a consciousness to drive beyond this known state into the unknown. But does the 'unknown' exist anymore? I don't think so. However, this does not deny the desire and the ambition and the urgency to be somewhere different with the work and all that that involves. So maybe experimentation is close to something about being different: being different to what is known and doable at that moment in time, either in grand, creative terms, changing the expectations of art forever, or in more intimate, small ways, within the realm of an individual artist's development, not necessarily for public consumption, or for audience response, or for critical analysis.

Is this as good as experimentation gets? To be different. I think so.

My second proposition is:
'Experimentation is inherent to the visual artist.'

The artist eventually recognises their preferred creative activities through a route of trial and error, of chance encounters, of influences, failures and exhilarating moments, and epiphanies of every possibility. Through the modernised and radicalised genres of landscape, still life, figuration, abstraction, and representation to the elite of Conceptualism, semiotics, deconstructionism, irony, post-irony, feminism and post-feminism, and everything else besides, the collective identity of art is diverse. However, its diversity is somehow within limits. Inevitably visible – a precondition of art, even if it is not visible, as with a sound work, for example, or a virtual work – an artwork is also inevitably contained. The work exists somewhere, even if it is virtual. And it is this 'somewhere' which is the containment and which is controlling and limiting.

However, the processes involved in the realisation of the work so that it can be 'somewhere' are inherently experimental. There are always unknowns in the production of work. Even with work designed and produced by chosen manufacturers to high specifications, there are surprises and the need to rethink. Although art can be very close to the rigours of product design, its origins are very different. The artist, from the conventional in pursuit of the orthodox, to those who subscribe to invention and contention, there is experimentation of some kind.

The point at which experimentation will always occur, whatever the quality and intention of the creative commitment, is at the beginning, at the outset of the process of production: the point when the first visible, physical decision is to be made, whatever that might be. It is the moment when the thinking becomes visible and physical. It is then, and only at that moment, that there is an experiment. That is because that first decision, however familiar it may be, is just that: a first decision, and at that moment has no precedence. In split-second timing, it probably will have precedence and it will be all too familiar, repetitive, another in a production line of works, etc., but for the briefest of moments it is an unknown as to what that first visible, physical gesture might be. And as an unknown, it also has the potential to be different, very different from anything the artist had either expected or known.

'Experimentation' is inherent to the moment of commitment from thought to the making visible of that thought. That moment will either generate possibilities and the work will be different, or it will turn into what is the same, what is already known as a process, what is infinitely repeatable and safe. The beginning of every work provides the artist with the choice of taking on risks or following what is known. Neither is better or worse than the other. The choice is dependent on what kind of need is there in that moment – the need for affirmation or the need for a different way.

APPENDIX TO PART 2

[...]

Another View: The Studio, the Working Process, and the Non-Exhibition

The emphasis placed on how artists prove themselves through exhibiting can be seen in relationship to what constitutes their creative activity. The exhibition is the result of a period of productivity. Where is this activity carried out? What processes are involved in order to realise the work for the exhibition?

It is clear from the diverse activities pursued by artists that the studio in the traditional sense has metamorphosed into anything from the kitchen table, the office desk, the bedsit through to the basic and cheapest unit available in a studio collective, and on to the large, converted warehouse space, customised to the requirements of a particular artist. Wherever and whatever form the studio takes, it declares a particular relationship to how work is produced and the processes involved in the production.

The relationship an artist has with the production of their work and the space they use for that production also generates a relationship artists develop towards exhibiting. The extremes are interesting: there is the methodical production of work which supplies the persistent demands generated by exhibiting commitments which is the lot of the successful artist. Then there is the equally methodical production of work by those artists with no exhibiting commitments who have to sustain their activity through determination and self-motivation. And there are the artists who wait until there is something to make work for, usually the exhibition, before they become involved and commit themselves to the demands of production.

This last-mentioned example exemplifies the importance attached to the exhibition as does the first-mentioned example. However, it is the middle example which exemplifies the artist and their activity in its most unequivocal form. It is this example which the other two stand in opposition to, regarding this way of being an artist as the worst-case scenario. No exhibition, then no proof of artistic worth? And it is this denigration of the pursuit of the artist, unattached to any particular commitment, which proposes such a paradox. Surely this kind of artist is potentially the 'freest', maybe not financially, but certainly creatively. And surely this is what contemporary art claims to champion. But of course, the 'freeness' is very selectively chosen and those artists who do not exhibit are excluded from the selection process at the outset. Their kind of 'freeness' is more of an embarrassment to the art world than exemplary. Why? Because, at its most specific, it is a law unto itself without the ambitions which the neediness of the current art world demands and expects. It is potentially a feud between two equally powerful, but diametrically opposed positions.

In view of the stark fact that most art produced will not be seen by anyone other than the artist, this raises the challenging question of what this unseen art is. I believe it forms an invisible foundation, the ultimate non-exhibition, which stands in silent witness to the noise of the proliferation of exhibitions which make up the current art scene so particular to London. These numerous exhibitions undoubtedly instigate a great sense of activity, a hunger to be out there, an ambition to be seen, but they are also too numerous to account for in any coherent way, which is no bad thing. Similarly the vast unseen, non-exhibition of those many artists working persistently in their studios, with no exhibitions forthcoming, consists of too many works to comprehend and to begin to categorise in any curatorially coherent way. The unseen non-exhibition is genuinely and authentically too diverse to belong anywhere other than where it is, in the studio.

Conceptually this unseen non-exhibition far outstrips any curated group show, with the many strategies employed by curators to make group shows coherent through themes and titles, or by challenging the themed approach with the anything-goes approach. This vast non-exhibition has no need for curatorial stances and positions. It just is what it is. And it remains unattended, unrecognised, and ignored. But despite such neglect, it carries on seemingly indifferent of such ignominy, preferring instead to be within its own world, the studio – wherever or whatever that might be – and supported by its audience of one, the artist him- or herself. Is there any better form of anarchy?

Barlow was the recipient of the Tate Britain Commission 2014. In 2012 she wrote an initial proposal for her work for the Duveen Galleries, which according to the brief would respond to the Tate's collection. The final work, titled *dock* (2014), was a vast and hugely ambitious installation which filled these enormous, grand galleries at the heart of Tate Britain, London. The conclusion of her proposal is reprinted here.

Tate Britain Commission: Conclusion from 'Artist Proposal'

2012

[...]

I considered that I had rejected the sculpture from the 1940s, 1950s, and early 1960s I had been introduced to when I was first at art school. However, looking back, it is clear to me that large forms and awkward structures have persisted throughout my fifty years of making sculpture, and their origins lie in my early encounters with those sculptures from the 1940s, 1950s, and 1960s.

My Duveen Galleries proposal is an opportunity to return to that early experience of sculpture (figs. 69, 115–19). I want to reclaim the 'lump' in a revitalised form, to suspend it, to have space circulating around it in an attempt to manipulate its weight and gravity. I want to reconsider the language of the 'hole' in relationship to invented form and the 'lump', where it is an inevitable result of the processes of making – where the uncompromising 'lump' form can be excavated to destruction, expanded, contracted, fractured, poured, drenched, smoothed, roughened, and can be left half-finished, polished, burnt, rebuilt. It can be coming or going, an object about to be or an object that has been. It allows a state of flux and for an unpredictable engagement in the processes of making, uncompromisingly and openly.

In addition, my questioning of how sculpture is viewed and experienced can be represented through the theatricality of the follies of fake balconies, staircases, and a stadium-style seating structure. But most importantly, the 'lump' forms, suspended at different heights will be freed from their usual, gravity-bound role of floor and plinth where half of their 'bodies' remain unseen. These 'lumps' will be hung in such a way that, as a group, every aspect of them will be revealed – top, bottom, inside, outside, front, back.

The Duveen floor space, the usual territory for sculpture to be located, will be empty. It will become the audience's territory, and as such, they will become protagonists on equal terms with the works suspended and hung above them.

First published as 'Artist Proposal': https://www.tate.org.uk/whats-on/tate-britain/exhibition/tate-britain-commission-2014-phyllida-barlow/exhibition-catalogue/proposal.

Barlow writes about her first studio visit in 1951, aged six, when she travelled to Paris with her mother, father, and siblings to reconnect with friends from before World War II. The studio belonged to the French artist-couple François-Xavier Lalanne (1927–2008) and Claude Lalanne (1924–2019), who were known as Les Lalanne. It was situated on Impasse Ronsin in Montparnasse, an artists' colony which at various times counted amongst its illustrious inhabitants Constantin Brâncuşi, Max Ernst, Niki de Saint-Phalle, and Jean Tinguely. The visit made a great impression on Barlow, and she describes how this memory was reawakened when she encountered their work again in 2013 while visiting the house of an American collector.

Fragmented Memories

2016

Paris, 1951:
a long journey through the night
a room, a kitchen – blue chairs – we sit huddled together
I am six years old
a candle has thick dribbles of wax accreting on the table
I pick at the wax and flick the pieces at Jean-Philippe
he is talking intensely to my mother
'stop doing that', she says to me

a dark passageway
a large doorway
exuberant greetings
everyone is embracing each other

my sister and I stand in the doorway and watch

hands are held high in the air in joy
laughter and noisy babble fill this place
where are we? and who are the people?

there is a painting on an easel halfway down the room
I am told the room is a studio
the painting is red and green
a thick black line is painted on top of the rectangles of red and green
the black line depicts a figure on a bicycle
the figure is a 'stick figure', childlike:
a vertical black line for the body, a black circle for the head
a bent black line for the leg on the pedal, and another for the other leg
two bent black lines are holding the handlebars
the black circle head is looking out of the picture

someone is stacking glasses in a pyramid shape
on a table further down the studio
he pours a drink into the glass on the top of the pyramid
the drink overflows into the glasses below

there is a huge crash – an explosion – and loud cries of alarm

my father has demolished the pyramid of glasses

there is shattered glass and drink everywhere

my mother says, 'you silly bugger'

my sister and I need a pee
we ask where the lavatory is

someone points to a shed in the yard
there is a wooden door
we push the door open
it is dark
the ground is soft and moist
the stench is of shit and piss
we clamp our hands over our mouths and noses

'where is the lavatory?'

my mother is there
'it's that hole', she says confidently

we stare in bewildered horror at the dark, encrusted orifice
sunk deep in the damp ground
'go there', she says, as if this is ordinary

we take it in turns to squat over the poisonous hole, holding each other's
hands for support, dreading any contact with the blackened scabs of shit

we emerge, gasping for air

we wander around the yard

the buildings have windows down to the ground
I press my face to the windows

these must be more studios

someone opens one of the windowed doors

we scurry back to the studio we know

later I learn that my parents returned to Paris in 1951 to meet up with Jean-Philippe Lalanne, and Pom Pom, and François-Xavier Lalanne, who they had not seen since before the war. Who did the studio belong to?

*

2013 – Palm Beach, Florida – my exhibition *Hoard* will open in December at the Norton Museum; it is a seven-day install.

We have a break from installing and are invited to have a swim at Jane Holzer's house; she is otherwise known as Warhol's muse 'Baby Jane'.

Her house is filled with exotic furniture: extraordinary wrought-iron chairs which curl and wind themselves into wild shapes; there is an animal cupboard; something which is made from sheepskin; there is a lamp adorned with metal cast leaves.

'Is this the Lalannes?', I ask Baby Jane.
'Yeah …', she drawls, 'it's all the Lalannes.'

First published as 'Fragmented Memories' in Adrian Dannatt, ed., *Impasse Ronsin* (New York: Paul Kasmin Gallery, 2016), 113. Also included in *Impasse Ronsin: Murder, Love, and Art in the Heart of Paris* (Basel: Museum Tinguely, 2020), 24–5.

Barlow describes the making of a series of works titled riff, each an enclosed set of shelves with twenty-five small sculptures inside. She offers an insight into the process of making small works, which she does alone. She writes of her use of offcuts, her choice of materials, and the actions and speed that characterise this activity.

Riff

2016

tell it how it is

cement, plaster, paper, cardboard, polystyrene, polyfoam board, wire, string, tape, plywood, fabric, carpet felt, wadding, upholstery foam, scrim, wire netting, steel mesh, wool, timber, paint, spray paint, filler, PU foam,

there is always waste –

plaster sets quickly, a lot is left in the bucket; it is setting too quickly to be used –

a bad judgement as to how much should have been mixed –

quick, use it up –

like cooking, mould the rapidly hardening plaster into dumplings – throw them into the corner – they can live there for a while – job done.

torn fabric, rolled-up canvas strips, ripped up tape, split timber, foamboard slivers, scrumpled wire mesh, paper, cardboard; mixed with broken offcuts of ply, razor-sharp cement fragments; pull them apart;

the Festool saw screeches unrelentingly; plywood and foam board are being cut into panels, then to be painted; it will become a large construction; but small pieces are the remains of this cutting/sawing process;

offcuts are accumulating; unforced, a slag heap is growing naturally; it has a beauty, different to the forced arrangement of the intended work – the cause of all the intensive labour commanding the centre space.

and the leftovers of cement and plaster –

it all becomes fodder for marginalised acts (fig. 90).

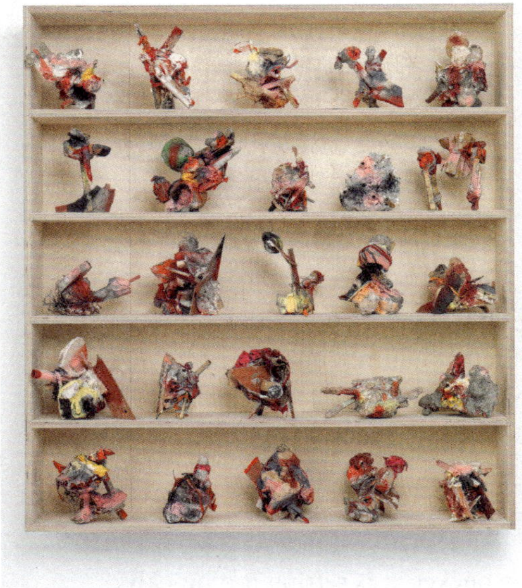

fig. 90 *untitled: riff, 3,* 2015–16

quick making – in the moment; peripheral, thoughtless, mindless; collaging, assemblaging – stop sooner rather than later – don't go back, move on;

no panic

not real sculpture.
but what is? why should I know or care –

small acts of making; hand-sized … squeeze, tie, wrap, stick, push, hold;

wait;

what are they?
what they are: momentary, unconsidered, nothingnesses, not anythings;

remains;

not anything, or anything less than not anything;

how to make nothing –

try it –

28 centimetres high by 28 centimetres deep by 28 centimetres wide –

(prop it up – stab the ply into the cemented polystyrene; it topples over; add another cement lump to the other end; tie it on with wool, then bind it with fabric strips; wait for the cement to set; five minutes; tedious; begin another – two scraps of ply; join them with plaster and scrim; add a strip of foam board – too long – slice it back; PU foam glues a polystyrene lump into the right angle of the two plywood scraps; lifeless; add a wire coil to hold the polystyrene in place; squeeze cement around the top of the polystyrene – a blob; the PU foam swells uncontrollably; let it; then add another plaster blob – mould it; prod it with a short length of offcut timber; bind with fabric and cement another timber offcut into the bottom of the polystyrene – the weight makes it stand up – that's better)

comical; drunken stand-up;

begin another;

a heap of half-moon plywood offcuts and a tangled mass of fabric ribbons have been dumped on the table; more fodder –
scrunch a ball of fabric with PU foam; cut off the top of the plastic bottle; stuff it with corrugated card; ram in the upholstery foam, and felt, and a timber shard; now it holds;

mix cement; wait, wait, wait; then five minutes to do what has to be done;

fold the cement; curl it into the crevice; bung the gap; weigh down the fragile timber strut – there it is;

now there are four.

each react – this one has to be lumpier, more rounded; this one more structural, stiff limbed; this one taller, languid; this one is OK;

paint – decoration; camouflage; concealment, cosmetic;

mark with spray paint;

territorial;

done.

In 1986 Barlow was invited to participate in *Third Generation*, an exhibition across various locations in and around Canterbury staged by curator Sandra Drew as part of the Canterbury Festival. Writing in 2018, just over thirty years later, Barlow recalls the exhibition and describes how her own contribution, *Threat*, which was sited in a wasteland, was vandalised. She alludes to a conference and the topic of feminism and refers to the debates amongst the participants, remembering the impetus to question orthodoxies and challenge authority that characterised this group and this time.

A Recollection (1986)

2018

where?
where to locate a work?

there was the cathedral – a proud and monumental location;
but not right –

others had already decided, and chosen their sites:

houses, peoples' homes, adopted to become intimate vitrines,
displaying personal possessions in the front windows –
a brilliant homage to those lives within;
there were corner spaces, out on the streets –
stubborn objects accosting unsuspecting passers-by;
and a plasticine wall –
such innovation;

but where … ?

out of the station, over a bridge which straddled a wasteland –
rough and unused;
ideal (fig. 91);

then the installing –
the rain poured down;

the stakes were hammered in;

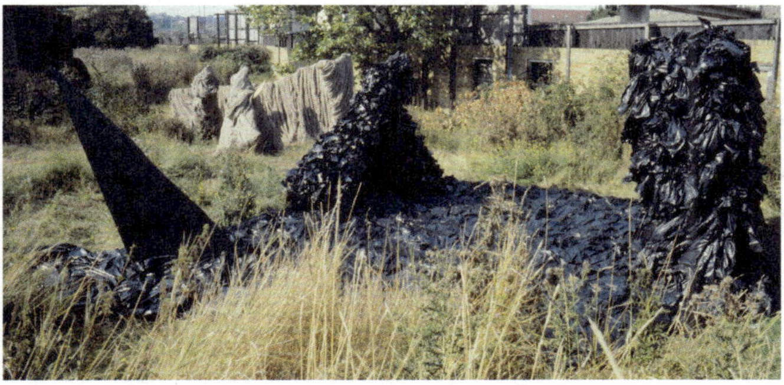

fig. 91 *Threat* (detail), 1986

fire-damaged carpet felt was draped and nailed to the stakes –
heavy, sodden folds, an entourage stalking the morass of black polythene,
spread out in layers;
bitumen-blackened paper, piled up to become a stooped, cave-like object,
and a savage fin plunged into the layers of black polythene …

this was more like street theatre,
a performance …
but a performance trapped in time …
sculpture as performance,
to be glimpsed,
to be walked past, on the bridge from the station –

what was it meant to be?
how do artists know what the subject of their work is?
the actions of making – layering, draping, dipping, squeezing, ramming,
stacking, piling, filling, emptying, folding, squashing, entering …
can these actions be the subject?

yes.

Kent Radio watched this installation process
from their studio overlooking the site –
'it's rubbish – come on everyone, let's burn it', chortled the DJ …

then worse, at the opening …
pilfered traffic cones perched jauntily on all the works
adorned the installation,
reducing it to a comic turn …

and then the humiliation of removing them, twenty, one by one,
in the full gaze of the amused public,
passing by on the bridge from the station;

but none of that matters;

at the conference, questions and assertions –
as women, what is our lineage?
how do women form their particular historical chain?

I didn't want to be part of a chain …

surely that was the orthodox approach to history –
but how could a different, and as yet unknown, history be revealed?
it must be through the power of individual lives –
those invisibilities, those misunderstood emotions,
those thwarted desires and ambitions;
and the glorious achievements:
from the deeply private and intimate to the heroic and the defiant;

and what will become of entrenched attitudes?
how can those social norms be opened out?
how can the much-hindered female expression become visible?
can humanity shed its craving for authority?

and, of course, there are other memories:

Sandra's generosity, her fortitude and conviction –
her kitchen table –
an unknowing stage for revelations and speculations,
with that focus on who are we? what do we want? what's stopping us?

and around that table, the strong characters,
their heartfelt determinations …
contentious, uneasy, competitive …

why was I so unsure?
their urgency for change –
yes, of course,
necessary, essential –

has it happened?
the questions persist,
and the answers continue to be silenced –

but at that time, in 1986 –
that exhibition, and what and who it represented,
signalled an energy to challenge authority,
to become a voice which had to be heard –
and yes, that voice has not been silenced …

First published in *From the Kitchen Table: Drew Gallery Projects 1984–90* (London: CGP London, 2018), 118–19.

In *Because It's Not There* Barlow offers an account of working in the studio and her approach to and experience of making. She begins by questioning the urge to make, the desire to fill space, and the relationship between object and space. She writes about choosing a working method for the piece she is to start and evokes the thrill of beginning and how, when the initial energy subsides, doubt can set in. She considers the language of failure, the idea of something 'working' and 'not working', and describes how she moves forward from disappointment to take the piece towards a successful resolution.

Because It's Not There

2018

the best thing about sculpture is that it doesn't necessarily have to have
a right way up
it also doesn't necessarily have to have an idea in order for it to come into
existence; also it doesn't have to have a subject
in fact, it doesn't have to have a lot of things
so why bother?
I mean, why bother to make sculpture?
the world is already full of stuff, natural and human-made,
useful and useless,
so why add to this?

unlike the question for which mountaineers have a ready answer –
why climb that mountain?
answer: because it's there – sculpture is the opposite:
why make?
answer: because there is nothing there.

two events:
an empty space and an urge to fill it
illogical and meaningless – and of no use;
the urge is about actions –
to pile up, spill, spread, push, crush, squeeze, hit, cut, saw, chop, slice, press,
mix, fold, stitch, pull, insert, remove, break, drag, drop, tie, knot, wind,
wrap, bind, bury,

this is an assassin's vocabulary;
but as much as this vocabulary is violent, it is also erotic;

and what of the empty space; why fill it?
why ruin the calmness of emptiness?

but something is there: the empty space and the potential to fill it are there;
it's a theatrical rendezvous between the emptiness and what will happen next;
and this tense encounter will generate more space – a new space,
or more accurately 360 degrees of spaces,

as the thing which will fill the space waits to be circumnavigated;
and now in this theatrical encounter, who or what owns which space
and how far does that ownership extend?
does the thing, the thing that is filling up the space, own all the space
or just the part it physically occupies;
and is the space, which was once empty and is now filled, altered –
does it behave differently?

is the space around the thing which fills the space active or passive?
does it take the space around it by surprise, exploding the space it does not occupy, rejecting it;
or does the thing distil what surrounds it,
making the space hug it to the point of claustrophobia;

and so the space, and the way it is devoured, becomes as much a material as the thing itself;
there is a stand-off between what is about to be devoured and the devourer;

but where is this action taking place?
is there a rehearsal, or is it a spontaneous event without preparation or practice?

in my experience of making sculpture, these are all possibilities:

the studio, or place of production,
provides the initial encounter between space and thing –
sometimes the thing is organised: it has an image and a set of thoughts
and intentions as to how it can be brought into existence;
actions will be important:
decisions as to what processes will be initiated to get the work going –
will it be constructed around some sort of armature, or lightweight material,
so the final work is a build-up of surfaces;
or will it be made from the centre outwards
so that the final surface is also what is contained within
but with both methods, the actions of pouring, spreading, squeezing, and pushing, etc., will be crucial to how the work develops

choosing a method and a process are all about reactions:
what went before, how was the previous work made?
then this one will be the opposite

the thrill of beginning a new work is one thing;
the first day is always fresh and brisk –

it seems easy and effortless;
the accumulation of materials is familiar but new –
plaster, cement, paper, scrim, fabric, cardboard, PU foam,
polystyrene, wire, ply –
they are building up swiftly;
something is happening; a form is forcing itself into existence;
it is bursting with the energy of the actions of piling up, squashing, pushing,
tying, wrapping, folding … these different materials, wet and dry,
are like clay …
they can be made to do anything

the actions become more confident, the materials more brutalised and forced,
the form is growing and taking on a life of its own;

its been a glorious day – fulfilling and dynamic
and here is the proof:
an explosive mound of inchoate, obdurate matter, smothered in cement and
plaster, clinging on to its shapelessness as best it can
is it as exciting as it felt? – surely it must be –
those actions were so right in what they were doing to each other
somehow that must come through?

doubt gnaws away at what was so thrilling –

and so now there is trouble:

GOING WRONG

and it's a reality check

the day had been a total immersion in the making;
there had been no pause for a contemplative appraisal
it was a high energy blast into the air with no preparation,
no thought, no subject
just the obsessive desire to be seduced by the acts of making;

the previous work had been well-planned, careful, and expedient
every part was lean and exposed – the opposite to today's explosive tirade;

why was this contrasting process not working?
why was the energy and excitement not evident?
it was a lifeless thing, moribund,

suffocated under the weight of its zealous acts of production;

and how strange the language of failure is:
'it doesn't work; it's not right; it's not doing anything;
what's it meant to be? why would you want to do that?'
and there are many more with subtle critical undertones –
'who is it for? where will it go?'

failure and success are not the only possibilities.
there is a vast uncharted territory between these two extremes
where success or failure do not have a chance to compete;

today's work was not working;
and so now it is at the beginning of its existence;
the thrill of its first day of being made had evaporated
and been replaced by the tough realisation that this work needed time;
it had only just begun;

so now, what are its choices for beginning again?

sculpture does not have to have a right way up
this work, this non-explosive explosion can be rolled around;
turned this way and that;
and then broken up,
and then joined back together, but differently,
then added to, with cement
then broken again

I am searching for it to become something, but it is stubborn
I eviscerate it – removing all the polystyrene and cardboard
it is now more flexible
it is a skin of scrim, plaster, cement, paper, fabric
I don't know what to do with this skin
the bulk that it once was has been erased
and with that all the excitement of that first day of making
has been erased as well;

the emotion has shifted from thrill to disappointment;
but this isn't negative;
it is calming;

there is the agitation of wanting to get on with it

but that is different.
and what is 'it'?

do I mean the processes, or the sculpture?
or is it not a sculpture?
and what about the space the original work occupied? where is that now?

this skin, now lying abjectly on the floor, is the remains,
as such it has become a material in its own right,
a flank of compressed materials that can be folded, rolled, squashed
or simply hung up, suspended, as it is

I am now in this vast territory of exploration
where the extremes of failure and success are so far away they don't exist.

I want to make another surface;
a surface in its own right – not the remains of an eviscerated thing –
I am thinking about layers of surfaces becoming something –
to be rolled and folded – bound together – simple
I am making choices –

I am thinking about why art is referred to as 'working' and 'not working'
these are terms used for things that have the potential to breakdown,
like engines and machinery and, of course, computers
and implies that if something is 'not working' then it can be mended
and if it is working then no need to fix anything –
'if it's not broken, don't fix it'

so how does this apply to sculpture?
did the 'working, not working' reference emerge from
the Industrial Revolution?
did pre-Renaissance artists use the phrase 'working/not-working'
when looking at their work?

how does an artwork get mended? and do artworks break down?

the flank of squashed materials is neither working or not working –
it is in abeyance

before I begin the next surface,
I will squash and fold the skin surface lying so forlornly on the floor;

this skin surface is one metre square and heavy;

I pull the corners in; I fold in the new corners;
now I roll the bottom edge towards the centre;
it is bulky; it is impossible to hold;
I fold it again and it has taken on a rotund form;
the actions of rolling and folding are retained in the deep, sharp creases;
the folded edges make a split across the centre;
this split is dynamic; it implies that the thing is about to burst;
it is very solid, but not leaden
it has a sense of being caught between two states of movement –
splitting open and unrolling –
it is at rest but uneasily so – there is suspense and anything could happen,

it works

it has taken a day of waiting and watching;
and ten minutes of rolling and folding
to resolve the previous day's explosive high-energy actions.

CONVERSATIONS AND INTERVIEWS

This excerpt comes from the start of an interview conducted by Miles Thurlow and filmed during the preparations for Barlow's solo show *Peninsula* at BALTIC Centre for Contemporary Art, Gateshead, UK, in 2004–5. Barlow talks to Thurlow, at the time a member of the BALTIC team, about the artist as liar and the moment of walking away from the finished work. She describes the impossibility of comprehending the whole object in sculpture and compares this to music, painting, and film, and she elaborates on the idea of syntax and how this relates to the experience of the audience. She talks about touch, theatricality, and the histrionic object.

Interview with Miles Thurlow

2004

[...]

Phyllida Barlow: The idea that I desperately want to come up with something that does have a conclusion to it – I'm not somebody who wants to come into the gallery every day and carry on the process. So I have a sort of problem with the word process, and then I have a problem with the word 'sculpture', and then I also have a problem with the word 'exhibition'. So it's like I've constructed this fairly difficult occupation where all the usual givens I find difficult to accept and yet I also collude with them. I am having an exhibition, I've had loads of exhibitions, and I mustn't pretend that I don't actually drive the work to a conclusion. I'm fascinated by that conclusion. But I also see it as a moment when … A very brief moment when you see what you've done and that's it, it's almost after that, I'm more than ready to walk away from it and say, 'OK, that was it. I want to get on with the next thing because …' Maybe because certain things didn't quite work out in that, but I don't want to do them in that work, I want to do them in a new work.

So, I find my activity intellectually very slippery, very unresolved. And that, on one hand, may be something that keeps me interested but, on another hand, leads to a kind of peculiar state of dishonesty, which I'm very aware of and has made me very interested in the whole idea of artist as liar. And I think maybe sculptors – if that's what I am, those of us who manipulate materials and make things in the middle of spaces – are bound up with lying, big time. And that does fascinate me. And that's the only bit of intellectual positioning that I feel the slightest bit truthful about: is that I am a liar.

Miles Thurlow: You're an honest liar at that.

PB: Well, I don't even know if I'm that, because my love of the physical world, the physicality, and how the everyday – just looking through that window at the street and the way a wall can control somebody, the edge of a pavement can control something, a car going past, a cigarette butt, a bit of litter on the … You know, these things, from the huge to the tiny, make us use space in particular ways and that idea of space as a solid material also seems to me deeply fascinating and absolutely nothing to do with illusion or lying. But you

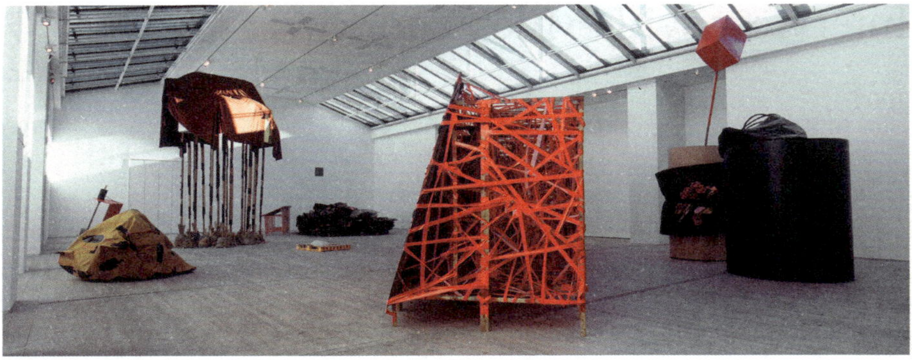

fig. 92 Installation view, *Peninsula*, BALTIC Centre for Contemporary Art, Gateshead, UK, 2004–5

need to lie in order to translate that back into the theatrical space of a gallery. Does that make sense to you?

MT: Why do you qualify that as lying or talk of it in those terms?

PB: Because maybe the space ... Say, the fourth floor of the BALTIC, it's a sort of given that loads of artists will use (figs. 92, 179). Therefore, my translation of that space is quite superficial in a way: it's about a particular moment in time. It's not going to become fixed in any way, somebody else will come in there and manipulate it. So it's a set of manipulations that are contrivances, that are there to do things to an audience. And that all suddenly seems really, to me, quite ... often quite peculiar in terms of the fact that what we're looking at is ordinary materials, you know, wood, paint, whatever. Even the most illusionistic of sculptures, it's still marble or wood or bronze. It's pretending. And I find that pretence both fascinating and deeply sort of disturbing as well.

MT: So the impermanence of the situation, in a way, is ... You have an uncomfortable relationship with that?

PB: Yes.

MT: In terms of you've got a certain set of circumstances that occur and that might be the point at which you feel that there is a dishonesty going, or a lie going on, and you're kind of presenting a circumstance as a solid fixed show –

PB: Yes, absolutely.

MT: That then will kind of disintegrate and fall apart and be moved or go somewhere else or exist in documentation that you feel somehow doesn't quite represent the experience of being within ... And that that kind of moment of actually being with the piece of work is a false ... It's a false and a true moment at the same time –

PB: Yes.

MT: Because it's going to move and change and dissipate.

PB: I think the moment that is most substantial is, for me, the moment when it is all up there and the decisions have been made and it is what it's going to be for the next few weeks or months or whatever. But it's an incredibly fleeting moment because once I become familiar with what is there, then all the doubts and the precariousnesses of those decisions start to come into play and that's when I'm more than willing to just walk away from it.

So I think I've never quite reconciled myself to my own work as a sculptural phenomenon. I can do it with a Bruce Nauman, for instance, describing what it's actually like walking round a Nauman, one of those circular pieces. It's quite extraordinary because what are you actually describing, you know? And you can't see the whole work at any one time, you can only see it in stages. OK, when you come into the gallery, you might see an image of the whole work, but that's very different from actually approaching it, stalking it, getting up close to it, and then seeing all the sort of shredded pieces of material that are holding these forms together, and the props and the wedges. It's like a lot of words that are gradually beginning to form a sentence. And I think it is, to me, very comparable to listening to a piece of music, which I think is an incredibly complicated intellectual process, that at the end of that piece of music, it's all gone. So what have you then got at the end of that piece of music? And to me, walking round a Nauman or an Alberto Giacometti is very similar. You're never quite sure of what the actual thing is that you've grasped.

You're very aware of your own physical self, walking round. I remember thinking of that Jacob Epstein, *Jacob and the Angel*, that huge, hideous alabaster piece, quite amazing, where trying to think of the front of that work when you're at the back of it is really quite mentally taxing. It's like you almost can't pull the whole thing together at any one time. Like listening to a massive symphony by Gustav Mahler, you know? You're in the present tense the whole time whilst you're going through it, and then it's suddenly all in the past tense because it's gone. And that was what I was meaning earlier about this syntax of tense in terms of how one makes sculpture. I do feel it's very different from painting, where the act of looking at a painting, which I absolutely love, is one of the painting is on the wall, it's already occupying a very official institutional space, it's on the wall of a building. And you stand in front of it and you walk up to it and then you walk away from it, it's like a sort of backwards and forwards in a very particular kind of corridor space. If you do that with sculpture, you're missing something.

MT: Because you can't get away from it, in a sense. It's always –

PB: Absolutely. Yes. So you're always in the present tense with sculpture, you know? And then the moment you're trying to deal with the past tense, you start to have problems, I think, of reconstructing it. But with a painting, I think it can deal with the syntax of tense because you can kind of peruse backwards and forwards, much more like reading a text or something where you can accumulate the information and make it have a kind of substantial order in your head. I think it's very difficult to do that with sculpture, sculpture defies that.

MT: So, jumping again slightly, but how do you feel about film in –

PB: Well, I think film and sculpture are absolutely *[signals 'entwined' with her hands]*. That's why you get so many video artists coming out of sculpture areas or the two become incredibly … And photography, they all become very related because the camera, if it's not going to be fixed like this camera in one position *[indicates camera filming them]*, it's going to trace the object round and round, move. It is acting as a kind of physical stalker of the object.

MT: Is that connected with your idea of lying, or … ?

PB: Yes, it is, because I think the way we claim the space in an exhibition is, to me, essentially theatrical in that the audience, in a way, is expected to behave in a certain way with these things. It seems to me interesting that, on the whole, people don't touch paintings. There's an agreement with an audience that a painting on a wall isn't touched, but sculpture has no such claim. And you've described what it's like at BALTIC, having to try to control people's behaviour. I find that incredibly interesting because I think the problem I have with this whole thing of touch is that if touch can become a language, that you then as a viewer say, 'Why do I want to touch it? Is it because it looks wet or dry, or gooey or sticky?' If that moment can be caught and really given to the viewer as a positive thing rather than having to reach out and touch Meret Oppenheim's fur teacup, you're left with this limbo land of desiring to touch that teacup. That seems like a really extraordinary language to try and promote and advocate rather than trying to conclude that language with the touch itself, which to me, totally destroys the whole point of having made this thing in that kind of way in the first place.

MT: So, the 'do not touch' is a really important thing?

PB: It is for me, in the same way that in the theatre, on the whole, we don't leap up on to the stage and say, 'Look, I don't agree with you', or whatever it is you might want to say. You understand that you sit in those chairs and you watch the performance, and of course, there are all sorts of ways in which theatre has challenged that and there are all sorts of ways in which we try and challenge that with installation and sculpture. And obviously it leads to all sorts of problems, but then that's what it's all about. But I think the theatricality of an object is because it's demanding this attention on one hand, but trying to control very much about how its attention is dealt with and received. So, it is a sort of spoiled-brat syndrome in lots of ways, or histrionic or hysterical, all those kinds of words can be applied to even things like Richard Serra, in my opinion, or Donald Judd. I don't think because they're Minimalists, if they are Minimalists, they become not tarred with the same brush of a histrionic object. I think a lot of Judd's work is very histrionic.

MT: Can you explain what you mean by a histrionic object?

PB: It demands to be looked at in a very particular way with an understanding of the vernacular that it's using, the vernacular of industry being transferred into an art space and therefore, demanding to be seen in an elevated kind of way, even though it's using incredibly practical and expedient sorts of skills that are usually applied to … well, quite remarkable objects in their own right …

[…]

Various edits of this talk (as well as a short film) are available online, including an audio file on BALTIC+ at http://balticplus.uk/phyllida-barlow-in-conversation-with-miles-thurlow-part-2-c8289/.

This interview was conducted ahead of the pivotal two-person exhibition with Nairy Baghramian at the Serpentine Gallery, London, in 2010. Interviewed by Julia Peyton-Jones and Hans Ulrich Obrist, at the time co-directors of the Serpentine, they discuss Barlow's beginnings in art, her education, her experiences and influences from the 1960s, the language used to discuss art, 'banned' words, and the politics of emotion. Barlow considers feminism, gendered work, the questioning of authority, her collaborations with Jess Flood-Paddock and Baghramian, and outlines her works for the Serpentine. She talks about the evolution of her forms, her interest in theatricality and the stage, size and scale, light and sound, the importance of surprise, the destination of works, and her desire to make work where there is no audience.

Interview with Julia Peyton-Jones and Hans Ulrich Obrist

2010

Hans Ulrich Obrist: How did you come to art, or how did art come to you?

Phyllida Barlow: It happened in a very simple way: with a love of making things from a very early age in that late-1940s/1950s making-do and getting-by kind of culture when there wasn't a lot around. I made houses out of cardboard and matchboxes and turned conkers into chairs for them, and moss for beds, all those kinds of things. I just loved that. Collecting and making was an ever-present pastime. It was always there. When I went to Chelsea School of Art, I discovered clay, which was like a revelation. George Fullard, who was a memorable tutor at Chelsea during the 1960s and up until his premature death in 1973, introduced me to the work of Germaine Richier. He told me that Richier said clay is hysterical; that you have to watch what it does. If you touch it too much it dies, so you must hardly touch it. And when you look at Richier's work, you actually see these incredible variations of surface, from wonderful highly polished shoulders through to creases and crumples of clay that she's just let move across the form. I think I was completely taken up by that physicality of a material that didn't immediately dictate an image. I was drawn into the material and maybe an image would emerge, but it wasn't the immediate relationship. Even when I was painting, I think it was how the paint traversed the canvas, rather than seeking to make a landscape or whatever it was, that interested me.

Julia Peyton-Jones: Were these clay objects pots or receptacles, or were they already sculpture?

PB: They were sculpture and were made in the life room. Chelsea was going through this enormous change as it entered the 1960s. Lawrence Gowing, who was then the head of Chelsea, imported quite a few people like Ian Stephenson, Patrick Caulfield, and others, including George Fullard. In sculpture there was Elisabeth Frink and there was Robert Clatworthy, names that have sort of faded into the mists of time. But they were fantastic teachers who weren't going to pay any kind of lip service to sculpture as an academic medium. They wanted to see people using clay as though it was almost like a building material rather than as a craft modelling material, so it was an exciting time to be at that particular art school. Even though it had no status in comparison to somewhere like St Martins or Newcastle – the art schools that really were radicalising art education – it had some incredible people in it.

JP-J: There seems, no matter what scale you're working on, always to be evidence of the hand in your work, which isn't true for all sculptors. Is that feeling that your hand is part of the work important for you?

PB: I want my hand to be there, but it's not a moral concern. It's not that I have this deep, sort of fundamentalist belief that sculpture has to be made by hand. My hand is there as an expedient way of doing something. The way in which the expression in the work comes about isn't through a need to be expressionist; it's through a need to find the most practical way of converting eight bags of plaster into a shape and the most economical way that might be done. So it's almost as though the least touch that can be delivered with that amount of material is what's important and, oddly enough, that gets read as being very hand-touched. If we think of Eva Hesse, we see this sense of touch in the work, but actually the materials were so lethal that she hardly touched them at all. Those liquid-to-solid materials can be extremely difficult to touch, and the resins would be dangerous as well. And we think of John McCracken's work in the opposite way, and yet every inch of that work is touched. So there is this paradox about hot and cold touch. McCracken's early work is actually boiling hot, whereas Hesse's is freezing cold.

HUO: You came out of art school at a moment when the New Generation sculptors were very dominant in the UK: Anthony Caro, Phillip King, and William Tucker, to name a few. I've had many conversations with Gilbert & George, who came out of art school more or less at the same time as you, and who were also confronted by this dominating generation of formalist modern sculptors. That was the beginning of their Living Sculptures. You also in some way marked a difference from this generation that preceded you; it would be interesting to know, from your point of view, how it was when you entered the art world, who were important models for you and also, when you feel that you really made your first autonomous work and could say, 'This is my language'.

PB: Yes, I remember vividly Gilbert & George's performance of *Singing Sculpture* which they did at a space on Glebe Place in Chelsea. That was different. That changed everything for me. But a bit before that I think, for me, it was a crisis. In seeing one of the New Generation shows that included David Annesley, Mike Bolus, Tucker, and Caro, I had a feeling that actually not a lot had changed and I couldn't get my head around it. At that time, 1965–6,

I was also beginning to look at contemporary work produced beyond the UK, in Italy and the US. I started to really look at Arte Povera, and someone showed me a Louise Bourgeois catalogue of her wooden totems, and – in connection with the New Generation exhibitions – it was like, 'Something's not adding up here'. Actually, Bruce McLean summed it up brilliantly. He described the New Generation as 'Henry Moore with stripes on'. With no insult to them, I think. But yes, some of the work took my breath away – Phillip King's large *Genghis Khan* piece really did – but there was still something about the British sense of the craft-meets-art moment that the Europeans and the Americans had somehow driven a great big wedge into. And the British were still very conservative.

There was a young artist at that time called Derrick Woodham. He made these sort of crushed shapes, beautifully modelled out of clay, then cast in fibreglass and resin. He sanded the resin for hours and days on end and then superbly painted them. They're painted sculptures, but they're also sculpted paintings. I think this rupture between painting and sculpture was the sort of British moment, but in my opinion it was not comparable to what was happening with Arte Povera, with Gordon Matta-Clark, or Alan Saret, Giuseppe Penone, Alighiero Boetti, Mario Merz, and generally with works from artists abroad who were throwing away the maps, so to speak. Works like Robert Smithson's *Asphalt Rundown* intrigued me and my response was, 'Oh, so this is sculpture, this is what is possible, this is what it's all about.' It just made me feel like a grain of sand in an almighty desert: that there was something so much bigger. I think out of that and looking at works like Robert Morris's thread-waste piece *Untitled* (1968), I began to realise that anti-form was just fantastic. In Britain that was still not particularly acceptable. But then, of course, there were exceptions – you've got Barry Flanagan's beautiful folded hessian piece *Pile 3*.

HUO: Were there other British artists, in addition to Barry Flanagan, who were using this language?

PB: You were getting people really manoeuvring themselves around that language – people like Martin Naylor and Carl Plackman. Absolutely fantastic artists.

JP-J: Many of these artists have exhibited here, of course. They're part of the Serpentine's history.

PB: This is what's so fascinating. There was this teacher called Peter Atkins (now Peter Kardia), who ran this course that was called, or has become known as, 'The Locked Room', at St Martins. It was commemorated recently in an exhibition at Ambika P3 at the University of Westminster. What I remember hearing at the time – and this may have been more rumour than fact – was that students went into The Locked Room and there was a polystyrene chunk, a glove, and a hammer, and if you wanted to make something, you had to put the glove on, pick the hammer up, and do it. Also, there was something about students only being allowed out of the room at certain times.

JP-J: That's extremely radical.

PB: This was the innovation of Kardia and Garth Evans. That's another name. Richard Deacon and many others were taught by Kardia. But living through that era for me was like going under the radar. I didn't agree with Victor Burgin that painting is nothing more than pigment daubed on woven fabric, or whatever it was he said, or with this kind of violent, aggressive intellectual position against what seemed to me to be the making of art. To me, it was too fascistic and, I thought, incredibly macho and I wasn't then speaking as a feminist; it was more like these were games to me. You were getting it from so many sides. Talking to David Batchelor the other day was very interesting. We discussed how getting rid of the conventional and traditional ways of talking about art was liberating and I said, 'Yes it was, but bringing it back now is also quite exciting' – so now it's possible to talk with a revived critical perception about things like creativity, expression, or emotion without everybody gagging in disgust.

JP-J: Is the word 'spirituality' yet possible?

PB: That was another one we were thinking about, actually.

JP-J: That's the taboo of all taboos.

PB: Absolutely. But also 'inspiration'. It's a really interesting list of words, and we all know why we wanted to get rid of them, because the words are meaningless unless you actually raise the critical bar and say 'Let's take each of these words one at a time and see what they are, and where they are leading.'

HUO: You've discussed your work in terms of the 'politics of emotion'. Could you explain what that means?

PB: It comes out of looking at these banned words, and their problematic associations with dead-end belief systems rooted in the past, and the need to be critically focused on how these words could be used. Those banned words were stranded without any critical apparatus to support them. Then I began to think, 'What's so bad about saying the word "emotion"?' I think it's because it becomes a convenient place to hide. To say, 'my work comes from my emotions' is just absolutely meaningless. Everybody's does to some extent. I began to think about how having an emotion is triggered by an event or a response and about what that event or response is. In some ways, that event or response has all sorts of social conditions attached to it, which then are very political, with a small 'p'. So if one is upset, hurt, offended, delighted, excited, or whatever, it isn't just down to one's own personality, it's the whole cultural framework that's led one to have those kinds of responses. That's how I see emotions as having a political resonance – not that there's a manifesto attached to them; it's just that they're not isolated things.

HUO: The political dimension in your work is something Nairy Baghramian described when she wrote for *Artforum*. She's discussed your work in terms of a 'feminist occupation of space'. I was wondering if you could talk about your relationship or connection to feminism?

PB: My relationship with feminism is complicated and something I feel in some ways that I've avoided. So when feminism was beginning to become both subject and content of some artists' work from the late 1960s onwards, I felt very alienated from that. I was someone who, for better or for worse, came out of an extremely male tradition of sculpture and who has always loved the phallocentric object, the quest to find the object that's trying to release itself from gravity through its uprightness and through its erectness or however you want to describe it. The obsession with fragmentation, with smashing this tradition, with destroying it, was to me only one very small part of a way of proceeding creatively. So I couldn't fully take on the idea that you knew your subject, you didn't have to find your subject, which is what I suppose has been my dilemma. To suddenly say the subject was feminism just seemed to me enormously problematic and I think I've had that problem with political art all the way through: where the subject is put ahead of how you might deal with other attractions, revulsions, those kinds of responses and choices about the world around you.

So feminism was a difficult one for me, although not from the bigger social point of view that identified vital things that obviously needed to be achieved for the rights of women. But then, that also would be true of the rights of human beings as a whole. So to me, there was, and is, a vast humanitarian question there as well. I do think work is gendered. But the more personal the process of discovering a gender for the work, or issues about gender, the more interested I am. The way decisions can be ignited beyond manifestos, doctrines, and theories is what inspires me. The female occupation of space could begin with an emotional response about a relationship to a certain kind of behaviour.

My occupation of space through my work, where my work acts on my behalf, evidences a questioning of authority. I'm interested in how spaces can be imbued with authority, often an inherited masculine authority which is reflected in the building in which the work is sited. Architecture can be, for me, problematic in this respect. I am never sure what the difference is between building and architecture. But my interest in size and dimension and in making works that are bigger than myself is connected to arguing with space. It, space, is as much a material as the things that I place in that space. Perhaps this combative response to space is in essence female, being protective and defensive at the same time. I wouldn't be able to define it beyond that, but I understand where Nairy's coming from with it.

JP-J: It's interesting to ask you to respond to Nairy's idea of a feminist occupation of space because, of course, these two positions are going to be brought together at the Serpentine for your exhibition. What do you think are the similarities and indeed differences in your two practices?

PB: I think Nairy turns space inside out and to me that's her political intervention in a space. So that the sequence of frames, the sequence of openings and closings, blind alleys and shuttings-off that she sets up is a kind of taking the framework of the institution and almost turning it inside out so that we're left with just the skeleton. There's this openness of air and light breathing through her work, and even the colours and the surfaces do that. Her work is alarmed and wired. You feel it's almost dangerous to get near it, whereas I think my work is more imploded. There's a density about my work that also, perhaps, comes with an interest in weight and gravity, and, paradoxically, about disrupting the inevitable forces of gravity with the very stuff that makes it what it is, mass and materiality. I think Nairy's work releases gravity, whereas my work absorbs it. There are these big differences and there's a very interesting misfit between the works. I suddenly thought – that might be quite an interesting title.

HUO: Misfits?

PB: Yes. I think the misfit is where the resonance between the work is going to happen; not through trying to pacify any awkwardness but by actually taking it on.

JP-J: Your works are two sides of the same coin, really. That's what makes it interesting.

PB: One is empty and the other is full, but not in a literal sense; in a physical, material sense.

HUO: It's interesting to come back to your contribution to this show. We started out with how you came into art. But there have been what I would call a series of epiphanies involving the invention of your different types of sculptures. In the exhibition, we're going to show many of these types – as a survey, because it's your first institutional show in London. We'll have the tube, the grid, the blobs, among others. Can you tell us about the works you've made for the show and what each of these had as its epiphany?

PB: The biggest epiphany for me has always been rooted in the fact that the sculptural language, whether that's in a painting or a film, a piece of furniture, or a conversation, isn't about the subject but about the negotiation, about the interaction initiated by the 'object', the thing – whatever that might be. It's almost as though the thing itself is hardly seen. The thing is an obstacle that you negotiate your way around. And that negotiation, that walking around, that perusing, means that you constantly lose the image. I think that's my relationship with sculpture: although it's very image-based, there is something about its relationship with the space. So if we begin with the central room, the north gallery, reaching up into that high, domed space and remembering works that have done that before, there's something about the way you're taken up into that space (figs. 48, 93). You're actually physically tracing this thing and then there's this object that's leading you there like a trail. I find that sequence really fascinating: that there's a symbiosis between you as the viewer and your physical engagement with how the objects, sculptures, alert you to the space they both occupy and leave empty. That's what the objects that use height are doing.

The second epiphany, maybe, is the ramp with the drums on it, where it's taking very familiar forms and, in the process of making, allowing those forms to become autonomous, to become themselves and not just necessarily referencing something else (fig. 94). They're almost like generic forms; there's the ramp and then on the end of it there are two drums that are two coils of hardboard. So there's a way of using the ramp as an object in itself but also as something that disrupts the drums. Everything has this edge of disrupting the familiar with an unfamiliar gesture or positioning.

Untitled: fences (fig. 95) comes from an obsession with grids that goes way back to one of my very early works, *Shedmesh* from 1975 (fig. 13), which was stacks of painters' stretchers tied together with canvas. The grid has really travelled right the way through, since 1975, so even now the fence works are a kind of variation on that theme: a form that's apparently transparent but is also incredibly solid and rigid.

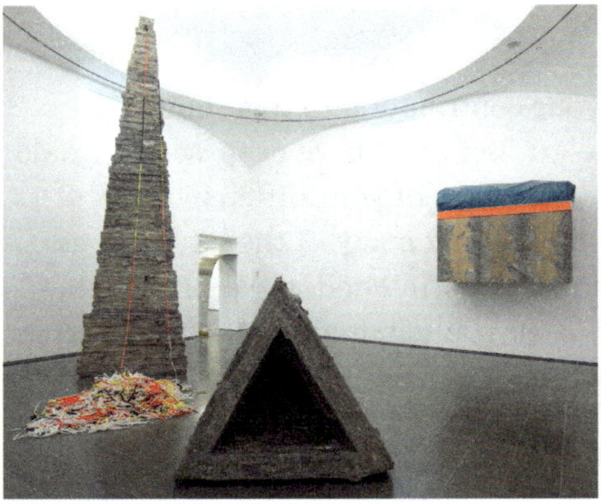

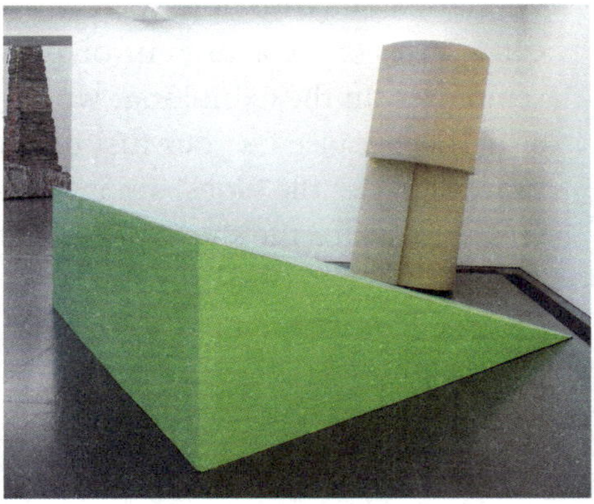

LEFT TO RIGHT:
figs. 93–4 Installation views, *Nairy Baghramian and Phyllida Barlow*, Serpentine Gallery, London, 2010

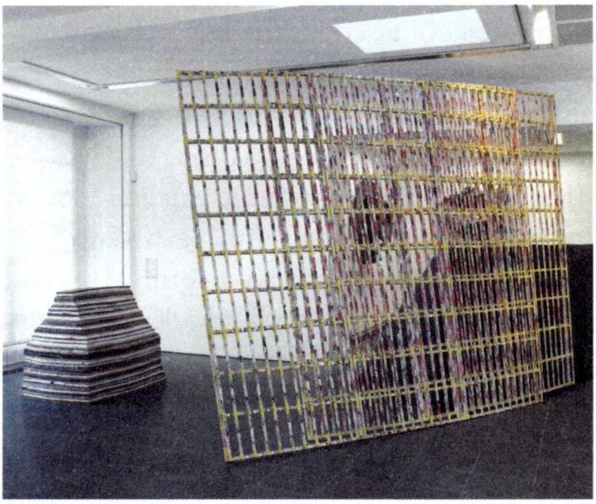

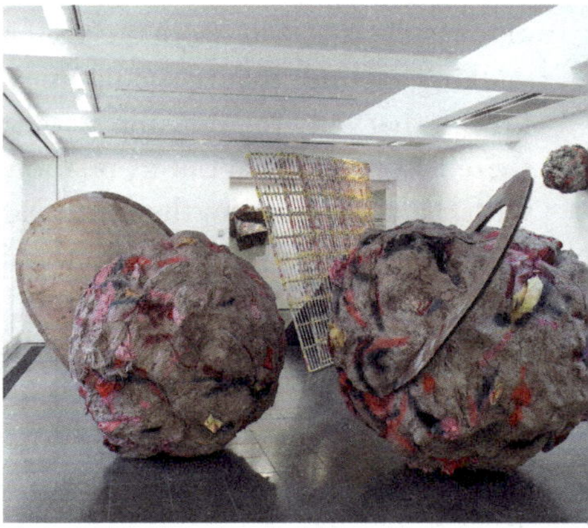

ABOVE LEFT TO RIGHT:
figs. 95–6 Installation views, *Nairy Baghramian and Phyllida Barlow*, Serpentine Gallery, London, 2010

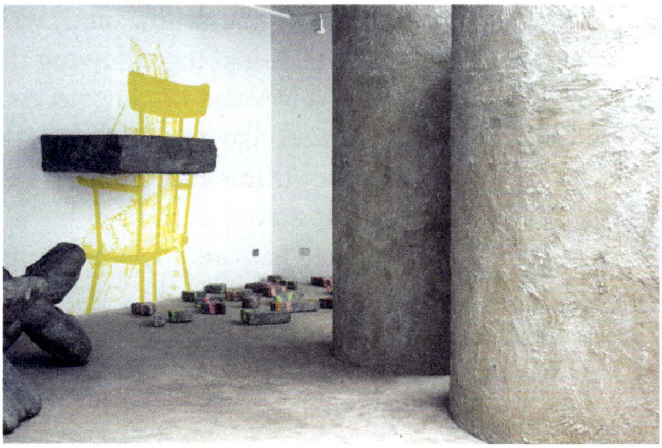

LEFT:
fig. 97 Installation view, *Phyllida Barlow/Jess Flood-Paddock*, The Russian Club Gallery, London, 2009

Then there are also *untitled: blob 1*, *untitled: blob 2*, and *untitled: double act* (fig. 96), which are all about a very immediate way of dealing with the material that I was speaking about earlier on: the least you can do to build up a sense of mass.

JP-J: In terms of collaboration, part of the genesis of this show was our visit to your exhibition at the Russian Club Gallery, where you presented your work alongside Jess Flood-Paddock, a student of yours (fig. 97). Is collaboration important to you in your work?

PB: No, it's not, actually. However, I should qualify that by saying that the way I work with assistants has to be collaborative. By which I mean that the instructions I give and how they are interpreted and acted upon by assistants is itself a creative process with many changes, suggestions, and trial and error processes where we are all in it together, but under my direction. It can be tense and unrelenting as my processes are physically demanding, and often repetitive, and on a large scale. The collaboration with Jess was completely up to the Russian Club. They chose us as their double show. It was chance that Jess was able to work in the space for a longer time than I was because I had other shows on, so I couldn't be there. I said to Jess, 'I want to do something very quickly.' That was when I went in and put these two huge drums in and clad them in cement. I asked Jess to react to them in any way she wanted: use them as a foil or as a form of dislike, hatred, antagonism. I said, 'You can even break them up and take them away; it doesn't matter, but I have to finish some other work, so why don't you have a few weeks in here?' So she brought loads of paintings, loads of stuff, and it was all going round and round in circles; she has an amazing way of thinking and collecting information that's utterly different from my own. In the end, she made the wall painting of a cat. I think it's turned its back on the sculptures, like it's saying, 'No, I don't want these.' I loved it because I have a kind of love-hate relationship with sculpture. Its history can reflect a self-regarding and inward-looking art form, so it seemed like the perfect gesture. And it prompted me to then bring other work into the space and allow the show to evolve – to allow Jess's cat to be the critic of the uncompromising solidity and pedantic qualities of my sculpture.

JP-J: There's something of the same kind of discussion with this exhibition – you've already talked about the different approaches to weight and gravity in your work and in Nairy's. That difference is very apparent, and that resonance is really felt.

PB: Nairy and I had a long conversation about collaboration. Because it hasn't been possible to work in the space together over a long period of time, the collaborative frisson can't happen in that way; it's got to happen in another way. It's been difficult to fathom what that is through conversations on the phone and in fairly quick meetings. That hasn't been so easy. It's been difficult to find out where the catalyst is between our two ways of working. But on the other hand, I think, exactly as you say, that kind of reciprocity between something that's full of air, very charged in that sense, and something that isn't, has been very important. I sense that Nairy doesn't make those same kinds of comparisons. Hers is a much more intellectual, politicised kind of comparison, which is interesting.

HUO: You have strong ties and connections to a younger generation of artists.

PB: Yes.

HUO: You've taught for many years and you're one of the most influential teachers in the UK of the last four decades. How does one teach art? And how has your teaching and pedagogy influenced your own practice?

PB: To me, the whole relationship with younger artists, and increasingly so over the last decade, has been about asking: 'What are we testing out and how are we testing it out and where does the test end up? Does the test have a conclusion or is it ongoing?' It's not so much about whether something is good or bad, or right or wrong, but more about how we examine it. It's a thinking process for students and tutors alike. It's almost as though those barriers between teacher and student get broken down because you're both in this together. You're both asking: 'What is an idea? And how is this so-called idea going to come into the world? Why does it need to come into the world? Where is our work going to end up? Who is it for? Who is our audience?'

Especially since we're no longer in the twentieth century; it's become even more exhilarating. The twentieth century has become viewable as a containable object. It's full of things, not all of them marvellous, in fact the reverse, socially, environmentally, politically, and creatively. I think, therefore, all artists are, in a way, in quite a predicament about our relationship with the twentieth century. I think there's a great sense of shared experience, regardless of age. We're trying to be in the now and yet there's this huge presence of something that's gone and the question of how we then relate to that. For me, constantly being surprised is so important. However familiar it is, whether it's clay or video or digital art or whatever, it's the surprise: 'My God! Somebody's done that!'

Take Tim Head, for instance, and his digital paintings. He's showing at Kettle's Yard at the moment. His digital paintings are fantastic. The work combines the rawness of the medium itself with an immersive, tactile, and overwhelming physical experience. The rawness in particular is a very unusual quality to generate through this medium. For me, even though I'm familiar with a lot of my ways of doing things, it's important to challenge that and question it by asking: 'Is there another way of doing this?' So it's been challenging to make the work for this show because I've been able to say: 'Maybe this is an anthology or a survey but maybe it's also about keeping that feeling of being surprised, and being taken by surprise, and not just repeating myself or saying the same thing more than once.' It's great when it happens.

JP-J: You create new works for each exhibition, or you remake works for each exhibition; that's a very labour-intensive process.

PB: Yes, and I think the time has come to question that process. I've been working with Dominic Eichler and Michel Ziegler of Silberkuppe in Berlin, and they're challenging that process and enabling me to question it. We are forming a new kind of premise for how I might change, beginning with keeping works rather than destroying them, while allowing the same sense of adventure to be retained in a work.

JP-J: Indeed, because every time you make it you can edit and change it.

PB: Yes.

JP-J: That's, of course, something that most artists can't do because the work is finished. Do you find that the work changes significantly from the first time you make it to the most recent version?

PB: Yes. The ramps are a theme that's been ongoing for more than twenty years. They were platforms and they've become ramps, so there is an evolution of the form. They were initially related to stages, like theatrical stages. Now the stage has become sloped and the objects are slipping off the stage. There are these performative qualities in the way I'm using some of these familiar themes.

HUO: Could you talk about these links to performativity, theatre, and about that idea of narrative in your installations?

PB: Take the BALTIC show from 2004–5 (figs. 92, 179): it was an epiphany to make the work for that fourth-floor gallery space, because it has two viewing points: one from the fifth floor where the space is seen from above, looked down on, and the other where it is entered, like going onstage. The narrative of being on the top floor and looking down on the space and the narrative of how the space itself could be entered and negotiated was incredibly important. Again, it was this looking up, looking down, looking across, looking through that was, in a way, the subject of the work. That related to where previous works had used some kind of platform with objects locked into them or on them or under them and I saw it as a sort of stage play, with the objects and viewers as the protagonists.

HUO: The objects were locked into the platforms?

PB: I would cut out sections of the platform and push the objects in. It was like translating the plinth into a kind of stage that would then invite that sense of a very static performance. The thing that moved would, of course, be the audience, which is unusual because audiences are usually fixed. It was like pulling the stage out into the central space, the space usually occupied by the audience, and then allowing the audience to be mobile around this stage that had originated as a plinth and has now become a ramp. That led me to think of sculpture as incredibly theatrical, just as a medium. It demands this rapport, like the meeting of protagonists within the space of the gallery or wherever it might be. It's an encounter that's theatrical, if that makes sense.

JP-J: Absolutely. The whole question of scale is very interesting in relation to the Serpentine. There's a feeling that the energy is almost uncontainable within the form that you make for it and if you couple that with the idea that you've precisely remade these pieces so that they may be only a few centimetres from the ceiling, for example, this is a very particular position to take in terms of the Serpentine's space and how your work is going to be seen. Could you tell us a little more about that?

PB: To me, there's scale and there's size. I'd say scale is artifice: it's inviting people to perceive something differently from its actual size. What I'm interested in is dimension and size and the idea that a dimension is a very controlling aspect of a physical environment. A sculptural object can interact with that control and actually tease it, so that it becomes a bit provocative. Size can also extend my own physical reach. It's not about a heroic bigness; it's actually the adventure of going beyond my own physical capacity that excites me. It's maybe why we want to climb trees or climb mountains; it may be why we want to walk that extra mile round the lake. It's about the adventure of going just that little bit further with something. To me, these things are to do with size and the things that control size and how space is controlled through size.

Scale is very different, and it's been interesting looking at all these recent programmes on Henry Moore, which I've found incredibly moving because they come from such a specific space and time of British art. Moore uses the word 'scale' a lot and it's because he's creating this extraordinary pictorial illusion. For somebody who believes so much in sculpture, to me it's like an anachronism. If you're here, this thing looks enormous, but it's not enormous compared with the tree that's a hundred metres away or something in a shipyard up in the North East. Even Richard Serra's pieces, which look massive at Gagosian, are still competing with real hugeness out in the world beyond.

JP-J: You've programmed a music event at Café Oto in connection with this show. What interests you about what you're doing there?

PB: To me it's very clear. With the things I do, the word 'sculpture' always comes up. That's great. I'm absolutely passionate about this medium and this subject, whatever you call it, and whether it can be defined, or whether it has boundaries now or doesn't have boundaries, and anything goes – and who cares anyway. So I thought, 'Why don't I do something that's completely outside my comfort zone?' Because I know so many youngish musicians – some aren't musicians, they're artists who are using sound as a material – and it just extends a notion of the sculptural language away from my own repertoire of physicality. It's just to take the opportunity to do something that's not familiar to me critically and trying to embrace that, and the excitement of giving a whole range of sound artists a small opportunity at Café Oto to do that. It's beyond my radar, so again it's to keep this excitement about this subject alive.

JP-J: Do you feel that sound integrates into your work in any other way or is this a completely separate kind of venture?

PB: Well, I think objects do have sound embedded in them. The issue of light is also important. I always think being able to look at and experience sculpture without gallery lights on is the best. Having a natural progression from dawn to dusk as an inherent part of the looking experience is revelatory and I equate that with something to do with sound. The silence of sculpture is uncanny, and actually walking around it where the noise comes from your own footsteps or your own body is like an imageless experience.

HUO: What are your unrealised projects? Do you have any you couldn't do, which were too expensive, too big, technically not possible, censored, or self-censored?

PB: Yes and no. I'm interested in making and locating work in remote places, whether that is an outside site or inside, but where I am the only audience for the work, and its future is uncertain. The work might only last a few minutes, or decay slowly, but it wouldn't matter. Uncertainty can be exciting and risky in relationship to making work, and therefore challenging and generative. I'm very attracted to the coastline. It is an edge and boundary, the meeting between land and sea, that is in a constant state of flux – a site that reinvents itself in accordance with tides, weather, and geology. But there are tricky issues to consider if such a fragile environment is to be used as a site for making and locating work. It has all the potential to be a selfish and indulgent project. I don't want to add to pollution, but I'd love to do something where the work gets lost in the sea when the tide comes in – to take a ramp down to the coast, for instance. I have thrown things in the Thames, just because it's fascinated me as a destination for a work. There are homes with art in them, there are galleries, there are bank foyers; there are these destination sites. So what's the worst-case scenario? Is it to actually throw a work away? Or would you be giving it a place that's restless, a non-place? I don't know what happened to the things I threw in the Thames, but it was liberating, and it was part of a whole ongoing series of objects that I would place around London on lamp posts, street furniture, and other things.

I was thinking about Michael Landy's *Art Bin*. It made me think about using bins that are already there, like bins in parks or recycling centres or on the street, and just filling them up. This work had the potential to take on lots of issues that question and go beyond the gallery: public space, futility, and commercialism – issues that I'm interested in. Did that piece have to be in a gallery? You sometimes feel that the constraints on art are polite and that there could be another way of doing things. That, for me, is constantly a huge desire: to do work where there is no audience.

First published as 'Interview with Phyllida Barlow by Julia Peyton-Jones and Hans Ulrich Obrist', in Kathryn Rattee and Melissa Larner, eds., *Nairy Baghramian & Phyllida Barlow* (London: Serpentine Gallery; Cologne: Verlag der Buchhandlung Walther König, 2010), 49–68.

On 17 October 2011 Barlow participated in a conversation with Professor Tamar Garb and Professor Briony Fer, at the Centre for the Study of Contemporary Art, University College London, to coincide with her debut exhibition with Hauser & Wirth at the old bank space on Piccadilly in London. Included here is an introduction to the exhibition that Barlow gave at the start of the event, in which she talks through the works, her approach to making the show, and the thinking behind her decisions. The first part of the ensuing discussion between the three participants is also included and centres around Barlow's issues with the words 'body' and 'viewer', and the role of the audience.

Conversation with Briony Fer and Tamar Garb

2011

Phyllida Barlow: [...] I just want to introduce you to the show [...]. The main resource for the show was, of course, this extraordinary space. This Lutyens space, of the bank on Piccadilly, which to me, is an absolute gift for anyone who makes sculpture.[1] I don't know if people still use the word 'sculpture'. I've always used it. And, of course, over the years I have been condemned for using it, and then celebrated for using it. And then condemned again for using it. Seems to be one of those words like all the visual arts, they have to be condemned as dead and then be allowed to be born again. But to me, as a sculptor, the space itself is a 360-degree spiral space. So you're never at rest in the space. The minute you go in, you're in what I think is really the inside of a plinth, this wooden constructed space, which I wanted to get above. So my first premise was not to be too concerned with imagery, but to be concerned with reaching, stretching, pushing, probing, going down and into, coming out of, going up again, and using the spiral staircase as a kind of connecting tissue between the spaces. And the actual images to begin with weren't so important. The one thing I also didn't want to get involved in was any kind of forced innovation or banging my head against the wall to be new. I just wanted to use a kind of familiarity of works that I had done before, and not feel under any pressure to make the work be sort of sensational in any kind of way.

So the first space was really to create two positions. One position where you go in and maybe you don't quite know what you're looking at, because the objects are reaching up into this space that really intrigued me (fig. 98). Which is a very typically Lutyens space, where he brings the light into the top part of the building. And that was where I wanted to make the, so to speak, objects be situated. And then to use the plinth space, the wooden space, as the means for elevating those objects. Then at that point, there's a choice. You can either go upstairs or take this tiny little staircase downstairs. So the syntax, the actual grammar of the building was really important. Rather than there being a narrative with a beginning, a middle, and an end, there was a spatial narrative. And so for me, my way of thinking was to actually go down into the much less formal space, the space which is the kind of underbelly, and use that as a very crowded, filled-up space and to pursue a complete lack of logic between all the objects.

I suppose I'm really interested in this kind of denial of a subject. I think that probably I use the words 'form', 'subject', and 'content' in completely the wrong way. But to me, the work doesn't really have a subject, but it has a series of actions and spatial relationships. So down in the basement I don't think there's any particular logical relationship with these works (fig. 99). It's just about placing and interrupting and creating a kind of dynamic that's in complete contrast within the different rooms down there. There are ten spaces in this gallery, and therefore it was a formidable amount of work to make each space very active and have its own independence from the space that you had just been in.

So most of the works have some kind of action that goes with them, like this is sort of crushed and piled (fig. 100). And then the other room right at the end is kind of blocked, tilted, and in a way I think quite absurd (figs. 55, 101). And then of course it's going up the little stairs on to the balcony, where I wanted something that was invisible from the space below. And these works, which are called 'broken shelves', are usually made from all the debris that accumulates in the studio and just get made like drawings, in a way (fig. 102). And I wanted it to be more like a landmark that you came in, so you would look that way and then turn and look at the other works. The view from the balcony is very important, because it shows the tops of those big blocks that you saw when you first came into the space (figs. 54, 103).

And then into the next spaces, to me, they very much refer to plinths and to the formality of the room (fig. 104). And I've made these before. I made them at the Serpentine. But I wanted to remake them, mainly because I accumulate a lot of waste materials and for me it's very important to use up these materials. And the idea of stacking and accumulating, so that they become like empty plinths, and kind of relate to the edge of the space there. And then a distraction, with the work on the wall. Small works are very important because they're done in my studio at home. And they're the very intimate aspect of how I make work, whereas the other works are made collectively with me and about anything between five and ten people helping me.

And then this room at the end (fig. 105), what was great about this, and I have Sara Harrison to thank, really, for this, was the removal men just brought the … No, they're not called 'removal men', are they?

Audience member: Art handlers.

PB: They're called 'art handlers'. The art handlers just brought these in and stacked them. And we went in there and that was virtually how it was left. There was a minimum amount of arranging. And I think that was quite inspirational to realise that that side of the work, which I think is enormously

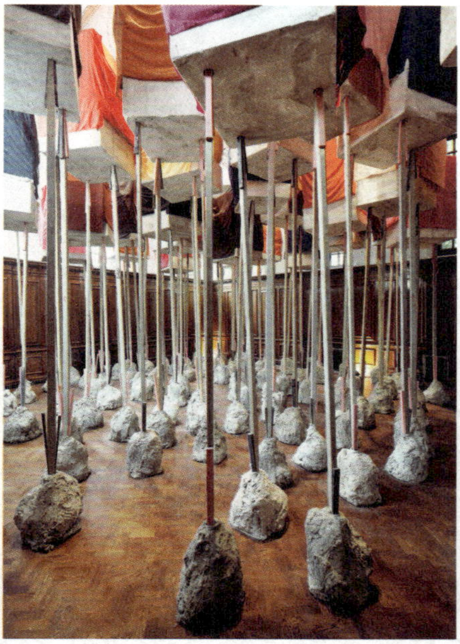

LEFT:
fig. 98 RIG: *untitled; blocks*, 2011

BELOW:
fig. 99 RIG: *untitled; hoops*, 2011

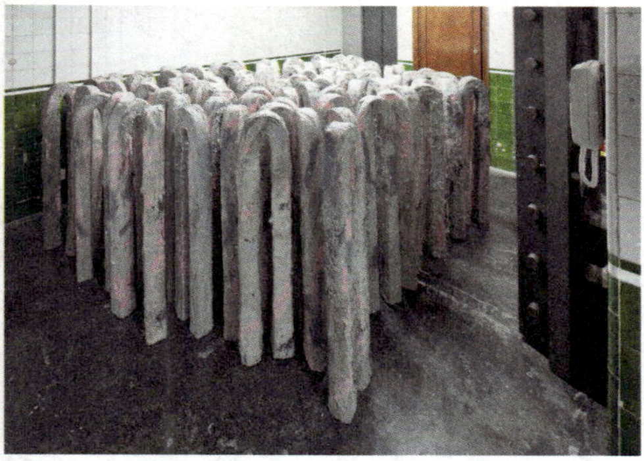

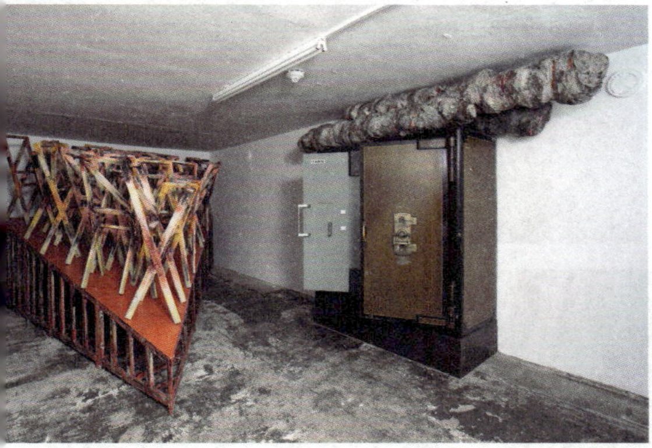

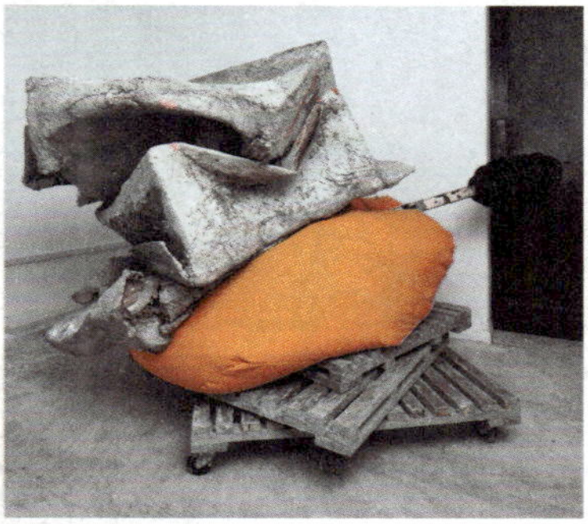

ABOVE LEFT TO RIGHT:
fig. 100 RIG: *untitled; stagechairs*, 2011,
and RIG: *untitled; tubes*, 2011
fig. 101 RIG: *untitled; crushedboxfeud*, 2011

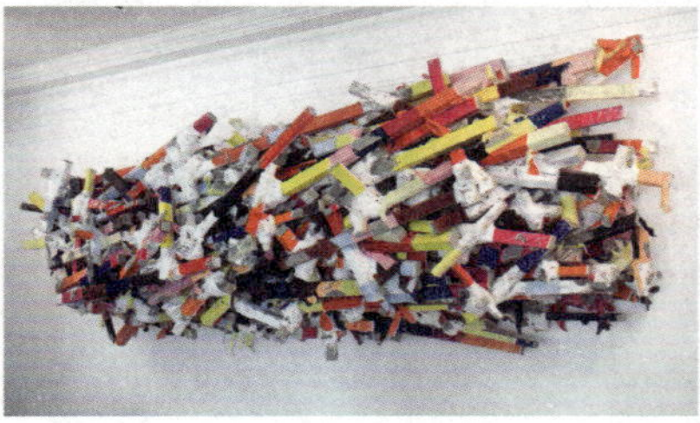

ABOVE:
fig. 102 RIG: *untitled; broken shelf 3*, 2011

RIGHT:
fig. 103 RIG: *untitled; broken shelf 3*, 2011,
and RIG: *untitled; blocks*, 2011

All images on this page are installation views, *Phyllida Barlow: RIG*, Hauser & Wirth Piccadilly, London, 2011

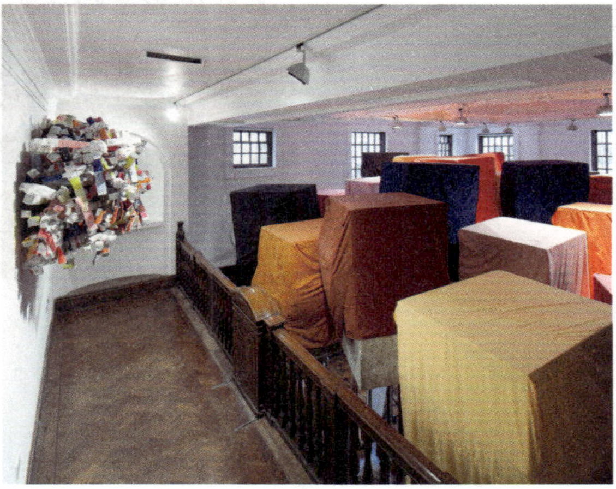

BELOW:
fig. 104 RIG: *untitled; hive 2*, 2011, RIG: *untitled; hive 3*, 2011, and RIG: *untitled; twist*, 2011

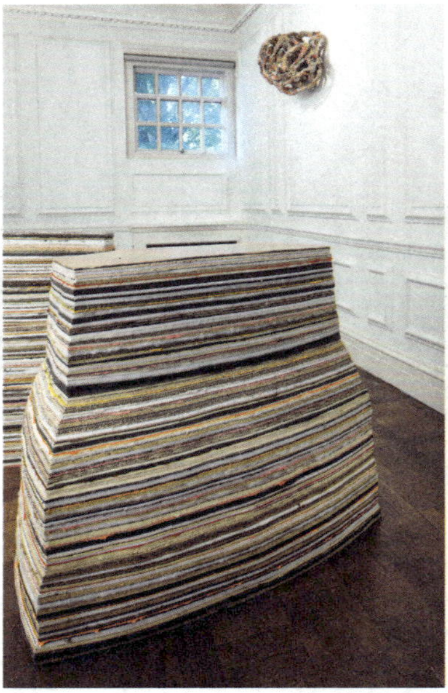

BELOW:
fig. 105 RIG: *untitled; emptyunits*, 2011

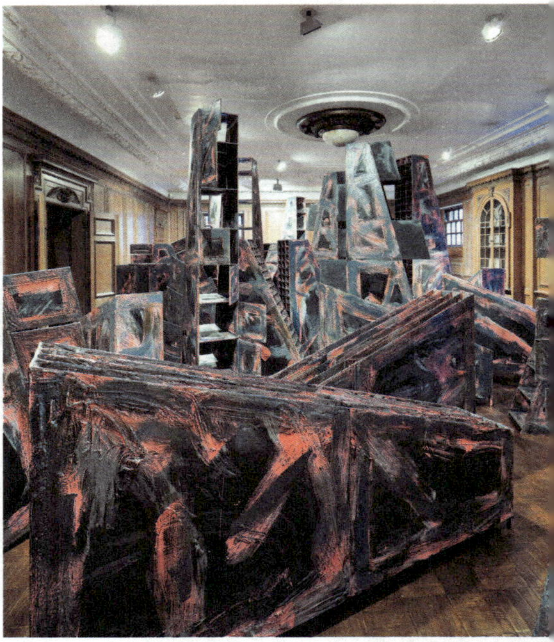

RIGHT:
fig. 106 RIG: *untitled; pompoms*, 2011

All images on this page are installation views, *Phyllida Barlow: RIG*, Hauser & Wirth Piccadilly, London, 2011

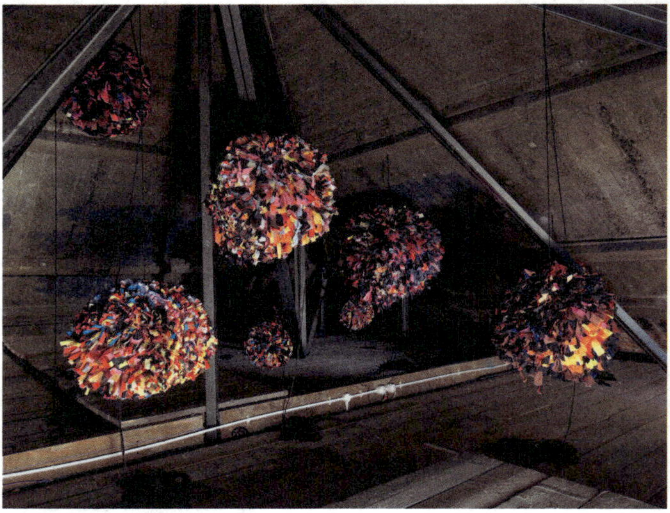

problematic, trying to make something look very random, could actually be handed over to someone else.

And then the sort of silly aspect of the work was maybe these pompoms up in the attic (fig. 106). So for me, everything is about a kind of spatial narrative, I said, rather than a subject that I can name. I hoped that each space would, in a way, inflect a different kind of mood or atmosphere. So that's that.

Tamar Garb: Well, of course it's very strange to look and to experience the show via that little PowerPoint, because the effect of the show is such that one is so in it, one experiences it so much as a body in a space, that seeing it translated into an image and a flat surface is a very, very strange experience. And so I wonder whether we could start off by just thinking through, for you, the relationship of the body to the work. It is a work that so much makes one think about one's own body, as a viewer. The obstruction to viewing and being in that space. And so, could you extend it a little bit more and talk to us a little bit about what you think of, in relation to the body either of the viewer or of the maker or makers, in relation to these very extraordinary objects that you make?

PB: I never know what 'the body' is. And when was it first talked about? My work's about the body. What does that mean? I have absolutely no idea. It's like that difference between 'nude' and 'naked'. And I think therefore talking about it as bodily, it's certainly not something I think about. I think about the actions that I'm capable of doing physically, but I don't think of my body in that way. In fact it sort of fills me with deep horror. But I know that it's something that I'm failing to sort of take on as an issue. But I think what I see it in relationship to is a series of protagonists. That the sculptures are protagonists, the space itself is a protagonist. And initially myself, I'm a protagonist in trying to activate these things, which I know you, Briony, have written about in your essay for the Serpentine.[2] That the things are not necessarily consciously particularly images, but they're more like events that can do what I want them to do in the space. So the protagonists, if that's a body, then the protagonists and how they are going to be able to walk around these objects, look up, look down, look through, bump into, you know, manoeuvre themselves, that's more … Maybe that relates to theatre and other forms of experience like that.

Briony Fer: Can I just add a question to that, Phyllida? Because the other word that I think you didn't like very much was 'viewer'. And in some ways, the viewer or the spectator you renamed that the 'protagonist'. If you resisted the idea that it might be about the body, you also want to resist in some way that it's about viewing, or simply about viewing. I wondered what that meant to you, that word. Because I think it's interesting why that's not a word that has much currency for you.

PB: Because I think when, for me, the act of making these things is so … it's challenging, and it requires incredible planning and manoeuvring of things. Therefore the idea of the viewer gets completely lost in that process. It becomes a collection of decisions and actions, a lot of which get changed and reordered in order to gain the thing that I'm trying to do in the first instance. So that initial activator is me. And then there's a kind of hope that those actions will attract or engage others.

TG: One of the words you used in thinking about the people who might experience your work, whether they're viewers or spectators, was the 'interloper'. And that interested me a lot, because it's almost a feeling as if one is trespassing on a world which is both meant and not meant to be seen or experienced. And you used this word when we were talking the other day, of the person who comes to experience this work as an interloper. So it's as if there's some private world, in a way, that one is intruding on. Why is that, do you think?

PB: I think it's a fascination with my kind of denial of making work for an audience. And wanting to keep something of the intimacy of how you make work right up to the last minute. So we were talking about wanting to bring the studio to the exhibition space, rather than finish the work and then the exhibition occurs. It's perhaps trying to keep several aspects of the making process in a great state of flux, right up to the last minute. And that is actually quite performative. So that the idea of suddenly cutting that off, and there being a moment where that ends, and then you open the doors and the audience comes in, seems to me, I mean, it just seems to me problematic in a way that it probably isn't problematic. It's just something that I have in my head.

TG: My experience, and it'd be interesting after this to see whether this was other people's experience of being in the space, is one of extreme physical discomfort, some of the time. In the ground floor, one is looking up all the time and you basically get a sore neck because the orientation is this orientation upwards. And sometimes it's even quite precarious. You bump into things. There isn't quite enough space. You go into this attic to see those glorious pompoms, suspended in the eaves, and you have to climb up this incredibly precarious staircase, and then you have to come down it backwards and risk falling. So there is a sense in which the whole configuration of your encounter with the space is something which both tantalises and teases and brings you in, and yet keeps you out all the time, and that's part of what's so riveting about it for me.

PB: I think that also is about whether we are onstage, backstage, or whatever. And the gallery space as a stage space intrigues me. So there's a point where, to me, the objects and who is manoeuvring themselves around the objects, there isn't actually any differentiation between those two characters or protagonists, as I say.

[...]

1. In 2003 Hauser & Wirth opened its first London gallery in the 1922 bank building designed by the English architect Sir Edwin Lutyens (1869–1944).
2. Briony Fer, 'Barriers for Thinking', in Kathryn Rattee and Melissa Larner, eds., *Nairy Baghramian & Phyllida Barlow* (London: Serpentine Gallery; Cologne: Verlag der Buchhandlung Walther König, 2010), 69–73.

This interview between ARTSEEN editor John Yau and Barlow was conducted by phone, soon after the opening of *RIG*, her debut exhibition with Hauser & Wirth at their space on Piccadilly in London in autumn 2011. Barlow and Yau converse about *RIG*, permanence and impermanence, the 1960s, absurdity, and subject, content, and form. They discuss notions of Englishness in relation to art and compare the American and British approaches to painting the body. They also talk about video art and technological advances and the problems of repeating a gesture.

Interview with John Yau

2011

John Yau: The first question I want to ask you is about the title *RIG*, which is both a noun and a verb, and which has a number of meanings in slang. I think that that gets to something about your thinking about sculpture. We tend to think of 'sculpture' as a noun, but it seems to me that you've introduced the verb into it. Does that make sense?

Phyllida Barlow: Great, yes, it makes sense. 'Rigging something up' implies a kind of temporary gesture. I think the verb 'to rig' is both to fix something slightly fraudulent but also to improvise with a way of fixing something. And then that's in complete contrast to something like an oil rig.

JY: One of the things about your work has always been that there's a temporariness to it, that you make it out of different, unlikely materials, and at the end of the exhibition you take it all apart. Some people think of sculpture as this permanent thing – you know, Donald Judd, Richard Serra, and Frank Stella – and they might think that you're doing something that subverts that idea of sculpture.

PB: I'm sometimes slightly bewildered by that response. Yes, I'm aware of perhaps subverting permanence, but I think that has a very long tradition, a tradition as long as that of monumentality. It's just on a different route, maybe through theatre and through travelling players or something like that. You've got the whole idea of improvised capture of space, which always mimicked the ceremonial or the monumental. I also think of Eva Hesse, or many other artists of that era, say, 1964 or even earlier, 1959, through to, say, the late 1970s. There are many improvised works going on and impermanent work being executed that are of a monumental nature but stand in contradiction to the Minimalist solidity or staticness that is conveyed through Judd.

JY: Would you say that there are at least two kinds of practice going on from the late 1950s to the present, and that one focuses on permanence, while the other one examines something more impermanent, transitory, and temporary as a way of thinking?

PB: When I began making sculpture in the early 1960s, there was already a collision and a friction between different intellectual and practical approaches to sculpture – one was rooted in Marcel Duchamp and the other possibly in Pablo Picasso. The Duchampian trajectory seems to have claimed the high intellectual ground and the other a more physical and material relationship with making. Of course, in actuality all this breaks down and both positions fuse. But I think there was a kind of stand-off between these two positions, which took hold during the late 1960s and 1970s with the Conceptual Art movement and Minimalism. However, between these two, the more gestural makers – for example, Eva Hesse, Robert Morris, Mario Merz, Piero Manzoni, Louise Bourgeois – were much more pertinent to me. For me, their work related as much to Surrealism as to the labels of Minimalism, Conceptualism, or Arte Povera. Their work employed accumulative processes with materials akin to Picasso's assemblage works and Kurt Schwitters's *Merzbau*.

So, yes, when I came into sculpture in the early 1960s, the most enduring impact that decade had on me was the questioning of what constituted sculptural language, and the challenges that were instigated against sculpture's identity as a permanent form.

My epiphany of what could be sculpture was to use waste materials. I used anything and everything from paper, polythene, cardboard, fabric, and many other 'sheet' materials, which could easily be cut, torn, ripped, sliced. For me, these were in opposition to the labour-intensity of the sculpture processes I had been so doggedly taught at art school, and which defined sculpture as sculpture – carving, casting, welding, construction. I have to say that I now savour and respect those processes and I am deeply grateful for having learnt them. They have given me independence and the opportunity to rebel against them, and to explore other approaches to making.

JY: For *RIG*, you were able to install your work in a building designed by the great English architect Edwin Lutyens. You had the whole building to use from the basement to the top floor. Is that correct?

PB: Yes, to the attic.

JY: You must have had some idea of what you were going to do, but, at the same time, I think a lot of it must have just come about with you trying to do something to the space of the building, to the walls, to how we move through that building, its different spaces.

PB: That's exactly it. The building has an incredible spatial narrative. You enter and there is this oak-panelled room that conveys authority. The oak panelling goes up to about half of the walls, and then there are bare walls after that, with windows. I saw that interior space, with its formal wooden panelling and floor, as a plinth. That relationship made me want to extend something up into the ceiling. As you enter, you are in an enclosed wooden space, but when you look up you are somehow liberated from this very, very solid space; you are liberated into the light, which gives on to the clouds and the sky. It's a very clever architectural space (fig. 98). And then the spatial narrative continues down a tiny staircase into the vault, where there is a collection of small rooms that aren't in particularly good condition (figs. 55, 99–101). So there is this underground space, and then the opposite of that is when you go up on to a balcony (figs. 54, 103), which overlooks that formal, first space, then into the very formal bank room (fig. 105), then eventually the attic (fig. 106). So it's a very particular narrative around the building spatially. It's a gift to anyone who makes sculpture because you're naturally on a kind of 360-degree circumnavigation of the building, and therefore of the work it would contain. For me it was really exciting to know that the work would, in a way, be very much about that 'walking around' experience that is so particular to sculpture, not just one-point viewing positions.

JY: But at the same time that you want people to circumnavigate the space, and the space around your work, it seems to me you wanted the narrative that might come from that also to be open-ended, not to be authoritarian the way I think certain sculptures and architectural spaces have a kind of authoritarian presence. You make us aware that these pieces are temporary, like the shelf that you made of all these small pieces, so it becomes an impossible shelf, which interacts with our own understanding of what function things have (fig. 102). I don't know if that makes sense, but I felt like there's a lot of that going on in your work.

PB: I think absurdity is inevitable. I think sculpture is an absurd discipline, beyond all others. Beyond film, beyond painting, beyond poetry. It occupies space, which in a crowded world would be better occupied by things that could serve people either more discreetly or in a better way. Sculpture stands vulnerable to attack for its absolutely unequivocal uselessness, and that to me is its tremendous strength – that it takes up the kind of spaces that we as human beings either want to reach and do something with or actually takes up the space that we might be occupying, and therefore to appropriate those spaces with something that's inert, heavy, and where its syntax is quite disruptive and broken, like the broken shelf, to me is gloriously absurd – that's its subject. Its rupture is its subject. The actions of making that are the script for this absurdity, have become the subject of the work, and apart from that I do not have a subject.

JY: But you have written about and spoken about artists who do have subjects. I mean, your essay 'The Sneeze of Louise', on Louise Bourgeois, is brilliant (see pages 324–35). You talked about her work in a way that got to the subject matter. This prompted me to look at your work through your view of Louise Bourgeois, but I felt refuted, and I thought, well that's interesting.

PB: I remember we talked about this when we first met in London and you were incredibly eloquent about it – the Holy Trinity of subject, content, and form. I think I'm still a traditional formalist, digging away at where the actions of form carry with them subject. You know the subject of destruction or the subject of breakage, and then the content is, to me, the different kinds of materials that can behave in different ways according to that subject. So the broken shelf, which is made up of offcuts of bits of armature which are then wrapped in fabric, almost as a sort of bandage to mend them, and then put together in this very ad hoc, speedy, quick way is, to me, very much about breakage and then repair – those two things carrying for me enormous content and emotive subjects.

JY: There is also a room where everything came out of the corner in a sharp angle (fig. 100). I feel like there's a lot of emotional content to your work, but it's not nameable according to some story that we associate with emotional content.

PB: Well, that would be fantastic – and of course we've been through two decades of intense subject-led work in the UK in particular. There is a huge infatuation with the ability of language to direct the intention of the work. I mean Damien Hirst's shark is a fantastic example of that. Hate him or love him, he really gave incredible substance to that way of working. It's certainly not my way of working. I would want to be the opposite of that, where things are in limbo in terms of being able to pin them down, but the act of making and the visual content of the work somehow creates a kind of link to quite specific emotional states, usually not particularly comfortable ones because I suppose they're the ones that interest me.

JY: If you think of YBA artists like Jake and Dinos Chapman, Marc Quinn, Tracey Emin, and others, the thing that I would say about them is that theirs is a very literary-based art. It's based on a narrative or a story, and I always felt that that was, in part, the legacy of England being a literary country.

PB: Absolutely. I absolutely agree, and a highly institutionalised country, and institutions need names, and names are language. I think there's a whole thesis there that on the one hand is very embracing of, you know, the radical – if the radical can be named and institutionalised, it will be in this country. Whether it's through the royal this or the royal that – you know, all these institutions that have 'royal' in front of them – or in quite eccentric institutions that are set up by individuals, you know, this or that philosophical, scientific, or religious society – these kind of rogue institutions are trying to accommodate the huge diversity of thinking. So that's an incredibly language-based approach to organising the human condition. Maybe it happens in all countries, I don't know – or in all cultures, I should say.

JY: I don't know. But one thing that's always struck me about English painting that seems very different from, let's say, American painting, is that if you think of the work of Jenny Saville, Lucian Freud, Francis Bacon, Leon Kossoff, they have a very different relationship to the body. It's portly Falstaff, who believes life is a charade. It's the wounded body, the abject body. And Americans don't want a body, but an image. It's why so many people love Andy Warhol; these are not bodies he shows us, but images of faces without bodies, or in his 'car crash' paintings, bodies without faces. They are disconnected. English painting comes from a different culture, and it has a different relationship to the body. This must also influence you as a sculptor.

PB: Really interesting. I wonder whether the Andy Warhol example is a statement of a kind of cultural pronouncement, of 'we're here', 'this is what we are'. Whereas the British English version is much more generic, much more born out of the landscape of a small nation, and therefore the body is not so particular in some ways. Think of Saville or Freud, and even Kossoff, who, I think is absolutely fantastic. I put him in a slightly different category because it's almost as if he's dissolving the body into paint. But Freud and Saville – both seem as though the body is archetypal to them. I mean, huge, rolling mounds of flesh and paint all together. Whereas Warhol is almost catalysing the sense of rashness of a land that's constantly discovering itself, almost as though there were – to use a really clichéd word – this necessity for absolute identity, completely different from anything else in the world, whereas the British one seems to me to be much more – I don't know – the only word I can think of is 'generic'. These are bodies that have their origin in and continue to be an inheritance from the Renaissance. Of course, they're unique, but they're not singular and didactic in the way that those startling images from Andy Warhol were and are. By the way, Richard Hamilton died. Did you hear that?

JY: No, I didn't.

PB: Just on the news – what time is it in New York?

JY: It's 2:30.

PB: Have you had lunch?

JY: No.

PB: Well, he must have died today. I heard it on the six o'clock news about an hour ago. I mean, there's an interesting example of someone who could not in my mind be anything else other than English. You think of Andy Warhol and you think of the way he was unafraid to deliver an image as an absolute autonomous thing, self-consciously of its time, off the street, and unashamedly exploitative of everyday banality. Then you think of the complexity of Richard Hamilton's paintings, with their footnote-type commentary. I mean, they're beautiful, but they're not about delivering a singular punch. And compare that to a James Rosenquist. I remember when I first saw a Rosenquist, I thought it was the most staggeringly wonderful thing I'd ever seen. You just knew there was nothing like that going on in Europe or the UK. It was completely and magnificently drastic in terms of being the complete opposite of the inward-lookingness that I think British art can be.

JY: I think of your work as being among the most drastic and non-literary work being made in England right now.

PB: The thing is that it is completely sculpture. It's absolutely, to me, rooted in the love of bringing into the world things that haven't been there before. The idea that they're going to somehow create – or I would hope that they're going to create – a difficulty with space and their location in space. I feel I am incredibly traditional, but to me the traditions are really exciting in the way that they can be kicked around a bit and re-examined. It's fascinating, the fact that people have used similar materials for absolutely thousands of years and constantly updated how to use those materials with such a tiny repertoire of technique: casting, modelling, clay, plaster, carving, assemblage. Even if we go into more sophisticated materials like plastics and all sorts of other things, inherently we're still dealing with very few actual techniques: modelling, moulding, or collaging. Then I suppose those two disciplines of painting and sculpture, this is what they're locked into, unlike video or digital stuff or whatever, which are still struggling to find coherency. There's the technology, fantastic, high-definition, this, that, and the other, but you still sit in a blackened room to look at it and it's stuck with its limitations in a way that painting and sculpture are not. Though I daresay that would make some people furious.

JY: It's true – you have to go somewhere and sit in a dark room, behind a thick curtain or blanket. If painting and sculpture are stuck in the white box – which I don't think they are – then you can say that video and film are stuck in a black box.

PB: Absolutely, yes. I mean, we've seen Bill Viola projections and they're fascinating, but to me they have a creative desperation about them, of trying to make this thing of the projection expand outside its frame. Tony Oursler does it very well, and I think they all do it superbly well, but I think there's still a problem with these things being so connected to painting in some ways. It's almost like going back to 16mm or Super 8 – such a shame those particular forms have gone actually because they were so much more physical.

JY: Right, and portable in a way.

PB: Yes, exactly, and the theme of light and everything, even the sound. I'm sure it's very tedious for people involved in video to hear this kind of stuff because I think it sounds so nostalgic, but I'm not particularly nostalgic for it. I think it's that the more the technology of video and other digital forms gets heightened, I'm not sure that it does anything more for the creative side, or the creative manipulation of that medium. It just seems to make more and more demands, to become more and more in the thrall of the technology rather than actually being able to almost overwhelm it in some way. And I think, someone like Robert Smithson and what he produced in the 1960s and 1970s – it's just such an ongoing extraordinary challenge to anyone making sculpture, people who are attracted to large sculpture. I don't see video as having yet arrived at that kind of snapping point. We're left to kind of pick up the pieces after those works, thank you very much! We still want to make this stuff! What the hell do we make after those kind of huge gestures that Smithson made that remain sort of monumental, in terms of throwing down a challenge?

JY: It's interesting that you use the word 'gesture' because I think it really is about whether or not you make a gesture, a drastic one, if you will, which is different than employing a process or technique over and over again, like Bernard Frize. I was just reading a review of someone who didn't want to make a stand so he used a light associated with computers because in a way it's just something very bland and commonplace.

PB: Right. How many times have we heard that? I mean they're all very good artists so I'm not having a go. For many years Keith Tyson used a computer as a means for making decisions of what images he would throw together. I suppose what interests me about that is, in a way, isn't that what imagination is meant to do? Isn't that what human imagination is meant to do? Isn't that what the challenge is? I like the fact that Tyson's work is a proposition to challenge the role of imagination – that's important. You try to push your imagination into places that look at randomness and try to encourage different ways of thinking about it. But it does seem to me that you willingly replace one regime with another when you hand things over to computers. I just find it odd.

JY: Yes, and also that a gesture is something that at its very best is unrepeatable unless you end up becoming a mimic of yourself, which is not good.

PB: I think that actually in terms of my work it's very relevant. There is an aspect of what I do where I'm worried about the gesture becoming exactly what you said – a sort of one-off thing, which then becomes repeatable and editionable and all the rest of it. That is when I have to take some sort of action to ensure that if I'm going to remake a work it's got to be in a very, very knowing way. It's no longer about the gesture; it would have to be about something else, and that seems, to me, important. You're right – the gesture is by definition something that can happen only once, but if you start to repeat it, it becomes a repeated gesture and it changes because it has a sort of accumulation of knowledge that begins to come into play. It's no longer a surprising action. It becomes learnt.

JY: We talked about this in our first conversation, about the notion of the repeated gesture, what happens when it, or anything else, becomes a style, a signature, or branding – a word that's now being used. It seems in your work that you have found ways to resist that, or push back against it, even though we're all limited as human beings so there's something almost futile about pushing against it. After all, we do accumulate history, methods, and knowledge, and yet at the same time we have to push back against them.

PB: I think that's something that I've not done, which is to revisit work that I've destroyed or from which I've used the materials again. But now I'm in the position to actually revisit work. In this current work at the gallery particularly, there's a whole room full of empty furniture units: cupboards and lockers and shelves (fig. 105). About thirteen years ago I made just two single pieces like that. It was really quite intense, revisiting that work, and salvaging from the memory of making that work a completely new work altogether. I think that's something I'm interested in going into more and more – how previous work, earlier works, might now come back, how I will be able to revisit them as an entirely new experience.

JY: To make it fresh?

PB: Yes.

JY: And are you working on another show? Are you thinking about another show?

PB: Another two shows. One at the Haus der Kunst in Munich and the other at the Museum Ludwig.

JY: And when will those shows be?

PB: The show in Munich opens on 11 November and the exhibition in Cologne opens 17 December. It's Kaspar König's last show before he retires.

JY: And are there any plans to show in New York City?

PB: There may be, but I think it's still under wraps, for autumn 2012.

First published as 'Phyllida Barlow with John Yau', *The Brooklyn Rail* (October 2011): 26–9; https://brooklynrail.org/2011/10/art/phyllida-barlow-with-john-yau.

This interview, conducted over email with curator Gary Carrion-Murayari, was included in *siege*, the publication accompanying the New Museum show of the same name, held in New York in 2012.
It begins by Barlow outlining the works she made in response to the fourth-floor exhibition space. She writes about the shifts she witnessed in sculpture in the 1970s, recalling certain exhibitions and events, the different exhibition and catalogue aesthetics of that period, and the change she has observed since then to thinking about the audience in a more accommodating way. She considers the urban environment – and specifically London – and its relationship to her work. Carrion-Murayari suggests that her drawings function as premonitions, which she takes on, discussing how they translate into her sculptures.

Interview with Gary Carrion-Murayari

2012

Gary Carrion-Murayari: Balconies, stages, stockades, and arches are all elements that have appeared in your work in some form in the past, but what made you return to them for this particular installation at the New Museum? I'm also wondering how you approached and tried to reimagine the often-challenging space of our fourth-floor gallery?

Phyllida Barlow: When I entered the fourth-floor gallery from the elevator I didn't know whether I was at the front or the back of the space. The more I thought about it, the more stage-like the space became. Consequently, I wanted to make the entrance from the elevator be the back of the space, like entering backstage. The front would then be the furthest wall from the gallery entrance, so I was intrigued by the idea of turning the space around.

Having become inspired by thinking of the space as reversible, other concerns then began to present themselves. The height of the gallery is awkward and, for me, emphasises the theatrical qualities of the dimensions of the space – high-ceilinged but proportionately not equalled by its length and width – which make it seem stunted and stage-like. But more importantly, I want to disrupt how the space is viewed on entering. Using the height seemed the most dramatic way to do this. The arches are formally very different to the architecture of the room and in conflict with it … or that is what I hope (figs. 56, 107). As well as turning the space around, I want to bring an 'exterior' world inside. By using height, floor, obstacles, corners, collisions, etc., I hope this will forestall and block how the space can be viewed all at once.

Although I have made a small cluster of the arch forms for *RIG* at Hauser & Wirth, on Piccadilly, London (fig. 99), I have not made them on this scale before. This transforms them (I hope) from something tomb-like into absurdly monumental forms that are kitsch and fake … and, of course, very theatrical. The huge, black balcony will also be placed high up, utilising the height of the space to complement the height of the arches, but will be something predatory and clumsy – a kind of folly.

The stage, the tarpaulins, and crushed boxes are all forms used before but, as with the arches, not in the way I will be locating them for *siege*. In contrast to the upright formalism of the arches and the brutal, clumsy shape of the balcony, both reaching up to the ceiling, the collection of stuff, shapes, and forms which make up the stage work will be a collision … a kind of car crash which spreads out from the stage form and will be very floor-bound.

The stockade has evolved into a crushed, dense work which will be an interruption between the arches and the balcony at floor level but which will have a height of about 150 centimetres (fig. 108). My intention is to create a narrative within the cramped space of the fourth floor, forcing the works to take advantage of the height and to explore the remaining terrain at floor level with unpredictable obstacles and spillages – exploiting both formal and anti-formal qualities.

GC-M: I'm interested in this notion of treating the gallery as a kind of stage and the performative roles that both the objects and the viewers play. Clearly, the terms and the debates around the theatricality of sculpture have changed since you started making work, so I'm wondering if you feel that the audience experiences your work or interacts with it in a different way today as opposed to in the 1970s? And, if so, has this affected the way you think about or approach your work?

PB: For me, the 1970s were a time of fracture both in art and in society through the grim political and economic circumstances. I am certain that the latter had a crucial impact on the former, not only in the inception of so-called Conceptual Art but in the way artists operated beyond institutional frameworks – seeking out alternative and different ways to make work and to release it from its site of production, or, more importantly for me, to incorporate its methods of production into its final incarnation, location, and destination.

There were several exhibitions which were important in 'breaking' sculpture – its formal qualities were, literally, dispersed throughout the space. One exhibition, titled *Art Spectrum*, in 1971, was held in the large hall of Alexandra Palace – a Victorian exhibition centre. The space was vast – high as well as wide and long. There were performances as well as installations, except I don't remember them being referred to as 'installations' – they were just what they were and usually referred to as 'sculpture'. The work I exhibited was *Sofa, floor & drawings* (fig. 109). It was reassuring to be in an exhibition where this work's theatricality and disparate assemblage of conflicting media were acceptable.

Marc Camille Chaimowicz, Martin Naylor, piles of shoes, a stretched-latex screen, Barry Flanagan giving every artist fifty pence, someone pouring cement from the top of a tree, another destroying their work in situ: it was a chance to displace sculpture from its history. In particular, its British history – a lot of the work demonstrated how artists, including myself, were looking for a release. Arte Povera, in particular, and artists from the US, such as

Robert Smithson, Robert Morris, Eva Hesse, as well as the Judson Dance Theater events and the Claes Oldenburg happenings, were providing the impetus to break away from the formalism inherited through Henry Moore/Barbara Hepworth, and even the New Generation British sculptors of the mid-1960s, and the burgeoning impact of Anthony Caro, as well as other 'heavy metal' sculptors.

This 'breakage' – and the breakaway – within sculpture freed up the space of the event in terms of both the making and the location of the work. The studio, wherever or whatever that might be, became the vibrant repository of the work's unpredictable qualities, allowing there to be infinite beginnings, middles, and ends. Nothing was finite. Such potential for opening up what sculpture could be, where its fragmentation into many versions, including the uncertainty as to its finished state, made both the space of its production (not necessarily the studio) and its site of exhibition (not necessarily the gallery) entirely up to the artist.

I remember performances on the Tube which included readings, dance, and coloured rectangles being placed randomly throughout the length of the train, and drawings which used the length of the Tube and its duration of travel as the means to an end … now these things sound clichéd and overused, but then it was liberating.

Then there was the big Royal Academy sculpture exhibition in 1972, *British Sculptors '72*, with two, then high-profile, young British artists dominating that exhibition – Martin Naylor and Carl Plackman – who, individually, took over a gallery each and made works which involved and sabotaged the whole space. The audience/viewers were forced to step over, walk across, etc., the works. And the works themselves invited detailed scrutiny where magnifying glasses, trip wires, mirrors, and other obstacles that complicated the act of looking were imposed upon the space and the viewer.

In London, dance and live performance were beginning to merge. And there were many dance/movement performances which incorporated 'costume' as a performative intervention in its own right. Merce Cunningham's collaboration with Robert Rauschenberg and John Cage, which was staged in the West End, was thrilling and, for me, was the culmination of breaking sculpture away from its doggedly formalistic inheritance.

One issue that fascinates me is the concern for the 'audience'. This seems to have become imploded into the notion of 'attracting' an audience – something I find repellent. And something I do not remember as being any concern during the 1960s and 1970s. In fact, the more a viewer/audience could be antagonised the better, and the more remote the work could be the better ('remote' both physically and geographically, as well as in separating itself from a known audience, or, conversely, imposing itself

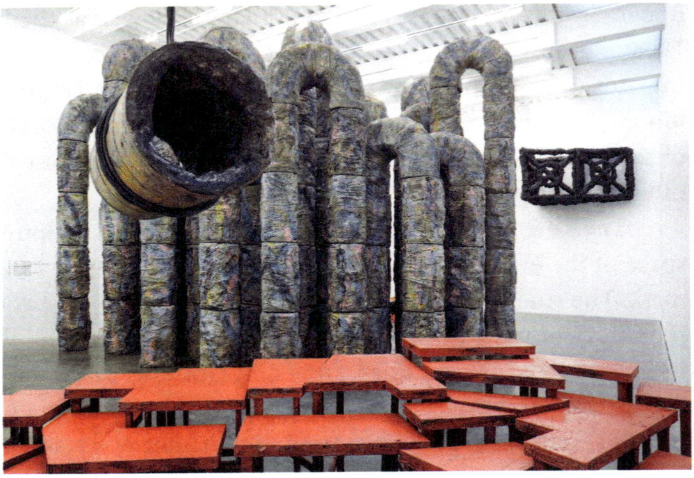

RIGHT AND BELOW:
figs. 107–8 Installation views, *Phyllida Barlow: siege*, New Museum, New York, 2012

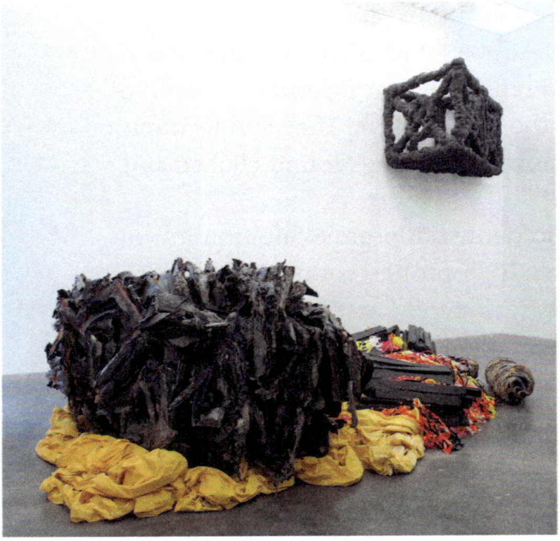

BELOW:
fig. 109 *Sofa, floor & drawings*, 1970–1

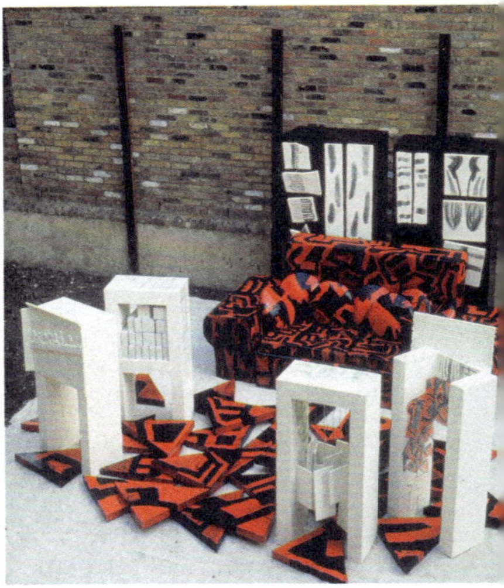

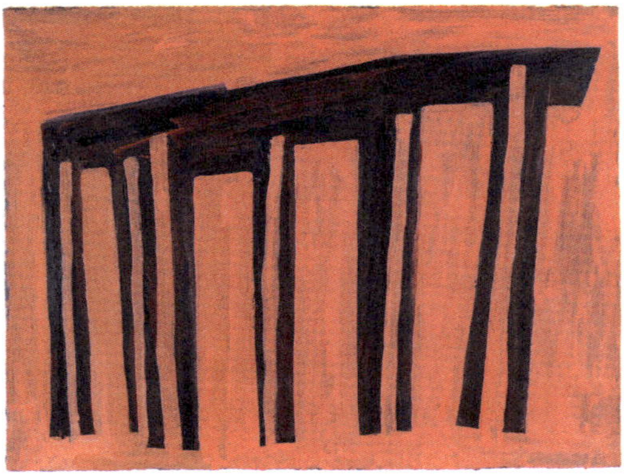

LEFT:
fig. 110 *untitled: arches*, 2012

on an uninitiated and unsuspecting audience). The experience was focused, for better or worse, on the artist and the work. The preferred audience was like-minded, fellow artists. Maybe I have romanticised this, but I do not remember the concern, which has centred on 'who is it for?' and has dominated so much public art, gallery art, and art production for so long (since the late 1980s/early 1990s), as having any relevance in the 1970s.

Therefore, my relationship with a potential audience/viewer is generated from myself as the primary viewer: What is my relationship to what I am doing? Is it awkward, difficult, enjoyable, laborious, boring, too complicated, quick, simple … ? How does this relationship affect what I want to do? How can I reach up there? How can I be surprised? What would happen if I crammed that corner, spilt this stuff, placed that very high up, balanced this on that? Undoubtedly, it's a selfish approach but it is about a relationship that's generated through the process of making and the desire to turn the eventual site for the work into something more than just an act of presentation.

Sculpture as theatre (rather than as theatrical) is a resource which transforms me from passive to active participant, from the process of production through to the highly performative act of installing the work – and it is during the work's installation that I not only experience it in its entirety for the first time but also become fully aware of its potential to have a relationship beyond myself. Once the work is installed, I seem to lose interest. Perhaps this is the moment when the work is handed over and it is no longer mine.

Of course, it is all very different with smaller works. These are, in many ways, more conventional. And I am looking a lot at those discredited sculptors of the 1940s and 1950s – particularly Europeans – because they now seem more radical than anyone else. Making smaller works and drawing is private and intimate. But the act of *doing* is similar to the larger works. However, a result happens within minutes – the work emerges quickly; changes can be executed immediately. Thinking and doing become synchronised. Time becomes a material. Speed becomes sensual and exhilarating, and essential. It is a different kind of theatricality.

GC-M: There are many younger sculptors who attempt to work between performance and sculpture or to create work where the performing body is somehow inscribed in the work, which obviously isn't a new interest. As someone who has worked closely with young artists over the years, has it been surprising to see an interest in it return or has your opinion or understanding of it changed?

PB: Working with young artists is salutary. The histories from the 1960s and 1970s seem less than useless for them. Their bravado and clarity are astonishing and admirable. But the climate in which they are forced to operate is harsh. The exhibition seems to be the event which determines their motivation: 'exhibition = alive; no exhibition = dead'. The performative as an integral part of the work's presentation and its status as an object seem very different now to then. Now it does seem to be very categorical; there is a critical necessity for an artwork to have an audience, as if they are bound together at source: art and audience; audience and art. This is very different to how my relationship with the performative roles of object and viewer has evolved.

How can young artists contend with this orthodoxy of prioritising the audience without shooting themselves in the foot (or the audience for that matter) – the worst-case scenario being that there is absolutely no interest in their work, and no destination for their work? I am sure that the necessity to arouse interest from an audience during the 1960s and 1970s was not a consideration for myself and other artists. Maybe, again, I am being arrogant, over-romantic, etc., but there was a different urgency – and, for me, it was a raw enthusiasm that struggled to attach itself to any particular notion of destination or result. It was a time of asking 'what if … ?' and 'not knowing' was more enriching than conviction. However, eventually 'not knowing' became just as much a conviction and just as problematic as 'knowing' … nothing stands still.

A question I ask myself is whether art's relationship with institutions has increased and become more delineated. Has art become more institutionalised with the knock-on effect of psychologically making artists more needy, more aware of seeking approval? But this is countered by the clarity of intention and sharp focus, and knowledge that young artists have, and which makes them canny, highly competitive, and ambitious.

An interest in what and who artists are, and what they do and how they do it, beyond, before, and without the exhibition seems to carry no authority. But for me it is fundamental. It is my focus and my interest. The young artists I have worked with in the past and work with now find this old-fashioned … and they are right, it is!

GC-M: I want to follow up about the context of your work in the 1970s and how you translate certain influences or energies into your work now. It was interesting to hear that Judson and Oldenburg affected you at the time – there is an exhibition up in New York right now about the New York happenings, and one of the things that comes across is the way in which the textures of those environments were such an extension of the particular landscape of New York City in the 1960s and how difficult that texture is to translate into a contemporary exhibition. In terms of your own practice, how important is London to your work?

PB: Your reference to the texture of a city is a wonderfully cunning way of creating a different interpretation of the urban environment. It cleverly avoids the pitfalls that images of the 1960s/1970s usually trigger: nostalgia and a longing to turn back the clock, etc. The grime and grit, which are inherent qualities of the images and documentation from those times, do have a particular atmosphere. I am looking at a catalogue from 1969 – *The Art of the Real: An Aspect of American Painting and Sculpture, 1948–1968*. It accompanied the exhibition of the same title which came from MoMA, New York, to the Tate Gallery, London, in 1969. I remember thoroughly enjoying the exhibition. However, it was when I looked at the catalogue later, in the 1990s, that I fully registered the impact of how art represents itself through its photographic catalogue image. In particular, the image of *Die* (1962) by Tony Smith made me laugh out loud. It was the joy of looking at an image without the self-conscious style of the contemporary catalogue orthodoxy that was so appealing.

Of course, I had not noticed the aberration of presenting the iconic Minimalist sculpture (of 'too small to be a monument, too big to be an object' fame) when I acquired the catalogue in 1969. Grimy black-and-white photographs were the norm and presenting an image of a work against a backdrop of urban, domestic, or studio clutter was also a norm for catalogues and any other kinds of publicity. Smith's *Die* is photographed in what seems to be a back garden; the sculpture itself has a stain around its lower surface; it is squashed into the frame with an excess of space above and below the object filled by a gravel terrain and an array of overhanging and out-of-focus foliage from the surrounding trees. Such an image would not pass for catalogue presentation today. I am sure that it would be deemed essential that this iconic sculpture would be best served placed in an environment cleansed of all interference from everyday life and preferably framed by a sterile white border which could mimic the cleansed space of the white-cube gallery.

Without doubt, the professionalism and technical achievements of today's catalogues distinguish themselves as serving the art within them in vivid and utterly appropriate ways. But are they too democratic? The HD/digital images give an overbearing equality to everything, which is beguiling but distancing and timeless. However, my comments are not intended to be judgemental or moral, and certainly not nostalgic for a return to the black-and-white images of yesteryear!

The griminess and the darkness inherent to black-and-white photography does evoke a different age with very different expectations for how and what constituted an exhibition. I like the confused, crowded, and cluttered use of the gallery spaces that I not only remember but which the images within exhibition catalogues reveal from that time. Maybe the lack of style evidenced the necessity for survivalism: the work should be robust enough to exist in its own right and not because of its style of presentation … somehow that lack of presentation skill is like the city: things are just there. I am interested in 'waking up' the things that are just there, giving different status to the behaviour of objects which are both familiar but strangely invisible within the cluttered, crowded visual noise of urban/London life. It is not just a process of culling images from the urban environment; more importantly for me, it is the behaviour of things which I want to emulate. My intention is to quell the image, obliterate it, and to make it of secondary importance to how the object that contains the image functions in relationship to the space, to other objects, myself initially, and finally others who might encounter it.

Returning to your expression of the 'textures' of the environments represented by images from the 1960s and 1970s, there is also a kind of 'truth to materials' which resonates from those images. For me, these images provide the clues to the palimpsest of surfaces that constitute everyday life. These surfaces are the decorative adornments to shapes and forms, and I want this layering of surfaces, and the accompanying textures, to be a part of my work, and how it is made. I want the two – surface and the shape/form beneath – to be both attached and separated within a single object. For example, the arches are built in a simple, expedient way with the minimum of technicalities. The surfaces which clad these simple forms do not add anything more formally to the original shapes. The scrim and cement cladding, which is then painted with daubs of colour, is more decorative and in excess of requirement than enhancing the original forms. In fact, the daubs of colour are a distraction to the arch structure. The surfaces I adopt for the works are essentially decoration. But it is decoration which is dependent on, and in conflict with, both the structure of the object which lies beneath and the process of how the surface is accumulated: the palimpsest of scrim, cement, paint, varnish …

The urban environment provides me with a versatile resource to observe how objects, including the human object, arrange themselves, both knowingly and unknowingly. It is the collision between the 'things' – urban things – which provoke hierarchies and the way we want to disobey these hierarchies, or conform to them, which brings these usually passive-aggressive things into our consciousness. Perhaps when street demonstrations erupt, then the dormant behaviour of what constitutes our urban environment wakes up and reveals itself in its most extreme form – the hierarchy of familiar things is used to further the cause of the demonstrators, and not left to be the passive controllers, as is their usual role – things are torn up and thrown, burnt, crashed, crushed.

Barriers, barricades, street furniture, curbs, pavements, security cameras, street lighting, roadworks, building works, traffic … all of these and much more provide the controls for how the urban environment functions and how an all-embracing authority asserts itself. These human-made physical interventions proclaim how our behaviour is guided and led in order to use the urban space efficiently. But such interventions are also highly political: 'things' are prioritised apparently with no consensus; public spaces become privatised; how we move around becomes increasingly but subtly controlled; this is the paranoia of the city … the watched and the watching and the watcher …

This emotive interpretation of how the city behaves evidences its layers and surfaces in another way other than visual. I'm interested in the subjective interpretations of how a city behaves, its psychological and political impact which its behaviour has on all things that inhabit the city – human or otherwise – and for me the city in question is London.

I have always lived and worked in London. It is an impossible place where nothing works but everything works; where it sprawls but is dense; where it can gleam but is dark; where there is newness but it is also decaying …

I have a memory which identifies something of this reference you make to the textures of the city. In the early 1950s, my father decided to take myself and my older sister and brother on a tour of the East End of London. He had done his medical training in the East End before the war and wanted to show us what had happened to this part of London since his training. We drove down to the docks and along Mile End Road and Whitechapel Road and into the surrounding localities … he showed us the bombed-out areas which he had known well. The devastation was ubiquitous apart from the evidence of the slow reconstruction which was taking place. I don't know what kind of impact this strange tour has had but it is fixed in my mind. I do know that the constant changes inscribed within the urban environment form a particular archaeology which absorbs present, past, and future: damage, reparation, renewal, reconstruction – these are in an ever-evolving life cycle which mirrors the decay and renewal of the natural environment. The urban and the natural reflect and reciprocate each other, where there is no perfect moment. My relationship with the processes of making somehow reflects this restlessness where I am never sure when enough is enough – there is always this craving to add another layer, or to break something down again – to destroy, repair, and rebuild. It is to affirm and authenticate the conflict between the shape and its structure in relationship to its surface and therefore its texture.

GC-M: Is the translation or transformation that happens in your work – between images, objects, or materials from the world outside of the studio and your finished sculptures – purely intuitive at this point?

PB: I am usually in a conflicted position of having to deploy practicalities and expedience, which are then combined with the irrationality of guesswork to advance the transformation and translation processes. The 'original' thing that initiated the chain reaction disappears in the face of the raw confrontation of how to make it – how to build it, with what, what size, what weight, what posture, where? – and as such the so-called 'original' is consumed.

The catalyst for the work is through guesswork rather than intuition. Guesswork is a remarkable and hugely underrated process: it seems to rely on previous experience and knowledge but is also only too eager to challenge these and test them out with the conclusion always under threat. It promotes risk and a refusal to explain and justify, and a respect for a lack of logic.

GC-M: Your description of the deceptiveness of photography as well as your emphasis on the role of guesswork point to the challenges of picturing the installation you're going to make in the museum space. So much of the experience of the sculptures is yet to be realised, but one thing we do have are some of the drawings you've done for the sculptures. Although they are schematic diagrams, they have an amazingly identical weight and presence. I've been thinking of them as kind of dreams or premonitions of the actual sculptures, but I'm interested in how they function for you during the sculptural process and what they are able or unable to convey about the sculptures once they are made and installed?

PB: It must be nerve-racking for curators trying to project proposals of work into the space. For the artist, it is an exploration – artist as explorer. The drawings are instructions. They provide information about materials, methods of making, and dimensions. Although they may not appear like this.

For some of the preparatory drawings there are connections to previous works. With these, I may have an idea as to how the work could look in its final incarnation. For new works with no back history, the drawings are speculative.

However, nothing prepares me for the confrontation of the space with the work. And it is in that order because in the initial meeting of the two, the space is dominant. I think my rather crude, simple drawing style, which I use for the preparatory drawings, emboldens the potential works as they appear on paper, giving them maximum strength as images, in preparation for this meeting between the space and the work.

The drawings for the New Museum are intended to be as clear as possible about what is to be made. But they are premonitions. I had not thought of this word before. It is very pertinent and an exciting way of thinking about the drawings.

For me, a premonition has a psychic association. It's visionary, with a heightened awareness of something which is about to happen. There is even a sense of foreboding. Certainly, at the stage when the drawings are executed, there is no actual, physical work – it still has to happen, and the more ambitious the work is, the greater the sense of foreboding. The drawings seem threatening, demanding that they be fulfilled. In many ways the drawings are misleading. For example, the drawing of the arches cannot demonstrate the height of them (fig. 110). Instead, they remain cartoon versions of what I hope will actually emerge in the gallery space.

Perhaps, in an everyday sense, not many premonitions get fulfilled. But the expectancy and the strong sense of the impending event, and something which is 'about to be', is dramatic. The drawings are produced with an intent that is full of hope. The production process does erode that positivity to some extent. The reality of translating the drawings into actual, physical objects demands reality checks, which can be at odds with what is on paper. I do encourage this process, where the original – the drawing and the premonition – have to meet the reality of the materiality of the production process and the resulting practicalities of weight, gravity, stability, structure, breakage, surface. And although that original flare of hope gets displaced, it becomes translated into the reality of the work itself.

I have always wanted to counteract the pragmatic activity and demands of making sculpture with the recognition of what goes on in my head – the absurd and unrealistic ambitions for the work, the juxtapositions of size, placing, and relationships between things – which, for me, often has filmic and Surrealist references (Andrei Tarkovsky, Robert Bresson, Alain Resnais, Michelangelo Antonioni, Luis Buñuel, Miklós Jancsó, Max Ernst, Giorgio de Chirico, Francis Picabia).

My drawings often originate from half-remembered things. I want to use the process of faulty memory as a way to allow these things to forget their origins and become something new. It is liberating to identify the preliminary processes of producing the work as a state of premonition. Importantly, and maybe this is a difference between a dreamlike state and a premonition, the latter has a sense of fleeting and ephemeral temporality. It is quick. Whereas a dreamlike state is slower and more enduring.

The drawn thing, whatever it might be, begins to play a part where its behavioural qualities offer a potential for enactment, playing a role, which is all in the future. As such, they cannot be anything more than an approximation of what might actually get made. Finally, when the work is actually being installed, what is there in the space – the works that make the exhibition – are approximations of a now remote 'original'.

I understand approximation as a creative act. It is an escape from truth, and permits lying and fibbing as a forceful resource. The objects, which eventually make it, are stand-ins, substitutes, and understudies for something barely remembered and usually forgotten. The final realisation of the work is a premonition fulfilled, but surprisingly and unpredictably. There can be no relationship to the original thought, idea, or even the drawings. The premonition and the final event have a relationship but not a predestined one, and I welcome this schism between the initiation of the work and its final realisation.

First published in Gary Carrion-Murayari, ed., *Phyllida Barlow: Siege*, (New York: New Museum, 2012), 10–37.

This edited interview with journalist Lutz Bernhardt was conducted in person in 2012 for Barlow's exhibition *BRINK* at the Ludwig Forum für Internationale Kunst in Aachen, Germany, and included in the eponymous publication. Barlow was the winner of the Kunstpreis Aachen that year. Beginning with her choice of title, Barlow discusses the exhibition in Aachen and her interest in demonstrations, fanaticism and dogmas, and time. They talk about capitalism and the art market, overlooked artists, and the aging of artworks.

Interview with Lutz Bernhardt

2012

[...]

Lutz Bernhardt: What does the exhibition title *BRINK* refer to?

Phyllida Barlow: 'Brink' means something on the edge. Something which is precarious – and it is either about to happen as an event, or it just stays in a state of tension. But these aren't necessarily bad things and they're not necessarily good things, it's just a very particular place and a very particular moment.

LB: At first I thought more of an abyss, connecting it to disaster. People are confronted by trials, like cancer or war ...

PB: I think the issue of war and disaster and the whole evidence of war and disaster, the damage and the collapse of an environment, whether it's a natural disaster or human disaster ... I have a morbid fascination for that, yes. But I think there is always the aftermath; there is always a process beyond an event, which is where something will begin to change, for better or worse. So although the title *BRINK* is about an edge, the border zone, it's not necessarily seen as a final event. It's more a proposition of time and place, of maybe where we are as human beings now, but which will inevitably change. Which is a very big statement to make. And I don't think this exhibition necessarily sums all that up. [...] But it's about something that maybe is on all our minds at any one time. About where the world is going and where we are going, how we, and our influences, are evolving. And I think also in a more practical way this space here in the Ludwig Forum is very extreme with great diversity. It's a very interesting space because there is an enormous amount of light coming in. Then there is this deep space in the middle. And then this platform around this sunken space, it has a sense of the brink about it. It has a sense of edge. And all these different spatial attributes, as well as the light, were inspirations for the work.

LB: How exactly has the architecture of the Ludwig Forum influenced your work?

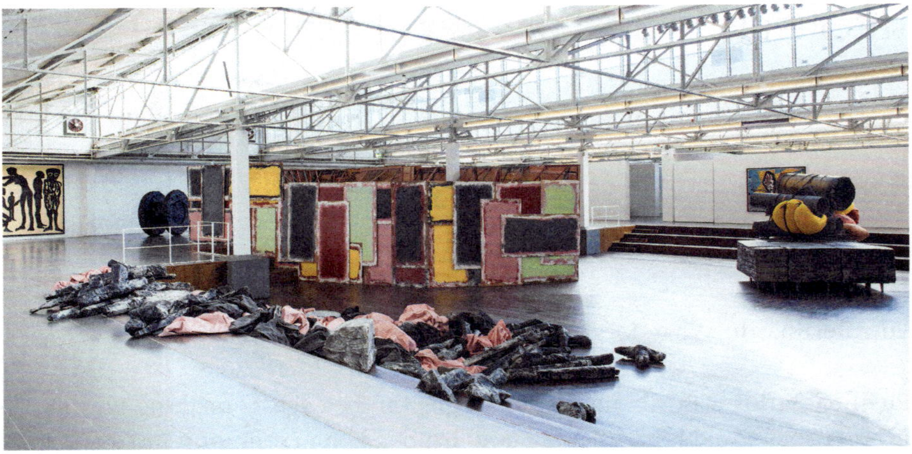

fig. 111 Installation view, *Phyllida Barlow: BRINK*, Ludwig Forum für Internationale Kunst, Aachen, Germany, 2012

PB: The main influence was the actual physical arrangement of the space, the articulated roof, and the steps going down to this lower space. These were very important physical aspects of how the work could be looked at and how it could engage with and interrupt these qualities (figs. 58, 111, 124).

LB: In your works you explore everyday phenomena you observe on the street: construction sites, traffic flows, but also other movements in public space like protests. What is it about them that attracts you? Is it the communication, the information flow?

PB: The issue of the street, although it's important, is only an example of where there is information and resources for the way we have relationships to objects that are already in the world. Whether there are moving objects like traffic or still objects like barriers and pavements and signs. It's the way that we behave in relationship to these objects and the way in which these objects behave in relationship to us. And maybe it's that behaviour that I find sculptural. But I think these things also occur in the natural environment. So it's trying to take these obstacles, these things that we take for granted in our daily lives, but which are very physical, and controlling, as a resource for the way I would like to relate to sculpture, and how sculpture can behave in a space.

LB: How does that fit into the art context, specifically here in the exhibition?

PB: Because I'm playing with several things. One is the placard which is about information – about telling something very powerful (fig. 57). Or it could be telling something that's quite ordinary. So it plays many different roles, it acts in many different ways. And then making them behave like paintings, they become ambivalent as to what they are. And it's interesting that they are always identified as placards. There isn't really anything there that suggests they are placards, other than the shape. So it's more how a shape conveys such strong information even though there is nothing on the shape that tells you it is a placard. And I suppose again I like that slippage of objects, where they slip from something clear … they slip from a very clear identity to something that maybe isn't that clear.

LB: You arrange these placards like the aftermath scene to a demonstration, a demonstration that is broken up, perhaps has been ended violently …

PB: Yes. It's the time when they no longer have that use, but have the evidence of a use. And I think that's the part of the cycle of destruction and then something beginning again – the cycles of destruction and regeneration. Or the aftermath of an event. And we are left wondering what the next thing is, what the next event is.

LB: You reuse parts of your works. You recycle the material. Is this part of art or a practical aspect?

PB: Some of these materials might come back to the studio and I will use them again for other works, yes. I think maybe the stockade (fig. 111) …

LB: What made it so important?

PB: Oh … it's not that it's more important. It's just … it's been problematic, technically, building this work. And I will maybe think again about how to do it. So it could be too difficult to make it again with these painted boards, which have become incredibly fragile and unstable. It would have to be remade in some other way. This is a work that I've made three times before in different forms, but for some reason this time it's been very difficult getting it to behave correctly.

LB: Your recycling is not a political statement …

PB: The politics of the work have much more to do with questions of why make sculpture at all, why bring into the world, a world already full of things, yet more things. To me sculpture's relationship with obstruction and also occupying the space that we could occupy, is where I think there is a political issue for me. Yes, the sculptural object's occupation of space – which space, what, where, and how – is political.

LB: For example, to come back to it, the demonstration.

PB: Yes, if you take a demonstration it intervenes in a dramatic way. The demonstration takes over familiar public spaces and uses them in an unfamiliar way – the crowd of people walking through the streets and the organisation of it. It has a language of its own, it's a very particular language that the demonstration has, and when it starts to break down into riots and chaos, it becomes a collapse as well as a development of that language. I'm interested in how, for me, it's something about sculpture that parallels this. It's a very romantic view, I know. But I think sculpture is quite outrageous in its use of space; and then how it is removed or it breaks down or it becomes something else – this changing identity of sculpture depending on its context or its ephemerality, is theatrical in a reciprocal way to the demonstration – the street demonstration. It is a parallel experience – again it's about the behaviour. It's generic. It's a generic idea that the remains of human activity all contain different kinds of messages. And become different kinds of awful, or awesome, or mundane physical evidence.

LB: The same applies to those staged mass gatherings designed to support authoritarian rulers or mega events in sport.

PB: Yes … which comes with its own political baggage as well. If you think of the Olympics and then what happens to the Olympic sites, the buildings … I saw a fascinating program on the swimming pools from past Olympic Games, and they were all unused, or a lot of them had been changed and now had different uses. They were very abject places, having been places of celebration. They'd become places of memories. These wonderful swimming pools with high diving boards … but they were not used because they were too expensive to maintain. So it's like the glory of these things collapsing into something else. It's about this constant cycle of change that I think has fascinated me. And wanting sculpture to have that possibility.

LB: Is the finished sculpture a snapshot of the whole process?

PB: Yes – I want the process of making sculpture and its final identity to always be very open. The process is so open. There's a freedom of making, however repetitive, and hard work it is. There is a freedom of how it might be, how it could be, all these possibilities … And then it comes to the exhibition space, and decisions get made. But then it's still being able to think about the life beyond that work that excites me as well. So it's an ongoing process. But the final decisions which become the exhibition are a false conclusion. I wouldn't say it's a kind of death. But it might seem as if there was only ever one point in the possibilities for these things. I enjoy that moment, that final decision of where things get positioned, located, and arranged, but I also begin to think what the next moment is. Maybe this is some kind of influence from film.

LB: Works of art do not need to physically last for eternity. But what does that mean for thinking about values, attitudes, and currents in art?

PB: Values, all values – sociological, economic, artistic, cultural – are changing enormously at the moment. There is conventionality and orthodoxy in art. And what is sought to be permanent, maybe it's fantastic. It's wonderful to be able to look at things that have a certain length of time behind them, four, five centuries, and they are still there. But I think we live in very different volatile times where information globally is taken in within five seconds. It's difficult to hold on to that sense of time as always being a long time. There are many different times, quick times, long times … and many expressions revolving around time – 'a waste of time' or 'time passing quickly' or 'making time', or 'taking time', or 'a stitch in time saves nine' (an English proverb) … or time is going to pass very slowly. We talk about time in many different ways; and I think this is a very important thing for me in terms of making. Making things quickly or being very slow and laborious produce different results.

LB: Is there a stronger compulsion today in art to conform to fashions or even dogmas which it is better not to question?

PB: We see that a lot, we see extremes of that, like in religion, fanatical religions, you know, I mean all religions, not just the ones that get a reputation like Islam. But all religions have their fanatical side. And it's just the same with politics unfortunately. These dogmas terrify me, and I think dogmas have also emerged in the visual arts. I think there has been a very big drive for things to be solved commercially in the visual arts. And not solved experimentally or through the ambition for the work. Instead there has been the cult of the individual overriding the significance of the work, if you know what I mean.

LB: What's your relationship to the art market?

PB: I'm very grateful for having sold work, and I am actually selling work for the first time in my life in the last two years. And my life as an artist has changed a lot for me without doubt. And you could say: why can't artists have a reasonable income or a decent way of living? Why should they be expected to be starving in a garret and not have the benefit from the income of selling their work? And putting it to a very positive use. It doesn't have to be something that controls the work. It could be something that actually enables the work to develop. And I think that's what it's been for me. It's been a huge means for developing all aspects of the work. Not just the big works but the small works and the drawings. I have just much more time to do this, which has been incredible. But I think the art market can get a bad reputation of being something that is very controlling of how artists relate to their work. But I don't think this is always the case …

LB: Because in the end it's about making money.

PB: Yes, it's a capitalist-driven activity. I think it's always been there in art. It comes in many disguised forms, whether it's a magnificent fresco in a church in the fifteenth century. But it is still in a way driven by a form of capitalism. And it's quite difficult to detach art from it. There are many ways of disguising it. But it can also be a means for enabling a kind of political disturbance as well. It's a strangely all-embracing form of capitalism when it comes to the art market. That it could be supporting dissident artists, it could be supporting artists who have remained in really appalling political situations, and it could be extremely degenerating, corrupt. It goes across the whole spectrum …

LB: The art market functions like the investment business. The price rises when demand goes up. Doesn't it make you angry that speculators determine what constitutes quality?

PB: I think there is that, but there are the museums, there are other more – if you like – more generous aspects of the art market that are involved as well. Yes, there are these individuals. But they are very particular, they have their time. Then I think their time goes and other individuals move in … But then you look around this museum and you look at these incredible works. And that's all driven by the art market. My biggest criticism is about all the artists who aren't known. Who are they? Where are they? Why are they unknown? That's a huge question for me. Maybe because I've spent a lot of my time as an artist being relatively unknown. I know what it's like. It's intriguing that so much about becoming known as an artist is based on luck. And there are a lot of amazing artists who will not get exhibitions, they won't be heard of, they won't win prizes, you know. The small group of artists who are seen is very different from the enormous group of artists who aren't seen. Most artists' work is not seen and that is a very harsh fact.

LB: But who is responsible for this?

PB: In the end, artists are responsible for getting their work seen. And it depends on how you define how a work is seen, by whom, where, when – it doesn't have to be in a gallery or in an exhibition. So it is the artist's responsibility to initiate how to get their work seen, however tough that might be, and however hopeless. And they are doing it! They try to get shows, they try to do this, and they are rejected. So there is something going on that is very tight, about how artists get a foot in the door and get their work seen. I do think there can be too much dependency on artists who already have reputations and not enough research given to discovering artists without much of an exhibition record but who have kept working. I know not all artists can be shown, but it sometimes seems to me that the powers that be find it difficult to break new ground, to get behind the scenes and see artists who are maybe like me [...] in their sixties who should be seen. They've been doing it all their life. It's complicated ... But it's an issue that fascinates me ...

LB: Last year you were admitted to the Royal Academy, an institution that is cause for controversy amongst artists. Did you hesitate?

PB: I think it's been incredible to have that support, which I didn't know I was getting. So to have refused it – which a lot of artists do, they refused to have this – seemed to me contrary, it seemed as though I was rejecting people who actually stood up and said, 'we want her.' That seemed to me ungenerous. But I think it's complicated to be a member of this institution because of this idea of the royal issue.

LB: What does the Aachen Art Prize mean to you?

PB: It means recognition beyond the United Kingdom. It means some recognition in Germany, which is fantastic. I think I have always thought that German culture is the most expansive and the most diverse out of the European countries. It seems there is such a huge range of culture involved in Germany. And such a depth – it's music, it's writing, it's film, it's poetry, it's visual arts, and a huge range of experimentation has always come out of Germany during my lifetime. Huge political changes as well, obviously, during the 1960s and 1970s, quite dangerous political situations with Baader-Meinhof and other very active groups of people. That, I think, was also very much related to making art. And how art might be shown, might not be shown, did art always need a building or could it be liberated from a place? These questions were big questions that came out of Germany.

When all is said and done, the things that remain are the evidence of what people have done. What they have achieved. Whether it's just a pair of shoes lying in the streets, or a delicate fresco. Somebody made those somewhere … Or whether it's a placard … In the same way as archaeological remains do, they present these enormous questions about the times in which people lived, and the persistent drive to create.

I think if you go around the Ludwig Forum in Aachen, and you go into the room where the 1960s work is, it is extraordinary, because it's aged in a particular way: what was then new technology and experimentation has become nostalgic and distant, like relics. Everything has become distressed, worn out … it has a different quality to when it was made – in its time, and now it is out of its time, but still so resonant and relevant. There are these old processes, for example the 35mm camera techniques, which are now half-remembered, and even forgotten. These works are still telling us about those times, vividly, loudly, and importantly but they have become documents … they have become historical.

Therefore art has an extraordinary sense of time embedded within it. And however much it is seen as a luxury, which it isn't, it is a necessity. It is the uncontrollable urge human beings have to take action, to do things that aren't necessarily about something having a use. It's a compulsion. And it is evidence of a particular time by a particular individual. I feel very strongly about that.

First published in *Phyllida Barlow: Brink* (Aachen: Ludwig Forum für Internationale Kunst; London: König Books, 2013), 89–96.

This Modern Art Notes Podcast interview with Tyler Green took place by telephone in 2013 at the time of the Carnegie International. In this edited version Barlow and Green discuss the origins of the work *untitled: upturnedhouse* (2012), which is held in the Carnegie's collection, and its pairing with a painting by Willem de Kooning. Barlow discusses the artist influences from early in her career including Eva Hesse, Robert Morris, and Louise Nevelson, and she talks about masculine and feminine ways of working, her use of paint, and the importance of speed. They discuss the *Objects for …* series, her affinity with Franz West, the appeal of different shapes, and the fact that most of her sculptures no longer exist.

Interview with Tyler Green

2013

Tyler Green: Phyllida Barlow, welcome to the Modern Art Notes Podcast.

Phyllida Barlow: Thank you.

TG: You have several significant pieces in the Carnegie International, and along with an exhibition this past summer at the Des Moines Art Center, they serve almost as an introduction of your work to American audiences. Let's start at the Carnegie: *upturnedhouse*, the sculpture up on the second floor of the museum, is one of the most awesome things I've seen in a long time (fig. 112). It addresses about twenty things at once: painting, sculpture, natural disaster, the metaphor of a world turned upside down, all kinds of things. I'd like to ask you about it by posing to you a question that I understand you pose to your students or posed to your students when you were a teacher. And that is, what kind of experiment is *upturnedhouse*, and does it have a conclusion?

PB: That's a great question. I'll begin at the end. The conclusion, in a way, emerged. The problem I have with making sculpture is that I don't necessarily have a conclusion in mind. Therefore, endings, finishings, conclusions tend to creep up on the work rather than on me. It is very much a relationship, making a piece of work, that begins recently with as little knowledge as possible. That seems to be my preferred position to take, so that I'm not working closely with an image, but more with a collection of maybe quite disparate components. There is then the task of trying to make these components come together. Maybe that's what the experiment is in the first place.

I have told this anecdote about these three upturned houses I've made: one that was shown in London, the second that was shown at Hauser & Wirth in New York this time last year, that has now found a home in the Carnegie Museum, and the third upturned house, which is *brokenupturnedhouse*, which will be shown at the Norton Museum in a few weeks' time (fig. 68). But the whole process of beginning these upturned houses came from a description I heard on British radio, which was a reporter, a journalist, going back to New Orleans about four weeks after Katrina had struck and interviewing a man who went to find his house. And he hadn't been able to get out to the place where he knew his house was, obviously, because it was under

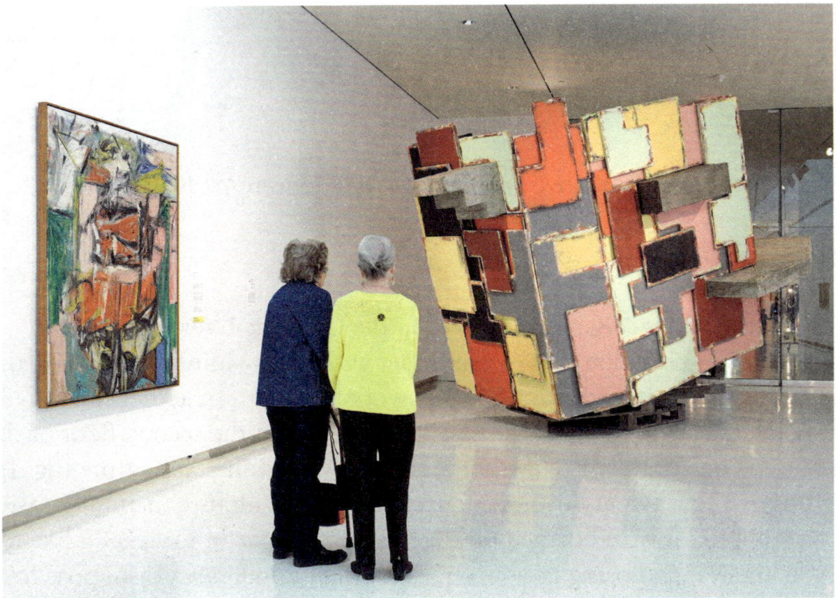

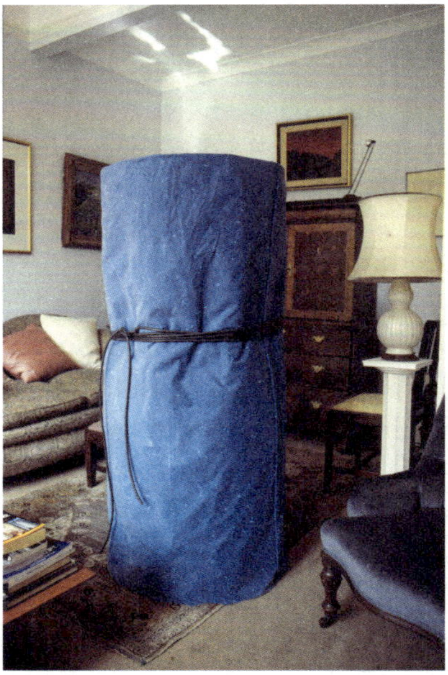

ABOVE:
fig. 112 **Phyllida Barlow**
untitled: upturnedhouse, 2012, and
Willem de Kooning
Woman VI, 1953, installation view,
2013 Carnegie International,
Carnegie Museum of Art,
Pittsburgh, US, 2013–14

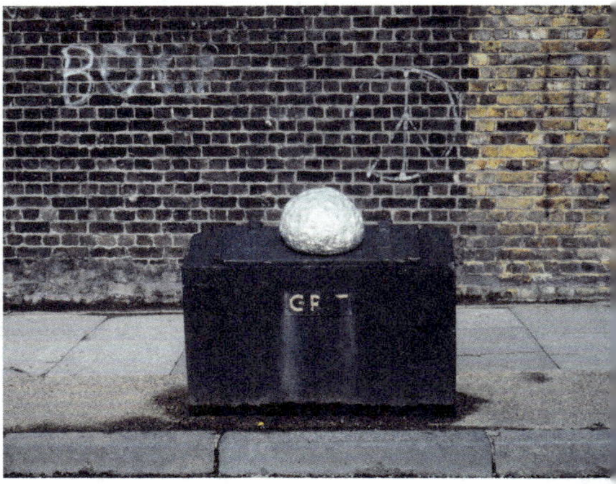

LEFT TO RIGHT:
fig. 113 *Object for the sitting room*, 1994
fig. 114 *Object for a street grit bin*, 1995

water and under this thick, black silt. And this man described, in quite extraordinary terms, how he waded down the road, which he knew was the road to the part of New Orleans where he lived. And he got deeper and deeper into this black silt, until he was quite bewildered about the location. But then he spotted this solitary tree, and he knew that tree, even though it was stripped of all its leaves, he knew it was the tree on the corner of the street where he lived, but there was nothing but ferocious, savage debris everywhere. But when he walked a bit further down the street, or, rather, waded down the street through this thick mud, he saw this house that was his house. Now, what was so extraordinary about his description was that he didn't actually mention, as far as I can remember, the word 'house'. Now that, to me, is a very sculptural experience, where you divest the object of its literal association. His description of walking round was what he called his 'home', or where he had lived. Of course, I can't remember it completely accurately, but I was completely beguiled by the fact that he was describing, in these extraordinary terms, this building that was now on its roof. It had been turned completely head over heels. And the way he described it was, to me, as though he was walking around a sculpture. Now, perhaps this is rather exploitative of me to take this man's genuine grief and horror at the force of what this Hurricane Katrina had done to his home. For me, to then take it and convert that beautiful description he gave of meeting up with his home after such devastation, for me to then take that and turn it into an artwork, I still feel very confused about how I have used devastation, both human-made devastation and naturally made devastation, as a resource for my work. But what was so utterly compelling about this man's description was that it so vividly gave me information for how I wanted to bring together a collection of components, and try and make this upturned structure in the way that he had described.

TG: *Upturnedhouse* includes a number of materials that you've been playing with for a while, things like plywood and what looks like shipping pallets, cement. So is the experiment taking that story and – to use a slightly hokey word – 'inspiration', and matching it to the materials that have interested you for a while?

PB: I think the experiment was to let go of the story, so there wasn't a literal description behind the work, but to more take the fragments of information that came out of the story, the boards, the corners of the house, its sense of balancing on its roof, the word 'balance', 'corners', 'broken'. I can't remember the literal list of words that he gave, but there was enough there to act as a trigger for me to say that whole idea with sculpture, that you can turn it around, you can rotate it, you can hang it or lie it down or stand it up.

You can do all these things with the objectness of sculpture and discover different ways of understanding the shape in front of you. It's incredibly basic, but that, I think, was the experiment. To bring these fragments of material information together and try to make something coherent, that had the qualities of being upturned.

TG: And I'm guessing that this piece is also related to a part of your installation BRINK at the Ludwig in Aachen a couple of years ago. Could you, I guess, quickly describe the relevant part of that installation and tell us how you made that idea malleable enough to become something else?

PB: The space in Aachen is actually quite extraordinary. It's these louvred windows, which are all glass lit. They're all glazed. It's an old umbrella factory, so it's all on one floor. But in the middle of this huge space, there is a drop down in the floor level, by about a metre, about over a yard deep. So there's a deep, sunken area of floor, and then a raised area all around it, so it's a dramatic space, in a way, that's all lit from above. I wanted to draw into this central space, almost as though it was a performative space, quite disparate objects that literally played off each other, however one interprets the word 'play'. Almost as though there was either a game or something theatrical going on. And one of the aspects of it was to actually enclose one section of the space around a column. So I used the idea of a boarded-up area, something that maybe, again, operated in a double way, very much as a collection of painted surfaces that would parody painting in some way, or, in a way, honour painting. And that they would take on a very formal architectural, slightly ad hoc quality. That space would then play off a very open fence structure that was on the opposite side of this sunken area. Then, various other components would be around or placed in relationship to those two main pieces (figs. 58, 111, 124).

TG: It looks, from the photographs of the installation in Aachen, that you can look over and into that middle area you're describing. At the Carnegie, if you're tall enough, you can kind of do that. I'm tall, so I kind of could. I wonder if that's part of the idea that translated or travelled between the two pieces.

PB: Yes, I think the idea of an interior space fascinates me. You can look into the interior space of *upturnedhouse* by, instead of reaching up and over into it, you look under it. And I always have this thing about sculpture that, we're trained to look at things at eye level. The most ways in which art is displayed in museums takes on a kind of eye-level format. But the thing about sculpture is that you can stalk it and prowl around it and peer into it and become very voyeuristic about how you investigate a sculptural form. This sounds very manipulative and very controlling, but I would love the audience to be choreographed into that role, where they peep into or bend down and look under, and their own relationship to the work becomes an integral part of what that work is. That it's not just the upright figure going around it, but maybe someone bending on one side and someone very upright on the other side. Or somebody having to slightly duck under the concrete block that sticks out from the *upturnedhouse*. And the same with the very big piece outside (fig. 67). The fact that it's almost like, in a way, a small coppice or wood might be, that you walk around it and you see through it at times. Those things about how the work collaborates with the viewer in making the audience have some kind of active role in the looking experience, rather than just a passive role. I would hope that somebody might just bend down and look under *upturnedhouse* and see that interior, the rather raw, quite brutal kind of interior to *upturnedhouse*.

TG: I jumped and looked over the top. The outdoor piece is titled *TIP*. At the Carnegie, *upturnedhouse* is installed right next to Willem de Kooning's great, great, great *Woman VI* painting. Did you have any input into where the painting went, or was that a happy thing to discover?

PB: That was a curatorial decision by Daniel Baumann, and of course, I was absolutely thrilled because there is this extraordinary synchronicity between de Kooning's skirt-shaped squares of red and green – I think they are – and then the panels on *upturnedhouse*, so to me, it's a wonderful reciprocity between the two works.

TG: There's a real conversation going on between the palette de Kooning uses and the palette for your sculpture.

PB: Yes, it's extraordinary. I've always absolutely loved de Kooning's work, but what I really love is being able to see one at a time, not a great number of them all at once. I think, for me, his real intensity happens when you get one on quite a lot of space, as there is in the case at the Carnegie. I saw his retrospective, huge retrospective, in New York, which was absolutely fantastic, but like a lot of retrospectives we have now going round the world, they are huge meals to digest. Just that wonderful intensity of a one-to-one experience with just a single painting by such a great artist is always, for me, extremely revealing and very special. Because you can focus, I can focus, I can concentrate, and I can give it time.

TG: For listeners who haven't been to the Carnegie yet, *upturnedhouse* is in a corner. The de Kooning is to the left of it. Really the only two things that you see or can see are those two works, so you have that experience with the two of them there together. It's an amazing install.

So I want to go back in time a little bit. In a recent monograph on your work titled *Objects for … and Other Things* that was published in the UK, the main essay of the book is by Mark Godfrey, and he places your 1975 sculpture *Shedmesh* (fig. 178) – I hope I'm saying that right – in the context of then concurrent American developments in sculpture, in the context of artists such as Richard Serra, with whom you engage at the Carnegie, Sol LeWitt, Tony Smith, and so on.

So I'm wondering how much back then you were aware of what was happening in America, and how much you consciously chose to engage with American sculptors rather than a very particular British tradition that was beginning to peter out about then.

PB: Yes. That's a very significant way of describing it. I think, for my generation, maybe the tremendous history of craft meeting the figure meeting landscape – as we know is so strong in Henry Moore's work – is inherent to a certain kind of Britishness. I think, for me, there was something about making that was not being satisfied by the moral legacy of those traditions. I'm much more tolerant of them now!

TG: Well, you didn't have to overthrow them in the same way you did at the beginning of a career, right? At the beginning of a career, artists have different –

PB: Yes, I rather sort of relish and love returning to the works, the European works of the 1940s and 1950s now. I see in its post-war monstrosity something very relevant and very powerful now. But at the time, it seemed to be dogged with the necessity to be very, very good at doing these, what are incredible sculptural processes, but sometimes, good in a craft-based way. And what I suppose I started to be hugely attracted to was, say, with Arte Povera coming out of Italy, was the idea of a material as a gestural, performative … Or the qualities of materials possessing gesture and performative qualities. But were things in themselves and were ends in themselves, like Robert Morris's felt works or Alan Saret's crushed mesh pieces, of course, the discovery of Eva Hesse, which came quite late. The first works I saw of her were the very brightly coloured works from the time she stayed in Germany. Then by about 1971, which was very near the time she had died, I began to see, only in photographic form, the full range of her very, very fragile and perfectly poised works with latex, muslin, and fibreglass and resin. And it was as though a whole world had opened up, that sense of incredible touch, but touch that holds such a brief moment of time in it.

Rather than the laborious state of touch that maybe late Henry Moores had, where you feel every inch is laboured over, there would be with a Hesse this sense of a moment caught in time, and there was the evidence of it in these hanging works or the fragile, tubular works, that something had only just come into existence. For me, it wasn't to do with ephemerality, it was actually the opposite; it was to do with giving incredible permanence to something that was utterly fleeting. And that seemed like Robert Morris's steam pieces, which have the same extraordinary qualities for me as well. Where something absolutely permanent and held in its own time is not won through extensive labour, which wears its labour very heavily, but almost as though you're witnessing something that is there forever, but you don't quite know where it's come from. I thought that was just extraordinary in so many American artists' work of that time.

TG: Of course, that was a time when American sculpture was overwhelmingly dominated by men. A couple of exceptions: Eva Hesse, who you mentioned, and Anne Truitt, who brought colour into a medium that had become colourless really at that point in American sculpture history –

PB: There was Eva Hesse, there was Lynda Benglis, there was Judy Pfaff, there was the wonderful Lee Bontecou. There was Louise Nevelson, Louise Bourgeois. I mean …

TG: Some of whom showed more in Europe than they did in the United States at that point.

PB: Yes. Louise Nevelson, I really loved her work very early on, and just this whole idea of objects that could be held in the hand, that you then made these quite enormous assemblages with. That was a tremendous experience for me as well, a learning experience that largeness could often be acquired through incredible intimacy with something that you could hold in your hand and then through an accumulative process, you get this other size emerging.

TG: Since the mid-1970s, a lot of the work you made then has been discussed by critics as being particularly gendered, as being a presentation of a particularly non-male point of view, and I wonder if that was something you consciously thought about or –

PB: No.

TG: Or not, no. Just no.

PB: I find it very interesting and very paradoxical this, because I think I probably make work in quite – if there is a gendered way of making, I would say I make work in a masculine way, i.e., I'm quite brutal with materials.

TG: Certainly now, but as much then?

PB: I think so. There was a lot of ripping, tearing, pushing, cutting, breaking. Is that the definition of being masculine?!

TG: They are certainly aggressive verbs, and you can't talk about aggressive verbs in sculpture in the 1960s and 1970s without thinking of Richard Serra, and you can't think of Richard Serra without thinking of, you know –

PB: Yes. But I think it is a discussion that isn't completely resolved. I think female brutality is highly stigmatised in a way that's slightly different from male brutality. But it's there. Both genders have it, and I think when it's applied to artwork, whether it's a man or a woman, a male or a female artist doing it, it is a subject; it's a subject inherent to the work. I've often seen my work as being very without subject, but the actions that are inherent to how I make are a kind of subject, if that makes any sense. And I think that is probably very much about a female not using, in my case, I'm not using my gender as a subject, but I'm using a sense of motivation and drive to do something with the materials in front of me. That is extremely active on those materials, and therefore, it inevitably leads to something that has those masculine attributes. I think the other side of it, which is the caressing of materials with paint or dipping them or them being laid in layers. Again, I would ask, is that just the prerogative of the feminine? I don't know. It's such an unresolved discussion, and one that is endlessly fascinating.

TG: You've talked about using paint as someone might use plaster or clay, which is such a great idea. I think if I were an art student, that would probably determine my next twenty years, and I love it as an idea. Could you give us one or two of your favourite examples in your oeuvre of how you use paint as you might have used plaster or clay?

PB: Certainly with some early work, or … they weren't early works, I was forty at the time, in the 1980s, where I was using paint as a means by which I could join paper and cloth and upholstery foam together, so the paint was applied very thickly and then squeezed into these materials. Also, in the Aachen piece, and I'll be doing a similar piece for the Norton Museum of Art, I've taken fabric, and I've soaked it in paint, and then I've squeezed it into shapes and rolled it up so that it takes on quite a lot of shape-like qualities because of that (fig. 58). And these works with these painted canvasses and painted calico, it is, are often on the floor, as floor works, and have other works embedded in them. Then there was a work I did that was called *Depot* that was in 1995, where I joined wood together with a lot of paint. And oddly enough, in the Carnegie work outside, embedding the coloured ribbons in the cement, I saw the cement and the coloured ribbons almost as a sort of painterly gesture, as much as a formal or shape-like gesture. Just thinking about the clay thing and the paint – in a way, I would go so far as to say the way the paint is applied, even on *upturnedhouse*, with the coloured panels, is actually more like smearing a bland surface on to the wood. It's more like smearing it with a deposit to, in a way, encrust that whole shape, the architectural shape with an encrusting of something, colour in that case. I think paint is always a modelling material of some sort, even in its most simple form, as with those panels in *upturnedhouse*.

TG: In *upturnedhouse*, the way the paint is there reminds me of early Cézanne portraits, where he almost spackles paint on to faces. The other foundational principle or practice that I've read you talk about a lot, both in terms of your own work and what you communicate to students, and even to your own assistants now, is the idea of speed … And you talked a little bit about it a moment ago as maybe having something to do with Eva Hesse. I guess, could you quickly summarise why speed is important to you? But maybe, more importantly, what does it get into the work that you want people to see or feel or have in the work?

PB: I think … Do you mean the sense, the tempo of making something?

TG: Yes, and that you, as I understand it, have told your assistants to take one pass at something when they do it. Do it quickly, do it, and then on to the next.

PB: Yes, it's a conflicted role that I have, where I make small sculptures, which are very much made by me. And they're, in a way, often try-outs or tests, not necessarily literally for the bigger works, but they constantly stir things up. They're made very quickly, and I like to retain that sense that maybe something's not completely finished or is in a state of flux. That is something that is a very alive part of making sculpture for me. When it comes to transferring that way of making to these much larger works, it's fraught with the difficulty of how to make that experience of the tempo at which something is produced be an experience in its own right for the person who's doing it which might usually not be me. So it's how then I give that direction almost as a builder would be given directions as to how to treat a certain surface. To keep that direction as pragmatic as possible, that there's only one swipe of the hand with the cement or the scrim, which, I think, you call 'burlap' in the States; it's just dipped in very quickly, pulled out of the bucket, and just placed on the frame with one gesture. These are very, very simple directions, where I hope the assistant who's doing that can retain the material's immediacy, and it not become a copied mannerism of mine.

TG: I'm also really interested in your *Object for ...* series, which I don't think one has ever been installed in the US, but correct me if I'm wrong. It's a series that you made or started in the mid-1990s.

PB: The early 1990s. In about 1992 I began them.

TG: Can you describe what exactly the series is, I guess, to start our conversation about it?

PB: Yes. From about 1990 until about 1995, maybe even earlier than 1990, I was struggling with the work and with finding venues for the work to be shown. It wasn't a huge priority, because I think the exhibition culture is far more ferocious now. Being under the radar wasn't a particular problem for me, but it was a problem in terms of thinking about what the destination for artworks might be and could be. What happened to artworks that were bought? Where did they end up? Did they end up on people's pianos or on their televisions or on their tables? And what about the artwork that was inappropriate to such a destination. That began to fascinate me just as an idea. So the first thing I did was take works out and just place them on the street and on street furniture. And just out of curiosity as well, as a subplot, to see how long they were there and some of them actually lasted about eight or nine years, because there they were placed in situations where they were just immediately absorbed into the urban environment, like the way someone might chuck an old pair of shoes up, and it just lands on the edge of a building or something.

TG: Yes, and let me just fill this in a little bit for listeners. Sometimes, you would put things on top of maybe a stop-light control box or between lamp posts, or just really on top of a mailbox or something (figs. 21, 114, 177). Just kinds of –

PB: Yes, very, very casual places that appealed, really because they almost performed as a kind of plinth in a way, as much as anything else. There was a bit of humour in it. The gallery could be taken to the most mundane situation possible, and it would be, in a way, a very comfortable location for something that would then go unnoticed. The two things could inhabit the appropriated plinth, so to speak.

TG: In the domestic context, that plinth could be a TV or on top of a desk or just out in the middle of the living room (figs. 22, 176). *Object for the sitting room* is a blue tarp bound by a rubber hose just in the middle of the room (fig. 113).

PB: Yes, exactly, because as an idea, the artwork had been purchased, and then suddenly, there would be nowhere for it to go other than it to occupy, very inconveniently, that space. I do perhaps find it quite humorous as to what the artwork's space is in our time, in our twenty-first-century time. There are collectors who have amazing spaces for artworks, but there are also homes where the artworks are almost unnoticed, because they're fulfilling some other kind of role. I think there's a strange, I would call it almost an anthropological issue, rather than an art issue, as to where art ends up. I think that that's ongoingly fascinating, where the big Rothko has pride of place in some amazing home somewhere, or the reproduction of a Van Gogh is practically unnoticed in somebody's kitchen. I think there is an archive of where these artworks, where and what they are inhabiting, and what status they have there, which seems to me a wonderful kind of archaeology and an anthropology at the same time and maybe a sort of sociology as well, that is distinct from the art world from which these things have emerged in the first place.

TG: So the siting of these pieces was a core principle. It seems there are two things that are present in the *Object for …* series that I wanted to ask you about. The first one is either their relationship to Franz West's work or maybe Franz West's work's relationship to these pieces, and I wonder –

PB: Oh no. I think it would be … Franz West wouldn't have known about my work, but I certainly knew about his work. You're absolutely right, yes.

TG: Are these pieces, in some way, a specific attempt to engage with him? Or are they –

PB: No, no.

TG: Was that just part of the soup?

PB: I think it was, in a way, a strange meeting of similar concerns.

TG: Yes, I think, right down to some of the colours you use.

PB: Yes, I know that was absolutely not lifted from Franz West. I think when I first saw his work, which was probably surprisingly late, it was a shock. And of course, those kinds of creative meetings, they present a lot of concerns that are quite surprising. One is that there's somebody doing something a little bit like I'm doing, but much better, or whatever the thoughts are. They arouse this weird egocentric thing that artists have, a sort of competitive spirit, but also, a sense, 'Well, I'm going to slightly divert', or 'I'm going to take this on', or 'I'm going to absorb this', but really, 'I'm not going to travel down that same road. I've got to find a parallel road.' I'm not saying it was that close a coincidence between his and my work, but there was a profound effect that seeing his work had. Even in the Carnegie, I came across a fabulous piece.

TG: Oh, fabulous one. That's such a good one.

PB: You know the one there.

TG: Oh, I do. We'll have an image of it up on the website. Yes, it's a great West. It's also interesting to me that he got to where he got through central European modernism and through a specific engagement with Austrian art. And you got to where you got through a very different engagement. And yet, in this period in the mid- to late 1990s, you were kind of walking down the same street.

PB: Yes, it's strange, because I think, just talking in a very practical way, there's a way of using very traditional processes, like how you build an armature very quickly and very simply out of cheap wood and scrim, burlap, and plaster, that is almost generic. A collection of artists from around the world could all be making a start with trying to get a shape to exist in front of them. They might all begin in that way, and there would be, at a certain point, a remarkable shared language between the way they're making things and I think it's then the point at which you arrest that process of making with those kinds of materials that can make there be similarities in the ways the works are emerging. I mean, Franz West's works, the ones where you enter them or you're invited to enter them, the plaster is left in this very rich, half-finished state. I think you look at Medardo Rosso or even Auguste Rodin's ways in which he left bits of mould on his figures, there's a long history of artists being fascinated in that aliveness of materials that have a liquid state and then solidify, that invites a shared language between those artists.

TG: One of the artistic moves that's at the heart of the *Object for ...* series and that you've used ever since is the idea, if you will, of taking a cylinder or something round and binding it; binding that cylinder with rope or with tape or with rope and tape and paint. I wonder where that move comes from, why it's something you like, if you will, and why you keep going back to it over and over again?

PB: I think there are certain … The triangle, I love the triangle as a shape. Not necessarily the equilateral triangle, but a triangle that seems to either be able to be poised on its apex in some way and be very unbalanced, or it's sitting very solidly on one of its sides. I think, in contrast to that, a circular form is potentially a voluptuous form; it doesn't have a resting point so easily as a triangular form. That circular form also lends itself to both a horizontality and to an uprightness, but the roundness is an all-round roundness, and I think that's my attraction to it. I like the way a cylindrical form can be laid horizontally and then placed on top of something, maybe quite high up. I like the way it can actually lie on the floor and seem almost mobile at that point. The characteristics of cylindrical forms have both incredible stillness about them when they're caught or trapped or held, but also have that potential that they've just arrived there. They've rolled there or they've had movement in them, but it's been arrested. And then, in their upright form, they're asleep, they're dormant. It's a dormant shape for me.

TG: Until the last year or year and a half or so, you had been barely seen in the United States. There were a couple of shows in Dallas, and that's about it. Your early work, going back a couple of decades, was typically impermanent. It was made, it was dissembled, it was recycled into something else, and so on. I wonder if there are any of those early pieces that you, particularly with American audiences, could see, or that you think would be useful for American audiences to have the opportunity to see, to have a grounding for what came next?

PB: OK, I'll just try and approach this in a slightly different way. Of course, there is a loss. There's definitely a sense of loss with the work, but not in a tragic sense. I would say, when you go and hear a great performance or a wonderful performance that really moves you, I'm often perplexed by, What is it that you actually go away with? Because the thing itself has disappeared. I think there's been something about making sculpture that's been a bit like that, that the event itself, whether it was great or not, doesn't matter. Once it's done, certainly from my point of view as the artist, something has gone, and I've always felt that about making things. The sort of build-up, the making, the whole practicalities of making are one part of it, but the main part of it is the installing of it. There is a marriage between the space and all the actions that have to be done to get this thing installed.

And there is a great sense of performance in doing that. Then, quite honestly, I'm extremely relieved to walk away from it. Something has gone at that point. But you know, thinking back on the work and thinking back on all the works that no longer exist and maybe very much recalling them now, for some reason, I'm having to use memory a lot as a resource about those works. I wouldn't know where to begin with which ones are the most important, because maybe it's like a whole experience.

TG: There's a narrative, yes.

PB: Exactly, yes. Now that works are being kept, it's a very, very strange experience, because some of the works don't keep that well, and they take up huge amounts of storage space. There is an issue about whether some works are better as things that can be remade and then remade again. It's an interesting crossroads at the moment, as to what the nature is of some of these very, very big installations, what their longevity is.

[...]

The original podcast is available at https://manpodcast.com/portfolio/no-109-phyllida-barlow/.

This edited three-way conversation between Barlow, Briony Fer, professor of art history at University College London, and Fiona Bradley, director of the Fruitmarket Gallery, Edinburgh, took place at UCL on 9 June 2014. The event coincided with Barlow's commission, *dock*, for the Duveen Galleries at Tate Britain, London, and *Phyllida Barlow: Fifty Years of Drawings* at Hauser & Wirth London. Barlow discusses how she approached the Tate Britain Commission and her thoughts for the work. They discuss her education and early influences, the role of colour in both her sculptures and her drawings, and Barlow's idea that the walls represent authority, while the floor is an anarchic space. Barlow talks about losing control, her working process, and the rejection of the image. Included after the conversation are exchanges from the Q&A that followed, in which Frances Morris, director of Tate Modern, and Tamar Garb, professor of art history at UCL, further discuss *dock* with Barlow and its connection to art history.

Conversation with Fiona Bradley and Briony Fer

2014

[...]

Fiona Bradley: I wanted to start with your reply to the question that I asked you in *dock*, your installation for the Duveen Galleries at Tate Britain (figs. 69, 115–19). Seeing the works for the first time, I was almost overwhelmed by the impact they had in the space, and I wondered if you were too. I remember asking whether they were as surprising in the space for you as they were for me, now you had the chance to experience them materially for the first time. And you replied, 'No. Completely not.' I assumed your lack of surprise was to do with having had a model of the space in which you had been placing models of the sculptures for months, but no, you said, 'I already know them, because I drew them.' That was fascinating to me. It might be unfair to ask you to plunge right into that, but I'd love to know how you begin to take ownership of a space, so that when you put work in it, it doesn't take you by surprise. However do you do that?

Phyllida Barlow: Two things. Although the work might have some site-specific origins, it isn't actually site-specific. What makes it have that site-specificity is dimension, and the thing about the Duveen was my relationship with sculpture has always been that the image of sculpture constantly dissolves and gets lost, as you walk round it. A memory of it is a very elusive thing, and as much as you can grasp an image of it, the image actually disappears. So I wanted actually to play with that. Literally play with that, throughout the Duveen Galleries, by in a way putting the sculptures in a very suspended state, both literally and, to some extent, metaphorically. They are literally hung. I think that that idea made me very fearless about the space, in a sort of arrogant way. I just took hold of the space, and placed it in my head, and lived with it in my head for that eighteen months that the whole thing was being negotiated and prepared. So the space became something that was inhabiting me rather than me inhabiting it.

FB: And do you do that by walking around it? By spending time in it? By photographing it?

PB: No. Not photographing it, no, but more going there. But I didn't go there that often, actually, and I find that with spaces I prefer to go just a few times and then use something of the sensation of it, rather than the literal space itself. So the process of looking up, looking down, and through. At the time the Tate was being built and rebuilt, so it was very dark in there, and that was actually quite interesting, and it was also winter. It was dark and wintry, and in a way, foreboding. But I think that was like a material in itself. It was like a dark material. So for me it was taking hold of those things and making them my own, I suppose.

FB: Is it the idea of the space then, or the feel of the space?

PB: The feel of the space, both in an imaginative sense, what could be remembered from it, and also that sense of something being high and out of reach. I think the idea of using the out-of-reach spaces just does fascinate me. I actually suffer from appalling vertigo. I can't even stand on something that's two inches off the ground, but it's great making other people do that for me. I think height is something that I'm just intrigued by. The fact that there is a sort of tidemark in galleries, which is eye level, and then there's this wonderful space above it, which I think other artists can use in other ways. Like Alison Wilding's work, before mine. Perhaps my oldest friend was in the Duveen before I was, so it was very interesting. But she used that eye-level sense of the space, and then the space above was a kind of weight on the sculpture. Whereas I very much wanted to get up there and make sculpture be seen, certainly for myself, from underneath and at a distance. This thing of walking round sculpture as though it's a painting. I would love to make people crawl to have a look at sculpture, because I think there is a whole way of experiencing sculpture which doesn't necessarily just have to be an object. There are many things that are sculptural, that aren't actually objects, like time and gravity, and I don't think they necessarily are just experienced through that processional way of using a gallery quite passively, as a sort of promenading space.

FB: You've talked before about gravity being one of the primary materials of sculpture.

PB: Yes.

FB: I like that, as a notion that it's important to you that these things are coming down.

PB: Are held.

FB: But go down, rather than going up. They descend.

PB: Yes, and they're held. The thing about the Duveen … although it wasn't a surprise, because of the drawings, we did make a model. And you should see the model now, it's like something that's been through an earthquake. It's been trampled on and broken and smashed to pieces, just because I can't work with models. They're just too niggly and neat, and too precise, and I'm not a precise person, I like approximation. I'm an approximist. Guess it!

FB: Is it also because you want things to be in flux –

PB: Yes, exactly –

FB: – and things to continue to change?

PB: – and the structural engineers didn't appreciate that at all!

Briony Fer: This is the sculpture gallery of Tate Britain. It's a huge space, as everybody says. There would have traditionally been a proportionate relation between the scale of sculpture and that space. I wonder, scale is obviously hugely important in your work, to its effect. But I wonder just how important it is? We can say that it's huge –

PB: Yes. I think scale is an illusionary thing, but I think size is a real thing. I think I make things that are to do with what I can actually reach, and make, within the studio. Then, they're made in many components, so very quickly they become big in size. I think in terms of scale, they bear no comparison to, say, things in a shipyard or an aircraft hangar.

FB: Because those things don't look made by a person. Is it important to you that your works are made – and therefore, look made – by somebody? Is it important that the process of their making is visually embedded in them?

PB: Yes, and I find that quite a difficult thing to talk about, because of this 'the hand of the artist', the expressionist thing, and actually, nearly all those works don't have my hand on it. They have me directing, almost as though the thing has a kind of stage-like performative thing about it, where the works are hugely directed. That's quite a taxing role to have, as an artist, where I'm constantly demonstrating, and the demonstrations are then copied. Sometimes they go wrong, so we have to begin again. Hence, the work taking on this often quite brutalised, damaged quality, that in a way I see as

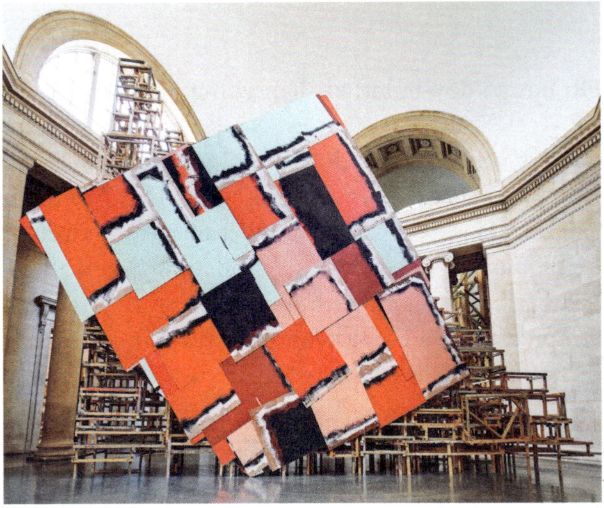

CLOCKWISE FROM RIGHT:
figs. 115–19 Installation views, *Phyllida Barlow: dock*, Tate Britain Commission, London, 2014

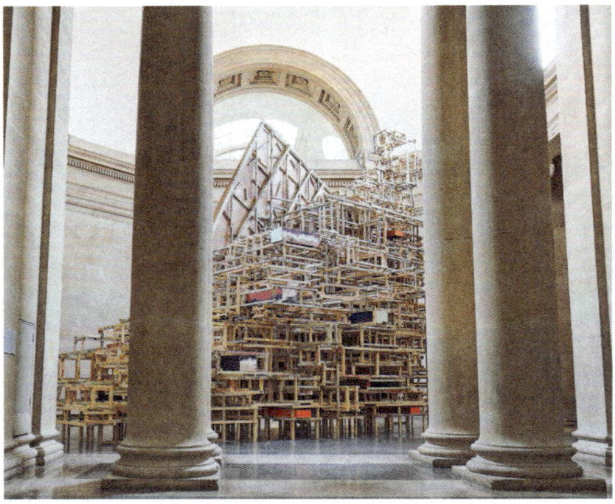

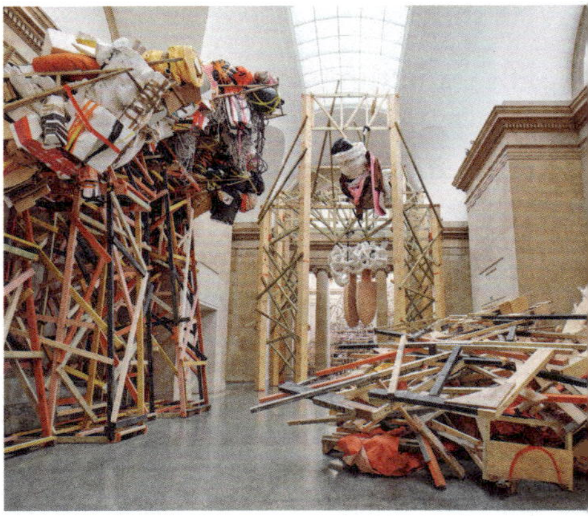

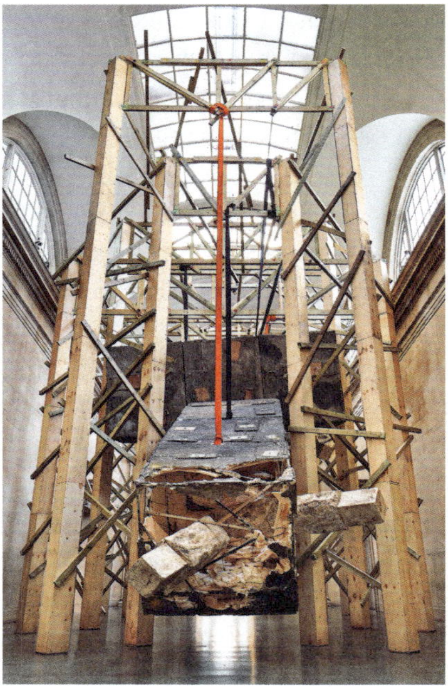

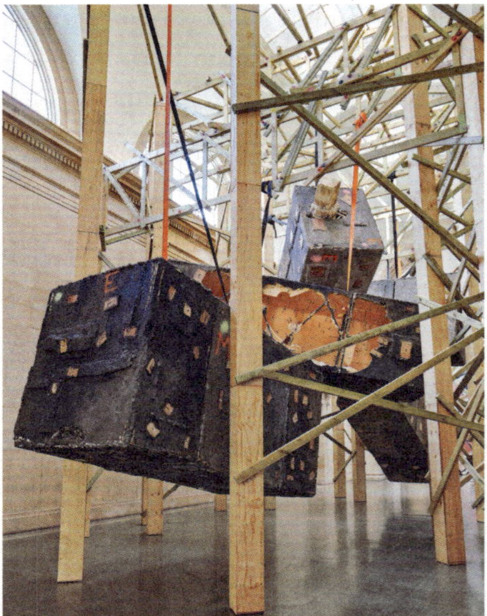

its reality, rather than as an expressionist mannerism. It's actually come from quite a real source, rather than a kind of 'faking it' source. Although, I have to say, I'm really interested in fakery as well.

BF: This is something that you've mentioned before, and it always really struck me and I kept it in my head. It came certainly to mind with the Duveen. You're interested in making things look rather like a ship in a bottle: how did it get there? So I guess that is about scale in the sense that it's too big to have come in the door, so there's that sense of it being fabricated and very clearly made. But the question of how is it made? How did it get there? It's almost as if it's landed. The aspect of wreckage, I suppose, that comes with that is very interesting and very much part of the effect.

PB: And very important to me. The idea of things elbowing their way into a space, I like very much. Maybe because I see that as something that is very animal, or human: how we acquire territory for ourselves, both emotionally and psychologically, and even politically. I think therefore objects, to me, they're taking over our space. If this object wasn't there [*indicates table*], it could be used by us, and I think sculpture always has that problem. It's greedy, and sort of inherently obtrusive and histrionic in how it grabs the space that we might otherwise have. I think politically that's obviously had a difficult history. It's been accused of all sorts of things. I actually see it as a very positive thing. That it's evidence of our state of existence. The way it is there, uncompromisingly.

FB: Because when the space is occupied by your sculptures, we move around in the space in a different way.

[...]

PB: When I'm making these, or we, the team is making these in the studio, I'm not actually thinking of the audience, I'm thinking of how do I want to see this in the Duveen. And then there's a hope that maybe that will be how an audience will be choreographed into –

FB: Because you are the first audience. The relationship that the sculptures are going to have with human beings starts with you.

PB: Yes.

FB: But not because you're making it for you, and you don't really want anyone else to see it. They're not private things.

PB: No. Not at all. These aren't.

BF: On the other hand, there is this sense of a lot of the titles of your earlier work. I'm thinking of works like *siege*, rather randomly drawing on that idea of almost a kind of siege mentality, or something that invokes a habitat, or some kind of first structure, but is also this catastrophic kind of remaindered ... Are these shelters? Well, kind of not, or –

PB: Or, are they coming, or are they going? That's my feeling about sculpture, and also maybe about our environments. Are things on their way out, or their way in, and how do we know the difference?

FB: Do you want them to be poised between the two, then? For there to be a sense that they've come, and they're going to go, and we've just caught them?

PB: Yes, exactly. I think that's what really interests me about the process of making, is a kind of place where more could happen. Or less could happen. And that is something that, for me, is a very compelling thing about using very ordinary materials, and I think –

FB: Because more will happen, won't it, to these? They're not finished. These materials have not finished making meaning for you.

PB: No. They'll probably be in the Fruitmarket. [...] In a completely new form.

BF: So at the end of its life, as it were, it will be dismantled and these materials will be recycled?

PB: Yes.

BF: Obviously a lot of your earlier work was dismantled, and therefore exists only in these photographic records.

PB: Yes.

BF: The temporality is therefore necessarily temporary, would you say?

PB: Yes, it was a very important part of beginning to sort out my relationship with sculpture, and the whole way in which sculpture was taught in the 1960s. Not necessarily at St Martins, which was then quite radical, or beginning to be radical, but certainly at Chelsea. And then here [the Slade] was an absolute nightmare. You know, in a dark basement being constantly told you were no bloody good, especially because you're a woman. I don't want to raise all that stuff, but it was an extremely archaic regime here. But, I am actually extremely grateful for the things I learned about sculpture, when sculpture was actually taught as a discipline. You learnt it. And you either passed it, or you failed it. And I constantly failed it until I came across clay and plaster. I think that's because they were very close to a kind of immediate gestural way of working, and they had their own life, which I had to compete with, in terms of making.

FB: Is it a no-tools thing?

PB: Yes, absolutely.

FB: So you work with your hands?

PB: Well, actually the clay … Both Elisabeth Frink and George Fullard said, 'Don't touch the clay,' and they would quote Germaine Richier, who said, 'Clay is a hysterical medium. The more you touch it, the more it screams.' That just made an incredible impression on me, that you could actually just do a swipe. And if you look at her work, you can see it in those … Well, the Tate has got those amazing *Orages*.

BF: Were you interested in Richier, at that –

PB: Oh, yes.

BF: At the end of the 1960s, I think, you encountered Eva Hesse's work?

PB: Yes.

BF: Or was it earlier?

PB: 1965. Somehow, I saw … She was in Germany then, wasn't she? So it was the works that were on at Hauser & Wirth that I saw [*Eva Hesse: 1965*, Hauser & Wirth London, 2013].

BF: So you actually saw them in –

PB: No, I actually saw them as black-and-white images, which sounds extraordinary. So I began to get to know that there was something that was extremely non-British, and I just fell upon it, because it was like being offered a new territory of exploration. That you could throw things. You could tie things. There wasn't a morality. I think it was the morality about making that I was, very early on, beginning to find absolutely intolerable.

FB: That it shouldn't be seen, the making?

PB: It shouldn't be seen at all. Or if it was going to be seen, it would be seen in a very specific kind of way, like through the skill of the bronze casting, or the cheese-grater marks of Henry Moore, were a real issue. But, in order to get to that point, you had to be able to carve, and you had to be able to do all these other things that were to do with making sculpture. So I think sculpture was very much about a craft process. And then looking at Eva Hesse, and then seeing the Arte Povera artists emerge, Piero Manzoni and people, it was just like, oh my God, there is another way of thinking about what an object is and what the status of an object is.

BF: I'm really interested in that moment. Partly because it seemed like a moment when we might retrospectively think of the sabotage of the art object and the thingness of it. That moment of Conceptualism in the later 1960s, as much here, as elsewhere. There is this moment for Eva Hesse, when after this year in Germany where she's making these highly coloured reliefs, a lot of which were shown at Hauser & Wirth last year, she goes back to New York, and she finds sculpture, and she abandons colour. And they're all monochrome.

PB: She has that incredible correspondence with Sol LeWitt about whiteness, doesn't she? [...] I just thought that was an absolutely fantastic discussion.

BF: And that necessity to, in some way ... In a way, as Mel Bochner says, to do something akin to what's happening within Conceptualism, and the sabotage of the object, but to do it through sculpture. I know that the time scale is not exactly the same or exactly parallel, but there's a way in which your various moves, early in your working life, and the work that you were making absolutely never abandons colour. Well, I suppose there are the drawings in the show at the gallery, where they suddenly become monochrome, the drawings of the 1970s. But the way in which colour functions for you, with sculpture, as opposed to against it. Or, is there some kind of antagonism, or battling-out between painting and sculpture? In the drawings, perhaps some of that is also being seen. But it's a very different response to the problematising of the relationship between painting and sculpture that we might think about in the US context, for instance, in the middle of the 1960s. It seems that colour and sculpture, as well as abstraction and figuration in a way, from the beginning never were entirely incompatible, oppositional elements. That, now, seems very timely of course, but at the time must have been really out of kilter with what other people were doing.

PB: Not in terms of the New Generation show in 1965, with Phillip King and the others where King showed *Genghis Khan* and *Tra-La-La*. So, there was that explosion of –

BF: Colour.

[…]

PB: Sculpture with colour.

[…]

FB: […] The early, very highly coloured drawings, are they to do with that kind of sculpture? Are the drawings where colour started to be something you could work with?

PB: I think the colour has always been about trying to emphasise and trying to differentiate between one edge and another, whereas I found the pencil, although fantastic, didn't do enough for me. So the colour and the way of painting has always been, in a way, quite practical and expedient. It's been about trying to state that this is where this begins.

FB: Right, so this is here, and this is here.

PB: Yes, exactly.

FB: And this is how you'd walk around it, if it was an object.

PB: Yes, absolutely. It also comes from maybe just being absolutely fascinated by early colour sculpture from the early part of the twentieth century. And wondering where that went to, in the black hole of the twentieth century. World War II obviously obliterated a lot, in a funny kind of way. It had to reinvent itself, which it did in the 1960s, and rediscovered some of the things that had been.

BF: You mentioned Pablo Picasso's *Glass of Absinthe*. But in a way, I take the point that Phillip King, Anthony Caro, coloured sculpture was there, but I guess it's something about painterly colour maybe that your work has. I don't know whether you would call it painterly, but it's not the kind of colour that –

PB: Yes, it was.

BF: … in a Caro, or in a Phillip King. Even though one of the drawings in the gallery almost has the Phillip King in there. But it's something maybe about the painterly, maybe something about painting and sculpture.

PB: It is.

BF: It seems like a kind of elephant in the room, to me, because you don't want to … These are not paintings, these are drawings. They're on paper. But the stroke, or something about the tactility, would that associate with a kind of bodily engagement with colour, or …

PB: We talked a bit about the order in which you see things and name things. I mean, is this a table before one sees it as a fake wood table, or a yellow table, or whatever colour? How do we create that order in our heads, about things? I think, for me, colour was very much about trying to almost compete with the form, because the formal qualities of things is what I've loved. That's where a sort of passion is. The roundedness of something, or the straightness of something, or the fallen-over-ness of something. But then the colour, in a way, is almost competing with that in a hierarchical sense.

FB: Or does colour help us see that? If we're looking at a sculpture of yours, does the colour confuse the bit of our brain that wants it to resolve itself into a table or a structure?

PB: Exactly, yes.

FB: The colour actually makes it look like a round thing, or a falling-over thing, rather than something we might recognise from somewhere else?

PB: It's a bit like a pointing device, in a way.

FB: Yes, so is colour doing the same thing that it's doing in the drawings? Saying, 'Look at this bit, and then look at that bit'?

PB: Yes. That's how I see it. But also I'm not afraid … I don't find it problematic that maybe sometimes the surfaces and the colour is almost akin to decoration, even though it might be a smear or a smudge. It's an additive thing so that it's surplus to requirement, in a way. To me it's actually emphasising something, and that's what the colour is doing.

FB: We talked earlier about the kinds of colours. Briony was mentioning the kinds of colours you used, and you said you used colours that draw attention to themselves. That are attention-seeking.

PB: Yes.

FB: I love the idea that a sculpture should be attention-seeking.

PB: Because I think it is …

FB: Do you think it inevitably is, so you might as well go with it?

PB: I think it's inevitably theatrical. Inevitably. I think as Germaine Richier said, it's quite an hysterical art form. Both in terms of hysterically funny, but also hysterically tragic. I think a lot of sculpture is there to be walked past. In a very peculiar way, becomes invisible. I'm thinking of the Richard Serra in Broadgate, which almost disappears into the environment. I think certainly public sculpture can do that extraordinary thing of becoming as invisible as anything else on the street becomes. Invisible until you fall over it, or something, or it bumps into you.

FB: And then you realise how absurd it is that we live with all these sculptural objects, the bollards, the street furniture, and we don't notice them as objects any more than we notice a great big Serra or, in our case in Edinburgh, two very large giraffes that I walk past every day.

PB: I also wonder whether painting – I know this is a very traditional, conventional view of painting – but because it occupies the wall space, there's somehow a formality there, that's very specific. Walls, to me, are the signature of authority in terms of architecture and buildings, whereas I think floors are more … In a way, they're absolutely essential! But they are more ambiguous in how they can be used and filled. Walls definitely are dividing spaces and controlling spaces, in terms of how you move around a building. In terms of art, they're traditionally the space that's known to be for paintings, whereas sculpture … […] I mean it's like parking a Caro as though it's a sofa, in the corner of a room, and I find that way of trying to keep sculpture out of the way … It's actually really interesting. Because I think that floor space is potentially, in my mind, an anarchic space. It's a space occupied by people, and other things that can interrupt people, but the wall space is actually … This isn't a reflection on … It's a much safer space, in a way, for where art can go.

BF: There is the sense that you're using the space that the architectural frame gives you, but you seem to bring, in terms of a lot of the things that have maybe inspired you visually over the years, the kind of mess or chaos of the street, like skips or in some of the drawings there are what seems resonant of those orange plastic sheets that shroud scaffolding. Or, you talked about pink, in terms of the colour of street signs, and all this bringing the outside into the inside, in a way, and messing up those borders. But it seemed that the, as it were, the life of the street, and the way in which boulders, or bollards, or barriers, they're often things that stop you moving around.
Is that, again, what you think sculpture is like? Some sort of big bollard?

PB: Yes. I suppose it's its obstinacy. Are there two things? Is there sculptural language and is there sculpture? Is sculptural language far more … I was going to use the word 'diffuse', in the sense that maybe weather can be sculptural, in the sense that it can affect us physically. Whereas a sculptural object is far more specific. I think it's the sculptural language that I'm interested in, and how things take us over or control us in all sorts of ways. As well as objects, I mean they obviously fascinate me, but I think there are certain things that accompany those objects that are in a way, about decision-making. Why do we have to cross the road here? What is that doing there? How is it that that building has gone up, and no one knows how the hell it got there? These things that are underlying the decision makings about objects. Which, I think sculpture has that problem. Therefore the sculptural object on the street that's just an everyday thing fascinates me because it's so loaded, if you begin to unravel it. And then, there's things that have a mood, like the weather, that I see also as very sculptural, but more about a language of sculpture. I don't know if that makes any sense. I think there's a differentiation.

FB: I was going to ask you about control. Your objects seem somehow to have an agency of their own. You talk about street furniture, and that clearly has an agency. We do what we're told, by objects.

PB: Yes, exactly.

FB: The fact that although these objects have been made by people, now it is the objects telling us what to do. We cross on the zebra crossing. The lines tell us to do that.

PB: Yes.

FB: But I wonder, do you like to keep in control of your objects?

PB: No. Although I think it's hell, I think that kind of losing control … which is sort of what I'm in the middle of now, with the next show. […] Especially if you're working with a team of people, so it's almost like a collaboration. So it is like being in the middle of directing something, and suddenly nobody knows what the script is.

FB: Because the object is taking over. The object has its own rules.

PB: Yes, it's taking over, and in a way that is possibly not what anyone expected. And so that's quite difficult. At that point, I probably don't know whether it's working or not.

FB: Is that the point that you always have to get to?

PB: Yes, I think I do.

FB: That point where all of it's about to fall apart.

PB: I think that's what was, in a way, the difficulty with the Duveen. Working at that height, and on that scale. That's why it wasn't a surprise when it all went in there, because so much of it had been worked through in some form or other, almost like a rehearsal. We couldn't actually see any of the work in its entirety, but there were plenty of rehearsals about how things went together. So, when the performance came there wasn't that surprise, because there had been those rehearsals.

FB: In terms of bravery and fear, and success and failure, is it a sense that the work has already failed, so it can be free to fail again, if that's what it's going to do? Is that part of the success of the work?

PB: Yes, I love failure. I think it's a fantastic place to inhabit. I sort of hate the word 'success'. It's bandied around, isn't it? […] Children are expected to be successful, and I think, 'For God's sakes!'

FB: Well, first we want them to be happy, then we want them to be successful, don't we? And we think that they're linked somehow.

PB: I don't mean to be like a miserable-ist, but I think why not enjoy something about failure, because it is a sort of freedom to be able to do that. You know, the Tate gave that opportunity, which I think is an act of incredible courage on their part.

FB: Courage on theirs, but not on yours?

PB: No.

FB: You talked about not being brave.

PB: No, I'm not brave at all. I think I'm just doing what I've always done. I don't see myself as … I think as an artist you have to occasionally … well, not occasionally, a lot, see it from the curator's point of view. That they're taking as many risks as you are, as an artist. And that's quite an interesting symbiotic relationship.

FB: I suppose so, and maybe the audience is taking the biggest risk of all, coming in and trusting that they're being manipulated by the artist around this object, and they're going to get something out of it. Do you care about the audience? Do you care about the visitor? That sounds terrible – 'Is it all about you?' I don't mean that you don't care about the audience, but can you bear to think about the audience when you're thinking things up? When you're thinking about how you're going to make something?

PB: I find it intensely irritating, having to think … I don't know at what moment you're meant to, as an artist, think about the audience. And I certainly can't think about the audience when I'm producing the work, and the work is in production. But I think the minute it hits that space, and it's all in pieces, and there's this incredible energy, driving energy, to get it to perform, because that's what is being asked, then gradually this sense of audience begins. What was incredible was setting up the Duveen works. It's very open, so I could hear what the public were thinking. That was quite amazing, listening to their comments.

FB: Did they think you were the scaffolder, putting the thing up?

PB: I don't know what they thought. But you could lean on the metal barriers, and you could just hear people's passing comments, and it's very revealing.

FB: It's a whole new dimension to the idea of work as performative, isn't it? We've talked about it having time and action embedded in it, but I have never thought about it as a public performance, your work.

PB: But it is, isn't it?

BF: Before we open it up to discussion with the audience, I wanted to broach one last issue, which I guess relates to the fact that you said you'd been doing this a very long time, and it's become very visible to us. You've had a suite of really extraordinary exhibitions, including these, but it's really that question that we, I think, are all interested in, which is what is the significance now of the kind of artist that you are? You've spoken very eloquently about a sculptural vocabulary and that your sense of making work comes out of this trajectory that began in the 1960s, and obviously you've been making work throughout that's come to a much greater public visibility. Not that it wasn't before. We were thinking about the significance of making and the 'stuff of art'. What I referred to before as the smell of the studio, that your work certainly has. And how you see that yourself. What it is about making. What it is about having this very physical relationship with the work. Why, in the context of our current conditions, when in a way we inhabit this image culture. We're saturated by images, and yet you and your work, I think I was getting the feeling that you want your work to, in some way, antagonise the image. That you're not a producer of images, in some way, and I wonder why that might be interesting now.

PB: Yes, the rejection of the image, I think is incredibly difficult to do. But that's where I begin my work. When I want to make something, I very often don't know what the hell it is I want to make. I just have the impulse to make. I think this is an incredibly difficult position to advocate, because it doesn't have a subject, and it doesn't have meaning in the sense that I think is more and more, a kind of necessity of art. I don't know where it's come from, but it seems to be. It's just like a bodily function. So often the works might begin with just mixing materials, or picking materials up, or using things that are lying around in the studio, and just literally playing around with them and seeing whether that then leads somewhere. Now, I don't find that a very convincing thing to be telling people. It doesn't ring true in some way, but it's just the way it is for me. Then it is a question of what is this going to become? I think that sense of something becoming something is what intrigues me. But I don't have a subject. I have lots of references about damage, and reparation, and regeneration. A kind of cycle of decay and regeneration. That fascinates me, because maybe that's what my generation has witnessed, seeing London in ruins, and then seeing it come up, and then fall down again. It's just a constantly changing thing, and it's the same with nature, it's part of us, that cycle. Therefore, for me, something about making is the same process. A constant state of change. But I think the idea of beginning something with great clarity is not the most interesting way for me to begin. I sort of long for it, because I think it would make life easier, but it's not the way I make things. I don't know. I think I'm an incredibly traditional, ordinary artist in that respect, and therefore I don't know whether it has any interest for anyone at all, in the current climate. So, that's my response.

BF: Perhaps the return of that kind of intense materiality, or watching something make itself and unmake itself, which is I think one of the interesting aspects of your work, it might relate in odd and curious ways to other work that is getting made, that might take different forms.

PB: Absolutely, yes.

BF: And, I find it quite interesting that although you come from such a sculptural base, so much to do with the medium, that in many ways perhaps we might think of your work in relationship to the work of other artists, that actually is in entirely different media. It's actually something more structural, or something about a necessity for a kind of resist. Or, it's certainly very strange materials and temporalities that you present us with, that fail to fit what we think we know, and certainly what we are being told about the world that we inhabit. So even, it's kind of belonging to a time of sculpture, almost cuts against the grain of the on-message sense of what art is meant to do.

PB: I think there was a time when that idea of talking about sculpture was almost sort of banned, in some way. Sculpture just wasn't within the vocabulary of fine art. It was just fine art, and I'm OK with that, from an educational point of view. But I'm not OK with it for myself. I would never inflict sculpture on my worst enemies! I hate it and love it, in equal doses, and I think its history is often dire. I think there's a whole classification of sculpture, maybe Gian Lorenzo Bernini is an example, where I think it's more about painting, than sculpture. Etc., etc., etc. So, the history, for me, is wobbly.

FB: [...] Running a gallery, I look a lot at audiences looking at art ... Things which happen in the gallery, things which happen right there in front of you, have a currency and a primacy to them, which is certainly what in my experience younger artists making things now want to look at. And audiences looking at things now want to look at. And it seems to me that your work is absolutely doing this. Whether it's riding some kind of zeitgeist, or whatever, it's absolutely of this moment where we want objects to come out and get us, and help us understand other things. Help us navigate the world. As we navigate our way around your sculptures, so we're going to go out there and navigate our way through everything else.

PB: Yes, and I think that's interesting in the sense that in a way, sculpture, despite its brutal reality, is probably the most fake of all the arts, because it isn't the thing that you then encounter, for real in the world, that that thing has reminded you of, or has prompted you to …

FB: Except that it totally is, because we navigate our way around stuff all the time.

PB: Yes, exactly, but because it's framed by a gallery, or a space, or whatever it is, it's onstage. I know I've talked about this before, but I never really understood that phrase. What is it? When you go to the theatre, you suspend …

BF: Disbelief.

FB: Disbelief.

PB: Suspend disbelief, is it? Or do you suspend belief? I never know which.

FB: I think it's disbelief. I'm not sure why though.

BF: Disbelief, yes.

PB: I never can quite tell what the difference is between suspending disbelief and suspending belief, because they sort of end up in the same place. To me, sculpture has that trickery about it. I mean, a bronze is an extraordinary thing, because it's just a skin with a great, big, black, hollow, hole in the middle. So, it's pretending.

[…]

Frances Morris: It's a follow-up question, really. I've always thought that you've been incredibly generous about what you might call your influences. So many artists refuse to talk about other artists, or don't want to see their work in the context of this time, or whatever time they're making work. I just wondered in relation to that, with the Duveens, you referred to the memory of other projects in those spaces. With all of us who have visited those spaces over the years, they're kind of haunted.

PB: Yes.

FM: I can almost see the marks where –

PB: The Serra.

FM: – and I love that patina of age. It's sort of kissing the hand of history. But more than that, I wondered whether as a British artist who has taught sculpture over a long period of time, who's sought to be very knowledgeable about their peers and their antecedents, whether it was particularly special for you or meaningful, or whether it inflected the work in any way to be at the centre of this trajectory of the history of art. You're kind of surrounded by this chronological, slow history unfolding. There is Anthony Caro, you can see through the door. It seemed to me, maybe I was reading too much into it, but it seemed to me there was a sort of secret history unfolding.

PB: Oh yes, there was. Absolutely. The Caro thing was very fortuitous, in that it was on the right, if you're going down, of where the big panel sculpture was, and it was quite inspirational, because it was there from quite early on when I was planning for the Duveen. It seemed like a sort of landmark, to in a way use, if that isn't being too insulting to him. I mean, I certainly wouldn't want to … I'm not making a facetious comment about those other artists, but there are things like invented form, which has become … Or, I think had a kind of rocky history, bad history. It's seen as sort of the ultimate thing to achieve, as a sculptor. The form that's all writhing and twisted. So, that interested me, and that's very much in that hanging, white plaster one. And, there are these constant references, the whole time. The sort of damaged containers (figs. 117–18). These obviously, well, obviously to me, referred to Minimalism, and so … yes.

FB: But they are like the Serra, aren't they, hoisted up?

PB: Well yes, it is a kind of potted history of …

Tamar Garb: At the same time there's something so extraordinarily contrary about the materials that you're using. The sense of the ephemeral, and the mobilisation of the ugly and the wasted, and the industrial, and those things. So you have the sense of the tradition, but at the same time you have this extraordinary feeling that it's imploding in front of your eyes. I think that, that's what, for me, was so wonderful and rich about it. Especially those big, Minimalist-like blocks in which you actually see the Styrofoam, or whatever it is, and you want to go and break off a piece.

[…]

PB: But that's what I was meaning about if a Donald Judd or a Robert Morris is the real thing, then these are pretend versions. Briony was talking about amateurism earlier on. These are almost like the amateur versions, and that's why, if they get knocked, and one has been knocked, and it's got this graze on one side, but I like that. They were made with that in mind, because they are made out of these non-lasting materials. A kind of pastiche. They're a shadow play of the versions that they came from, and because I've loved that work so passionately, and it is a passion. It's been something of trying to absorb that into the Duveen.

[...]

On the occasion of the solo exhibition *demo* at the Kunsthalle Zürich, Barlow took part in a conversation with director/curator Daniel Baumann on 3 February 2017. The event begins with an introduction by Barlow in which she outlines her approach to the exhibition, which occupies the upstairs and downstairs spaces of the Kunsthalle, and she explains how each floor relates to the other. She talks about 'the idea' and the trinity of form, content, and subject, her idea of leaving the work unfinished, and her mistrust of perfectionism. This leads into an open discussion steered by Baumann, with questions from the audience, edited here to include exchanges covering the difference between the words 'object' and 'sculpture', narrative, audience, and different possible ways of viewing an artwork.

Conversation with Daniel Baumann

2017

Phyllida Barlow: I thought I would begin the talk whilst images of earlier work are showing by talking about how I came to think about this exhibition. And what my relationship is with this thing called an idea, which I think as artists we hold in high esteem, but which I find enormously problematic. Because I never know whether the idea actually survives, and there's something about that which makes me enjoy the kind of lack of logic, that I might start with something called an idea, but very rapidly, it breaks down. And very rapidly, I realise that I leave an audience with often quite a bewildering array of objects that can seem somewhat illogical and haphazard in the choice of what they are.

But the idea for this exhibition was very exciting because Daniel offered the opportunity to use this upstairs space with the proviso that it was going to be renovated, it was going to be torn down, it was going to be rebuilt, and there was some problem with the building on that front. That immediately appealed to me because my process of making is very much about building and damage and deconstructing the object as much as remaking the object, so there seemed to be a sort of fragile relationship there that was actually to do with that process. So it seemed as though there was a way in which I could use this upstairs building as a reference for the way I make work, which is to begin to make something, and to try and find out what the object is that I'm trying to make (fig. 78). And then it goes through these changes of often being destroyed and then remade, and so finishing work can actually be quite problematic. That's in quite severe contrast to works that actually have a very clear image, a lot of which are downstairs, where I'm sort of confident about what the work is going to be, but maybe not particularly confident about the method of making it (figs. 77, 120).

I think some of these issues relate to a conversation that perhaps we can have at the end about the trinity of issues that I think most artists deal with, which are form, content, and subject, and the order in which we might play with those three issues. Whether an artist is more inclined to put subject first, then the content, i.e., what the materials are and what goes into the work, and then the form, which for me is how the work actually takes on its existence. And, for me, I think my work is very much led by form, and I'm constantly trying to hunt down what the subject might be. But in this case [...] the subject was very much given with the building being broken down, so that was the start.

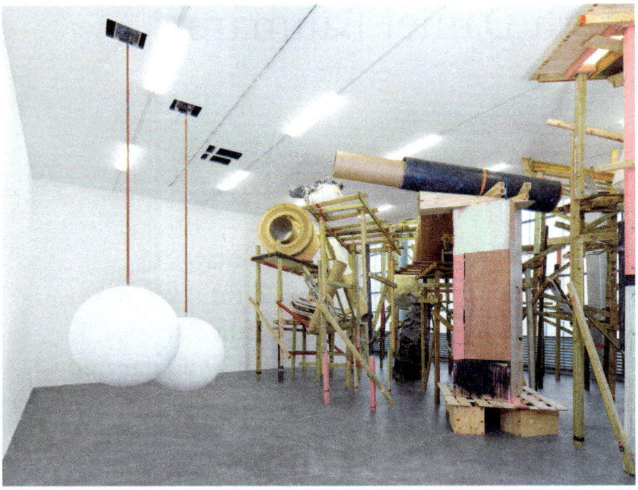

fig. 120 Installation view, *demo*, Kunsthalle Zürich, 2016

That then led to downstairs being, in my mind … and this is where I find the whole idea of 'the idea', a folly, a kind of trap that myself as an artist – I know there are a lot of artists who are very confident about what the idea is, and they can process it very methodically – but I can't. But in this case, the idea was that the work downstairs would be an indication of things that change, things that have an inherent fragility, an instability about them, and that are shadowing another possibility for those objects. So the condition I made for all the objects that were made downstairs was that they would all be half-made, half-finished, which in a way accounts for their temporary aesthetic. The aesthetic is very raw and open, there are no mysteries as to what the materials are, or in a way, how they're finished. But that idea of them being a kind of shadow of something that might have something more permanent elsewhere, that their other identity could be a more permanent version of themselves is an idea that belongs to me, and I have no real faith in the fact that that idea would ever convey itself to an audience.

So to me, the kind of destruction of the idea, the getting rid of the idea is incredibly important, and allowing the work to take form almost independently of having an idea, and so that's very much how these works downstairs all began to evolve. They're a kind of huge mixture of things that are quite familiar when you look at them, and then thrown into that, I think there are shapes that have just grown out of a process where I was trying to find out what that shape might become. Then there are actual cast forms where the process of making them allowed the shape to make itself, and that was a very exciting thing to be involved in technically. And then there are other things that seem to almost have no logic whatsoever, like the profiles of the pianos. I was trying to explain at supper just now what they are. I think those shapes have … probably are almost like symbolic forms that are in a way trying to identify something where we do this thing of when we see an image, we immediately say, 'Oh, that's a piano,' or whatever it is, 'That's a chair.' But when is it not a piano? And in this case, they're not pianos even though they have that image of a piano. I think for me as a sculptor, I very much like that play on the fakery of sculpture. Where things are pretending to be things. Where there's a huge amount of play-acting, things acting out being objects that I have actually observed in the world or have a great fascination for, but actually know perfectly well that they're not those objects. And how the act of making removes things more and more and more from their source of inspiration. So again, for me, that references this kind of slow collapse of the idea and what I hope is something else taking place.

Again, the idea of putting these objects very high up on these stilted structures was, in my mind, reaching up to this space here. So there was this sort of sense that these objects and the work was knocking on the ceiling of something that was above. Now how on earth an audience is meant to know that, I have no idea, but perhaps that's also where I think for myself, it's incredibly important that I don't get stuck with trying to prove the logic of something, but maybe allow this other event, which is almost like a theatrical event, take place, so that the work, what it is, just takes over from the original thought process even though that original thought process was very important.

I'm very curious now, having come back to it, to know what the audience thinks of the show, what the problems are. Does anyone here really hate it? I'd like to hear from them. Sometimes it's incredibly ... I don't know, a critic once wrote about my work that it was disgusting. It was the most incredibly vivid piece of writing. In fact, it was a brilliant piece of writing even though it was condemning the work to eternal hell! And in his hatred of the work, he actually spoke a lot of truths about it. The vivid description of why he disliked it was exactly what I wanted it to be. So I think often a passionate response at both ends of the spectrum is very stimulating.

But the point of this introduction was to really describe how the original joy of coming here and being able to work with two spaces, one on top of the other, triggered a whole load of ideas, a whole load of words like 'shadow play', 'dislocation', 'fracture', 'breakage', 'damage'. A lot of quite strong words that also, in my mind, played around with the notion of sculpture as a whole succession for me, of phantom states, of a phantom being. Almost like a ghostlike evidence of my experience in the world, that I can never actually make the reality of the experience, but I can play around with things that can be substitutes for that. And in this case, it was very much about the fact that a space was being broken down, and how that was a kind of and is a kind of metaphor for so much that we know that is going on in the world around, but maybe also in our own lives. I don't mean that in a tragic sense, but things don't go to plan, and I think I find breakage and damage actually very beautiful. I don't find it a hideous thing that's got to be shoved away. I mean, obviously in the vast humanitarian crises that are happening in the world, it is hideous and it is shocking. But I think in our everyday lives that the trivial incidents that happen, that don't run to plan I find fascinating. I find them in comparison to perfectionism, which I find deeply disturbing and troubling, I find they're much more interesting. Why the break in something causes so much disturbance, and perfectionism is the thing that's revered and considered the thing to achieve. So I was immediately very much in the thrall of working in a building, especially a gallery building, which on the whole are meant to have their own forms of perfectionism. But this one was going through the state of change, and for me, that was an incredibly exciting challenge that reciprocated my ways of working, the ways I tend to use and make work.

Daniel Baumann: So maybe there are questions already here, somebody who would like to throw in a critique? Positive or negative, or an opinion, or a simple question to Phyllida. Please, if you wish to do so, ask now. There will be other occasions, but it shouldn't be just a monologue or dialogue between the two of us.

Audience 1: A very simple question. You spoke about the term 'object', and then you said your 'sculpture'. Tell me, what is the difference for you between the term 'object' and why do you choose it for this kind of work and not 'sculpture'?

PB: As I was saying it, I was thinking, 'Oh.' Brilliant, yes. Brilliant question. You've found out! No, I tend not to use the word 'object', and I have no idea why that came out of my mouth. I think it's also actually self-consciousness. Maybe since the 1960s, the word 'sculpture' and what it represents has had a lot of trouble. It's caused a lot of problems. Maybe because there's a history, a modernist history that was very, very serious about what was good and what was bad sculpture. What was right, and what was wrong sculpture. And I was very much taught with that approach, 'That's good and that's bad,' and I hated it. It made me incredibly rebellious. And then during the 1960s as sculpture expanded into so much else, the word 'sculpture' almost stopped being used and people talked about 'making' or they talked about 'object-making'. To me, an object when I just simplify it is much more an image. Where a sculpture is an evolving thing. Where there isn't any one image to it, you have to walk round it and round it, and you can never quite hold what the image of it is because it changes at every point. I think what I'm really interested in is sculptural language rather than saying, 'This is sculpture and that isn't sculpture.' I think the weather can be sculpture, or a smell can be sculpture. I mean, I'm sure we all know this, in this room, that a sculpture isn't just a material object thing. But when I think of objects, I think of an image.

[...]

Audience 2: I don't know if the question really makes sense, but I was wondering if we could think about narrative, the term 'narrative', a little bit together maybe. Because of course it's an all-encompassing spatial work. The idea of narrative in the classical sense that maybe even involves walking round the sculpture might now not work anymore. Or what is the narrative? Is the event actually taking place? Are there many events? Just how do space and narrative and the idea of sculpture or maybe a break with the classical idea of sculpture, where do these things come together?

PB: To me, it is a spatial narrative. It's whether the space is controlling the work or the work is controlling the space. And for me, this is always an exciting challenge to take on. So the idea of making the work go through the three galleries was the narrative, and also repeating shapes so that maybe this idea of sculpture being something that you can never quite get hold of, or that's my relationship. Even if I make things out of cement and they're incredibly heavy, I still think there's a huge ephemerality there because of the process of walking round, or the way in which the space at that moment invites you to walk around as much as the objects do. So that's one narrative. The other narrative is when I'm in the studio making these things with, say, three or four assistants, I'm only thinking about the process of making the sculpture, the process of its possibility of where it's going to go. The minute it all arrives, it's like being told I'm Hamlet and I've got to go on now and be Hamlet, and I haven't even read the play. It's almost a moment of absolute terror because the difference between making the work in the studio and then bringing the studio to the space, then the performance has got to be almost invented on the spot. So there isn't a literal narrative, but I hope there's a spatial and formal narrative that is very, actually quite spontaneously made up in the week that I have to install the work.

Audience 2: What about the audience then?

[...]

PB: The audience at that moment becomes crucial. Yes, they are the protagonists. It's as if there are three performers: the space, the sculptures, and the audience. My ideal is that the three are working together. That's what I want, but whether that ... again, it's that kind of grandiose artist's idea, you never know whether it actually happens or not, but that's the intention. But the idea of a narrative being almost an empty space intrigues me. I find that fascinating.

DB: I just wanted to add something to this. I think one of the reasons beside the forms and the challenges and the size of the sculptures, I always felt that your work is a bit nastier than how you present it or than how we think it is. So there's a lot of manipulation going on, not in a bad or nasty or negative way, but I think we're very much guided through space by these sculptures, and then it actually gives these sculptures a lot of power that they don't show, because they look like, 'Oh, I happened to come here. I stand here now for a moment and I'm going away.' But I actually think the way we walk, you see people walking in here, and then they go on the stage and they look through the holes and then they go back. They are like actors in a play. It's just we don't realise it. And it's only maybe afterwards when you go home and all of a sudden you think, 'Oh, wait a second. That thing told me something to do. It is a perfect choreography, I just didn't realise it.' [...] So I think that was something I was very much impressed by – the way they pretend to be something, which they actually are, but they're also a lot of other things. And these other things, they linger on, at least that's what happened with me. They linger on even weeks or months after the show because it kind of comes back into my mind at very strange moments.

Audience 3: I wanted to actually ask you about those structures downstairs. It was interesting to hear you say that they're knocking on the ceiling, but they have for me this vertiginous quality that's like flying buttresses, and I just wondered if you could say something about the ecstasy of height.

PB: Well, I think I've become over the years, and have been for many years, interested in how we look at sculpture and how sculpture and a lot of art occupies the same space that we occupy. So there's a very, what I would call comfortable relationship between how we encounter artwork. And then it fascinates me that especially with something like sculpture, it doesn't take on all the space, that we're not physically prompted to look up or round or underneath these things. Sculpture is the whole object, it doesn't in a way have a top, bottom, or sides, it's a whole thing.

And therefore, that made me very curious, probably about thirty years ago, to try and install work so that there would be a surprising view of what the object was that I think in a way reflects something of how we look at nature, how we look at the urban environment. That we're often looking up or through or beyond just the immediate head-height kind of experience, and that this could be reflected in how we can enter an exhibition. And again, it's about who's controlling what. Is the space controlling us and the way we look at art, or is the art controlling the space and us? So it's that symbiotic relationship.

But vertiginousness fascinates me. Also there's that same thing of when you're standing on the mountain – I suddenly feel very nervous about saying that word in Switzerland! When you're standing on the mountain, you can't actually see the mountain. And I also feel that there's something quite sculptural about how does the object disappear and how does it reappear? That when you're at a distance from things you can see them, but when you're actually absolutely close up, you can't. So I think that has a lot to do with this placing things high up, and vertiginousness intrigues me as a physical experience because I can't stand on a chair without … So it's very much about a kind of envy to be able to do physical things that I'm not capable of doing.

DB: Also downstairs when you come in and you see the first structure, and then when you go, you lose all control. So it is a bit of vertigo as an experience of height but of control of space. And the same here. Actually, your brain tries, when you look through the holes, your brain tries to make a unit out of what you see, and you never succeed. So that is also … it can create a vertigo moment or a moment also of dissatisfaction, which I think is interesting because what we expect from art is being satisfied. Or from films or from books. And when we're not satisfied, we basically think it's a bad book or a bad film, but maybe it's actually a really interesting film because it doesn't give you what you expect. And that's what's happening here and downstairs.

PB: But I think the glimpse, which is a word I love, where you can just catch something for a moment, and what you retain from that. I find that fascinating. I think I make work that can be seen very quickly. We just went downstairs to see the Rodney Graham show [*Rodney Graham: Media Studies*, Hauser & Wirth Zürich, 2017], I don't know if any of you have seen it? The lightboxes are just absolutely fantastic, I think. And you can't take your eyes off them. You just are riveted by them. I think my work is the absolute opposite. It isn't riveting. And you can walk through it extremely quickly, and maybe there are things that then linger from having walked through it quickly, and I'm sort of fine with that, you know? It's a different way of presenting art or making art or getting involved in art. Certainly when I did the Tate show, which was down the Duveen Gallery, I don't know if any of you have been to it – it is a long, eighty-metre hall, and it's a passageway so that everybody walks through it – and I purposefully used that as a way in which the work would be walked past. It would be work made to be walked past rather than to be, as in the Rodney Graham case, where you really want to stop and you just want to study these intriguing images and every detail of them.

[...]

A video of this talk is available at http://kunsthallezurich.ch/en/articles/video-artist-talk-phyllida-barlow-daniel-baumann.

This is an excerpt from a conversation that took place between art critic, journalist, and broadcaster Alastair Sooke and Barlow at the Chatsworth Festival at Chatsworth House, Bakewell, UK, on 22–24 September 2017. Included here are the parts of the conversation which focus on Barlow's then recent experiences representing Great Britain at the Venice Biennale in 2017. They discuss what it means to represent one's country, and Barlow outlines her approach to and ideas behind the Venice work and how this experience made her reconsider aspects of her thinking about sculpture.

Conversation with Alastair Sooke

2017

[...]

Alastair Sooke: It's a great accolade, I'm assuming, for an artist to be asked to represent their country and to be at Venice. Was it something that was just an unadulterated pleasure when you were invited to do it, or did you slightly think, 'Ah'? It's also a big stage and possibly quite a daunting thing to do?

Phyllida Barlow: I think there were several things going on in the sense that politically, it seems a very fractured, complex time globally. And although the honour is unquestionable, there is also a burden of how to approach that honour, which is also interesting. And when I was installing, because it's a group show, the Biennale, it's not a solo show, it's a group show, you've got Japan, you've got Canada, Germany, France, so you're not on your own, and meeting all of these other artists and all of the artists were scratching their heads and saying, 'Where are we globally? What do these individual countries mean?'

AS: Of course, this shifts enormously over time, as well.

PB: Yes.

AS: I mean, the Biennale's been running since what, the 1890s, I think, and the spot of the Pavilion is incredible at the end of this avenue in the Giardini (fig. 121) [...] and it completely reflects Britain's time and place in the world –

PB: Absolutely.

AS: – one hundred years ago, but maybe not so much today.

PB: No. No, it's a proper colonial building. It's right next door to Germany and right next door to France. So it was great meeting those artists. And the Canadian pavilion. Everybody was talking about the mood in which they were awarded this tremendous privilege of representing their countries for the Venice Biennale and the unease about an individual point of view of what it means to represent your country and whether you can carry that as a subject within the work. And of course, most of the artists were saying, 'No, you can't.' What you can do is respond to various, very individual things about that commission. And for me, it was the space. For me it was in a way making a work at a troubled time but also combining that with a great sense of celebration that so many countries were all together, in this together. I found that hugely important. Not just me, but everyone was … there was the privilege of meeting all of these artists from so many different corners of the world.

AS: I think the word 'celebration' is key to me. This, like all of your work, has this tremendous vigour and exuberance and a delight, and a joyfulness, I feel as well as, as we can maybe come on to, perhaps referring to fractured times, troubling times. You're talking about when you're there, you're meeting other artists, you've already conceived of the work, you're making it in situ. Talk us through the process to get to that point. Did you fly out to have a close look at the pavilion itself?

PB: Oh, yes, and there was the architecture biennale in situ, so the main features of the inside of that pavilion, the British Pavilion, were all concealed. So it was a question of then unpeeling that, which is a very insulting thing to do to somebody else's exhibition. But to get to the raw state of the building, and to in a way look at its location with these other extraordinary buildings. It's like a kind of theme park in a way. There's no point in avoiding that or denying that. The fact that the pavilions do carry the trace of each country's political past, you know the Russian one has a sort of Soviet feeling about it, the Finnish/Scandinavian one has something that's very stereotypically Scandinavian about it. They carry the imprint of their national identities quite strongly.

AS: When you left after that visit, some of these forms that we see now, are you already imagining their shape, their appearance, how they will be, or is it a slightly different sense of the work you have at that stage?

PB: Yes, at that stage, I definitely wanted to erupt out of the pavilion in a sort of gesture of a country that might be kind of shrinking itself. And then, the idea of trying to explode. But I don't think that was the subject of the work. It was a gesture of how to, in a way, make a sculptural event happen that was very much about moving outside the building and taking occupation of that space outside. […] These baubles almost decorate the front of the pavilion (figs. 79, 122). But I think for me, looking at a space, it's always like the beginning of an adventure, because I want to explore the parts of the space

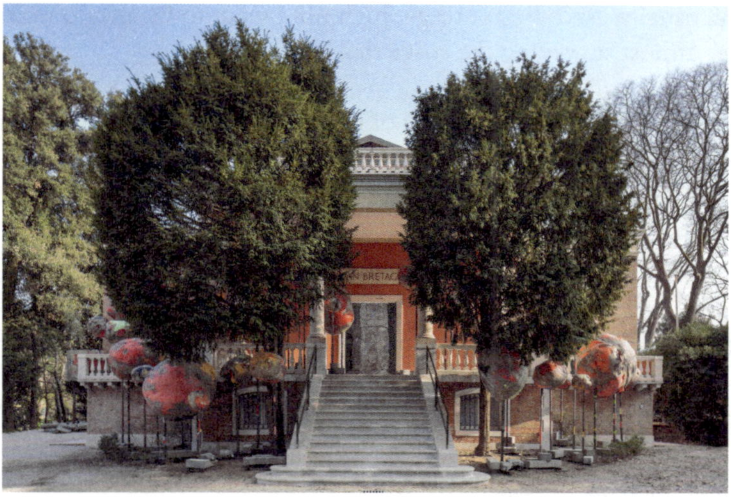

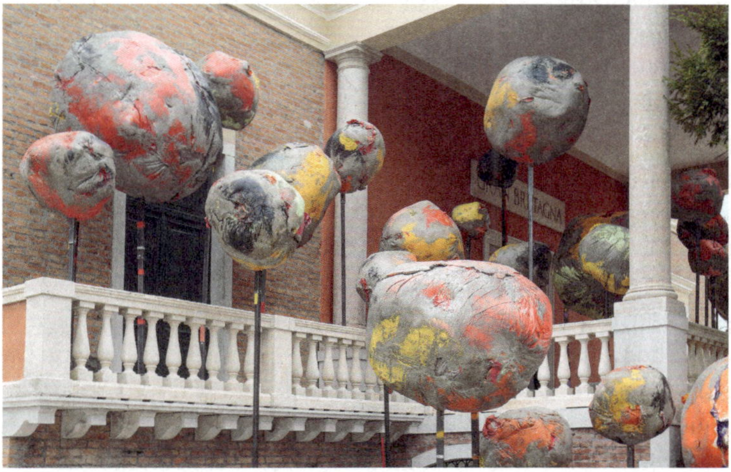

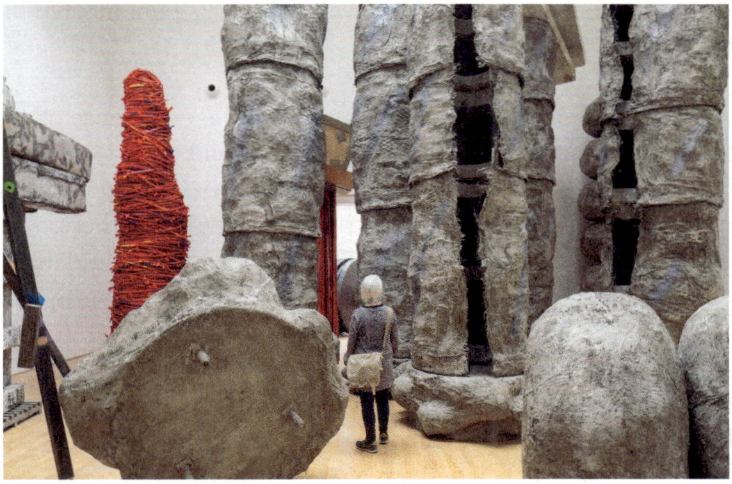

TOP TO BOTTOM:
figs. 121–3 Installation views, *Phyllida Barlow: folly*, British Pavilion, 57th Venice Biennale, 2017

that aren't usually used. I want to get high up. I want to be able to make the sculptures almost surveying the space that they're in.

AS: It was very noticeable that many of the forms inside are tree-trunk-like (figs. 80, 123).

PB: Yes.

AS: In that sense, they really go up to the top and use the height of the building. And it completely changes how you feel as a viewer. You're not really looking at a nice, polite bronze just in front of you, it's something which is much more immersive. [...] Because quite often with your work, I feel like sometimes people use the phrase 'stage set' or say that it has a theatrical component, and it feels like performance is important. I know you're a big fan of slapstick comedy and of classic silent movies in that vein. Is that something that you were thinking of trying to play with in Venice?

PB: Not in this particular case, but I was very much interested in the theatre aspect of the way the pavilion is beautifully designed with a sort of central courtyard, and then, a way you can walk through the whole spaces circumnavigating that central space. So, to me, that was immediately a kind of theatrical way of negotiating a space. The idea of surprise seemed very important, that each room would not reveal itself in its entirety, there would be things to find and discover, whether they were low down or high up. And that would, I hope, keep an audience in a way guessing, and maybe keep the audience on the move. That this possibly wasn't an exhibition where you stand and ponder. It was an exhibition where you're on the go, and it might even take you five minutes to go round the whole thing. But to me, that's not a bad thing, but that in a way is ... Well, what gets remembered kind of survives –

AS: Do you think also it feels in a way that reflects the experience of making the work? I say that, because I remember meeting you before for this interview ... You live in North London, and you have a small studio, which is at the side of the house. And you used a very similar phrase standing in there, you said, 'This is not a place to think and ponder. There are no creature comforts here.' It's a place where you go in, and I guess, work fairly quickly, swiftly.

PB: Yes.

AS: So, for you, when you see the finished work, do you feel there's a remnant of that swiftness, that urgency perhaps to the creation of it?

PB: Yes, I'm temperamentally impatient and want to get the thing done, strike while the iron's hot. There isn't time to speculate on whether it's the right idea. In a way, there's a lot of guesswork. Guessing, and then, acting. I'm sure it goes back to having small children and knowing that I only had maybe a couple of hours in the studio. I'm going back thirty, forty years, but it was an incredible training for me to take action and get on with it. It's not foolproof. There are many mistakes in working like that, and getting these columns to behave properly was a pretty arduous experience.

AS: Because a lot of your work foregrounds this quite precarious quality. And feels as though it really could topple. Are there several experiments? Is there a process of iteration where you're making things that are actually falling down?

PB: The experiments with these, which is exactly what I'm doing in the studio at the moment again, is something that drives me mad. I'm not good at it. It's just everything is made, and then has to be tested out, then taken apart, and then made again and tested out. And there was a process from about August until October 2016 when we were just trying out how to make these things be able to be accumulated on top of each other and that they were –

AS: And this was with a team of people?

PB: Yes, this was with six assistants, which includes my studio manager, who is a welder, which is just amazing, so we can do welded things on the spot. I don't have to send them away to a fabricator, so that we can make these adjustments in situ in the studio. It is a luxury to have that.

[…]

PB: Since Venice, going back to your first question about that responsibility and what that honour is. I think being an artist who has a single discipline, i.e., sculpture, and it can be named as that, and being surrounded by pavilions of such extraordinary works, the German pavilion with its fantastic glass stage, the dogs, the nude figures around on the floor underneath you as you walk. And then the French pavilion with the recording studios, the Canadian pavilion with the fountains –

AS: And these are the three that are just there.

PB: There, yes.

AS: I mean, they're really close.

PB: And then, suddenly, bang, you hit sculpture. And I started to think, 'Oh, God. This is so dull.' And I think it has made me feel vulnerable in the sense that you –

AS: I'm surprised to hear you say that.

PB: Being in love with this thing of sculpture and its ugliness, its obdurateness, its lack of … Once it's in a place, it's there. And its history through Arte Povera or whatever it might be, there are many artists who have tried to repudiate that obdurate quality about it. But it's also made me think about painting a lot, and is there now an opportunity to actually push the painterly side of the work much further, or my own relationship with painting much further? So in a way, the Venice experience has brought me to a kind of crossroads. It's great to be challenged and to be constantly challenged and not just see a massive event like Venice as a kind of, 'Yeah, well that's it', you know?

AS: The culmination –

PB: Yes.

AS: And then, you can rest on your laurels.

PB: Yes, I can't. In fact, it's had the opposite effect.

[…]

Published in the magazine *Border Crossings* in December 2018, this far-ranging, in-depth phone interview (reprinted here in an edited version) with art critic and academic Robert Enright covers Barlow's interest in working big, the relationship between objects and their settings, and her increased interest in the single object post-Venice. They reference projects from the last years in Aachen, Pittsburgh, the Tate Britain Commission, and the Venice Biennale. They discuss the theatrical and the absurd, authority, titles, meaning and naming, the simile and the metaphor, phantoms, spatial narrative, certainty, and chaos. Barlow talks about her processes and embracing different clashing languages.

Interview with Robert Enright

2018

[…]

Robert Enright: You have never been intimidated by scale. What was it in your character that made you want to take on space the way you did?

Phyllida Barlow: I think it's the adventure of objects or even things that are not objects, like weather or landscape or temperature, all sorts of things that are bigger than myself, things that are all-enveloping. What began to fascinate me was how a work occupies a space and what its role is there; it can reach high up, and it can have the potential to fall over, it can stretch, or it can unravel. So it was a curiosity about the object as a sentient thing that emulated my own curiosity about experiences that are bigger than myself physically and maybe psychologically as well. It wasn't so much about championing huge sculpture as it was the adventure of reaching up there, or reaching across there, or of something blocking or interrupting that reach. They were quite aggressive ways of changing how I was thinking about space or about human interaction with space.

RE: You don't view sculpture in an autonomous context as much as a relational one. So it is the relationship of one piece to another that engages you. How, then, in an exhibition like BRINK, would I think of my movement through the separate sculptures?

PB: That's interesting. The space is in this amazing museum in Aachen, and the exhibition space is four steps down in a sunken area (figs. 58, 111, 124). It was very important for you to see the sculptures from above as well as at eye level when you got down into the space with them. So I hoped there were those kinds of invitation to the viewer to move into the work. They were very separate pieces in BRINK, and I wanted each one to have a special relationship to the space around it. I was hoping the viewer would be encouraged to move in relationship to the objects that would both lure them into the space or prevent them from doing that, so they would have to go on a different route. To me, viewers always become protagonists on equal footing with the sculptures they are looking at. So the way in which the works are set up in a space becomes very performative to me. That show was much more than a set of autonomous works that cropped up in awkward relationships to the step-down space that was there.

RE: You talk about the theatrical, and you're drawn to the dramatic. In a sense, you 'stage' the individual pieces inside the exhibition.

PB: That's a much more succinct way of putting it. Yes, they are staged, and they're staged in a way to rebuff and to form relationships with each other, ones that are both in contrast to and in empathy with each other. It is very much about working out what each sculpture will do to the one that's nearest to or opposite it. So the installing process is always quite fraught. It's like a performative act finding out whether objects will tolerate each other.

RE: One of the most successful examples of that theatrical encounter was what you were able to do with *folly* in the British Pavilion (figs. 79–80, 121–3). Did the architectural space encourage you to set up entrances and exits?

PB: That was exactly what I wanted. In a way, I wanted the work to erupt and surprise. The British Pavilion is a polite pastiche of a building, and it seemed exciting to try to explore it well beyond its confines. The height of it was quite important in blocking off what was actually quite a small building and having it collapse and unfold at the same time. The spaces open up and close up all the way round but in this very theatrical way.

RE: And you even extend it outside the building. Your installation begins before the viewer even enters the building.

PB: Yes. It was very enjoyable to make those absurd objects. I'm not actually sure what they are, but I wanted to add that element of absurdity. Years ago we went to see *Ubu Roi*, the play by Alfred Jarry, and its bombastic absurdity attracted me. I've always been attracted to the incongruous, the out-of-sync, to something that doesn't quite fit, or that you can't quite gauge what it is. That state of unknowing is both pleasurable and uncomfortable.

RE: When I first saw *untitled: balcony* from 2012 (figs. 107–8), I thought of Manet, but as I came to recognise how much you love theatre, it occurred to me that I should have been thinking of Shakespeare's *Romeo and Juliet* rather than painting.

PB: It comes from a fascination with architectural conceits that are almost like gestures to grandeur. But balconies come in all kinds of forms; there are grandiose balconies but there are also social housing balconies, these

RIGHT:
fig. 124 Installation view, *Phyllida Barlow: BRINK*, Ludwig Forum für Internationale Kunst, Aachen, Germany, 2012; foreground: *untitled: stackedobjectsonapiano*, 2012; background: *untitled: leaningfence*, 2012

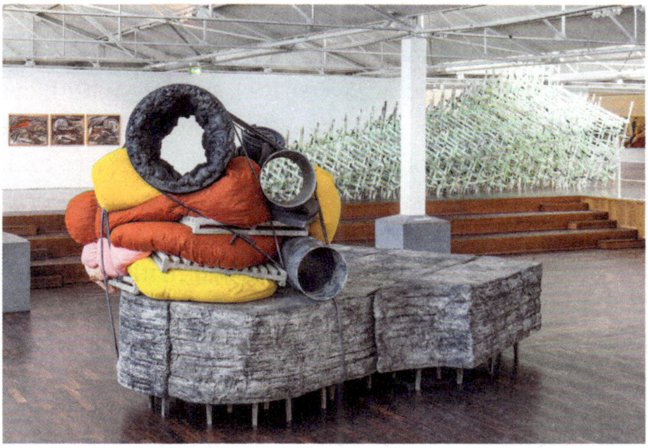

BELOW:
fig. 125 *untitled: bottle rack*, 2007

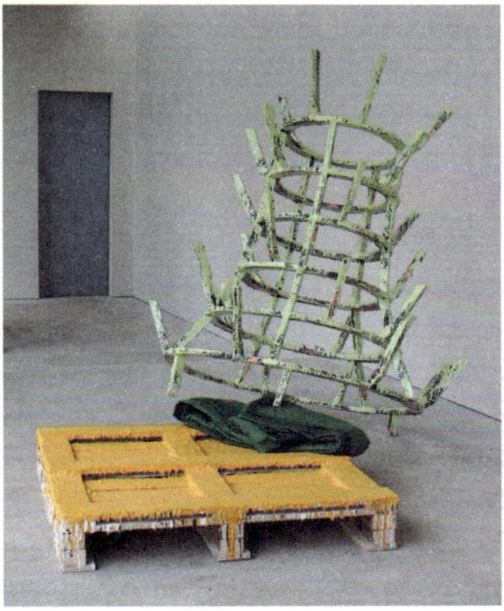

BELOW:
fig. 126 *untitled: folly; pianostack/anvil; 2016/2017*, 2016–17

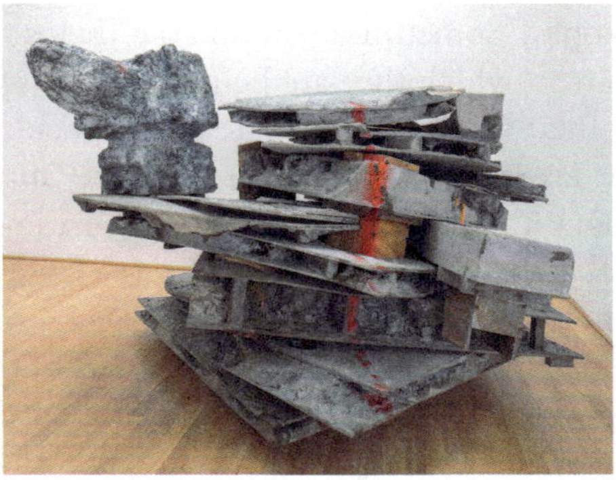

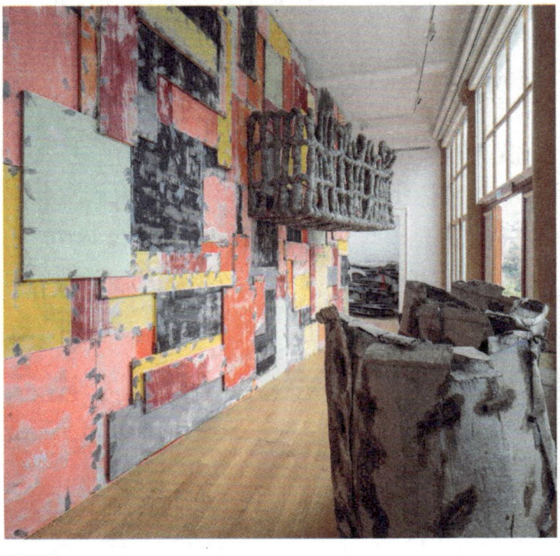

ABOVE:
fig. 127 Installation view, *Phyllida Barlow: folly*, British Pavilion, 57th Venice Biennale, 2017

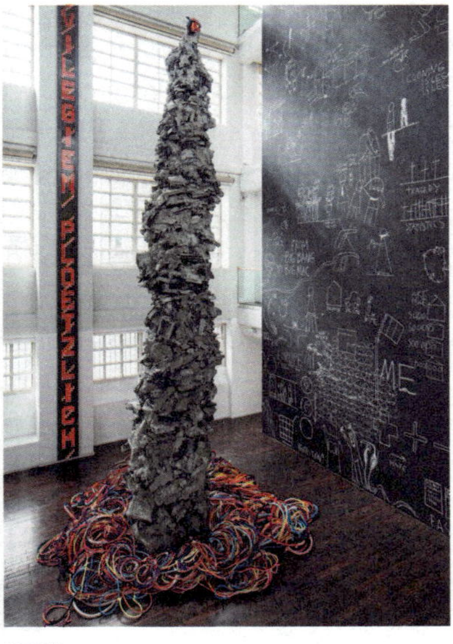

ABOVE:
fig. 128 *untitled: sadmonument*, 2012, installation view, *Phyllida Barlow: BRINK*, Ludwig Forum für Internationale Kunst, Aachen, Germany, 2012

extraordinary extra spaces that extend the living accommodations and often get used as basic storage spaces, bulging with bicycles and prams and God knows what. I like the idea of the building being extended beyond its interior to the exterior. But in another way they are follies, especially the Baroque balconies that you get in Vienna that don't look as if they can be used. But they do aspire to some kind of grandeur. I'm intrigued by them as architectural props. The theatrical is automatically inherent. And it's operatic.

RE: You do have this tendency to want to take the mickey out of grandeur, and at Tate Britain you go full on in that direction.

PB: Yes. I don't know what I would call it, but it is a kind of resistance or questioning of what and who has authority. When you see these monuments and statues all over cities like London, you naturally ask, 'Who are all these people?' Sometimes you find out they have done appalling things in various wars in which they are being idealised as heroes – people who sent millions to their death, etc. So there is this paradox about authority that goes back to my art-school days, which were very male-orientated. I wasn't too bothered about it. I did have a lot of determination and was prepared to be quite isolated and almost able to observe from the edges. But there were also people who were very supportive, so it's not a bad-luck story at all. It's just one of witnessing social change, being part of that social change and recognising how ingrained certain attitudes were. I think that was what made me have a real questioning of who owns authority and how it comes about.

RE: The titles of your exhibitions pose questions as much as they provide answers. I'm thinking of the precariousness of a name like *BRINK* or the ambiguity of the title *folly*. Even the naming of your work questions the notion of certainty. Are you suspicious about the idea of certainty?

PB: That's very observant and helpful. Yes, I'm suspicious of certainty. And it's not that continual doubt is a good thing. If it's cultivated it can lead to a kind of fear of what to do. But I think that doubt as a presence is very interesting, and I see it as a partner to certainty in a way, as a reciprocating condition.

RE: You talk about the 'slippage of objects' where no clear meanings emerge and where other meanings can arise ambiguously. If meaning can slip around, then you can't get caught within a framework that is too tidy.

PB: Yes. I challenge anyone to make something that doesn't have meaning. When you begin with a piece of paper and a pencil, you're already on some kind of semiotic trail. Of course the observations of the world around are very important to me, but are they just figures to be able to start something? I think they are, and the thing that gets made or the thing that gets drawn displaces that original experience quite quickly. There isn't a lingering need to hang on to that. It's almost as if I want the thing I'm making to lead me somewhere that is a long way from that original moment of seeing, like a fleeting witnessing of an object or a surface, and then using that as an ignition point and waiting to see where it lands.

RE: You seem to have decided that sculpture is a 'collection of redundant things', as you say, but that they do have associations and metaphors attached to them. In that sense meaning is embedded in the making.

PB: Yes, it is. I think my enemy is the simile, that it is like something. Of course, that is impossible to avoid. But the aspiration is for the metaphor. It is this; it is crushed; it is about to fall. It has these qualities that are not about image or an actual thing, but about a condition that it's in. I think achieving that is asking a lot and I'm not sure I've got there yet.

RE: One of the most compelling things about your work is the way you invest it with a sense of precarious balance. It's obvious in a piece like *leaningfence* (fig. 124). But so many of your sculptures – *TIP*, for example (fig. 67) – have this feeling of being carefully balanced in space. What is so attractive about that precarity?

PB: I think it is what you were saying about certainty. It's about the in-between, about things that are redundant, but you don't quite know what they're about to become through their redundancy. It's also to do with naming: when something is redundant and is no longer useful, what name does it have? I'm sitting in an industrial space, and they're just chucking out all these broken pallets, so they're no longer pallets in a functional sense. So what have they become? They're in a sort of limbo land, uncertain about their identity. That also happens with the way things lose their actual state of permanency, through redundancy, through age and through time. They begin to tilt or lean or even fall over. In nature, a tree crashes to the ground and becomes a fallen tree. Eventually it will no longer have the identity of a tree. I find that fascinating, these eons of time while things go through slow change or they happen in a split second. It intrigues me to try to use that.

RE: When you mention pallets, I'm reminded of your piece called *untitled: bottle rack* from 2007 (fig. 125). Of course, when you see the rack you can't help but feel the reference to Marcel Duchamp, but then you add the yellow pallet and the green fabric drop cloth. So we're in Duchamp land and then we're also in Isa Genzken land. Do you want to invoke other artists in your own sculptures?

PB: Duchamp does set a benchmark for artists that I find very difficult. What he did was to completely change the way an artist might relate to the world and how that becomes a work of art. There's no going back, but as the decades pass, Duchamp becomes more and more a kind of academic prop. I hate to say this, but I think he provides this intellectual and academic status to how we think about art. I regard it as very problematic that his work is seen as the highest intellectual status. I'm curious about how one might challenge that. I see Duchamp as a kind of opposing force. I'm glad that he's there but I'm not in any way, shape, or form of that Duchampian genetic strain.

RE: I'm going to go back briefly to *TIP* and make a curious suggestion. Those red sticks seem to be advancing on the museum entrance as if they're involved in some kind of military deployment. It reminded me of Paolo Uccello's *Battle of San Romano*. It has this sense of structure combined with a hint of imminent danger.

PB: Those are qualities that I'm interested in although I wasn't necessarily thinking of it as an attack on the museum. There is a Richard Serra right next to it, so I thought of something that was a companion to the Serra but that had a different force and energy, something that was fragmented but that became whole, and that was horizontal as well as vertical. So I saw it as an element of chaos, of disorder quite meticulously arranged. Putting that work up was like doing a painting. I was standing there and directing where these uprights went. The actual building of it in situ was exhilarating and nerve-racking. It's not a whole sculpture that gets moved in by cranes. I was playing with that opposition to the Serra and with something like a spillage, with an eruption of what a museum contains. But the artists who have been important to me are Eva Hesse and Gordon Matta-Clark, the early Robert Morris, Louise Nevelson, Louise Bourgeois, Judy Pfaff, Lee Bontecou, and Rebecca Horn. I think there are also a lot of artists who looked at chaos and said, I can't do that. Artists can't do absolute chaos. That's for nature and for cataclysmic human disasters in war. We can imitate it, or we can emulate it in some other way, which goes back to your point about metaphor. You know, the idea that you're going to take on nature and the havoc it wreaks. I mean, nature doesn't think I'm going to wreak havoc; it's just nature. Look at the carnage after tsunamis and hurricanes; art can't do that. We can photograph it and film it, but to try to make one's art be like that won't happen. So there has to be a way of understanding what objecthood is, and how something thrown to the ground or torn or shredded becomes a state in itself. It may remind us of those things, but it absolutely isn't those things.

RE: Your work raises interesting questions about process. There are times when I think it is not so much assembled as scattered in space. Which makes me ask, how predetermined is your process? I know there were drawings for each of the rooms in *folly*. Do you always know where the piece is going to go, or is the piece discovered in its making?

PB: I think my preferred state of play is that I don't know anything. But there's a tautology with these high-profile exhibitions. It becomes important for the people who are administrating these things to know something about where the work is going. I've fallen afoul of that, and it does create huge problems for everybody, and problems mean money. I've had to learn to say that by such and such a date I know what's going where, so that people can put things in motion. At the British Council it was necessary to have a plan, and while one room changed, on the whole it was close to what I had originally conceived. In the end the massive undertaking of the Venice Biennale and the amount of work it involved caused me to reconsider what I'd done, and I have to admit it was almost as though I had a revulsion to my own work after Venice. Since then I've been trying out different routes that allow more simple gestures to be more fully exposed rather than having the fabrication and the manufacturing process be so incredibly full-on. In Venice the labour attached to the making and the use of the handmade was raised almost to a punitive extreme, and stepping back and relinquishing some of that seemed to address some kind of finale.

RE: That's especially interesting because you have referred to 'the fragile edge of losing control'. Again, it seems a question of giving yourself permission inside the making of a piece rather than having it conform to some predetermined notion about what it should be.

PB: Yes, there is that push me/pull me thing. There might be something I want to do, a binding with plaster or various pieces of steel, and then the process involves watching them gradually take form, even though I'm not sure of the outcome. The outcome will reveal itself. It's reclaiming the action of the thing leading the work rather than knowing that the things are going to be very tall and column-like. So, yes, it is inviting change and action more full-bloodedly back into the work. And there were many works in Venice that did have a sense of not quite knowing where they were going. That's my preferred state of working but it doesn't always end up like that.

RE: The middle name of a three-part piece called *crashedlintelbrokensculpturepaintedtarps* seems to imply that composition, for you, isn't just about making but also about unmaking. What I'm trying to get at is the way in which the making of the work is also an unravelling and whether that can be productive for you.

PB: Definitely. In the third room in Venice, there's an anvil sitting on a stack of stuff, and the stack began as totally different objects that got destroyed (fig. 126). They were going to go in the front of the pavilion but that wasn't allowed. I began to make them and was told where I had planned to locate them was common ground that couldn't be owned by anyone. I didn't quite know what the rules were. They were being processed as these grand-piano-like objects and they were being broken down in order to be chucked out. So we stacked them on top of each other, and it seemed a simple and satisfactory solution. So, yes, the unmaking and the making are very symbiotic. For me, sculpture is not necessarily finite; it's almost as if some of the work is caught halfway between its beginning and its end. It's almost a state of expediency to say, 'That's it.' Again, I'm back to certainty and uncertainty. I'm not completely convinced it is it, but it's certainly as good as it gets at that moment and there is a sense that if it goes any further, it will just become rubble. Sometimes there is a tension about knowing where to stop.

RE: When you're making a piece or a series of sculptures, whether in Des Moines or New York or Aachen, do you find the materials in the place, or do you more often take the material you need to the location and then make the piece there?

PB: For the last eight years most of the work emerges from the studio in various sections or in pieces and then gets assembled on-site, so I don't get materials there. The last one I did like that was in Nuremberg for the show at the Kunstverein in 2011 (fig. 52).

RE: One of the tensions that comes up in your practice is whether the space dominates the work or the work the space.

PB: For a long time sculpture as a commodity was not on the agenda for me at all, and therefore this idea of staging and the theatricality of the experience were such a stark contrast to the actual making of the work, which is private and has its shambolic moments. Then when the work is actually delivered to the site, it's suddenly as though the performance has begun, and these new tensions arise. It's as if the work actually begins when it gets to the space and my relationship to and memories of the space will then be put to the test. The script gets thrown away and a whole new generative process of making begins. It's not so much about placing an object and revering that object's placement as it is about its relationship to the space. Is the space dominant or is the object dominant; does the space become as much an object as the object itself? There are so many issues that begin to stake their claim in how this performance is going to take shape. This is the fascination I have with the totality of the whole experience rather than with the notion of the single dominant object. But I have to say that I am becoming interested in allowing a single object to have more space to play in. What seems to have emerged after Venice is a relooking at what space and the object do together and how my language can expand and evolve that relationship.

RE: I want to know how painting and drawing fit into your sculptural production. You have said that sculpture began as a dialogue with painting, and it seems like painting has remained a constant aspect of your practice. Is that an accurate assessment?

PB: Yes, it is but it's not through avoiding it. I'm not sure that I regard my drawings, which happen to use paint, as paintings. I still see them very much as drawings, but to actually turn them into paintings is a development that I very much want to pursue. I want to go bigger and see what happens when they are no longer these drawings. I'm not quite sure how to explain it, but there seems to be a mental process that makes them be that. It's almost as if I'm trying to find something out about them and drawing is the closest way for me to get out what is going on in my head. Maybe I see painting as a more evolved form where there is some knowledge of how certain things can work together, and that it is no longer about guesswork. The way I am using colour and the way I am using paint are very much about speculation and guesswork. It is a very direct way of thinking about what I'm making or what I'm going to make.

RE: When I saw *stockade* (fig. 111) I thought it was a colourful *Merzbau*. It has a collage sense, too. Was there a way to get into *stockade*, or was it hermetic and so you could only walk around it?

PB: No, you couldn't get into it. The only point of looking was from the staircase that went up through it and then you got a glimpse inside. But what you say about the *Merzbau* is interesting. Again, it was very much about creating a space that the viewer could be in as a protagonist. It was about making a very conscious experience of walking around, so that in my mind what was being walked around was invisible, but there was also a sense of its interior that you saw as you walked up the stairs. So there was a sense of speculation about the inside of this object when you're on the outside, but you are still on the inside because you are in a building. A bit like the balcony on the inside. Again, I was hoping to play with the protagonist/viewer's being involved in a theatrical event without a script or a plot or anything. Wandering around backstage at a theatre is one of the most fascinating experiences because everything is about to happen.

RE: The other thing you realise is that everything is a construction, a world made for your entertainment, and that it is all smoke and mirrors.

PB: Exactly. I do think sculpture is a bit fake. The whole thing of bringing into the world these objects that compete with all the other objects in the world is a bit of a sham. They're kind of pretenders, and I love that. It intrigues me.

RE: You said about *folly* that it 'began to unfold in a way that was almost natural.' So do you end up telling yourself stories about the relationship between and among the pieces in an exhibition? What is this notion of narrative that you're talking about that is so intriguing to you?

PB: It's a spatial narrative. The filled-up space, the half-empty space, the maybe-once-occupied space, the left-behind space, the space that's in waiting. You know, those kind of attic or basement spaces, or thoroughfare spaces, or intimidating spaces. The characteristics can be enhanced or argued with through what is done to them – that's what I see as the narrative rather than an actual story. Maybe in Venice it was the full space, almost like a redundant museum with objects-in-waiting, followed by a folly space with the balcony (fig. 127). The characteristics of each space related very much to the one that was before and the one that was about to be encountered.

RE: You've talked about the desire you have to employ all the different languages of sculpture. As you have made more and more work, does the vocabulary expand, or does it become a reduced one that you want to focus on?

PB: I suppose there is an historical thing about that. When I was busy rejecting so much of the modernist vernacular of the 1920s, 1930s, 1940s, and 1950s, I began to realise that it was deeply ingrained within me, it was innate and there was a real love of that sculpture. I actually realised that I wanted to concede and say yes to these rounded forms of Barbara Hepworth and the nooks and crannies of Henry Moore and to extraordinary French sculptors like Ossip Zadkine. Very awkward, ugly things had a real fascination for me, and rather than claiming that Arte Povera changed everything for me, I could embrace all these different languages and not be afraid to use extremely difficult, awkward sculptural languages. I could enjoy them as much as I might enjoy some Minimalism or the very gestural aspects of Arte Povera. Now I'm sorting out and prioritising things in a different way where the simpler the work, the more particular it can be about that clash of mixed and very different languages. They can all be used and they all have some huge value to me. I don't have to have a preference or a hierarchy.

RE: When I saw the *arches* at the New Museum in 2012, I thought they were a cross between three-dimensional, late Philip Guston, and Stonehenge. There was something so awkwardly chthonic about them. The reason I mention Guston is that you have talked about your embrace of the not-attractive, the deliberately not-refined, and Guston is the progenitor of a radical shift in the way that painting could be made.

PB: People often mention him in reference to my work. He's been there and I've increasingly loved his work but I've never been consciously influenced by him. He's not like Franz West or early Bourgeois or Hesse. I've looked at and absorbed his work, but I've never said I need to emulate him. In some ways he is just there naturally. He was a radical artist but not in the usual way, not in setting out to reinvent the wheel like Duchamp or Jackson Pollock but more obliquely. Those artists are increasingly interesting me more than the great game changers.

RE: You say your need in sculpture is for a constant cycle of change. Because you reuse material, you are manifesting that cycle in a material way. But is there something philosophical about your commitment to change that goes beyond a material preoccupation?

PB: Yes, there is. The whole process of using materials that become fixed and then forcing them to change takes on a formidable presence when you work with uncertainty. I'm working with the sense that there may be a lot that I don't know about what I am doing and that sometimes I don't know where the end or the finish is. All these aspects of the object emerging go against the ways in which objects are produced or made in the rest of the world. When you're making a car or a chair, you've got to know what you're doing to end up with that thing. Sculpture seems to enjoy this special category of making where you don't have to know those things. I embrace that and want to take it on. It means that changes of mind and changes of direction are inherent, and I am constantly asking whether this is the way to go, or is that the way to go. When I say I had a revulsion to the Venice works, that doesn't mean it was time to have a breakdown. Quite the opposite. It was time to ask a series of questions. What is a single object for someone who's always made objects in groups, or in relationship to the space? What can a single object do when it's encountered, when it is just the two protagonists? I'm very excited by discovering how that works out. What I cherish about sculpture is its obduracy but also its relationship to action. I want to keep those two very opposing conditions in full play whilst I'm challenging all sorts of other things about the way I make work.

RE: You have that lovely idea about what you call 'the phantom state of objects' that can come from either dreams or memories. What do you mean by that? I don't want to say it's a trope because I know you're not fond of them, but there is something very poetic about the phrase.

PB: I think we can all find associations with things; it's the nature of verbal language and the nature of semiotics. Even if we don't know what something is, we say it is like this or it is like that. I'm sure it's the human way of surviving. But to make things that might have an origin in the world but through the act of making they become something else is like making a phantom for me. It seems to resonate with some kind of familiarity, but it can't be that thing because it is not functioning as that thing, or it is somehow masquerading as that thing. Like the columns in Venice: they're not real columns; they're not theatre columns; they're not a whole load of things and that lets them take on this phantom quality. I would say you can look at a Constantin Brâncuşi head or a Brâncuşi stacked object and you're truly groping for some kind of relationship. It's not difficult to have a relationship with them, but to actually know what the verbal equivalent is to these things is tricky. Naming them is very difficult.

RE: You have a totemic work called *untitled: sadmonument* (fig. 128), and you have this idea of 'tragic monuments'. It makes me wonder if in some sense you are a chronicler of a lost time, and that despite its exuberance and intensity and passion, your work has an elegiac quality.

PB: This is complicated. Although I can't make a great emotional claim, the shadow of World War II is a very long shadow, and its generational impact doesn't go away. It's odd how it lingers and resurfaces in various forms. I think my emotional relationship with power and what the act of making things is in relationship to that is a quite tangled emotional web. Maybe there is even some weird guilt about making sculpture. You know, these things involve everything I shouldn't be involved in – there's masculinity and aggression, there's materials that pollute, there's materiality, expense, there's probably even indulgence. The list is endless. But at the same time there is something about making things that are unlike anything else in the world and that are irrefutable in their lack of use that seems necessary, that is an element of positivity. Maybe the abject monument, the monument that's fallen, the monument that no longer serves its purpose, is a reminder of a futility that, in its own way, is positive. Futility isn't just a negative quality; it enables positive things to emerge. Opposites are always intriguing.

First published as 'All Sorts of Things That Are Bigger Than Myself: The Sculptural World of Phyllida Barlow', *Border Crossings* 148 (December 2018): 34–46.

ON DRAWING

This very brief text by Barlow outlines the role of drawing in her practice and was published in the exhibition catalogue for *British Sculptors: Attitudes to Drawing* held at Sunderland Arts Centre, Sunderland, UK, in 1974. Barlow's work was included in this group show alongside artists such as Michael Craig-Martin, Barry Flanagan, and Elisabeth Frink. Written when she was thirty years old, her text is reprinted here to show the remarkable consistency with which Barlow has approached her work.

My Drawing

1974

My drawing is a relaxed activity compared to the heavy work of making sculpture. It is often only just a more intense form of doodling and scribbling. Ideas begin from landscape, rooms, figures, and piles of rubbish and debris that I have seen, but the action of making marks seems to take over from the original observation.

The marks on paper attempt to form themselves into makeable objects but they are objects which have no reality as regards technical problems and material. The drawings provide the clues as to what I should make – they are not reproductions on paper of finished sculptures.

The quickness with which an image can be formed through the unfolding of line and bright blocks of colour is an end in itself. The enjoyment of this is an escape from sculpture where I can never achieve this kind of immediacy.

First published in Edward Lucie-Smith, *British Sculptors: Attitudes to Drawing* (Sunderland: Sunderland Arts Centre, 1974), unpaginated.

Published in *Saatchi Gallery Magazine, Art & Music* in 2011, this text is a poetic description of the way in which Barlow approaches making works on paper – an activity which lies at the very core of her practice.

A Brilliant Way of Looking: A Brief Account of Making a Drawing

2011

Drawing
is
doing whatever I want
Usually at the end of the day
when exhausted
often until late
into the early hours
Make it up
Refute logic
Defy gravity
Remove location
Remove materials (for making)
Could be timber, ply, plaster, cement, paint,
Always sculpture
Test reality
Plot how to make
Work it out
Choose materials
Seek out information
Be undecided
Be decided
See differences
Change size
Change position
Change point of view
Be pictorial
Forget sculpture
Be solid
Be vague
Be curious
Use weight
Or weightlessness
Make it sculptural
Solid

Or unsculptural
Wet
Paint
Draw into
Be surprised
Do it again
Paint it out
Begin again
Colour is shape
Edges
Of colour against colour
Shapes
Edgelessness
Something up against something else
Be quick
Stop sooner
Wait
Next time
Go over
One line
Stop

First published as 'A Brilliant Way of Looking: A Brief Account of Making a Drawing', *The Saatchi Gallery Magazine, Art & Music* (2011), 32.

This interview with curator Sophie Raikes, extracted from various spoken and written conversations in February 2012, focusses on Barlow's drawing practice. It was included in volume 65 of the Henry Moore Institute Essays on Sculpture series, *Bad Copies: The Drawings of Phyllida Barlow*, which accompanied an exhibition of her drawings at Leeds Art Gallery in 2012. Barlow talks about being taught drawing at Chelsea College of Arts, London, and the Slade School of Fine Art, London, detailing some of the advice she was given and teachers she encountered. She speaks of drawing as a daily activity and describes her use of sketchbooks. She cites 2001 as a turning point for the role of drawing in her work, discusses her use of paint, her studio set-up, and notes that she does not want her drawings to be illustrations for sculptures.

Interview with Sophie Raikes

2012

Sophie Raikes: You have spoken extensively about your experiences at art school in interviews and lectures. I would like to specifically ask you about how you learnt to draw. I am particularly interested in your experiences at Chelsea School of Art, where you studied between 1960 and 1963, and the Slade School of Fine Art, where you were based between 1963 and 1966. What was the attitude at Chelsea and the Slade to drawing? How were materials, subject matter, and technique addressed? How did you respond to the approaches of your tutors?

Phyllida Barlow: I have never thought of myself as being good at drawing. Henry Moore in fact confirmed this when he looked at my drawings in an interview for the Boise Travel Scholarship in 1963. Moore told me: 'You need to do a lot more drawing – practice a lot.' My problem was with life drawing. I think I did not, and still do not, have the ability to concentrate on the study of something. I probably use my memory more than direct observational experience. However there was some wonderful and memorable advice given to me by the likes of artists Michael Andrews, Liz Frink, Robert Clatworthy, Lawrence Gowing, and Myles Murphy, who taught me. Older tutors would always draw on your drawing, and that, for me, came as a huge relief.

A wonderful, completely deaf artist, Vivian Pitchforth, taught by 'correcting' the students' drawings in complete silence. It was Mike Andrews who suggested working from the inside of the form of the figure and forgetting about the edge, or outline, recommending: 'Just let the figure emerge from the inside, without the edges.' I found that advice liberating, but my drawings were still terrible. And it was Myles Murphy, a Euston Road painter, who suggested I look at Matisse's drawings because, when looked at closely, there were surprises. You would see not just one line but many, as well as many which had been erased. You can see his thinking, not just wanting a likeness, but also wanting the drawing to exist in its own right. The drawings are so much more than simple linear representations, they hold form in all of that empty space. The idea of empty space in a drawing being full of form was thrilling.

Then there was Ian Stephenson, hotfoot from Newcastle, and the experimental ideas of teaching initiated by Victor Pasmore and Richard Hamilton. Ian Stephenson set up a whole course at Chelsea where there was no life drawing. Instead, actions were used repetitively. These included writing, dropping, spilling, tearing, scratching, working with mirror images, working with your eyes shut, using your left hand or right hand (the one you usually didn't use). A whole host of other methods were instigated as ways of working. It was powerful stuff at the time. Some students were absolutely horrified, but what he was doing was to become significant in how and what foundation courses were to offer artists at a later date. It became clear that for me drawing should be developed outside of the life room and that memory was important – the act of remembering something, recalling selected qualities so that the choice, and how to choose, became a significant creative act. Eventually I found that it was the process of drawing for sculpture that became particularly important.

George Fullard was a great inspiration. He was, though, against the idea of sculptors' drawings being illustrations of a proposed work. Sometimes I do feel that my drawings have been and can be 'illustrations' for sculptures. I don't want them to be this. Maybe the reason I have used painterly processes when drawing has been to avoid illustration and develop qualities of what a proposed sculpture might entail through the use of colour as much as line. Colour provides a kind of mass, which can be abstract as well as image. Fullard quoted Picasso frequently, always recommending his drawings as immediate and spontaneous thoughts that could be turned into anything, sculpture or painting, or could just remain themselves. Fullard was intrigued by how children draw. He always issued a severe warning to not try to draw like a child, rather to draw without trying too hard. He advised not to try and make a great drawing, but to keep the process as intimate and as close to the action of drawing as possible. Fullard would recommend drawing when exhausted, as then you would edit out all the fuss and be only able to do what was essential.

When I arrived at the Slade in 1963 I missed the inspirational teaching I had experienced at Chelsea. It was replaced by a rather moral attitude to drawing. William Coldstream was, surprisingly, the least of the moralists. He recommended that there were very few criteria for measuring a good drawing from a bad drawing. Coldstream had instigated a visiting artists programme – Larry Rivers was the visiting artist at the time I was studying. Rivers came to the studio I was in and looked at my drawings. 'Are you British?' he asked. I admitted that I was, and he said, 'well these are very un-British drawings, keep going, they are OK, and could get better.' I was too stunned to ask what a British drawing was and what an un-British drawing could possibly be. But it was a boost to my confidence, and it felt good. That was in about 1964.

There is one anecdote I love because it sums up for me the incredible authority and timelessness of drawing. I was at the Slade teaching around the early 1990s and having a coffee with a colleague, a wonderful tutor and artist, Norman Norris. We were looking at a photograph that was on the front page of *The Times* newspaper. The photograph showed some spectacular cave drawings of bison and deer that had been recently discovered in the south of France. These drawings were estimated as being thirty thousand years old. Norman was silent and thoughtful for some time. Then he turned to me and said: 'Has drawing got any better?'

SR: You have also spoken of drawing being a daily activity. Could you say what this means in practice?

PB: I do some kind of drawing a lot. It is not a duty. Or a necessity. Or a self-conscious habit. It is just a simple activity. Sometimes it is a reminder, sometimes just a fidgety thing – something to do. When I have had fallow times I still continued to doodle on scraps of paper, in the margins of things I was meant to be writing for teaching purposes and on anything else that was to hand. I have about five or six sketchbooks on the go at any one time, scattered in different rooms and in my studios. The sketchbook activity is purposefully disorganised to keep things open and to make sure that it does not become too important.

The sketchbooks contain anything, from lists of materials, telephone numbers, names, shopping lists for Sainsbury's supermarket, memos and diagrams, drawings, workings-out. Consequently interesting drawings are few and far between, they are there buried in amongst everything else. There is always something I want to get down as a quick drawing. Forgetting is useful. It is a kind of editing. If it can't be remembered then it didn't have to be remembered and will probably come up again at another time. Some things have reoccurred again and again over the decades – enclosed spaces, stacked towers, heaped objects, placards, and hoardings, amorphous shapes, folded shapes, broken things, ramps, fences, grids, barriers. Is it unusual to draw the whole time?

Since about 2001 drawing has become a very important part of how I make the sculptures. It all began with coming to a complete standstill with making sculpture in the summer of 2001, after *British Art Show 5*. The work I had made for that exhibition was titled *after dark into black* (fig. 129). I was thrilled with making the work and the whole drama of installing the work in the Dean Gallery, Edinburgh. But after the excitement of it all coming together I was disappointed. Also embarrassed. It was such a histrionic work, so attention seeking. I wanted to run away from it. Then during that summer of 2001, I had a strong desire to make something in opposition to *after dark into black* – to pour stuff, fill things up, break things, squash, push, pile up, to be formless and edgeless. But it was all too difficult. The amount

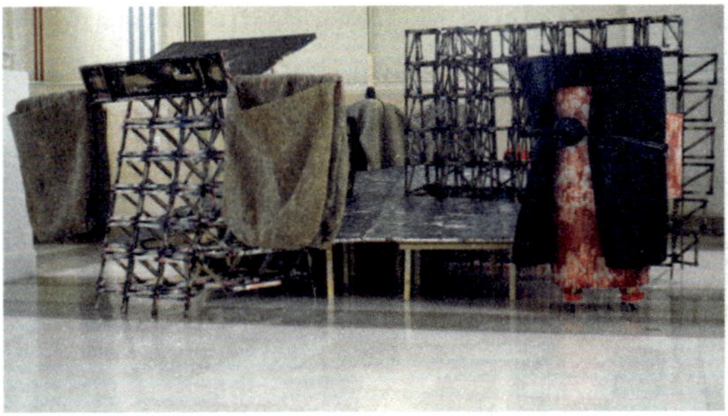 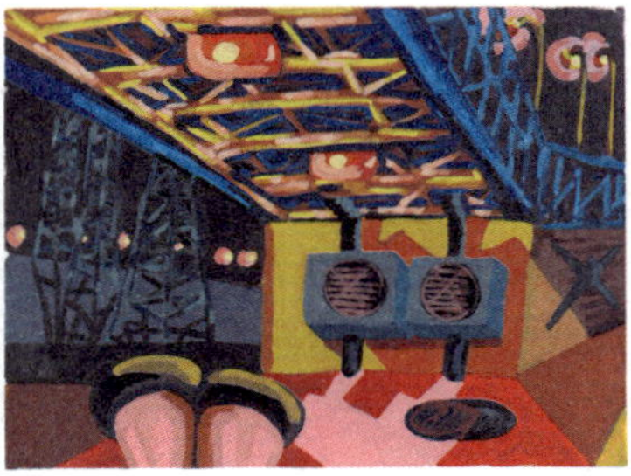

LEFT TO RIGHT:
fig. 129 *after dark into black*, 2000–1
fig. 130 *untitled*, 2001

of materials was absurd, and the weight of the works became a limitation in itself. Nothing was happening with all these actions and the studio was becoming unmanageable. It was like the worst kind of loss of control – not a loss of control in a good way where things are discovered and surprises happen, but in a desperate, unproductive way where I was repeating actions from before and getting nowhere.

I began to photograph things out on the street and especially on walks with our dog on Walthamstow Marshes, along the canal, and in other urban spaces. But the things I photographed I wanted as isolated objects, for them to be sculptures in the making. I did not want the other things that were included in the photographs, such as people, hedges, trees, and pathways. I then stopped taking photographs, and instead made small impromptu drawings in sketchbooks. These combined with remembering images, objects, views, and so on, became the resource for about sixty drawings I produced during that summer of 2001. They were very formulaic. All were done on watercolour paper with acrylic. All fill the entire sheet. All were the same size (approximately fifty-eight by seventy-two centimetres), and all were landscape (figs. 130, 139).

I felt I was hanging on to a creative drive by the skin of my teeth. My longing to be making dominated this time. However these drawings culled from 'urban' walks were a turning point. They formed themselves into an archive of observed things. For a few years following this summer the resulting drawings were the basis for many sculptural works in many venues, culminating in the works I showed at the BALTIC and *SKIT* at Bloomberg.

Making those drawings set a precedent. It has now become essential for me to get thoughts about possible works down as directly and as quickly as possible. It is a way of testing out a possible work's potential for realisation: how it might or could be, as well as what, where, how big or small; as well as asking what kind of object it is, how much space it needs or owns. Then the proposed work begins to evolve on the paper with the pushing and spreading and liquidity of the paint and changes happen. The paper has become a space. The acrylic allows both edges and mass to argue with each other. Images can become overwhelmed by blurred gestures, or can be more pronounced and as such, be a guide for how to proceed with the physical and material-making. I never know what will happen; I never know whether a drawing will be a kind of speculative 'thing' or something clear and obvious as to what it is.

I have called these works made since 2001 'coloured drawings'. They are not paintings. They retain something casual, on the margins and at the periphery of those works that demand a lot of organisation, which become more resolved and are more time consuming. These coloured drawings come about in the same way as the smaller works: quick, intimate, open to change and spontaneous decision, and irrational changes of mind and direction.

So, yes, now, I can feel bereft if I do not have drawings on the go. Since retiring from teaching in 2009, with more time to make work, it has become something of a driven feeling to make the drawings. I am always excited to know if I can make something which is a surprise, that is not what I expected, that turns out to be something I didn't know about. This is rare, but always a thrill and a challenge that today might be the day when it happens.

SR: What is the role of your studio, that is, your home studio, in your drawing practice? I am interested in how it operates both as a place for making drawings and also how it works in imaginative terms?

PB: As the children have gradually left home, various rooms at home have become available. Inevitably these have become 'studios' for both Fabian, my husband, and myself. The house is a series of working and living spaces. It has not had any upkeep attention paid to it for many years, since 1985 to be exact. Consequently it is a working environment more than just a domestic place and shows the wear and tear and degeneration which time has thrown at it.

My drawing space is a basement room. I like it because I can use it at any time and for any amount of time – a quick burst or more prolonged sessions. It is a different space to my home sculpture studio, which is a long space down the side of the house, only two metres and eight centimetres wide. It was once a builder's store. Both this sculpture studio and my drawing studio are very private places – very different from my collaborative studio in Bermondsey where the large works are produced.

The sculpture studio at home is where smaller works are made, or come about. They are produced very like the drawings where I may not be sure as to what the work is going to be. I begin with offcuts: ply, paper, fabric, wire, mesh, timber, aluminium armature, plaster, cement, scrim, paint. Perhaps a bundle of offcuts suggest something or a work is made by just beginning, joining stuff together then taking it apart and breaking it. Some gestural actions can initiate these smaller works. The use of plaster and cement is important both as a material for modelling but also as a kind of 'paint' to build up the flat wire, mesh, and ply surfaces and give them more substance.

The drawing studio is always ready. The drawings are about bringing an outside world inside. The environment of making a domestic space into a working studio space is, for me, something I have done for years. Anywhere can become a working space. It is not difficult, as many domestic spaces are associated with labour, especially the kitchen. I don't need a 'special' studio for drawing, or for making the smaller works, and the drawing 'studio' does not generate an imaginative process as a space. I have to bring my imagination to the drawings.

Sometimes it happens, and sometimes it doesn't.

First published in *Bad Copies: The Drawings of Phyllida Barlow*, Henry Moore Institute Essays on Sculpture 65 (Hertfordshire: Henry Moore Foundation, 2012), 29–36.

Included in *Phyllida Barlow: Fifty Years of Drawings*, the publication which accompanied the eponymous exhibition at Hauser & Wirth London in 2014, Hans Ulrich Obrist and Barlow conducted this interview while looking through her drawing archive together in the summer of 2011. Going decade by decade from the 1960s to the present day, they consider the influences and concerns, the movements and artists that have shaped Barlow's drawing practice. They discuss the characteristics of her drawings from each decade, her approach to making them, and how they relate to her sculptures.

Interview with Hans Ulrich Obrist

2014

Phyllida Barlow: If I think of the sixties, and I think of New British Sculpture, and I think of Pop Art and Abstract Expressionism and the rise of Marcel Duchamp, I see these drawings within that context (fig. 131).

Hans Ulrich Obrist: When we did the interview with you for the show at the Serpentine Gallery (see pages 124–38) we spoke about this moment, at art school, when the new generation of sculptors was very dominant.

PB: Yes, I think also that I was getting very angry with my art-school education, that no one had talked about them really, or about what was happening in the States. That was like a closely guarded secret. When I began to realise that there was this thing … Well, it didn't even have a name then, I don't think – Arte Povera – but there were things happening in Europe and America that were so startling compared to what was the still very traditional sculptural language of the New Generation. It was like a complete epiphany.

HUO: These are sculptural drawings.

PB: Absolutely.

HUO: So when did you realise that you were a sculptor and not a painter?

PB: 1961 – I can date it.

HUO: 1961! Do you remember the day?

PB: I think it was in a life drawing class when I just realised that I didn't understand life drawing, and there was a tutor there who said, 'I think you should come into sculpture and use clay and forget about painting and working from the figure.'

HUO: And who was the tutor?

PB: George Fullard. You'd have to do a lot of research to find out about him.

But then, just before these, the idea of breaking up things, fracturing things, was very important.

HUO: There's also a Pop element in them, I suppose?

PB: Absolutely.

HUO: The colours are very Pop, and it was the moment of English Pop Art.

PB: Yes, which came from America. Everything either came from America or Europe. I always think of the English artistic era of the 1960s and 1970s as being a kind of hybrid, looking across the Atlantic or looking across the Channel!

HUO: So it wasn't about looking at one's own history that much?

PB: No, I think that actually came much later. I remember feeling really antagonistic towards Henry Moore and Barbara Hepworth, and having just been to the Hepworth Museum and seen those Hepworths, they are just fantastic. But, I think, at that time, it was about saying 'I don't want to belong to this British tradition, which seems so moral …'

HUO: So it marked a rupture of some sort?

PB: Yes, but I don't think I succeeded. I think I'm utterly entrenched in the sculptural …

HUO: In our previous conversation, you have said about your beginnings that you felt like not a lot had changed.

PB: I didn't think it had, and it was a realisation when I then looked at these drawings. I remember putting them away, almost in disgust, because what I then began to see was this idea of fracture and breaking up. I was actually looking at things like frames, and unravelling sculptural language, or attempting to. I never feel like I managed to, I think it's a love-hate relationship with it.

HUO: Everything is already in these first works?

PB: Absolutely, and that constant argument about where the argument is, and the breaking up of space. It's all in here, a longing to escape from sculpture. In the 1960s I had been looking at a lot of American anti-form, Eva Hesse as well.

HUO: So you were already aware, in the 1960s, of Eva Hesse?

PB: By 1969, yes. I remember just thinking, what on earth am I doing? Also I was realising that the material itself could do things, like what was happening with Arte Povera. Having done very tight drawings in the mid-1960s, by the late 1960s, I was breaking that all up, and seeing the space between things as very active and beginning to understand.

HUO: There was a new freedom all of a sudden. So in 1961 you came to sculpture. Was there a day when you suddenly felt free?

PB: I'm just trying to think, but I think it was after the New Generation. It was in the space between 1967 and 1970, looking at Barry Flanagan, meeting Barry Flanagan, meeting Richard Long … various other artists who were moving outside and reinvestigating sculptural language as something not just to do with those very powerful formal concerns – Moore and Hepworth.

HUO: And Gilbert & George, their groundbreaking invention of Living Sculptures … ?

PB: Absolutely, which of course I saw in 1970, on Glebe Place – the first one. I didn't want to make that kind of art, but that was fantastic.

HUO: When we worked on the Serpentine show, we talked a lot about sculpture and not drawing. So when you did these drawings in the 1960s, did you always also do sculpture, or was the drawing, at that time, the main focus?

PB: Yes, they were always connected.

HUO: There are so many drawings here in your archive. What is the role of drawing? Because it seems like an almost daily practice. When I visited your studio you said that you would draw all the time. But is it something preparatory for the sculptures, or do they come after the sculptures, or at the same time? What is the relationship between the drawings and the sculptures?

PB: It's before, during, and after.

HUO: In all directions?

PB: Yes. It's about information. I think that, for me, the problem with sculpture is its relationship to image. But the drawings, oddly enough, are both a way of trying to form an image but give some idea of how to proceed with the making process, and then there's a kind of anarchy against that. So the drawings are often doing something quite tight, and then breaking it all down. And that breaking down often happens when I'm in the middle of making it. So there's a restlessness that sets in, where I'm almost bored and frustrated with the making process, which can often be tedious actually! It needs something else to be thrown into the mix. The small works that we had at the Serpentine, the blobs, of course, were really, really wonderful to make – the putting the surface on the grids – because there's a result. But some of the building of frames, and then the next stage, and then the next stage … it's just …

HUO: Hard?

PB: Hard. It's labour.

HUO: So in this sense, the drawings are like luggage somehow.

PB: Absolutely, yes, that's a great way of putting it. Everything always seems to come from somewhere, like ruins or streets or open spaces. Often, it's about inside/outside; it's about bringing the open space into the inside, or taking the inside to the outside, oscillating between exterior worlds and interior worlds, whether that's landscapes or rooms (fig. 132).

HUO: It's interesting that already in the 1960s there is this turning-inside-out of space. This was very present in your Serpentine show. The inside-out and outside-in of space, with these rooms and …

PB: Yes. The Serpentine is an incredible space in that respect, isn't it? Because the outside really does come in, and that was the thing that so excited me about it.

HUO: And what's the connection to architecture and design? Because very often there are interiors, there are apartments, there are blocks, there are buildings.

PB: A lot of looking at the framing of architecture and then what goes through architecture. At this time I was also very interested in things like shop-window displays, as the kind of antithesis of architecture – things arranged within the framework of structures, and how that breaks down or makes these other kinds of spaces that are almost empty spaces, but they're contained by the things around them, whether that's furniture, or objects on display, or the façades of buildings.

LEFT:

fig. 131 untitled, 1965–6

BELOW:

fig. 132 untitled, 1967–70

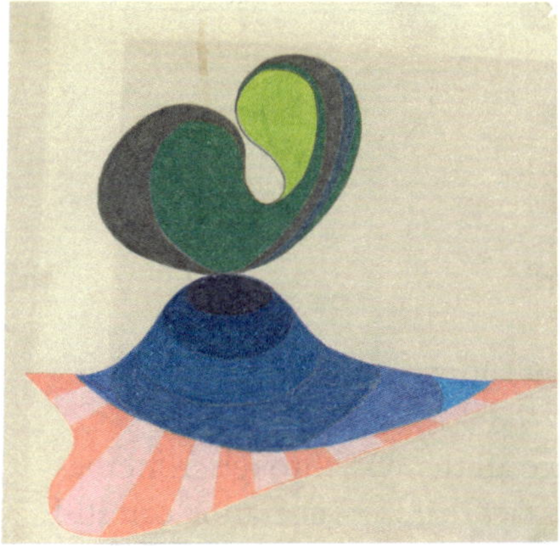

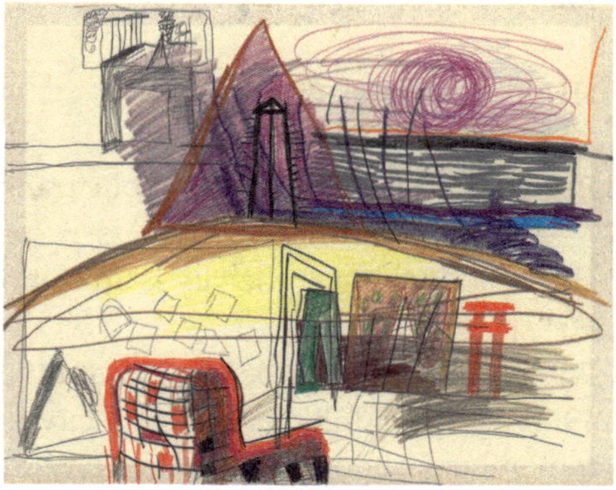

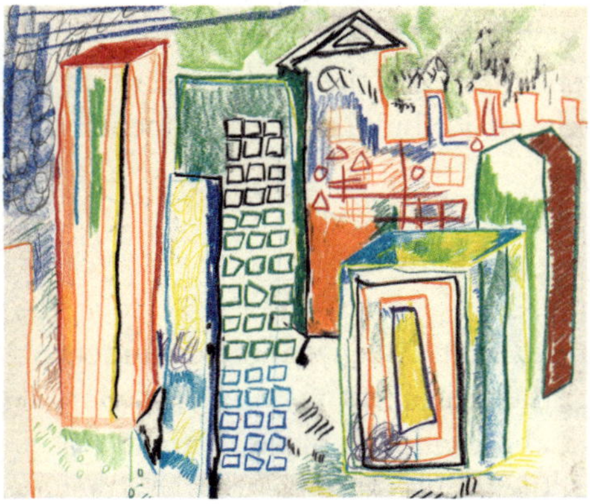

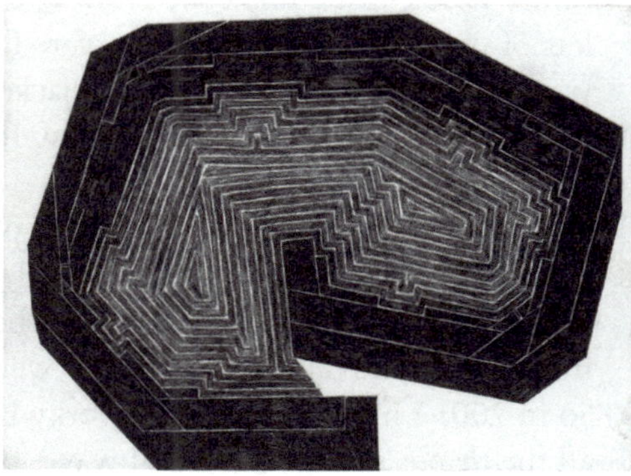

ABOVE:

fig. 133 untitled, 1968

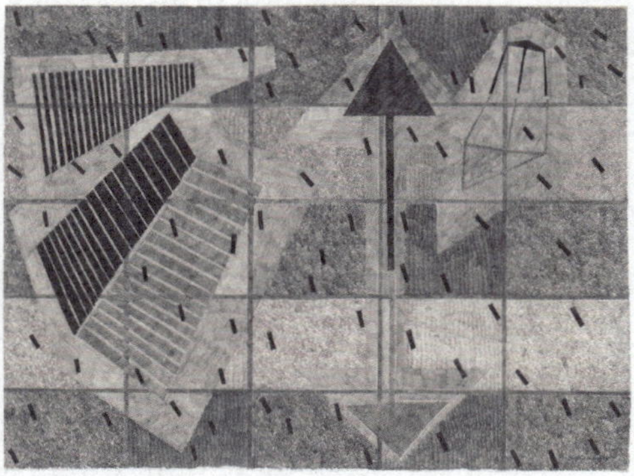

ABOVE:

fig. 134 untitled: looking down on enclosed space, 1977–80

LEFT:

fig. 135 untitled, 1975

HUO: Were you inspired by found situations?

PB: Yes, yes, very much so.

HUO: So you'd walk through London and look at …

PB: Absolutely, and that's ongoing.

HUO: Driving or walking?

PB: Walking … and buses, public transport.

HUO: So looking at the city is an important source of inspiration for you?

PB: Oh God, yes! It's been a major influence all the way through from the 1960s. And I think the changing city – the fact that my generation can still remember London as a bombed city, and then suddenly seeing it overnight in the 1960s, just completely cleared, and well-loved places that I suppose lots of people used to go to that were flattened, and just these odd places that you could live in were suddenly hijacked into major building developments. And this went on and on and on (fig. 133).

HUO: Do you document your walks, photographically or … ?

PB: No, no, I did, and then I stopped because I didn't like what the documents included, in the photographs. They weren't the things that I was interested in. So in 2001 I hit a bit of a wall, workwise, and I decided to make an archive of all the things – in a very literal way – of all the things that I saw on the street (figs. 130, 139). First of all, I photographed them all and then there would be people or things I didn't want.

HUO: So basically by drawing them you could eliminate the stuff you didn't want.

PB: Yes, so then I didn't use my camera at all and just used memory.

HUO: Memory, not the sketchbook?

PB: Sketchbook first, then memory, so all these things were just very quick notes. I don't know what I think of these drawings now, but it was an incredibly important thing to do, because it then led into the drawings that have been more current since the 2000s.

HUO: So something changed in the 2000s?

PB: Yes, exactly.

HUO: But before we get there, we were in the early 1970s, so what happened in the mid-1970s?

PB: Yes, the mid-1970s went into a bit of a … flat charcoal drawings …

HUO: But in the 1960s and 1970s, did you sell work to museums or galleries?

PB: No, nothing.

HUO: So you were completely outside the world of exhibitions?

PB: Yes. I think a lot of us were. We were doing things in a different way, and I think the obsession with exhibition and the obsession with being framed by a gallery is actually quite recent.

HUO: It's a 1980s thing, it started in the eighties?

PB: Right. Before then it was more about the studio.

HUO: So one can say that the work opened up and then in the mid-1970s it closed down again (figs. 134–5).

PB: And quite depressed. I didn't know what to …

HUO: Sort of a dark Constructivism.

PB: I think it was a very dark time for me.

HUO: There was a recession, and there was the oil crisis.

PB: Yes, but there were terrific things going on in the 1970s. Martin Naylor and Carl Plackman. Really significant British artists. So these were the 1970s drawings that were slightly more resolved versions of these ones.

HUO: They actually remind me of Władysław Strzemiński and Polish Constructivism.

PB: Well, that's exactly what I was looking at. I was looking at …

HUO: Also Katarzyna Kobro and Henrik Stażewski?

PB: Yes, and also, oddly enough, I was looking at a lot of textile artists that were coming from Poland, who were quite amazing. I've forgotten her name – huge woven things. I think I found them very liberating, after the didacticism of Conceptualism, Minimalism. It was as if these things were coming in one after the other. You hardly had time to absorb some of those … James Rosenquist, I remember absolutely loving Rosenquist, and then before I knew it, it was Donald Judd or somebody, and everyone was making their decisions about which one, and if you couldn't make your decision, and I couldn't, it was …

HUO: Yes, there were camps in the art world at that time.

PB: Yes.

HUO: And today?

PB: There are cliques, but they're more social than aesthetic.

[…]

HUO: Within a month you do dozens of sculptures – it's very impressive! That leads us back to your incredible working rhythms, because when I visited you for the first time, you said that in those days, in the 1970s, you had so many different lives. You had your family, your teaching. Then your artwork, and the day has twenty-four hours. And I was wondering how it all worked, and you said that even in the cold you would start work at four or five in the morning. So when did you then draw?

PB: Well, I think in the 1970s the drawing was really difficult. I found it very difficult. I think that was a time when I was drawing … I think it's always just been going on. There would always be a drawing, and there still is drawing on the go. They're a form of making, drawings. I think that what I have to admit and face up to as an artist is my being very traditional, and I think that always feels … I don't know … I think everything that has really inspired me has always been incredibly innovative, but I don't think I'm necessarily an innovator. I'm more somebody who picks up on innovations and makes use of them in some way. I think all roads do inevitably lead back to some kind of tradition. Tradition is incredibly different from convention or orthodoxy; tradition is actually, possibly to do with process, in my mind, more than just being very conventional.

HUO: It's a dynamic process!

PB: Absolutely.

HUO: For neuroscientists, memory is dynamic.

PB: Totally. Tradition is to do with memory, and how you might remember. It's not just about making a monument or a statue.

HUO: Another thing that I wanted to ask you before was to do with Poland. In both Polish Constructivism and Russian Constructivism, there were many women artists. In Russia, for example, there were Lyubov Popova and Natalia Goncharova; in Poland there was Katarzyna Kobro. And you told me about all the artists in England around at that time, and they were mostly men, and with the exception of Hepworth, the historic references are mostly men.

PB: But there were a lot of women students, and there was a feeling that there was something changing in terms of a kind of male-dominated history of sculpture. I think that by the 1970s that was incredibly energised, and there were two female processes. There was the feminist wave that was often to do with biological feminism and social feminism, and then there were actual ways of making that were paradoxical because people talked about sewing as being female, but then look at fashion designers and tailors and everybody – there are many brilliant male fashion designers. So those kind of didactic arguments just didn't work. Or, cooking was a female activity. It clearly isn't. The paradoxes within feminism and art have always been interesting, and women have often returned to the body as a site of feminist exchange, and I've not been particularly interested in that as just a female preserve. So to me it was quite a complex time, the 1970s, the 1980s. I think suddenly in the 1980s it all …

HUO: Blossomed.

PB: Yes, opened up again. The arguments became … not like camps, as you were saying, but more to do with social exploration.

HUO: How did you connect to Susan Hiller or Margaret Harrison and feminism?

PB: I didn't. I feel really ashamed in a way. No, there were some incidents that really perplexed me. My daughter was born in 1973, so that was in the absolute heart of feminist arguments within art schools, and that became quite complicated, I think, emotionally complicated maybe. There was a form of feminism that seemed to be based on masculinism, and then there was a form of feminism which began to evolve, which was utterly obsessed with being a woman, and all of these different camps I felt weren't interesting. I felt that the things that were interesting were to do with straightforward social justice and social equality, the social issues around women. They were the things that interested me.

HUO: So were there artists with whom you discussed these matters at that time? Who were the artists with whom you exchanged? You were not part of a movement or a group …

PB: I was very solitary at this time, very. I think that for both Fabian, my husband, and myself, that was quite a tricky time of not belonging comfortably to anything that was happening then. I think that for me Martin Naylor's work and Carl Plackman's work, first shown at the big Royal Academy show of around 1974, was where I felt there was a real engagement with a new evolution of sculptural language within British art.

HUO: How could one describe this?

PB: It's difficult. Well, you think of what was happening then, the performance artists – Rose Finn-Kelcey, people like her. And Andrew Wilson, when he came to look at these drawings a few weeks ago, he brought a thing called *Art Spectrum*. It was a catalogue for an exhibition that happened up at Alexandra Palace in 1971.

HUO: And you were in that?

PB: Yes (fig. 109). If you look at it you will see the complete survey of what was going on in British art, and there is actually everything from Op Art-type work to Finn-Kelcey's amazing flags that she put up outside Alexandra Palace. And Barry Flanagan gave every artist … what was it? It was 1971, so they were just doing decimalisation … he gave everybody 50p as his work of art.

[…]

HUO: Coming back to those drawings, you said the influence for this super-density came from craft and textiles.

PB: Yes, and also trying to get away from or escape from sculpture into something else.

HUO: Or find a detour. David Hockney told me he sometimes needs to do a detour. So he'll do a movie or a book or a text and then come back into painting.

PB: Yes, the detours for me are in the drawings. In drawing you can do anything. You can make this float in mid-air; you can make it have no weight.

HUO: You can defy gravity.

PB: Exactly. The minute you have materials you've got all those problems.

HUO: And after the mid-1970s, and these dark constructions, you said that it then lightened up again. So what would be the next phase, the late 1970s and early 1980s?

PB: I think there was a long gap between about 1979 and 1984, when there were probably just sketchbook drawings, and of course they're at home still.

HUO: So you've always had sketchbooks?

PB: Oh always, yes, and some of them just have one drawing in them and a shopping list. So they're not like some artists' sketchbooks. I was astonished to look at Alison Wilding's sketchbooks. They're meticulous, a really quite incredible archive of things. But mine are … I just pick them out at random, there's no sequence or anything. It's shambolic.

HUO: But that would be another interview we need to do one day! Today it's the interview about your drawings, but one day we should do an interview looking at your diaries. The drawings are not dated and are untitled, mostly?

PB: Yes, exactly. So the drawing just became very direct and very quick.

HUO: Some of them are almost instant drawings, right?

PB: Instant, absolutely instant (fig. 136).

HUO: Or, as Dieter Roth would have said, 'speed drawings'.

PB: They are speed drawings, yes. I think that a lot of the things that have been inherent for many years suddenly become consolidated during this

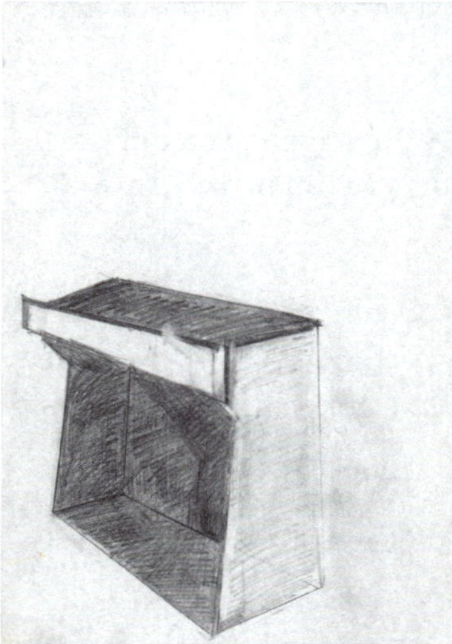

LEFT:
fig. 136 *untitled*, mid-1980s–early 1990s

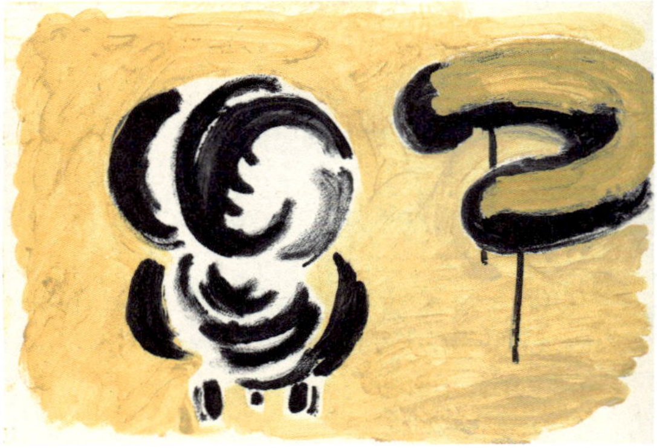

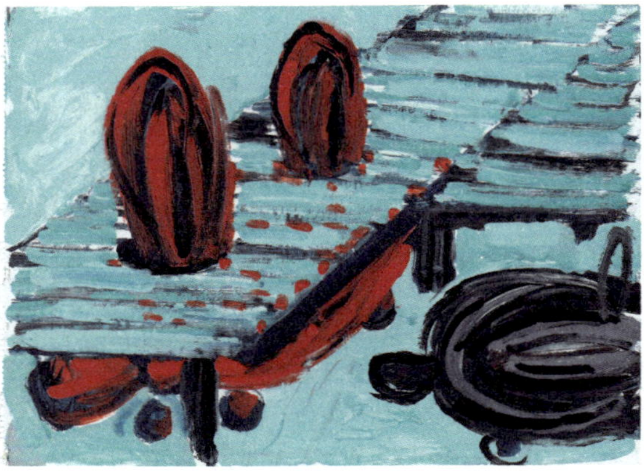

ABOVE:
fig. 137 *untitled*, 1980s–90s
LEFT:
fig. 138 *untitled*, late 1990s

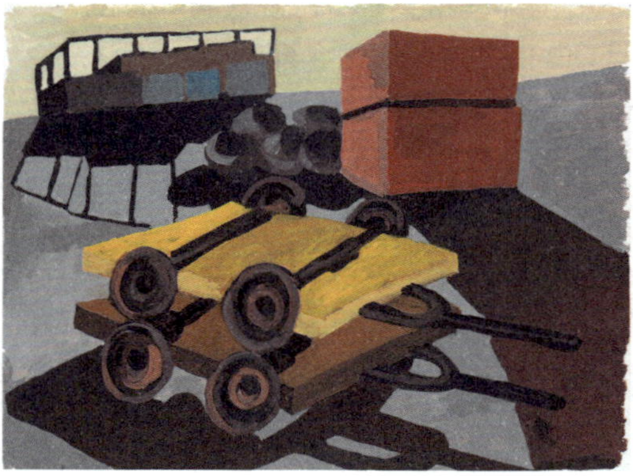

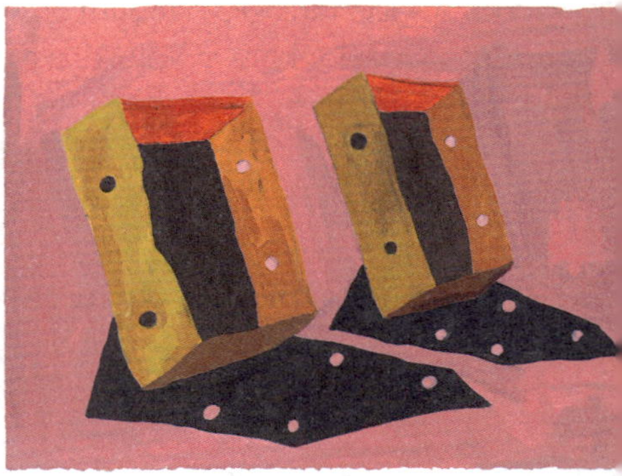

ABOVE LEFT TO RIGHT:
fig. 139 *untitled*, 2001
fig. 140 *untitled*, 2009–10

1980s-to-1990s period. It's as though I'm not particularly bothered about style or ways of doing things; it just happened. I think maybe frustration produced that, a kind of pressure of time. I was having to really go and make teaching a very major part of my work, just for income, so that the pressure on finding time to make work was very intense during that time, and therefore the drawings just …

HUO: So the pressure produced this more direct language?

PB: Absolutely.

HUO: There was less time. But it's interesting that part of this new velocity means that you also get away from the idea of drawing it all, and it becomes more about the use of colour. They're very painterly. Did you use acrylic?

PB: Yes, these are all acrylic.

HUO: So that's the thing in the eighties, the arrival of acrylic in the drawings. They're painted drawings (fig. 137).

PB: They are painted drawings, yes, and that's just stayed ever since.

HUO: Some have the feel of preparatory drawings for sculptures, and some have the feel of being really free. Let's talk more about the 1980s. Colours are back, as in the late 1960s drawings, but it's a different palette of colours somehow.

PB: Yes, I think I was beginning to be very interested in my memory of colours, and how those related to the present. To me, the way memory interfaces with the now and the then, the syntax of memory – that you're remembering in the present but that the content of the memory is in the past tense. The colour relates to that, the colours from the 1950s and the early 1960s have always remained important, I think, as well as colours that you see on the street, the yellows and the reds.

HUO: I'm curious because when you started, and there was all the British sculpture; there was the New Generation, and all of that, that struck you as different. You continued to work in a more solitary state throughout the seventies, but very intensely. Then the 1980s arrived, and suddenly there was this big phenomenon of British Sculpture …

PB: In two stages.

HUO: Did you connect to them? Did it change something? Was there suddenly a dialogue?

PB: I think that, for me, it was 'Thank God! Something's happened, something's broken!' I think, for me, there was also a little bit of disappointment at not being part of it, when I felt that I was actually part of it. I don't mean that in an arrogant or bitter way, I just mean that I felt that I was using all sorts of materials that became very evident in *The Sculpture Show* in 1983, at those two venues at the Hayward and the Serpentine.

HUO: And you were not part of that show?

PB: No. Richard Deacon was in that; Anish Kapoor's early works with the piles of pigment. So all of those artists who were very much about compounding the previous twenty years, in my opinion – things that had happened with Arte Povera, things that had happened under the guise of anti-form, but that actually became very formal. You think of Deacon's amazing early work, which I think is phenomenal – the galvanised pieces with loose pieces of canvas hanging off them.

HUO: So what happened in the late 1980s to 1990s? What changed then?

PB: It was evolutionary, I think. I was just curious about running between something that could possibly be a proposal for a sculpture, or something, but that wasn't, that was just itself. It's just constantly trying to enjoy a lack of resolution, to enjoy a kind of sculptural sensibility, but not have to drive it home in any particular way, and I think that was the epiphany in the 1980s and throughout the 1990s. I think that then the next epiphany was just enjoying the quality of the paint and moving it around the paper.

HUO: So the next step, you said, was to just enjoy that colour-freedom, colour-flow. These are the ones that I saw in the studio. You do many of those, and they're also very big. And that's why I thought it was interesting when in the late 1980s you had the packaging paper with the coloured background, because it anticipates you painting your own background. So it led to something quite essential, actually. Because what happens in the late 1990s is that they become like paintings, you paint the background (fig. 138). When did you start to do this?

PB: That really has happened since the late 1990s, 2000s.

HUO: And very often you do a monochromatic background, is that right? Does it start with the background, or does the background come at the end?

PB: Both. I think I see it as a space.

HUO: I also have the feeling that with the autonomy of the colour and the background being painted – they also become more autonomous from the sculptures in some way. They're autonomous works.

PB: Yes, that's what Penelope Curtis felt, actually, exactly that. She said that they were almost more grounded than the sculptures were.

HUO: What's the role of chance in all of this? The packing paper arrived by chance.

PB: Yes, I like chance, and I like accidents. I like doing things in the studio which are restagings of accidents, like pushing things off tables or knocking things over, or cutting through things so that they break. I enjoy that, and I think maybe those kinds of drawings are about obliterating, in some way. I think that what's happened throughout the 2000s is just a real need to do this activity that's more like … in some ways is quite connected to painting, I suppose. I don't think of them as paintings, I think of them as drawings. I think of them as drawings because of the speed with which I can do them.

HUO: One sees, during the 2000s, that you derived an ever-increasing pleasure from doing those. It became almost an addiction because you did more and more.

PB: It is an addiction. I think it's also a kind of confidence, which isn't necessarily a good thing. I like the exploration of doubt; a tentativeness.

HUO: One could say that in the mid-2000s the drawings become more sculptural. They become three-dimensional (figs. 139–40).

PB: Yes. But I find their relationship with painting really uncomfortable for some reason.

HUO: And that brings us to now. What's now?

PB: I'm very interested in that state of mind when you want to do something, but you actually don't know what to do. I think it's a very un-talked-about area of making art, this longing. 'Yes, I want this, and I don't even know what to call it!' So I just remember pouring this paint on to that paper there, and then gradually introducing other colours in layers, and this semi-geometric form emerged, and then at one point saying 'stop'. And I think knowing when and when not to stop is still very difficult to decide. I don't know whether things are finished or not, but that, for me, is when this way of drawing is at its most exciting. I think the archival drawings were just so mechanical. You know, the ones that were just of the street objects?

HUO: Yes.

PB: But this is something else. This is where I'm still in a state of quandary about the work, even when I can't go on with it any further.

HUO: So it's emerging.

PB: Emerging, exactly.

HUO: And also the doubt is in that sense still there.

PB: Well, for me, that's when something is really exciting. It's easy with that, because it just happens, but when you try and push it a bit further ... To me, what's incredible about them is what would have happened if there had been another piece of plaster on that? There's a moment when you think things are either going to really change something, or not change at all.

First published in *Phyllida Barlow: Fifty Years of Drawings* (Zurich: Hauser & Wirth and JRP/Ringier, 2014), 216–27.

ON TEACHING

Titled 'Learning Experience', this interview was published in *Frieze* magazine in September 2006. The curator Mark Godfrey, who at that time was a colleague at the Slade School of Fine Art, London, focuses on Barlow's experiences of art education, both as student and teacher. They discuss her time studying at Chelsea College of Arts, London, and at the Slade, her path through teaching, and her approach as a teacher. They talk about medium-based teaching, the place of theory in fine-art courses, the influence of the art market, and the risks of academicism and PhD culture.

Interview with Mark Godfrey

2006

Mark Godfrey: Can you tell me about your experience of art school as a student at Chelsea College of Art and Design and the Slade?

Phyllida Barlow: I was at Chelsea from 1960 to 1963 and the Slade from 1963 to 1966. I had no qualification from Chelsea because it was changing from the academic National Diploma in design award to a fine-arts diploma. It was a very exciting time. Then I came to the Slade, and it was a three-year diploma course. In terms of today's art education I don't have any qualification that equals the current BA, MA, or MFA. When I arrived at Chelsea, Lawrence Gowing was bringing in a lot of young successful artists, such as Patrick Caulfield, Ian Stephenson, and John Hoyland. Henry Moore had been teaching sculpture, and when he left, Gowing brought in the sculptor George Fullard, who'd been badly wounded in World War II, which had an enormous impact on his own work and on his ideas about art education. He was a brilliant visionary. Within days of arriving he'd stirred up a hornets' nest of intrigue, asking what a sculpture course, such as it was at Chelsea, might be.

MG: How had it been before he arrived there?

PB: We worked on the figure in clay, and the welding room was forbidden to women. Stone carving was taught in a very traditional way, as were all the sculpture skills; it was a skill-based school, which Fullard radically changed.

MG: In what way?

PB: He got rid of the life figure from the two sculpture studios and encouraged the use of salvaged materials. The King's Road at that time was going through a radical transformation. All the leases came to an end sometime in 1960 and 1961. Many of the old shops were being gutted to make way for the new boutiques like Mary Quant and Foale and Tuffin, so there was all this raw material just lying around. For Fullard the only use for a life class was if it was part of a process for thinking and examining what observation meant, not for creating a facsimile of what was in front of you.

MG: How were things when you arrived at the Slade?

PB: There was a feud going on between William Coldstream and the head of sculpture, Professor A. H. Gerard – both remarkable men in their own way. Gerard was very much about formal structures that could be discovered and visualised from nature. He was probably a very skilled carver, but I was in no mood for any of that.

MG: Were conservative pedagogical methods of any use to you?

PB: No, they were not. At the Slade, we were told to work from the figure, it was compulsory. I wanted to reinvent what sculpture could be, to experiment with weird, non-sculptural materials. It would have been easier to have made a complete break with sculpture altogether, in the way that Terry Atkinson was doing with his Fine Artz group, in relationship to painting. Because I was still working within the discipline of sculpture I was expected to comply rather than explore beyond the given formal and material boundaries of sculpture. So my first year at the Slade was depressing, but then the atmosphere became lively and rebellious. Larry Rivers did a residency, and Robert Rauschenberg visited. Thorold Dickinson, who was running the film course, was bringing in films that were completely ahead of their time and so different from the rigid language of sculpture and painting that was being taught. When I started teaching, it was film which inspired me most.

MG: When did you begin to teach?

PB: I got a job in 1966 at the Bristol School of Art and then went to Chelsea from 1967 to 1978. From the mid- to late 1960s to the early 1970s every art school was employing young tutors straight from art college. It was very exciting; groups like Art & Language were bubbling away, and lots of different art-school models were being developed. By 1978 my work was idiosyncratic and unfashionable, and I felt isolated. I had three children, so I left Chelsea and returned to teaching in 1983, now with five children, so I needed regular income. I got a job at Brighton with Alison Wilding, Edward Allington, Peter Randall-Page, and Eric Bainbridge. It was the most brilliant year I've ever had teaching.

MG: What made it so brilliant?

PB: We believed that the course should be based on a critical presence – nothing new in that, but we emphasised scrutinising the work as a group, where different points of view could flourish. From my point of view, I was also being educated by my colleagues, who were exhibiting internationally.

I was surprised to get the job because I was completely unknown, forty years old and at a fragile stage in my artistic development. The opportunity to work with these astonishing artists was beyond my wildest dreams, and they have remained great friends and hugely important to me.

MG: Who were your students during that year at Brighton?

PB: They included Rachel Whiteread, Steven Pippin, and Lee Andrews, who all went on to have fantastic success with their work.

MG: Where did you go then?

PB: I went to do a shared post at Camberwell in sculpture with a well-known artist, Brian Catling. The invitation was to change the content of the sculpture course, which we took very literally. Paul de Monchaux, the head of the sculpture course, had established an incredible course and was leaving. Our input seemed to rock the boat, in conjunction with Wendy Smith and John Hilliard running the painting area; and then Tony Carter joined and Stephen Johnson. We all injected completely new approaches into Camberwell, questioning what the subject, content, and form of sculpture could be.

MG: So then you went to teach at the Slade, and it was divided into sculpture, painting, and fine-art media. It still is. How do you defend such a structure in a post-medium age?

PB: I can only defend it so long as those three disciplines come together as a debate, to explore why somebody is able to define their activity, for example, as painting, and to relate that to sculpture, film, video, photography, performance, etc. Artists borrow and steal from each other left, right, and centre, and that's what makes the debates come alive. Practical reasons can also make distinctions important because some processes require clean spaces, others require spaces where a mess can be made, some require walls, some require an open space, etc. Most students work on the cusp between disciplines. That is the most exciting place to be, conceptually and in practical terms: where painting comes off the wall, where sculpture becomes a projection, such as a film, video, or slide, where projection becomes an object.

MG: What are the dangers for you of the art-school courses that are not structured around mediums?

PB: In the past twenty years, many art schools have changed to courses that are not medium/discipline-specific. I think this departure gave way to an emphasis on subject-led work. Form has definitely been a non-starter. There has been a loss of understanding of the relationship between the work and the space it occupies. A kind of homogeneity has evolved where there can be an indifference to what the status of the work is once it has left the studio, or its place of manufacture, and to how and why and with what the work relates to within the space it occupies. The exhibiting space can become a conventional backdrop, rather than a potential for challenging the work and the viewer. In courses organised around medium or disciplines, discussions about the use of space are promoted, and these raise many other issues, including the contentious issue of art as commodity. The all-in-one fine-art courses probably make sense but might miss out on debates which the medium-specific courses can shake up more effectively because issues are more blatantly exposed, less disguised.

MG: Do you think medium-based art degrees risk producing students who consider formal questions at the expense of attention to subject matter?

PB: Subject matter has dominated over form and content for some time, whatever the chosen discipline or medium. Knowing the subject of the work has been in the ascendance since the late 1980s. But things are changing. There is a surge of interest in making work in order to discover a subject.

MG: What do you regard as the role of the tutor in a one-on-one situation?

PB: It is essential to give myself up wholly to what the student has to say about the position they find themselves in, in relationship to their work, physically, emotionally, psychologically, socially, politically. It's important that the student is encouraged to articulate their creative position. This is very different from group teaching, which is becoming increasingly important in the form of group tutorials and seminars.

MG: What do you think is the role of the group tutorial?

PB: To enable students as a group to take on the formal and aesthetic issues of presentation, to understand its intentions, and to question the status of the work: is it finished or a work in progress? Is it political? What are the implications of the work being placed, located in a particular way? And of course, who is the work for? A group offers up a diversity of responses which come from the students, where disagreements can open up the complexity of the discussion and not close it down with a single point of view. Also, I think group teaching can disrupt moral judgements, for example, about hard work or political correctness, as well as creative judgements, and develop a more investigatory approach.

MG: What do you do with students who can't or won't address the questions you just mentioned? I've heard you talk about the right of the artist not to write about their work.

PB: I think that if somebody comes on a fine-art course, it has to be very clear that they're part of a group, even if they want to operate as a loner. I don't think everybody is able to articulate what they're doing, but I think the ones who really find it difficult are very different from the ones who don't want to or refuse and you have to find out why: it might be the beginning of developing a position, for example, where the work has to speak for itself. And then the question is: well, does the work speak for itself, or is this refusal to speak just defensive?

MG: When you see work in the studio that resembles work the student doesn't know about, at what point is it appropriate for you to inform them?

PB: Straight away, because what they're doing is contextualising their work, and there should be as few nasty shocks when they leave art school as possible, such as realising that their work is an unintentional pastiche of an artist's work they never knew about. As tutors we must inform in all kinds of ways. But you have to be open to getting it wrong. Perhaps you thought the work looked like a John Bock or a Peter Doig, and then you realise, through discussion, that the student has been engaged with a totally different kind of process, with totally different references.

MG: At what point do you remember students having to take art history and theory seminars and writing essays?

PB: It was about 1969. But it was in a very different form to what is usually taught now. Stuart Morgan, that remarkable critic and observer of twentieth-century art, spoke about being taught liberal studies – which is what history and theory courses were called then – in Brighton in the 1970s. One of the first student essays I remember seeing was delivered in a suitcase on wheels with a drawing of Donald Duck on it; when you opened the suitcase, it was like a jack-in-the-box, and the whole essay sprang out; it was a complete re-enactment of a Donald Duck cartoon, done as a critical work.

MG: So liberal studies were a component of the fine-arts course, and the students were writing essays?

PB: Yes, but not just on the history of art, which was rather despised.

MG: Now we have a history and theory component at the Slade. Do you see this as a necessary part of art-school education?

PB: On the one hand I think that students need a history and theory component whether they are naturally good at it or not. But there are students whose interests lie in questioning the state of contemporary art, who might be better served presenting their critical processes in a different form: as a lecture, forum, seminar, performance, recording, or documentary with greater emphasis on images than words. I think it is easy for academicism to creep in and yet, clearly, not all art students have this ability and they can become disadvantaged by the very system they have elected to join.

MG: How do you guard against that kind of establishment of orthodoxy among your students?

PB: Years ago I invited Richard Wentworth in to give the crit of the postgraduate-course final exhibition. He sent all the students a postcard asking them to 'name the orthodoxies that have influenced your work and your final exhibition', and not a single student understood the question. At the time, the work of the YBAs was taken as an orthodoxy, but Richard suggested that the students had the opportunity to examine and challenge the very orthodoxies that the YBA phenomenon had created. Now slacker art seems to appeal to a lot of students, perhaps because it signals a very quick way of doing things, and it is economically viable, and doable under all sorts of conditions including the bedsit! But you can guard against orthodoxies by encouraging students to really interrogate what's actually in front of them.

MG: Do you find students are increasingly directing their work towards commercially successful careers?

PB: By the early 1990s, the emergence of YBAs became a model for a certain kind of career ambition. These artists proved that you could make money out of your art, which of course other generations had not been able to do to that extent. At degree shows now, paintings and other wall-based work always sell quite well, but students have begun to assess and rigorously debate the limitations of commercialism. Degree shows are still filled with projections, performances, installations, which don't tend to sell. Students also realise that financial success can be isolating and can remove an artist from knowing what is going on at a grass-roots level, and there might be many surprises there with new ways of questioning and resourcing how to be an artist. Having said all this, it would be churlish not to celebrate a sale of work, and the possibility for students to recuperate the huge overdrafts they accrue. As someone who hasn't made money commercially from my work, I encourage students to address questions relating to their futures outside art school. 'Do you actually need a studio, because studios are expensive? Are you self-sufficient enough to actually get on with producing work in an economically viable way, and does this involve doing some God-awful job for three days a week?' Economically it's so tough to live in London and support yourself as an artist. There should be no snobbery at all about going on a teacher training course or something like that, which will give you an income to survive while you make your own work, albeit, in the little spare time you have.

MG: Are fewer artists going into teaching because they can be more easily supported by sales?

PB: When I started to teach, art schools were seen as a form of patronage. There was less emphasis on whether you showed your work or not: it was about having the space and time to make work within your own studio, and teaching afforded the means to do that. That whole culture of art schools being patrons has virtually disappeared without trace. A lot of artists who emerged at the YBA time said, 'We're not teaching; we're going to sell.' But I think some of them have had to come back to teaching. The financial success they had in the early years has not sustained itself, and they are looking for jobs in art schools and bring a wealth of experience from that time, which is fascinating.

MG: One reason to teach is to replenish your ideas about art-making. Are there any particular instances you can tell us about of the impact of teaching on the development of your practice?

PB: I think the evolution of the physical has influenced me, and I think being wrong-footed always intrigues me. I once made the mistake of referring to Bruce Nauman's work as pure sculpture, and a student, Jasper Joseph-Lester, went ballistic and said that you must never use the word 'pure' in relationship to the visual arts – it has fascistic connotations. I attempted to justify what I had said: in Nauman's sculptures of the 1980s, there is no single, ultimate viewing position; they prompt you to keep on moving around, under, and across them. But Jasper was right to challenge my use of the word, and he made me think more clearly.

MG: What do you predict will happen to fine-arts degree courses?

PB: One way I hope fine-art degree courses might change is to be more inclusive, less didactic about what is good and what is bad art and to take risks with the applicants who could be offered places on fine-art courses. Also, it is now critical and crucial to represent the cosmopolitan nature of a country like the UK within the student intake. Can a broader cross-section of society, culturally and economically, be tempted to apply to art schools? And what is meant by 'non-Western'? These are now very important issues, not just for art schools but for art as a whole.

MG: You've been worried about fine-arts degree courses becoming too academic. What do you perceive as the problems with this?

PB: There's a pressure on fine-art courses to include PhD courses and that can emphasise an over-theoretical approach to art supported by the economic fact that PhDs are the cheapest courses to fund as they require the least support … a supervisor and two or three meetings per year, and funding raised by the student in question. Very different from the much more expensive BA courses which require a lot of support: tutors, technical advisors, studios, workshops, etc. Too much emphasis on the theoretical can change the culture of fine-art courses by the influence from the PhD culture. It's seen hierarchically as though the PhD is the top with the BA or the foundation courses at the bottom. If there has got to be a hierarchy then it should be about how work is made, how it is to be shown, what it is examining, what questions it is provoking, what the nature of the experiment might be … these are issues which can be either adventurous or banal at any level. A PhD does not mean better art. In fact, it is often the opposite.

MG: If you were the head of an art school or the founder of a new art school where you didn't have to answer to any university requirements yet had to award a degree, how would you assess a three-year BA course?

PB: Maybe by simply granting students a pass or fail for their degree result. Perhaps to get rid of degrees altogether and place greater importance on being able to fail, to understand that as a crucial and critical part of making work. An imaginative, challenging, politicised, and contentious awareness of how to present work, not just as an exhibition but as particular to the requirements of the work, would, and is, a key issue of the art-school process. If some students elected to be silent, I think that would have to be accommodated, and, as mentioned before, to be understood as a statement in its own right, or as a protest, an act of repudiation … a rare event in art schools now because the financial stakes are high and parents are implicated in the funding of their children's higher education, which has put the brakes on single-minded acts of rebellion, so to speak. Parents are more likely to complain about their children's degree result than the student. It is a bizarre situation with students terrified of failure. But an art school has a responsibility to enable students to become articulate and confident about what they are presenting, because that's what they'll need when they leave.

MG: Do you think that in the UK and internationally there are too many fine-arts degrees creating too many artists?

PB: There's a 'stack 'em high, sell 'em cheap' educational ethos being nudged into place. It probably has something to do with government statistics, trying to drive down the unemployment figures by keeping as many young people as possible in education for as long as possible. However, what is interesting is that, however remote and economically up against it a fine-art course might be, you will still find exceptionally talented students on that course. Also, fine-art courses have the potential to prepare students for more than a life as a visual artist. Traditionally art schools were, and perhaps still are, the seedbeds for all kinds of creative promise, for writers, musicians, film directors, performers, organisers, administrators, curators, critics, educationalists, teachers, etc. It should not be underestimated what a rich resource an art-school education can be.

First published as 'Learning Experience', *Frieze* (September 2006), 168–75; https://frieze.com/article/learning-experience.

Barlow was interviewed by artist John Reardon at her home in June 2009 for his book *ch-ch-ch-changes: Artists Talk about Teaching*. She discusses the shifts in art education she has witnessed, including the new level of influence exerted by the art world, and she outlines her views on and approaches to teaching. They talk about failure, subject-led work, the challenge of balancing being an artist with family life, and Barlow's commission *stack* for the Southbank, London, in 2008. Barlow speaks about the respective responsibilities of teacher and student and responds to the question as to whether it is possible to teach art.

Interview with John Reardon

2009

John Reardon: In a recent article, Mark Godfrey introduces you as 'one of the most influential teachers and artists working in Britain today'. With a career spanning forty years ... you grimace?

Phyllida Barlow: I don't think that's true.

JR: Why do you think Godfrey would say that? Is it simply down to longevity, or do you bring a special kind of focus to teaching that produces particular kinds of results?

PB: It is a very expedient remark that tries to raise interest in the article, otherwise there would be no point in him writing it. From my point of view, I don't quite know where he would get that information from, other than rolling the credits of a few names that I've obviously had contact with over forty years. I feel that my kind of teaching – and there are a lot of us around – is that every day is a new day. You feel you have no history as a teacher, you almost feel you have no history as an artist. You enter the studio and the tutorial almost starts from scratch each time, and therefore you're in a process of constant renewal. I suppose that's the excitement of the teaching experience; that people like myself don't know how to use their own history. And it doesn't necessarily stand one in very good stead. It's unreliable, in as much as I don't have anything to rely on, everything is always different.

JR: Why do you think that is?

PB: Because I think there are so many changes with each decade, or five years, or even quicker now – two years. Each group of students is bringing an entirely new life cycle. If you just want to depend on something that happened to you over forty years, that is not anything I'm particularly interested in doing. I am genuinely interested in the here and now, and how that then relates to a whole history of knowledge and attempts to understand from the past. But I don't think the past leads, the individual leads.

JR: How do you keep it from becoming predictable? How do you go in there every day and start again?

PB: Unfortunately every teacher has their predictable emotional, passionate luggage, and the students are the first to recognise this. They know I might say something like 'take it outside, go and put it on a street corner', 'take it down to Euston Station', 'why not do this as a performance?', 'why are you videoing it, why not do the performance live?' They know I will say these things, or 'why have you put it there, why not stick it on the ceiling?' I can bore myself with my own repertoire of things, but I suppose that's directly connected to how I would treat the process of making in the studio. You know that nothing is reliable, you know an idea isn't reliable.

JR: In a conversation with Sacha Craddock about the making of *Peninsula* (figs. 92, 179), the work you did for the BALTIC Centre for Contemporary Art, you explained how the students you had working with you constantly reminded you of what you would say to them in their studio, but would do the opposite in yours.

PB: Yes. Touché!

JR: You taught people like Rachel Whiteread, Steven Pippin, and so on. Did they require much teaching?

PB: I don't think either Rachel or Steve Pippin would necessarily think of me as a particularly significant teacher. That particular year in Brighton, where I met them first – at the old Brighton Poly, before it became whatever it did become – there was an extraordinary head of sculpture who was retiring. Which is why Ed Allington and I got this kind of joint job there.

JR: Who was the head of sculpture?

PB: James Tower. He needs huge credit for his ability to select really interesting students. If you look at the history of Brighton during that early 1980s era, the artists and the students at the time, who became well-known artists, who went there, were astonishing. A lot of these things go, they disappear without a trace, and that's just the way it is. But in that particular year at Brighton, there was Rachel, there was Steve Pippin, there was another wonderful artist called Lee – gosh I've forgotten his name – Lee Andrews … and several others whose names have gone just for the moment. Alison Wilding was teaching in this group of people at Brighton as well. It was an astonishing eighteen months there, and then the whole system changed. Polytechnics went, the new universities started sprouting up left, right, and centre, and that regime disappeared. A new regime came in, but I was very lucky teaching with that team of people, to pick up that group of students who'd actually been selected by someone else. We were very lucky to just be there at that particular moment. In fact Rachel was far more indebted to Alison Wilding, Ed Allington, and Richard Wilson than me. She's become a good friend now, but at the time I was much more in a sort of supportive role than the sort of dynamic teacher. That has emerged later, actually.

JR: Do you think someone like Rachel arrived with everything she needed? Did she need to be there?

PB: Yes. I think so. Hugely so, yes. What the teaching context there gave was incredibly studio-based and produced a critical dynamic, between this extraordinary, exceptional group of staff, and Eric Bainbridge was also in that group. It was a really extraordinary circumstance to bring these five artists together. It provided a kind of critical breadth. Whether those students then, or really successful artists now, would ever really credit that, I don't know. It was such a fertile environment for ambition really, and motivation, to do things with the work. I can remember Eric Bainbridge, whom I admire hugely – I think he's one of the most exciting artists and teachers actually – looking at this girl's work. It was very clunky and awkward, and he just turned to her and said, 'well, why not stick all those bits together with bubblegum?' To make her completely rethink a way of doing something. He wasn't just being facetious; he was actually being really ahead of his time. If you think of what's happened to contemporary art since, you just know that that remark changed her life. Whether she became a famous artist or not, was neither here nor there – I don't think she did, I think she went off and did something completely different … But you can see somebody's inspired thinking.

JR: You were around at a time of some major figures in art education: George Fullard, William Coldstream at the Slade, Lawrence Gowing at Chelsea. Are there figures of that stature and creativity working in art education today? And, if so, where is their influence being felt?

PB: The influence now is coming from the art world itself, and this is the most complicated part of art education today; art has become so successful out there that it's now impacting, to some extent, on what happens within art schools in a way that maybe hasn't quite happened before. The giant educationalists, who really had visions about art schools becoming dynamic centres for the exchange of ideas, processes, and ways of thinking, both George Fullard and Lawrence Gowing, and, in a strange way, Coldstream were like that. They didn't see them as places that manufactured finished artists who could be delivered straight into the art world … they saw them as places where there could be an ongoing process of revealing and testing out, and changing and offering huge opportunity to people. Whereas now there is an intense pressure for young, emerging artists about surviving. That's very different from, say, twenty to thirty years ago. I wouldn't want to say it's a good or a bad thing; it's just a shift. You're looking at what's going on in the art world – outside of the art school – for information, for how to develop.

JR: And what effect is that having on the art school and educational system?

PB: It's making it incredibly economy-driven. It's making everyone very, very aware of the economies of being an art student, of how to relate that to economic survival after art school. I would say the running order when you leave is first how am I going to survive economically; then where am I going to survive economically; and, thirdly, how am I going to make my work? Whereas previously it was first, how am I going to make my work; then, how am I going to pay for it?; and last, where am I going to do that? 'Oh, in a shed in the middle of nowhere.' It's all reversed the other way, and this isn't a criticism; you can't blame people for that, because just trying to survive in London alone, as we all know, is a huge challenge.

JR: Is this the same for teachers?

PB: Yes, totally. The pressures, that is, for how to survive as an artist. Although the income from teaching does provide some kind of financial security but the responsibilities and accountabilities as a teacher are now under scrutiny in ways that were not so until comparatively recently. Teaching has offered a false security that has not done teachers, their work, or art schools any good. And in the end these accountability exercises were an inevitability to reveal complacency.

JR: You mentioned to Godfrey that there was a time when art schools were seen as a form of patronage. 'There was less emphasis on whether you showed your work or not: it was about having the space and time to make work within your own studio, and teaching afforded the means to do that. That whole culture of art schools being patrons has virtually disappeared without trace'. It now seems almost to be a career choice of a kind; you go to art school and you'll do the MA and PhD, and that's a way to continue being part of the system …

PB: Yes. I find it very difficult to talk about this aspect of it, and you maybe need to go to a higher authority, who really knows about it! The dogmatic feeling we have that there's the academic path, which gives you lots of job opportunities within academia, and so you plod on through. You do your BA, you maybe have a year out, you do your MA and you do your PhD, and then you're away, is deeply flawed as a concept for an artist. And maybe this has all come about through people actually saying, 'we don't have to call artists "artists" anymore, they can be anything …' It's a slightly politicised thing; are they just like everybody else? Well, of course we're just like everybody else, it's just we have this desire to make visible things that usually aren't visible, and therefore it's a kind of useless profession. Trying to make it thoroughly useful through this academic trajectory seems to give it a kind of pretension, where there are problems with honing the artist into this highly academic being, while they're going to become enormously theoretical through this process.

JR: At the expense of what?

PB: At the expense of the risk that their work at the coalface might have to experience. Although PhD students struggle to survive – they're trying to get funding, they're trying to do this, they're trying to do that – they're also under this kind of protective umbrella, which I think is very make-believe. The other route, which is taking artists straight to the art world, and the hugely competitive thing that it is now and what that entails, and how they battle it out with galleries everywhere, and showing in your bedroom cupboard etc., that's sort of fantastic in a way. But it's also not without its problems, in emphasising the exhibition as a sign that you're alive, 'yeah, I'm alive, I've got a show.' And if you don't have a show you're dead. So both paths for me have huge problems. Just to finish this off without being too boring; the path towards the art world and showing your work and trying to get a job that just tides you over a bit, those artists who are succeeding in that, they are showing, they do not want to do teaching jobs. They don't mind visiting, maybe doing something that's one day a week, but that's not going to pay for anything now. So you've got this huge rift building up, where the only real way that you can survive through teaching now is to do a full-time job. The part-time jobs don't pay.

JR: Was there a time when you got a different artist coming in to teach, that wouldn't come in now, because of something to do with what you call the industrialisation of education?

PB: Up to say the mid-1980s, the hierarchies in art schools were very much that there were these older people who were running the departments. They were rock solid in their jobs and maybe the work had taken a back seat over the years. You could go around to Sheffield, or visit numerous art schools, and you'd find these very reliable, solid characters whom the students would often treat in a very paternalistic kind of way. Yes, they were usually men, and what happened with the change in dynamic in art schools through the YBAs, through the whole rise of Thatcherism, the rise of an aggressive art market, is that educationally that whole system was challenged. So in answer to your question: I think the patronage thing went out of the window, because it had fallen foul of itself, it had shot itself in the foot. It was providing people with comfy incomes and stability, but it wasn't doing what it had set out to do originally twenty years earlier, in the 1960s, which was to foster this kind of huge creative resource. It sort of backfired on itself. And maybe there should never have been full-time jobs, maybe the patronage thing should have always been about three-year contracts, or something, so that it could have refuelled and revitalised itself. And the huge scrutiny that art schools are now under, or that education is under with the Research Assessment Exercise, although I think it's dreadful, there is a sense that you've got to be doing something in order to be able to teach it. That sleeping thing, where you had people who were really sleeping through education, who were running departments, but weren't doing any of their own work, has gone. That's been challenged in some way, maybe in the worst possible way. I don't want to sound as if I support the RAE, because I think these things are all cockeyed, but in answer to your question; the people who are visiting now are usually very successful artists that art schools are trying to get in. That wasn't what the visiting programmes were necessarily about so much previously.

JR: Just on what you said about the RAE; would you agree that, as an artist, you need a practice in order to teach?

PB: I think so.

JR: In what state does the practice have to be in?

PB: Good point. Very good point. The emphasis on the famous artist, who has zillions of exhibitions to their name, is obviously satisfying students' curiosity, and it's important to satisfy that. But there is a whole raft of other artists who are working in all sorts of other ways. I met this artist I have a huge respect for, who's an ex-Goldsmiths student, Liadin Cooke. We just met the other day at the Henry Moore Institute, where she's got a drawing, and this one superb drawing had taken her two years to do. She's been an artist, but not within this kind of massive production way of showing left, right, and centre. It's been a quiet, highly contemplative, very serious, intense activity, with a lot of thinking as well. Sometimes the London artist identity takes precedence over maybe many other forms of being an artist, some of which may be about not producing a single thing. And, my God, we should support that.

JR: While I agree there is a variety of ways of working, we should also acknowledge what kind of condition a practice needs to be in, in order to have a certain kind of vitality and value. And I'm not just talking about some sort of commercial value necessarily …

PB: It is a state of being. I would sum it up as that, where there is a deep sense of longing, and there isn't necessarily the product yet for that longing, but it's there and it needs that time and it needs that desire and it needs that process of deep introspection in order for something to then be catalysed. Those people can have a profound and lasting influence on balancing institutions and what goes on in them, but unfortunately at the moment they're a sort of breed that isn't evidenced within art schools. You see, it's not just about the rote production of work. A lot of these things that scrutinise education and judge it don't have a category for that, they don't know how to.

JR: You've put your finger on something else that came up with Mark Godfrey around a question of failure. When he asked you about what you'd do if you could run an art school for a day – one of those kinds of fantastical 'what if' questions – and, to paraphrase, you talked about acknowledging a certain kind of failure as being an implicit part of a process of working that's not so much acknowledged now.

PB: Failure, and we've got to examine what that word 'failure' means, because I see failure as a very positive thing, not as a negative thing. I see it as a whole process towards finding out about something. That if something doesn't work it carries an enormous amount of information with it. Whether you are then able to go on and make something work, I don't know, but that phrase of 'whether something works or not', is an extraordinary phrase: where does it come from? Does it come from the industrial revolution? Was it about discovering machinery? And the fact that it's the word 'work' that is associated with 'labour', in some way suggests there's a breakage when something doesn't work. I don't think there necessarily is a breakage. I think it's more that something hasn't fulfilled a kind of promise. That isn't necessarily an image in one's head, it can be as much a kind of sense of touch, or a driving towards something that doesn't yet have an image, or a visual identity, and that's what you're striving to discover. So the failure of it is that it hasn't quite happened yet, but I don't know what it should be. And that not-knowing state is often deemed a kind of failure; you must know what you want, you must know what your intentions are, you must know what your aims and objectives are. It's such a harsh, unforgiving language. And yet the not knowing can often be that, as an artist, you're not working necessarily with very vivid visual, cerebral processes. You're actually trying to find those, and that's why you want to make the stuff, or draw the stuff, or paint the stuff. So the failure thing to me is very much associated with that striving for, and that struggle. Two words that I know are very unfashionable. But there is something for me in the striving to find the visual thing that isn't yet in one's head. It just doesn't have a cerebral identity.

JR: Can I read you something? It's part of a statement you made where you say '… teaching reciprocates my activities as an artist, as does my family (I have five children, now grown up). Sculpture for me has been ephemeral and temporary, and dominating my experience has been an experimental approach to making and exhibiting where I have prioritised an interventionist approach of the here and now …' Looking across your work, there seems to me to be a number of themes that you constantly touch upon; the first, I would say, is the scourge of subject-led work, and maybe that goes back to the notion of failure. The second is how you got here. There's a certain kind of humility and self-effacement about how you got involved in this whole thing, and at the same time there's a kind of dissent, or scepticism, in your relationship to it. The third is sculpture as a theme, and the fourth is your family. I was just wondering what it all adds up to?

PB: This is not going to answer the question, but I can remember when I did a talk at Goldsmiths, and I then did a talk at Camberwell, they were quite close together. I had had four years out, because of the children, and life had got extremely tough in all sorts of ways economically. When I went back in, I was quite startled by the changes in that brief time that had happened. I left Chelsea in 1978, and then the twins came along, and that stopped me from going back into teaching. There were reasons I had to leave in 1978; one child was quite ill recurringly, and it was really becoming a nerve-racking process. So I left, and then the twins came along in 1981, and I then went back to teaching in 1984 at Brighton. By then I had five children, which was like a guilty secret, trying to not let people know this terrible fact of life. But I remember doing this talk at Goldsmiths, and then, when I got the job at Camberwell, it came up again, because I was describing how when the five of them were around it was very difficult to work. So I would go into the studio very late at night, and I actually hadn't got a clue what to make, so I'd turn all the lights off. I've described this many times in slide talks; it was a very, very pivotal moment, when making things not through an image, but through touch, which made me think about this whole issue of where the subject is in the work. Having described that when I did these slide talks, on two occasions students would say to me, 'well, what's more important to you: being a mother, or being an artist?' And I would just have to say being a mother. There was this recoiling in horror from the audience that one could actually say that – prioritise being a mother over being an artist.

JR: But why were you being asked to make a choice in the first place?

PB: Exactly. I didn't have the wits to say what you pointed out; it isn't about a choice, the two are actually reciprocal, although an impossible combination, and I wouldn't necessarily recommend it to anyone, because the split is a very cruel schism; they're both intensely creative processes, but they stand in absolute opposition to each other. One is selfish, and the other has to be selfless. The mix is not good. But being asked by these students I felt so put on the spot, and it was like I had to tell the truth under those circumstances. Where you're maybe picking up the dissent is the fact that there was a kind of feeling of inhumanity about the whole role of teaching in an art school, that was rooted in how you portrayed the artist as this ruthless ambitious creature, which of course is true to some extent, in order to survive, and therefore anything else that might soften that was considered a nauseating, or slightly repellent characteristic. Now things are very different. Things have changed in that respect.

JR: Is subject-led work still a scourge?

PB: No. The way in which I might want to initiate work is still through trying to find something, trying to find a form, trying to find an image, trying to find how these materials can become articulate and coherent, and that I won't know what the subject is. At the moment I'm just making these endless folded forms, and they look very sort of vaginal and lip-like and ear-like, or they look like folded cloth. And I hate that, because the image of them is too dominant. So a journey with them has begun, and I don't quite know where to make this folded form start to become absolutely itself, rather than having these other connotations. And maybe that shape is impossible without those connotations. So they're finding a subject, and I'm reneging on the subject that they've found. Another artist would begin with saying, 'well, I want this very kind of inward-looking shape and it's going to be very bodily and it's going to be very visceral.' They would be very confident about placing those qualities at the forefront of the process. There was a time during the 1990s when the image-based, pictorial object was so dominant. That's what I was thinking about when I was talking about subject-led work.

JR: Can you teach art?

PB: No, but you can provide an endless process of enquiry and debate and discussion and conversation around it. But can anyone do that? No, I think that there are two things in that question; one is the object itself, and the other is the privilege of meeting the person who's made that object, who then enables you to question the object through them. So, there's this three-party thing; the object becomes a prompt and a prop for understanding that individual's deepest thoughts, and I think that does require a certain kind of knowledge of the histories that that object might promote. Whether it's an object that's referring very much to the here and now in terms of the galleries, or whether there's a bit of Arte Povera in there, or a bit of Minimalism, a bit of Victorian kitsch. Having that knowledge, you can bring it to the individual and maybe wake them up a bit about those things, or they might already know those things very clearly ... That might have come over as really kind of arrogant; I just want to qualify that. When I'm saying 'that knowledge', I'm not assuming that that individual doesn't have that knowledge as well, but that kind of pooling of knowledges becomes very revealing in how you can then find out about emotional expressions that might be trying to be communicated through this object that's in front of you. If you're going to talk about kitsch, or Victorian figurative art, and this individual says, 'yes, that's exactly what I was referring to', it becomes a point of contact in how one would want to do that now.

JR: And what do you think is your responsibility as a teacher?

PB: For me, it's to ensure that a student feels they have a working process with which they can leave their BA degree course, in order to set themselves up as the artist of their choice, as the artist they want to be. And are there enough methodologies at their disposal to be able to do that within the economic restrictions that they're going to have to endure. So you're not just promoting them to use polished stainless steel and incredibly expensive materials. You've actually said; 'try this out in all these other ways, so that you can at least begin to realise ideas and thoughts in your heads in a very direct, expedient kind of way.'

JR: And the student's responsibility?

PB: I've always thought the student's responsibility was to want to do it, quite simply. That was it. It's almost the question you might ask those incoming students: 'do you really want to do this?'

fig. 141 *untitled: stack;* 2008, 2008

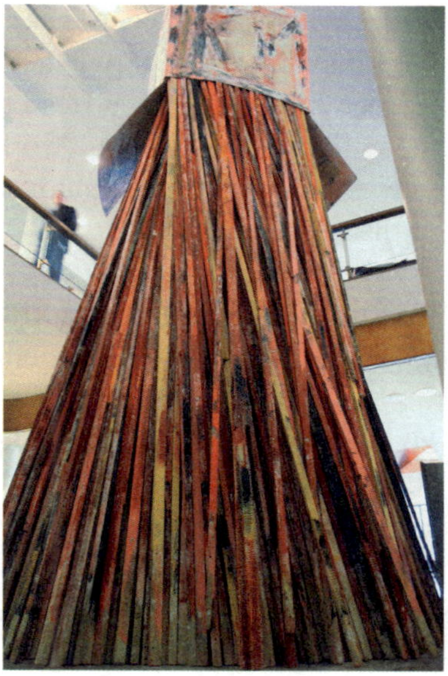

JR: Can I ask you something about the relationship of the school to the world? I'm thinking about this in relation to your commission *stack* for the Royal Festival Hall (fig. 141) …

PB: *Stack*, for me, is a bit of a failure. I'm afraid it doesn't completely work; its base is too big, and all sorts of things went slightly wrong with it, including having to cut off sixty centimetres at the top, so it doesn't quite go the height. But the location interests me, this idea of making something that big, which is then almost camouflaged into the Royal Festival Hall. What I'm almost suggesting with that work is that the public space is actually not just about a big glitzy kind of commissioned work. It's about an intervention, it's about drawing attention maybe to qualities of the space that wouldn't necessarily be looked at. Or using a space that's almost an unusable space, like a ship in a bottle, which is what the whole point of *stack* was. So those kind of things would, I hope, enable me to talk to students in a very open way about the hazards of taking on a really full-on kind of public space like the Southbank, but still having a kind of flexible relationship with it, and trying something out that may not necessarily work, but to not be afraid of that. Several people have said to me that piece doesn't work, and that's fine. I'm glad they've been honest with me, because I don't think it works, and as I say to the students, 'I'd give myself a low 2.2 for that.' I'm very grateful to the Southbank for giving me that opportunity, but it was a hazardous experience. It was a real roller-coaster ride, and I slightly lost my nerve with it. Therefore things, just at the last minute, went awry with it, and one has to live with that. You can't ask them to take it down again, so it's tricky. But I hope it provides students with a chance to be critical of their so-called teacher … If they ever wanted to talk about it, it would provide the context to say 'look this is a public work, and it hasn't completely worked, but it's interesting to have been put in that position; it's not just the protective space of the gallery.'

JR: The more you talk about this, the more I understand that when you talk about failure, you're actually talking about learning …

PB: Yes. It's so interesting, because when I was talking to Alison Wilding, about it not working, she said, 'No, it doesn't completely work.' But she said, 'Isn't it wonderful that we can still be learning?' And she's absolutely right. I think that's part of the risk, and if I seem sceptical, it's because I don't entirely believe in the degree show system. It's a whole load of other things that are buried in that experience. It's great that they can put on these shows, but the show isn't the thing that's going to count at all, unfortunately it's going to be many other things. It's like being an athlete, isn't it? A fantastic athlete, except they've got this dodgy tendon in their ankle, and getting the athlete who's absolutely completely all-in-one and can run the one hundred metres without hamstrings snapping and everything. The artist always has something. The very good degree show doesn't entirely convince me, because the sort of flaw that that person is going to have to overcome is the thing that's really interesting.

JR: Why I asked the question in the first place was something that came up around subject-led work, and what you think got lost, or misplaced, with the focus on subject-led work. You seemed to suggest that what got lost was an interrogation of context, or a set of relationships between the work and the world, so to speak. And somehow *stack* made me curious about what kind of relationship you understand the art-school should have with the world, and how this exchange should happen. How the world comes into the school, and how you take the work to the world …

PB: I saw the very dogmatic subject-led art as providing such a lot of equipment for theoretical semiotics, for semiotic language to be used. The object itself was just an equation for verbal language, providing a very fixed context, in which the object would be shown, for example in the white cube. So you got a whole cycle of things happening that were utterly dependent on each other. And then I began to see that the art school system, with the degree show as the culminating glory of that three- to four-year BA, or two-year MA thing, as absolutely reciprocal to that white-cube orthodoxy.

The object that went into it that would provide the theory, the verbal language, would provide the exchange. So something seemed to be going missing and it seemed to be this huge territory between the art school and the gallery. Or it seemed to be about the process of thinking, or dreaming, or making, or imagination, trusting – a whole load of words – and the kind of flow chart that would come out of those words just seemed to be vanishing. It's not that I want every artwork to show its process – I don't – but it's as though something of how the artist would come to the position of being able to realise a work was getting less and less recognition, or acknowledgement. It was more the delivery and the end product that was important, and the best way of showing that – which is absolutely true, one can't deny it – is the white-cube space. But it's not the only way, and it seems you don't always need a white-cube space to do what you've got to do as an artist. It's been like trying to give students the breadth of experience that moves beyond and outside of that, that I think is very important. Which is why something like the challenge of the Southbank was important, because it's the biggest antithesis to a white cube in terms of space. Not in terms of people – the white-cube space can attract huge numbers of people and the Southbank has huge numbers of people going through it. But they're apparently very different groups of people, so that was the challenge.

JR: And finally, how's the health of art education in the UK? Is it in robust health?

PB: Yes, I think it is. The problem is getting the younger artists into the art schools to teach. I know some really fantastic younger artists, and they will only visit. They're selling their work, they're kind of making ends meet through some other route. But intellectually and inspirationally and creatively, as people who can discuss work, they're fantastic. But they don't want that commitment, they don't want to be in that institutional framework. That is going to be an increasing problem.

First published in David Mollin and John Reardon, eds., *ch-ch-ch-changes: Artists Talk about Teaching* (London: Ridinghouse, 2009), 34–49.

In December 1997 Barlow was a participant in the project *Between the Visible and the Invisible* initiated and organised by Nilofar Akmut. Twelve artists from Australia, Germany, Japan, Pakistan, Singapore, the United Kingdom, and the United States travelled to Pakistan to work with students and tutors from all fine-art disciplines at the National College of Arts, Lahore. Writing twenty-three years later in 2020 Barlow recalls certain episodes from the trip. In the excerpts below, she remembers witnessing a life class and recounts her experience of leading a sculpture workshop for the students. Also included is her account of the tensions that emerged between the visiting and local tutors during what was for her an important and fascinating trip.

Lahore

2020

[...]

THE LIFE ROOM

F was an assistant to the project. He was a friendly young man, and an artist, healthily ambitious and keen to come to the UK and study at the Slade. We had many conversations from which I deduced his frustration with the art school in Lahore, and his hunger to be successful and make money from his art. This was difficult to unravel. His main focus was to find out which kind of art – what style, what subject – could be guaranteed to be successful, both financially and in terms of critical acclaim. These concerns reflected what he thought he would gain from coming to London and studying at the Slade. When I protested, and asked him to reconsider his ambitions, he became sulky and defiant. I told him he would not be accepted on to the Slade course if those were his only intentions. We had heated discussions where I suggested to him that, as a young artist, it was natural and, in some ways, necessary to want to be where the creative energies were at their most vibrant and of the moment, but, surely, he would want to discover how to interpret those creative energies on his own terms. He was only too clear that he did not want to have to 'waste time' experimenting and trying to find out what was relevant and particular to him – he wanted a brilliant teacher to tell him what direction to go in, a teacher who was famous and knew how to go about being a successful artist. Of course, he had learnt all about the YBAs and their Goldsmiths experience. He wanted to be part of that excitement and, as he thought, inevitable success. I reminded him that the YBAs were now well established, having been around for ten years.

And so we established a warm-hearted relationship based on arguments and contentious disagreements about art. One afternoon, he suggested we take a walk around the art school so I could see for myself its limitations from his point of view. We began the tour in the painting department of which I do not have much recollection. However, I do remember looking at a temporary display of paintings. The students had been set a composition project, and the works on display were to be marked and judged for their adherence to the rules of composition as imposed by the fine-art course.

The works were clichéd versions of familiar mid-twentieth-century, European styles, but particularly British. All the paintings were figurative, reflecting a very old-fashioned, academic, and dated approach to that genre. But most depressing was the careful obedience to what seemed to be composition rules. Figures were carefully ranked across the canvasses, forward facing, each correctly occupying exactly the right amount of space. The colours were faded greens and browns, muted reds and grey-blues. The dullness was all-pervading.

F was glum and despondent.

'Let's go to the sculpture life room', he said.

The life room was on the ground floor. Large windows spanned one side of the studio. Glazed double doors opened out on to the central grass quadrangle of the art school. F went ahead of me through the double doors to check whether it was appropriate for a visitor to enter. He returned to usher me into the bright, sunlit studio.

The studio was impressive. A large airy space, and with its high ceiling, timber walls painted dark green, and a timber floor, it had a nineteenth-century atmosphere. Shelves lined the walls crowded with moulds, portrait heads, busts, and life figures, rank upon rank, all, at first glance, similar.

A huge dais dominated the centre of the studio upon which a female model reclined. To my bewilderment, she was draped in a white muslin sheet. The material clung to her and was like a veil so that her naked body could be seen through the fabric. It was provocative – the supposed objective role of the life model had been transformed into something sexual: her breasts protruding into the cloth very suggestively, as was her stomach. Only her head was uncovered. I was horrified.

'What's going on?', I asked F. 'The muslin drape, what's it doing?'

F laughed, 'It's because nudity is banned so she has to be covered.'

I was angry. I was alarmed for the model. Did she realise what was being done to her? Was this the worst possible influence from British colonialism, that even with the arts the impact was corrupt?

'But this is turning the whole exercise into soft porn. It could be, might be interesting if there was some sort of intention, some sort of comment on sexuality, some conceptual reasoning – but clearly this is meant to be about study. It is so perverse.' I whispered, enraged.

The model took a break. When she stood up, I realised to my horror that the muslin was wet. F explained that the material would then cling to her body, rather than just lying on it, revealing more detail. This laborious attempt to both conceal and reveal was unbearable. The sexual implications, however unintentional, were difficult to tolerate. Again, there could be, and have been, many contexts where this relationship to the body has been a clear, artistic intention. Hellenic sculpture, through to the Renaissance, and up to the present day used the draped figure to enhance both beauty and sexuality, with many other distressing, sexist messages embedded in the imagery. But to see the life-room tradition become a vehicle for such corruption now, today, was difficult to comprehend. Yet again, I was caught in the colonial trap. The European tradition of the life room – its discipline, its prescriptive processes, its judgemental approach, its orthodoxies – all of these became indoctrinations within European art schools. But when combined with colonialism, then they became toxic.

F and I wandered round the life room inspecting the clay models the students were working on. The clay was smooth, and the life model had morphed into blurred effigies where the attempts to incorporate the wet muslin shroud with an accurate rendition of the body that lay beneath proved an impossible task. I tried to explain my disgust. I didn't want to offend the students, or F. But the more I wanted to identify what I thought was wrong, the more confused I became; and the more redundant I felt. If cultures can be fused and their salient qualities shared and absorbed, how is that to be initiated? By whom and what for?

But my disgust was not levelled at the model herself, or the students' endeavours, or the fact that working from the figure as translated from a European tradition to an Islamic culture could, ironically, end up being this provocatively draped, sexually implicit, life model – it was the ever-present shadow of colonialism that was plaguing me as much as I felt it was plaguing a cultural rapport between European artists and those from Pakistan.

Whichever way I turned to justify what we, as a group, were doing in Lahore with the students, we inevitably came head-to-head with the impact of colonialism. Our good intentions could not help but be interpreted as colonial.

SCULPTURE

The sculpture project I was responsible for initiating was to be centred around materials, improvisation, and the unknown. I was keen to open up 'making', in terms of sculpture, as being an encounter with the imagination and for there not to be a dependency on a pre-existing idea – to experiment with bringing into the world something that was nameless, that had no identity other than what it was, to be led by the process of making, to be surprised.

F was to assist me with setting up the project. We accumulated many materials, and I had requested materials that could be recycled, that were about to be thrown away, etc. – timber lengths, paper, cardboard, wire, chicken wire, offcuts of plywood, fabric. But there were immediately issues. In Lahore, and probably Pakistan as a whole, all materials were valued as having potential usefulness. Compared to what I was used to in London, there was a different attitude to these materials, and they were not rubbish. Whilst the Western attitude to the recycling of rubbish and waste, where the disposable culture is rife, has caused an 'out-of-sight, out-of-mind' relationship to anything that can be thrown away, in Lahore there was a highly organised culture of recycling which included salvaging, mending, reparation, and re-using. Rubbish, refuse, debris, waste – these were not necessarily to be cleared away and disposed of – these all had potential and value.

Therefore my introduction to making, with the emphasis on the unknown – to bring into the world something that had never been in the world before – fell upon deaf ears. Several students left, saying they did not understand and that they wanted to learn about sculpture – carving, casting, metal work. I began to panic. But F had an idea. He suggested we go to the market where everything and anything was available – where whole stalls were devoted to the sale of redundant domestic goods, used fabric, broken machinery, timber lengths salvaged from anywhere … He said, you name it and there would be stalls which would be selling it.

The students were excited and animated, thrilled to be taking the lead, to show me what was specific to their culture and their understanding of 'things'. I was equally thrilled and excited to visit such a rich resource.

The market did not disappoint and exceeded my wildest expectations. We began our tour at the bicycle stall. Every component of a bicycle was separated into different categories down to the smallest valve and screw. Bundles of used inner tubes were hung in great coils across the front of the stall, whilst loose spokes from bicycle wheels were stashed in baskets, as were the rubber grips from handlebars … saddles were piled in heaps, also springs, bike lights, pedals. For me, it was a wondrous feat of organisation – and an inspiration about the power of dismantling – the limbo created by removing the function of something, placing objects into a state of dormancy to be neither useless nor useful.

We went on to a used furniture stall, different from a second-hand furniture stall – all this furniture was beyond use but could still be salvaged. Here the furniture was being carefully taken apart and the sections of Formica surfaces, shelves, cupboard doors being stacked in a very orderly way. Again, every component of the furniture was being separated out: handles, knobs, door catches, locks, screws, wall fixings … all of these categorised and placed in their separate containers.

Onwards to stalls that specialised in buttons – a feast of glinting, shining colour in huge mounds, every conceivable kind of button to be found from Mickey Mouse buttons to humble, round, white shirt buttons. Huge decorative buttons had their own place, as did those buttons that could be distinguished by a fashion label – YSL, D&G, Armani … And another stall selling wool – whilst the stall owners' children unwound wool from second-hand knitwear, others wound the wool into figure-of-eight skeins and hung them up on butchers' hooks along the front of the stall. It all looked decorative and festive.

On and on we went and before we knew it, it was lunchtime. F suggested a good café, and I volunteered to treat everyone to lunch. The atmosphere was joyful, and the students were enchanting.

The café was crowded with many people F knew, and the food was delicious. It was a lovely occasion.

As we walked back to the art school, I was anxious about how I could develop the potential which visiting the market had prompted. I realised that I had to explain that the visit to the market had been an entirely new experience for me. And that it had opened my eyes to a different attitude to making from what I had proposed at the beginning of the day. I knew it was important to understand making from the students' perspective and not impose my relationship with making on to them.

I needed to initiate a discussion.

I began to talk to A. She was an older student. At my introductory talk that morning, she was very alert and keen – the only one! I told her that I was debating how to restart the project. She said she thought the whole point of the project was to bring to the students my experiences as an artist as a fresh point of view. She was insistent that I did not change what I had proposed but agreed that I could talk about how much the market had affected me and why. She was quick to respond to the idea of objects, things, being dismantled and losing their original identity so they became ghost objects in limbo.

When we had returned to the art school, we sat under the trees to talk about how to proceed. I now had a powerful ally in A. I told the group of students that the visit to the market had changed my attitude to what making could be in relationship to sculpture. That, although I would continue with the original intention of making something that had not been in the world before, that had no name, or meaning, that had come into existence through spontaneity, improvisation, urgency and 'making do', I wanted them to also show me what their relationship to objects was with particular reference to the visit to the market.

'Everything at the market – the piles of buttons, the knitting wool, the dismantled bicycle parts, everything had a name, and a value, even though they were redundant, but categorised and separated out for sale – these things, these objects, were asleep, so to speak. But they were also lying in wait, ready to be useful again. How do you unname a bicycle pedal, or an inner tube, or a row of Mickey Mouse buttons, and give them an entirely new existence?' I asked.

The students were cheerful and excited. 'Can we go and buy stuff from the market?', one student asked. For a moment, I thought, no ... I wanted them to begin with the empty space in front of them. But I changed my mind and told them that I had wanted to say 'No', and why – that I wanted them to begin with an empty space. To my surprise, none of the students then wanted to go back to the market.

F and A both contributed to the discussion, and it was agreed that we would begin the next day. The students wandered off, and F and A and I sat in the sunny art-school gardens.

'You see', F began, 'there is no real history of sculpture in Pakistan. We have the prehistoric artefacts and archaeological sites from the Indus valley civilisations, we have our music, our oral traditions of poetry, our architecture, our traditional miniature painting and calligraphy – but sculpture, no'.

'OK' I responded, 'then does making have any meaning? When I persistently refer to making what do the students think?' I asked.

'Oh, they're thinking of crafts – ceramics, woodcarving, stonecarving, embroidery, weaving, jewellery, leather work … anything that has a particular skill, that can make money!' F replied.

'For me, what you have proposed is an entirely new approach to sculpture,' began A. 'I have attended many lectures about art – and art from Europe and America, so I know what materiality means to European artists and the arguments which released new attitudes to making and materiality in 1960s Italy, and the influence it had further afield. I know how important Arte Povera was to the history of European art. I have thought about this a lot. I think there is a problem of transporting such a movement to a country like Pakistan. The references have a host of different meanings to those they have in Western cultures. To make Arte Povera in Pakistan should be inspirational and absolutely relevant – but it isn't. People want to escape into the beautifully made, the superbly crafted, things that have great skill and therefore great worth both economically and aesthetically. How do you say, to make "poor art" in a poor country where anything and everything can be salvaged and reused is like "coals to Newcastle"!'

A and I spent a lot of time together that week. She was inspirational company. She made beautiful poignant work – fired clay objects – and during the sculpture project week, she bound sticks in torn shards of fabric. She said, 'I keep on thinking of water-divining rods, but I know that is not what you want – you don't want a narrative. But in Pakistan everything has to have a narrative. It's ingrained and innate.'

I responded quickly, keen to adjust her interpretation of my argument. 'But you have discovered the divining-rod association through your act of binding the sticks, your act of making – and transforming. You weren't necessarily thinking of divining rods before you began. I think that's exactly what I am hoping can happen. And although you name them as divining rods, they are not divining rods. They are symbols of them … that's a whole other story!! Anyway, I don't want to impose – why should I? My desire to make sculpture which is free of naming and narrative is my interest, my problem … I don't want to force my interests on to all of you. I want to avoid all judgemental orthodoxies – you know, right/wrong, good/bad … it doesn't make sense to impose like that. This should be about different attitudes, different cultural experiences … and generosity.'

The students rallied to the project with great enthusiasm. I don't think I convinced them of the wonders, as I saw it, of the unnameable object. But I did witness their unreserved pleasure in the excitement of unpreconceived making, the pleasure of making on its terms, the discovery of materials, and stuff finding ways of coming together, using invention, spontaneity, and 'making do' as solutions … Yes, I did succeed in inspiring the students that these were all possibilities for opening up the imagination. And the students in turn introduced me to the uninhibited relevance of narrative.

What I did learn was that symbolism and narrative were all important to these students: that a split, timber offcut, dug into the ground, supporting a broken saucer, surrounded by pebbles weighing down beautifully cut paper shapes was all about this student discovering the time she became aware of no longer being a child, of becoming a woman. This student was veiled, so I only had her eyes to communicate with. Her narrative was intensely meaningful, and faultless, beyond criticism.

It was interesting that the females were far more productive than the male students. In fact the male students were uncomfortable from the start.

'They interpret the project as being "feminine"', was A's diagnosis, 'they want something more masculine – metal, steel, like Anthony Caro, David Smith, and Henry Moore. They want to be tough and heroic!'

F seemed somewhat unenthusiastic as well, saying, early on, that it wasn't his thing to make in this improvising way. He liked to have a 'concept' that he could be clear about – where making was well-planned and could equate with the concept. He was a great admirer of Marcel Duchamp. I asked him what and who a Pakistani Duchamp might be, what their work would be like, again in the light of the market experience.

F paused. The question perplexed him.

'Duchamp provided another way of looking at the world and what art could be in the world. I like his non-visual approach. I like the fact that he fuses language, image, and object, and mixes them up. Which comes first, language or image? How he questions how you see, and what you see. He makes language and image equal. That's what I want to do. Your unnaming issue is interesting but doesn't go far enough. It's still rooted in expression. I want to make – whatever that means – without the expressive gesture interfering. Jeff Koons, Damien Hirst – they're on top of it!'

At the end of the week the students presented their work. I requested that each student whose work was being presented should remain silent whilst the rest of us discussed what we were looking at. Then at the end of each presentation, the student in question could speak and reveal their experience, and what the work was to them.

The first two presentations went well. The third presentation was to be given by Z, a male student. He had been working at the far end of the outside space allocated for the project. I had talked to him about twice during the week. He always left early, and I was dubious about his interest and commitment to the project. His work, set up in the far corner, consisted of a scarecrow-figure, roughly assembled from a garden fork, a rough piece of wood, tied crossway to another piece of wood attached vertically to the garden fork. The assemblage was covered with various bits of clothing. It was a sinister image. I asked him if he was OK with remaining silent whilst we all discussed his work. He nodded dourly. Then M, another male student laughed and shouted at him in Urdu. F looked embarrassed. I asked him to translate. He reassured me saying that it was nothing. But the mood had shifted.

'Come on', I said, 'what did M say?'

'He was teasing, saying to Z – now you are taking orders from a woman.'

'That's OK', I said, but I had no idea why I said that.

I turned to Z, 'Do you have a problem?'

'No, no, no', he protested. 'Please continue with the discussion.'

I left it at that, but the afternoon had been blighted. The female students were subdued, even sulky. Maybe they wanted me to make more of the incident, to flush out sexism and prejudice, to find out why M should have said that to Z.

As we walked to the next presentation, I asked A what she thought.

'There is prejudice against women generally, and there is in this art school, from the students and the staff. Yes, some of the male staff are sexist, but its old-school sexism. It's not that it's harmless, it's just very patronising. That's why this workshop fortnight is so important to me, and to Naazish [Ata-ullah] as head of printmaking, and many of us female students who want to be artists and to be taken seriously. But there is this rising tide of fundamentalism, and some of the boys are beginning to adopt a kind of fundamentalist style. It's quite frightening because it maybe just a phase, a sort of angry young man phase, but it could turn into the real thing. The extreme politics are volatile and attractive to those lacking self-esteem. It gives them power – a power generated by male authoritarianism … it's all so depressingly regressive. I long to leave, go to America or the UK. But that's just a dream.'

I could tell she was upset.

'I am so sorry you had to contend with this', she continued.

'Let's make this next presentation fun and put that incident in its place …', I replied.

We came to B's work. It consisted of a fragile disc made from cardboard supported on a tripod of sticks. Wool had been wound around the disc to hold it in place on the tripod. There was a thin plywood circle fixed outside the cardboard disc. Wire had been pierced through the ply so that it hung down at regular intervals. Attached to the wire were signs and shapes delicately made from the wire. The whole object was placed in a flat dish filled with water and around the dish various clay objects were positioned.

I asked B if she would accept being silent whilst everyone discussed her work. She agreed, bright-eyed and eager.

I asked various students to comment. They answered obediently pointing out the work's delicacy, referring to its windmill-like structure, and that it could be made large, that it was architectural.

Z had taken up his usual position at the back of the group.

'Z', I said, 'you've been very quiet all afternoon. I would like to know what you think. Is there anything that you like or don't like about this work?'

He shrugged his shoulders insolently. Someone sniggered. 'Where do you think the centre of the work is … does it have a focus? What do you think?'

'I don't know. I don't really care. It has no meaning for me', he muttered.

'Does anyone else feel the same?' I asked.

'Oh no, I don't', H replied, a female student who had been a very positive presence throughout the week, 'I actually know what this work is about. But I can pretend I don't know! It's like a diagram, or a sketch. It doesn't have to be seen as a momentous decision. I like it because it is trying out something. For me it fulfils all that you talked about at the beginning of the workshop. Maybe, because I know what it's about, it has too much meaning. It isn't a meaningless object but for me the important thing is that it's made as if B was stuck in her bedroom at home and she is using anything that came to hand – it has its own beauty because of that. I can also see it being made in steel, to a large scale.'

'That's great. Thank you so much', I responded.

'I have a question – would you know that this is the work of a female?' I asked, hoping that this would be provocative.

'Perhaps you would like to answer this question, B, and come out of your silence?'

B took a moment to collect her thoughts.

'Actually', she pondered, 'when I look around at all the other works, they all have this fragile, ephemeral quality, as if they are not quite the real thing. Is that a female quality, something that only women do? That doesn't seem quite right to me. This way of working has given me a lot of freedom because this week hasn't been about making things well. It's been about trying things out, making do in any way we can as if we're stuck on a desert island and have to improvise with what's around. Yes, I agree with H, my work is like a diagram, or sketch, or even a model. It can now go in any direction. But whether it's a female work, I don't know … look at Z's work: it's all tied together with string, and there are things sewn on, and it's made really badly.' Everyone burst out laughing, even Z. 'Is it a female work? And what does that mean? Women can do anything when it comes to making – from sewing, cooking, all the usual domestic things, and farming, repairing their homes – building, fixing broken things … and they do all these daily chores with skill and facility.'

B's eyes were blazing now, she tossed her head, throwing back the ends of her hijab. She was angry.

'Your work, Z, is as female as mine,' she continued, 'I don't like your work – you have made a statue of a Taliban fighter; it's like a puppet; I think you are making a joke … I think you want to make fun of all of us. You are very rude and insulting.'

I stepped in to lift the discussion, 'That was an amazing speech, B. Very powerful. Thank you. Just tell me about your work. For me it has something of a sundial. In fact, as we look at it now, the shadows of the wire pieces are incredible … take a photograph and do some drawings … it has so much potential. But is it something specific? … These wire shapes look like words, and the designs on the cardboard disc are almost like signs of the zodiac. What is it? And would you make it enormous if you could?'

'I'm sorry' B said, 'this has been such an important week for some of us … there is a divide between us girls and the boys, that's our culture, our society, but we, as females, have ambitions, we want to have a future – we want respect.'

I began clapping and soon everyone joined in. The week had ended on a happy but contentious note.

A said, 'We never did find out what B's sculpture was about.'

But by that stage I don't think it mattered. She had been able to speak her mind and sculpture was the catalyst! What more could we want?

LOOKING BACK

I'm writing this in the midst of the global coronavirus outbreak. The date is 31 March 2020. Twenty-three years have passed since the Lahore International Workshop in December 1997.

Over the years, I have frequently thought about my visit to Lahore. Many moments repeat themselves over and over again. And although I have forgotten the names of many of the participants, vivid images of those remarkable people recur regularly. I have the mental possession of wonderful encounters, wonderful discussions, and above all, a much-valued introduction to a country and its culture that has left an indelible mark on my understanding of the political, social, and religious eruptions of the ensuing years.

[...]

At some point during the workshop at the art school, it became obvious to the group, and to Nilofar [Akmut], that for the regular tutors at the art school, what we, as artists from so many different countries, were bringing to the art school was unclear in its intentions and its cause. Many of these tutors were respected artists in their own right in Lahore. They were feeling excluded and disrespected by the group and the workshops and project initiatives, and the results were disruptive and unclear for students and staff: what we were doing seemed to them to be very 'Western', and inconsiderate of what they, the tutors, were trying to achieve. It was an imposition on the art school and all that it stood for – good drawing, good technique, good skills, good composition, and good subject. There was little tolerance for the fact that many of us in the group wanted to understand these values and that examining and questioning these was what we all wanted to do with our own endeavours as artists but also in our roles within education.

An informal meeting was arranged so that the regular tutors at the art school and the group could share their respective experiences. I do not remember the exact issues that were raised, but what I was left to ruminate on, was, as before, that the whole enterprise of initiating the international workshop at the art school, inevitably recalled a colonialist influence – that our projects were inherently from an entirely Western stance which had no methods or sensitivities for being inclusive of Pakistan's cultural histories and legacies.

Although I agreed with this, I could not help but find the criticism paradoxical: the work I saw in the painting department was undeniably rooted in a very English vernacular, an old-fashioned 1930s style of composition and use of colour, content, and aesthetics. It seemed extraordinary to me that these tutors were lamenting a lack of 'Pakistani' awareness when the work I had seen had all the hallmarks of very English aesthetic and formal values. The evening was awkward and unresolved.

I look back on that discussion with regret. I did not want there to be discord between the regular art-school staff and us visitors.

[...]

ON OTHER ARTISTS

Published in *Phyllida Barlow: Objects for … and Other Things*, 'The Sneeze of Louise' is adapted from a slide-illustrated lecture about French-American artist Louise Bourgeois (1911–2010). It relates to work Barlow saw in a number of exhibitions in 1995: the group show *Rites of Passage: Art for the End of the Century* at the Tate Gallery, London (now Tate Britain), and the solo shows *Louise Bourgeois: Sculptures, environnements, dessins, 1938–1995* at the Musée d'Art Moderne de la Ville de Paris, and *Louise Bourgeois: Sculpture* and *The Prints of Louise Bourgeois* both at the Museum of Modern Art, Oxford. The paper was given at a conference that coincided with the two exhibitions in Oxford and was included in the museum's publication on Bourgeois. Barlow discusses in detail Marcel Duchamp's *Why Not Sneeze, Rose Sélavy?* (1921), *Bourgeois's Cell (Eyes and Mirrors)* (1989–93) and *No Exit* (1989), and Man Ray's *Object to Be Destroyed* (1923) and their relationship to time. She references other works by Bourgeois – *Avenza Revisited II* (1968–9), *Spiral Woman* (1951–2), *Lair* (1986), *Maisons Fragiles* (1978), *Articulated Lair* (1986), and *Cumul I* (1969) – and their relation to one another. She considers Bourgeois's use of material, in particular plaster, the spiral form, suspension, and the sexual charge of Bourgeois's sculpture.

Louise Bourgeois: The Sneeze of Louise

1995

Whilst looking at Louise Bourgeois's *Cells* and *The Red Rooms* in the Musée de l'Art Moderne de la Ville de Paris and the Tate Gallery, London, I thought about the devices artists have used during this century to frame and contain disparate things so as to bring unlikely, opposing, or contrasting objects together as a unified experience – devices such as boxes, plinths, cages, and, of course recently, the ubiquitous vitrine.

I recalled Marcel Duchamp's *Why Not Sneeze, Rose Sélavy?* of 1921 (figs. 39, 142). As a small, neat object it is easy to remember. Its disparate collection of things are unified by a small, portable cage. The ring on top is just big enough for a finger to go through suggesting a container for the lightest of animals – small birds to be transported to and from market. It is therefore a portable object which, as such, clearly shows the signs of wear and tear.

It contains a collection of white cubes, apparently trapped. Though marble is a dense, heavy material, the cubes masquerade perfectly as cubes of sugar. Protruding into the cubes are two objects: a thermometer and a cuttlebone. The thermometer is an instrument which measures and records the changes in body temperature, registering sickness or health, but here, as it nestles and probes into the cool, deceitful cubes of marble sugar, what change is expected to be detected? Perhaps a rise in temperature would cause an explosion, and the small cage and its contents would fragment into a powder of sugary marble dust laced with beads of mercury, ground cuttlebone, tangled wire, and shards of glass.

Is this an object held in time, poised to explode? The thermometer waits in anticipation for any change which indicates the impending explosion. What is the role of the cuttlebone? What is a cuttlebone – something found washed up on seashores, or an object for pet birds to sharpen their beaks on? It is, in fact, the central bone of the cuttlefish, a squid-like animal which ejects ink when alarmed. Like the thermometer this residual object also indicates anticipation, but in its case it is the anticipation of fear, and the volatile consequences of that fear, an eruption of black ink. Gradually this small, portable cage-object becomes more and more like an ambiguous instrument with a sexuality which its title begins to reveal. More particularly, it reveals its absence of sex, its hoping for sex.

The sneeze, sometimes referred to as the next best thing to an orgasm, is the anticipated event and the disparate contents of the cage, in their different ways, mark time in anticipation of this longed-for, desired event.

BELOW LEFT TO RIGHT:

fig. 142 **Marcel Duchamp**
Why Not Sneeze, Rose Sélavy?, 1921/1964

fig. 143 **Louise Bourgeois**
Cell (Eyes and Mirrors), 1989–93

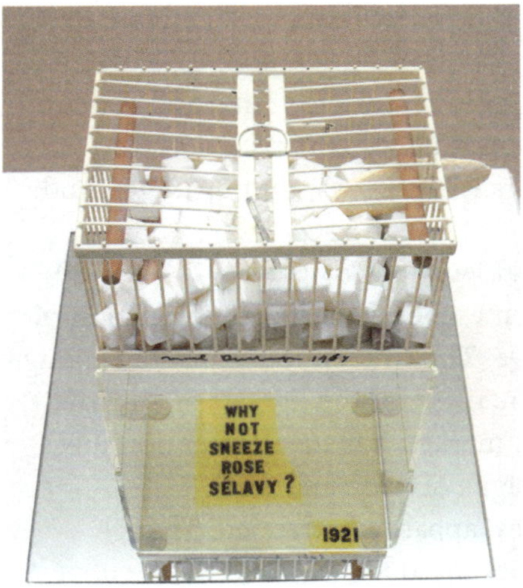

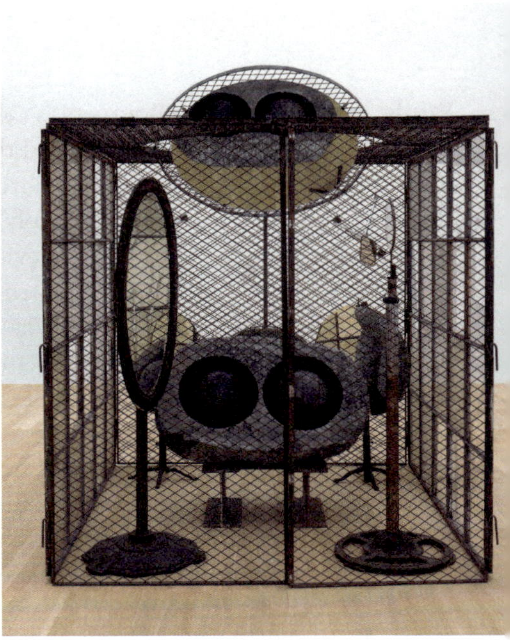

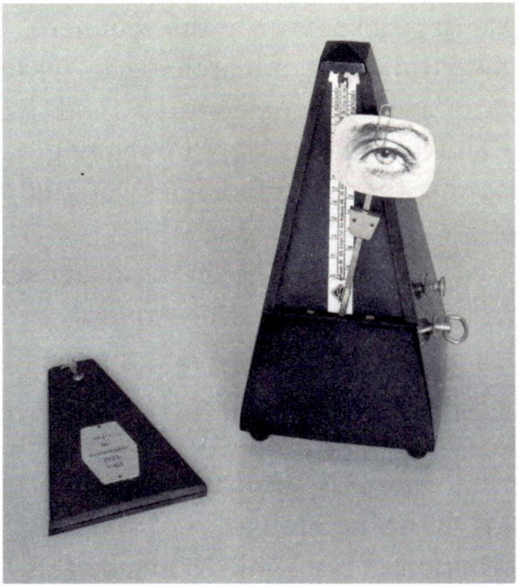

ABOVE:

fig. 144 **Man Ray**
Indestructible Object (originally titled *Object to Be Destroyed*), 1923/1933/1965

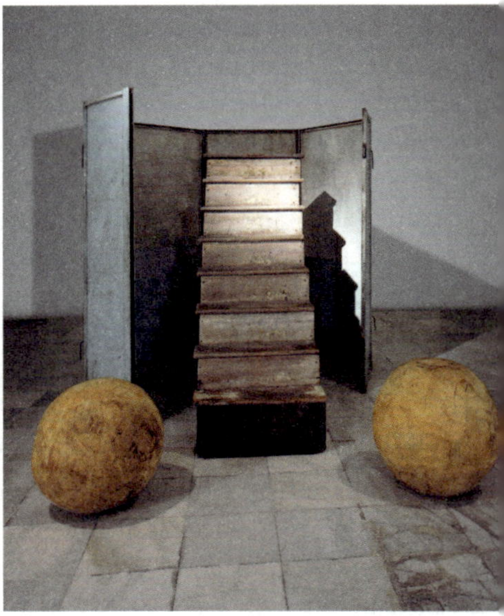

ABOVE:

fig. 145 **Louise Bourgeois**
No Exit, 1989

At the moment when the thermometer registers a change as the cool marble sugar cubes become hot and the cuttlebone recalls its former status as the rigid inner bone of the warning, ink-squirting, fleshy squid, the prolonged anticipation will be released in the craved-for orgasmic explosion of a sneeze. Bourgeois knew Duchamp and thought he was an unhappy man because '... all his life he felt that he could not have made a woman sexually happy'.[1] Perhaps this adds to the significance of this object's potent sexuality, for, as Bourgeois said in an interview with Christiane Meyer-Thoss, '... the sexual or the absence of sex is everything'.[2]

Duchamp's object is an object of measurement. It is in suspense, held in time, unfolding itself continuously at the same moment, a constant reminder of the longed-for and the about-to-be. Its tension is borne out of its implications of an unfulfilled sexual longing told by its disguising and playful symbols. 'All symbolic acts are pleasurable', said Bourgeois. 'People will not admit that.'[3] Though these symbols are playful, what they symbolise is painful: the fearful experience of sexual longing when it is reciprocated by a dreaded and awesome sexual unfulfillment. I can recall *Why Not Sneeze* ... as an image. It is easy to remember. The work of Bourgeois which reminded me of *Why Not Sneeze* ... I cannot recall as an image, and I find it difficult to remember. It demands that you are there with it.

The work I am referring to is *Cell (Eyes and Mirrors)* (1989–93; fig. 143). This work reveals itself as you approach it and walk around it. And it is as an unfolding space and as an unfolding object that it arouses response. These unfolding qualities are time-based and seem to refute an image for a physically sensual experience which is to do with time, place, and an all-pervading atmosphere of fear. It is the element of time which enables me to compare *Cell (Eyes and Mirrors)* with Duchamp's *Why Not Sneeze* ... . In both works I experience a suspension of time through objects which act as instruments of measurement.

With *Cell (Eyes and Mirrors)* the space unfolds as you walk around the sculpture. This is emphasised in the contrast between the predatory and watchful but unseeing gaze of the carved, breast-like granite eyes and the ever watchful, all-seeing gaze of the mirrors which seem to record, hold, and trap every movement beyond their immediate environment. As you walk around this sculpture you can experience an opposite view. As you look at, or more appropriately, watch the back of the granite eyes the front is revealed by the mirrors. This is a sculpture with eyes at the back of its head. As objects of continuous revelation the mirrors are instruments of surveillance which do not keep secrets, harsh devices of stark objectivity which capture, in real time, the presence of the viewer who becomes ensnared and trapped in the *Cell*'s interior space.

The mirrors are the gaze, the sight of the sightless granite. They are the instruments which register change. They monitor your changing movements and the unchanging movements of the objects they stand guard over within, just as the thermometer anticipates change in *Why Not Sneeze* … . The boundary or container for this sculpture – the derelict structure of salvaged window frames from disbanded factory or office – act as a grid. Grids imply systems of order, means for measuring. As Bourgeois has said: 'The grid is a very peaceful thing … everything has a place. Everything is welcome.'[4] Like the well-used container cage of *Why Not Sneeze* … , this worn and weathered container has recorded on it its passage through time. Both have time engrained within them and because of this they convey a sense of resignation. They can wait forever.

Cell (Eyes and Mirrors) is full of sight and no sight, a kind of blindness which is full of stillness, a state of waiting, but also of movement. The movements are caught in the reflective eyes of the mirrors which lie in wait to trap the stalking viewer and pull them into the gridded, interior space where 'everything has a place, everything is welcome'.[5] This blind and watchful anticipation is also full of fear, and, like *Why Not Sneeze* … , full of the absence of sex. This absence is suspended in time which itself constitutes the fear in *Cell (Eyes and Mirrors)*. Bourgeois says: 'My work is a very specific fight against fears, one at a time'.[6] Here absence of sex arises out of fear of the awesome potency of the sexual, implied by the ripe, breasted forms of the granite eyes, and their accompanying voyeuristic mirrors, rather than out of the fear of the awesome impotency of the sex of *Why Not Sneeze* … .

Man Ray's *Object to Be Destroyed* (1923; fig. 144) and Bourgeois's *No Exit* (1989; fig. 145) show how time can be manifested in objects and sculpture whose material and physical identities could seem to deny and to be incapable of referencing time. The forensic evidence of time in the sculptures of Bourgeois is as emotively significant as the artist's explicit use of sexually charged forms and surfaces. As in *Why Not Sneeze* … and *Cell (Eyes and Mirrors)*, a similar anticipatory sense of time through measurement is present in *Object to Be Destroyed* and *No Exit*. They are instruments of measurement. In the case of *Object to Be Destroyed* a metronome reveals time as a beat, a rhythm. Time becomes malleable because its rhythm can be altered from faster to slower and back again. Time appears to pass quickly or slowly or, if the metronome stops, to stand still. All compete with our notion of time as a constant.

This is an ominous instrument-object. Its alterable but unrelenting beat is emphasised by the ever-watchful photographic image of the eye, expediently attached to the metronome needle with a paper clip. Its cold, dreamy stare is both hypnotically alluring and fearsome in its concentration, an additional and accompanying menace to the rhythmic clockwork sound. It is an unavoidable reminder of a potential time bomb and a relentless advance towards a moment. This object's relevance to the sculpture of Bourgeois is through the everwatchful gaze of the image of the eye, and the association Bourgeois makes in her sculpture with watchfulness, sleep, and blindness. Implicit in these states is their relationship to sound, sound which alerts, awakens, and reveals.

The potential to describe sound through objects which can evoke or associate themselves with sound rather than through objects which make sound as in *Object to Be Destroyed* is evident in much of the sculpture of Bourgeois of which *No Exit* is one example. The staircase of *No Exit* acts as a grid on which the tread of a foot could measure and beat out the rhythm of a quick or slow pace. This potential for sound is embedded within the wooden staircase's material physicality. Formally, *No Exit* is a sculpture with a clearly identifiable front and a back. It has an interior and an exterior. Also, it is phallic: the column of stairs is accompanied by two carved wooden spheres set on either side. This phallic arrangement, so essential to much of her sculpture, can take on and become female with characteristics of breasts and vagina.

As you approach this work, the carved spheres seem to be rolled back, like a newly opened up tomb, inviting entry. You can walk around the staircase and into the space it occupies – very different from *Cell (Eyes and Mirrors)*. It is essential to do this in order to discover that at the back of the staircase is located a small hatch which reveals the space beneath the stairs. The ultimate secret space, it is the ideal hiding place, small, dark, and highly charged with childhood inquisitiveness and fears. This under-the-stair space is inhabited by two casts of hearts supported on a steel rod. These are the sound of this work colluding with the already implied sound of the footfall on the bare boards of the staircase. These casts act as a reminder of the beating, thumping heart. Like the footfall on the stair it can change in rhythm and pace, signalling a combination of pleasure and fear, of calm and agitation. It reciprocates the bare-boarded stairs' symbolic implications of the empty or deserted house, where anything and everything can lurk. The uncertainty where the staircase is going to or coming from evokes the dread of apprehension, the anticipation of the unexpected – a sound, a creaking board, or a movement, a fleeting shadow of something or someone unknown.

No Exit is full of suspicion. Arousing implications of time held and potential movement, its disparate elements are contained by a framed, screened space: the staircase is partly encircled by high wooden screens, offering another kind of unfolding space as experienced in *Cells (Eyes and Mirrors)*. Screens, with their implications of privacy and intimacy, do not protect this particular space because it can be entered. The viewer is lured in to walk around at leisure, to experience the shifting evocations of time and movement contained in the bare-boarded stairs and secret place beneath, and the could-be and the about-to-be sound of the pulsating heart and beating footfall.

The sculptural concerns of traditional formalism and material physicality paradoxically arouse their opposites, the powerful sensory and sensual responses of the non-physical and the non-material. The traditions inherent in the sculpture of Bourgeois are deeply rooted in the Palaeolithic and twentieth-century art of Europe. These traditions are exemplified by the sculpture of mid-twentieth-century European artists. This is the dark heart of European sculpture which, after World War II, sought a way to begin again by placing its trust in nature. Believing in nature as pure, simple, and innocent provided the incentive to establish new beginnings for artists through which they could eradicate the horrors of war and its accompanying despotic totalitarianism and the genocide of the then recent past.

Étienne Martin's wood carving *Large Couple* (1947; fig. 146), invents a primitive-styled expression which equates with those qualities of nature believed to herald a better, purer future. Its heavy forms, dark shadows, and cumbersome figuration are evidence of the grim aesthetics of mid-twentieth-century European sculpture, in which well-learnt, crafted sculpture techniques and a formalism identifiable with ancient art were doggedly and uninspiringly deployed. Bourgeois's *Avenza Revisited II* (1968–9; fig. 24) is comparable to the Martin work, but is redeemed by its fluidity, its spillage, and its sensual tactility, qualities which have the potential to give beauty to the monstrous.[7] The arched form is curled over on itself, like a massive wave, to form deep, cavernous, concave, folded spaces at the centre of the work, the reciprocal womblike form to the phallus/breast forms emerging as the top surface of the sculpture. These merged phallus/breast forms are endemic to her fifty years of making sculpture, from the totemic, breasted phallic sculptures of the 1940s and 1950s, through to the hanging and suspended *Fillette* (1968), the *Lairs*, and the numerous pendulous cast rubber forms of recent years (1990s). Within this autonomous object there is the merging of the feminine and the masculine, between the phallus and the breast, between the swelling, growing forms and the excavated, cavernous space beneath. The enclosed spaces of the more recent *Lairs* and *Cells* seem to have their origins in this monstrous object's interior space.

The glorious upheaval of the plaster forms of *Avenza Revisited II* so clearly portray Bourgeois's relationship with fear that it becomes alarming to try to identify what this object is. It seems to exemplify the power of an autonomous object which defies a rememberable identity. As I have already noted, objects and sculpture can be either recalled as some kind of image, or be impossible to recall and so demand that you are there to experience them. The experience of objects and sculpture is inextricably linked to the real time required to look, walk around, and consider. It is almost as if, in the absence of a human presence, the object would dissolve. This is very different from an object which presents itself as an image and can take on a pictorial equivalence.

The use of plaster is one of the liquid-to-solid materials with which Bourgeois has had a continued relationship. Through it she reveals her

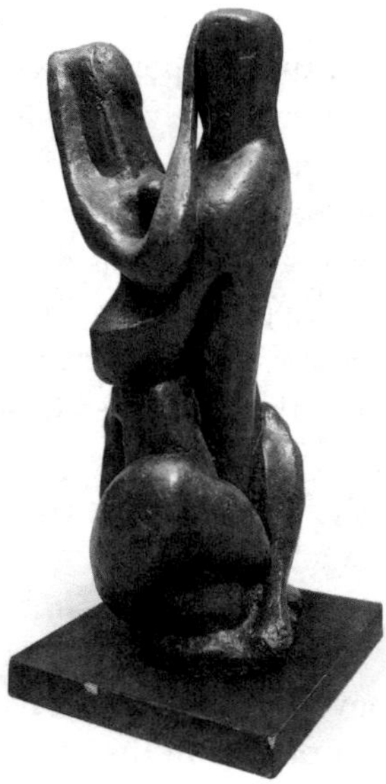

fig. 146 Étienne Martin
Large Couple, 1947

marks of making, such as striations of fingermarks drawn in the wet surface of the plaster during the process of modelling. Like all such marks they make evident her presence in the work, as if her emotions are drawn into the body of the sculpture. My subject, she says, is the rawness of the emotions, my medium is my materials. Plaster gives a lot to the doer. If you pour plaster it is going to set, go from liquid to solid, it has a life of its own, separate from the sculptor. The resistance of stone is total. Plaster and cement provide you with a kind of dialogue.[8]

Bourgeois's language with materials and form have a symbiosis with how emotions find physical outlets through the body. This is powerfully communicated in *Avenza Revisited II*. It is a kind of spewing up, a welling-over of stuff with her mark so clearly smeared into the setting plaster. It is fearless about the non-beautiful but it does give beauty to the monstrous, endowing the fat, full, and overflowing forms with sensuality. *Avenza Revisited II* shows how her subjectivity and her relationship with herself can be manifested through the most traditional of sculptural forms and techniques. 'I have complete confidence in the inner self; the outer one is of no concern to me.'[9] This sculpture is raw and hot, and her presence within it contrasts sharply with the distance she keeps from the more highly finished works where she employs a cool, mechanistic objectivity and her presence and closeness to the work is eradicated. *Avenza Revisited II* is wild in its confrontation and fearless in its nameless identity.

Spiral Woman (1951–2; fig. 147) is another example which clearly demonstrates the traditional roots of Bourgeois's sculpture. The spiral, at one time used to inhabit every sculpture department as the exercise which demonstrated how a twisted, turning form can reveal both its front and its back from any one point of view. The spiral with its turning of forms and space is more imaginatively achieved in *Cell (Eyes and Mirrors)* where the innovation of the mirrors reveals the back of the objects and their space from any one viewpoint. *Cell (Eyes and Mirrors)* is a kind of spiralled space. *Spiral Woman* is mundane. However, Bourgeois has continued to evolve the spiral form throughout her creative life as initiated in this earlier work. The fact that the spiral form of *Spiral Woman* is fixed to a metal support which holds it above the ground pre-empts the suspended form, such an important part of her repertoire which has distinguished the very differing identities for her sculpture. 'Horizontality is a desire to give up, to sleep and be passive, to retreat. Verticality is affirmation, an attempt at a peaceful compromise and a desire for acceptance. Hanging and floating are states of ambivalence and doubt.'[10]

Spiral Woman's simple construction of layered wood produces concave and convex forms. The excavated, cavernous forms of *Avenza Revisited II* could have their origins in the concave spaces created by the spiral forms of the sculptures of this earlier time, and are evolved in works such as *Nature Study (Velvet Eyes)* (1984), and the recent *Nature Study #5* (1995), with their deeply excavated spaces harbouring rounded, succulent forms. *Spiral Woman* does not touch the ground. The sculpture is placed in space surrounded on all sides by air, suggesting a kind of displacement. The object fixed on top of the sculpture implies a direction, like a compass needle, and gives this otherwise symmetrical object an asymmetry as well as disarming its abstract identity with a figurative implication. The extensive use of the spiral form, richly and inventively evolved, is an indication of the importance of the otherwise dull *Spiral Woman*.

The suspended form implied in *Spiral Woman* is fully realised in the hanging *Lair* (1986; fig. 148). This is the lair as a lure. Its pendulous form of solid, dense, black rubber surveys the space in which it hangs through its eye, a square, empty slot slicing through the bulbous body of the lair. The rounded form of *Lair*, now swollen, bellied out, and assertive, is evolved from the earlier carved wood, phallic totems. The eye, the square slot of empty space – ambiguous because where something should be there is nothing – penetrates the dense rubber substance but does not unfold an interior space. Instead the viewer is taken cleanly through the body of the object to the other side. This empty eye slot is the lure, pulling the viewer into its sight in order to be taken through, with not even a glimpse of an unexpected interior space, for there is none. *Spiral Woman*'s form turns anxiously in space. *Lair* confidently commands the space it inhabits, its empty eye turning on the space with radar precision. As with *Cell (Eyes and Mirrors)* the eye in *Lair* is also blind, but its absence is compensated for by its watchful menace which reciprocates its dark, predatory, suspended weight – a protectively sealed space which might harbour a deadly intent.

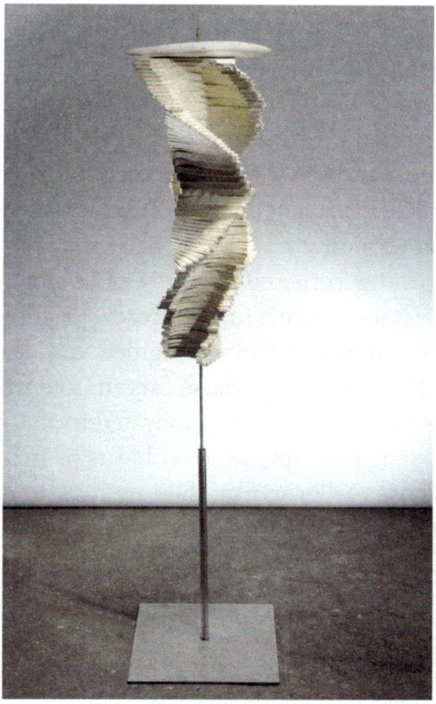

LEFT:
fig. 147 **Louise Bourgeois**
Spiral Woman, 1951–2

BELOW:
fig. 148 **Louise Bourgeois**
Lair, 1986

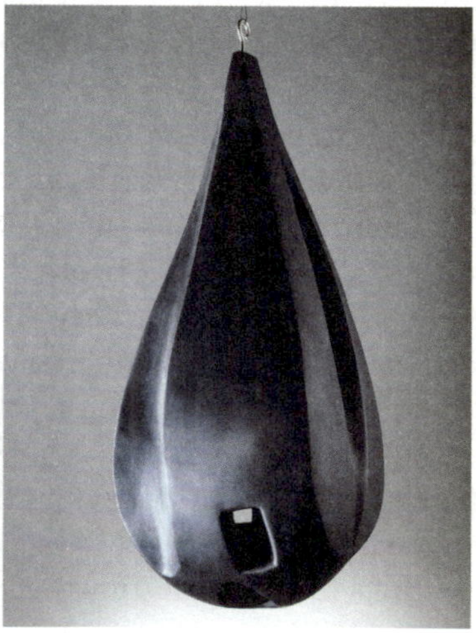

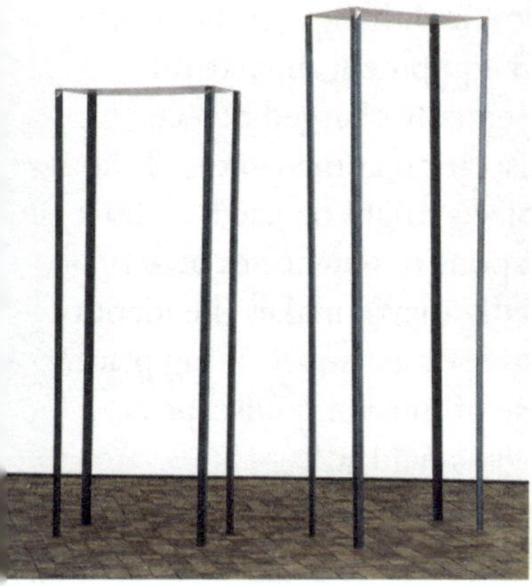

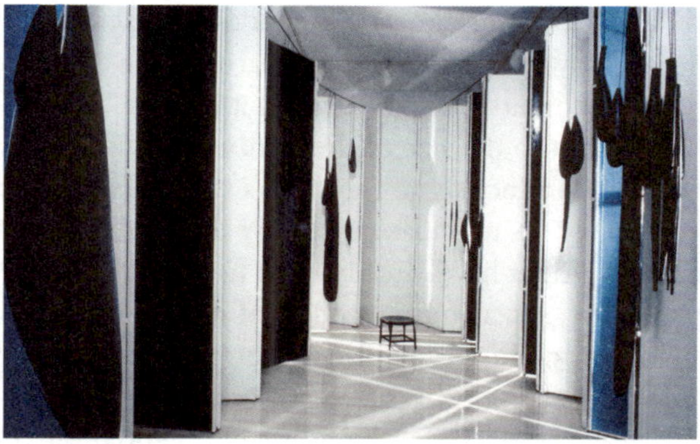

ABOVE LEFT TO RIGHT:
fig. 149 **Louise Bourgeois**
Maisons Fragiles, 1978
fig. 150 **Louise Bourgeois**
Articulated Lair (detail), 1986

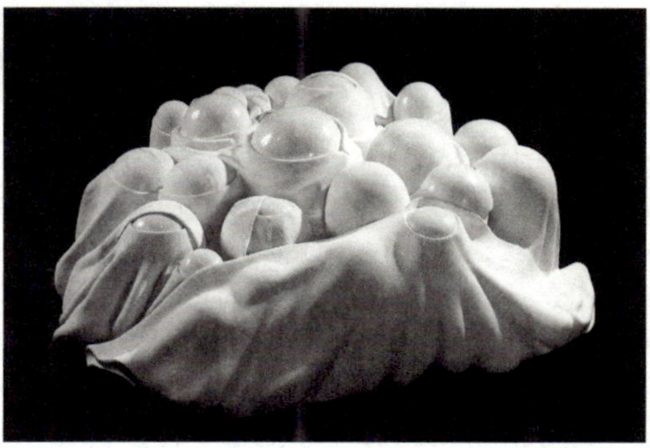

ABOVE:
fig. 151 **Louise Bourgeois**
Cumul I, 1969

Maisons Fragiles (1978; fig. 149), although an earlier work, could be the exoskeletal container of the bulbous form of *Lair*. Its lean but perilous structure contrasts starkly with the ubiquitous rounded forms of carved marble and cast rubber and offers the meanest support and the slightest protection. Its insecurity is enhanced by its unstable lilt and its gangling height which argue with its table-like identity and structural economy.

Articulated Lair (1986; fig. 150) merges the form and structure of *Lair* and *Maisons Fragiles* to become an interior landscape, a place full of dread – deathly calm and still. Like *Lair* it recalls, in an entirely new and reimagined way, the dark sculpture of the 1940s and 1950s. In *Articulated Lair* those carved, totemic, breasted, phallic forms have evolved into pendulous, ripe, elongated forms of dense, black, cast rubber. They are arranged simply as solo objects or in clusters, but instead of standing, as in those earlier works, they are now hung, housed, and supported within the angles of the tall articulated, steel screens. If the hanging *Lair* is the lair as a lure then *Articulated Lair* is the lair as a place, an interior landscape and, as with *Cell (Eyes and Mirrors)* and *No Exit*, it is suspended in time.

With its institutional, functional, painted-steel walls and its yawning, cavernous cathedral-like space, *Articulated Lair* is a place of waiting, a cleaned and modernised development of the excavated space of *Avenza Revisited II*. Most of all, however, it is a storage place for the equipment which hangs on the walls in dormant anticipation. And it is large, adult-sized equipment, in alarming contrast to the size of the diminutive stool. These sexually charged objects relate ominously to the child's stool which sits in isolation at the centre of the space. The anticipation of how these pendulous objects might be used, or how they might have already been used, perhaps as weapons of defence or attack, or as ripe, succulent reminders of delight (now morbidly inert), makes the identity of this child-visited place ambiguous. Is it a protective or an imprisoning place? Whichever it is, it is a place of waiting, whose sense of interior landscape is static and where all growth and potential for change is held still.

Like *No Exit*, *Articulated Lair* is also a sculptural object which can be walked around and walked through, enterable by one of two small doors incorporated into the structure. It has a similar rhythm of opening and closing forms as *No Exit*. The articulated screens are reminiscent of the articulated staircase. This lair is the ultimate secret place under the stairs but formidably enlarged to become that ominous space as experienced from a child's point of view. This is a place of total silence, a place of limbo and deathly suspense, without heartbeat or footfall, where the empty stool waits for the child.

If *Articulated Lair* is dormant then *Cumul I* (1969; fig. 151) is awakening. And if the sexuality in *Articulated Lair* is in deathly fear of its ominous, perhaps abusive, potency, then the sexuality in *Cumul I* is sensually awakening, an intoxication of drowsy rapture which creates a peaceful recognition of deep sex. The white marble is carved into a cocooning cloth: the enrobing cocoon of *Fillette* and of *Fragile Goddess* (1970) has become a membrane which now slips aside. Caressing the emerging phallic forms, it mutates into heavy-lidded eyes laden with sleep. *Articulated Lair* is a deathlike interior landscape. *Cumul I* answers with the landscape of bliss, confident in its sensual and sexual drowsiness, a dormancy changing to wakefulness.

The carved marble cluster of phallus/breast forms are not only emergent but also merging their male and female identities. This is a harmonious landscape, where the moment of dawn is captured, a moment of waking which reciprocates the horizontality of this sculpture and the relationship to horizontality which Bourgeois equates with sleep and the desire to give up, to succumb. For me, I interpret *Cumul I*'s desire to give up as an easy abandon and the desire to sleep as a state of bliss. I referred to *Avenza Revisited II* as a hot object in comparison to her precisely carved and smoothly surfaced marble and bronze sculptures. *Cumul I* is a superbly carved and smoothly surfaced sculpture, the result of calculated and precise technique. The whiteness has a cool purity redolent of a classical elegance and taste which the rounded, swelling, overtly sexual forms rudely challenge with an indolent kitsch.

'The Sneeze of Louise' is the sexual charge in the sculpture, unpredictable in how, where, and with what it will direct itself but rampant with an emotive and unashamed sculptural language: it exploits and explores the extremes of where she places herself in the work, intimately close or objectively and coldly at a distance.

Louise Bourgeois should have the last word: 'It is not an image I am seeking. It's not an idea. It is an emotion you want to recreate, an emotion of wanting, of giving, and of destroying.'[11]

1. 'Louise Bourgeois – In a Strange Way Things Are Getting Better', an interview with Francesco Bonami, *Flash Art* 27, no. 174 (January/February 1994), 39.
2. 'Louise Bourgeois: Self-Expression Is Sacred and Fatal – Statements', in Christiane Meyer-Thoss, ed., *Louise Bourgeois: Designing for Free Fall* (Zurich: Ammann Verlag, 1992), 189.
3. Meyer-Thoss, *Louise Bourgeois: Designing for Free Fall*, 200.
4. Meyer-Thoss, 73.
5. Meyer-Thoss, 73.
6. Meyer-Thoss, 128.
7. The original text referred to this work by its earlier title, *Untitled*. It was later renamed *Avenza Revisited II*.
8. Meyer-Thoss, 123.
9. Meyer-Thoss, 135.
10. Meyer-Thoss, 69.
11. Meyer-Thoss, 194.

First published in Ian Cole, ed., *Louise Bourgeois*, Museum of Modern Art Papers, vol. 1 (Oxford: Museum of Modern Art, 1996), 4–11. Reprinted in *Phyllida Barlow: Objects for … and Other Things* (London: Black Dog Publishing, 2004), 168–75, and Jon Wood and Julia Kelly, eds., *Contemporary Sculpture: Artists' Writings and Interviews* (Berlin: Hatje Cantz, 2019), 49–60.

This talk was given on 6 May 1998 at the Mappin Art Gallery in Sheffield, UK, on the occasion of the opening of the exhibition *George Fullard: Playing with Paradox*, which toured to Kettle's Yard, Cambridge. An edited version was included in *Tate Etc.* in autumn 2016 as 'My Teacher, George Fullard'. Barlow recounts her first encounter with the British artist George Fullard (1923–1973) on his arrival at Chelsea College of Arts in 1961 and the approach to teaching and the broad range of interests of this inspirational tutor. She discusses the views and ideas that shaped his own artistic practice, including the role of memory and his use of clay.

George Fullard: Touching the Past

1998

The date was 1961. It was a life class and each student was solemnly in attendance of their work: in fact, a portrait head class, the silence of such a class being palpable, broken only by the occasional squeaks of the modelling stands as they were turned, the shuffles of the students in their ritualistic movements around their work and the model, and the muffled sounds of the working of the clay: a monastic atmosphere rooted in a tireless history, but repressed and stultified by years of overuse and misuse.

Into this environment entered George, immaculate, brisk, sharp, watchful. He quizzically and shrewdly inspected our tired efforts, moving around the studio with decisive intensity, shadowed by the large, clumsy figure of Lawrence Gowing. 'Changes need to be made', muttered Gowing.

'Yes', responded George, 'the first being to find out why a head and not a foot.'

This comment, heard by all of us in that studio, including the model, was the alarm that woke us up; we were snapped out of a twilight world, protected by its ceremonies of unquestioned conventions of crafts and skills, and the lights were turned on. In that instance we were given the opportunity to look around and experience the shock of another reality.

Undoubtedly, this brief visit and its portentous overheard conversation precipitated an excitement of almost revolutionary fervour: we were about to not only witness but to be part of the end of a regime and the beginning of a new era.

George did not fail us. He far exceeded our wildest expectations, initiated by his insistence, on his first day, that we all convene to the pub where we remained until closing time, accompanied by the instruction: 'All talking should take place in the pub, not in the studio', followed at a later date by: 'As artists we should talk a lot because then anything that can't be talked about will get made.'

More, much more was to follow: worn-out processes were revitalised through new descriptions: casting was magical because, like a conjuring trick, an object is made to disappear and then reappear in a completely different material; welding was as facile as sticking with glue and should therefore only be used in an emergency; wood was alive; metal like paper and could be treated like fabric for dressmaking; and clay was mud. On and on it went, and the maxim of Picasso, 'Before you use a nail, you must reinvent it', became the motto by which we all began to exist.

The boundaries were being moved so drastically, and the excitement and the energy generated from the movements of those boundaries, have, I believe, set a precedent for all who had the good fortune of being there in those early days of George's association with Chelsea School of Art.

George established that the vision inherent to an art school has to come from within it and not from the rules imposed upon it from conventions and dogmas outside of it. Such external impositions, he believed, had neither relevance nor accountability from an individual who would be answerable for the kind of tyranny symptomatic of mindless, official authority.

George took total responsibility for his vision. He would never be the mouthpiece for an official stance. The suspicion he had for authority, and its academic influences on art, gave him a youthful vigour. He was an ally of his students and on the level with them, not easily so, always ahead of them, to challenge and motivate the vision each young artist possessed, and to strip away the collusion with rote learning which smacked of the academic traits he so loathed and mistrusted.

It is the potent memory that so many of us have of George, of his ability to have given to us through those vivid, demanding, abrasive, contentious, extremely funny, extremely venomous, extremely generous conversations that enabled us to look at the world about us as a rich potential for our own creativity: not to always turn to art, particularly the thoughtless labour of a visionless academic art, for confirmation, but to go elsewhere.

And so he talked of Buster Keaton's relationships to objects where Keaton's absurd, but absolutely familiar, incidents with inanimate things George was able to interpret and to reveal to us as sculptural, and Harold Lloyd's and Charlie Chaplin's games with accidents as essential information for understanding the accident with a work in progress in the studio, how to use this and exploit its potential. This was visionary information that has stayed with me, enhanced by further rich revelations: the drama of storytelling as with F. Scott Fitzgerald, how the awkwardness and pathos of the agonising and hopeless relationships described in *The Great Gatsby* and *Tender Is the Night* were made comparable to the awkwardness of how sculpture gets made, how things come together that never expected to come together. Or, in opposition to this, how seeming clichés within a Bing Crosby or Frank Sinatra song were, in fact, pure poetry, and again, as such were relevant to how we should understand how to use traditional materials of clay, plaster, wood, and metal, that the clichés of these materials were there to be manipulated, reinvented, not taken for granted.

And there was always more to come: cartoons, like *Tom and Jerry*, how the cruelty of these characters turned into comedy, a magical and deceptive contrivance that lures and deceives by one means in order to reveal something of another, which, again, every sculptor should be able to achieve.

The resources were limitless, but never predictable, and the focus was never out of sight: the diversity of experiences led to one thing which was able to embrace them all, that was sculpture, and there was always Picasso to prove the point.

George instilled a confidence that proclaimed contradiction as the propagator of creativity; by turning your back on what you were meant to be doing and looking elsewhere, you would find the clues for what you were *really* meant to be doing: 'Hard work is disastrous unless you are either exhausted or do not know what you are doing' and 'Draw very late at night when you are exhausted and then you will only draw what is really important.' All these memories of George confirm that *Playing with Paradox*, the title of this wonderful exhibition, is a succinct definition of how George worked as an artist and how that informed his teaching, that the two were together, or as he would constantly remind us: 'You cannot be a teacher as an artist, because you do not know what to teach because everything changes. Memory, and trying to remember is all we have.'

Memory, and its processes, were an important part of the subject of George's work, as narrative, as image, and as mood. He formed a deeply moving, as well as revelationary, alliance with memory, where his quest for memory was both thwarted and rewarded. And it seems to me that it was this conflict that made him refer to photography in the very particular terms that he did, often refuting the word 'photograph' for his preferred word 'snapshot', with its implications of a natural, domestic authenticity. George saw a relationship between the 'snapshot' and sculpture, where the act of capture was, to him, inherent in both.

This important, and highly personal, relationship to photography is, for me, a key to his work. There is an absolute stillness in the sculpture, comparable to the stillness of the frozen glimpse of light that creates the photographic image. It is like the stillness of time standing still where the particularity of a moment is caught and then trapped by the material and physical qualities of the sculpture. So the choice of materials and how to innovate with those materials was, for George, the crucial means for capturing, identifying the processes of making as processes of entrapment, requiring the hunter's skills of precision, decisiveness, accuracy, and timing.

And he often compared the terminology of the hunter's weapons, their guns, as having the same terminology as associated with the camera, such as to 'shoot a film', 'aim the camera', to 'catch an image on film', etc.

In the earlier clay sculptures turned bronzes, the timing of touch, another important quality of his work, enables these remarkable bronzes to be vigorous within their inherent stillness: the sense of weight, the massive weight of bronze competing with the lightest of interference from the rawness of the almost, paradoxically, seemingly untouched clay (fig. 152).

The bronze is given a very specific role: it is not a cosmetic vehicle; it has to work to justify its inclusion in these acts of distillation. The bronze is the trap, holding the clay at the moment it was relinquished, that it is relinquished by George from any further handling, a decisive moment when enough was enough, no more, no less.

Again, his understanding of clay was idiosyncratic, a highly personal contract between himself and this material, part love and part hate, part trust and part mistrust. 'You should only have to touch it once' was a remark that made me completely reconsider this mundane and then, much abused material.

Another comment he used was in fact a quote from Germaine Richier, a sculptor he admired and whose work he made known to many young artists, a comment which he felt was essential to the understanding of clay: 'Clay is hysterical', she said, 'it reacts to everything: take care when you touch it that it knows what you want!'

If George's relationship with clay was distinctive, so was his relationship with the extraordinary range of materials used in the constructed sculptures. Furthermore, how would George respond to all the current debates about appropriation and the readymade when he was so in advance of this debate? I cannot help laughing at what his response might have been, and the caustic venom which he would be able to inject into these debates: such thoughts as these signal not only what a continuing loss he is to art and artists but how, despite this sense of loss, how much of a presence he is capable of being, a presence which is so soundly evidenced by this remarkable exhibition.

As with the clay, there is, for me, the quality of stillness within the constructed works as well. In some of them, the more sculptural earlier

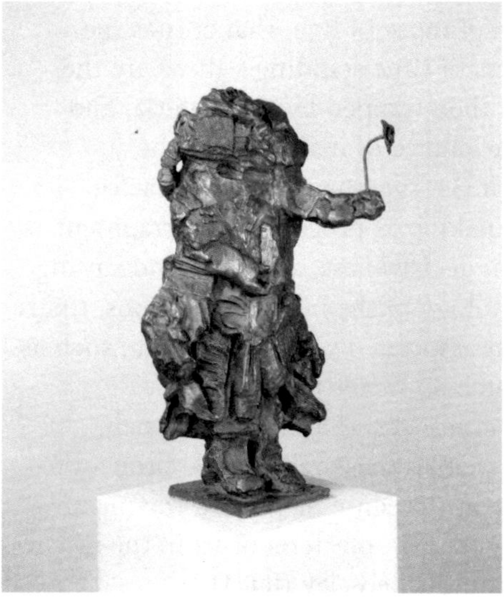

fig. 152 **George Fullard**
Infant with Flower, 1958/1960

constructions, it is the stillness of confrontation, a menacing pause prior to conflict, where the object itself stares back in antagonistic astonishment, frozen in a moment of fearful aggression, all stiff, sharp limbs of fallen table, closed doors, opened drawer, perched tabletop, and awkward leanings of severed skirting boards and floorboards, formally arranged as horizontals, verticals, and diagonals, so tensely compressed, where the edges of the work are as sharp and as cutting as the overlapping surfaces of the interiors.

Very different from the more pictorial seascapes. Here, for me, George's empathy with clichés, how their poetic potential could be linked to a relationship with a particular time, and a particular memory, have become the catalysts which could transform the banal into the sublime.

The blues and the whites of the painted metal might be clichés, snapshot clichés, but just as the folded paper hat is in fact painted metal and acts as a boat, so too is this 'play' with materials a game of pretending because the bliss of this idyll, this supposed cliché, is host to the sinking ship, and the scene is held forever at a moment of lingering doubt. The snapshot has been monumentalised, but delicately so, with minimal translation from the fragility of a snapshot, perhaps a snapshot of a memory, to the permanence of materials of folded aluminium sheet and steel sheet, of cast bronze, and of painted wood. There is no respite from this moment. The story refuses to end, and we are left to look and look, reciprocating the long look out to sea which the sea provokes in us all, and which these particular works contrive to make us do.

And so these works complement the powerful retort of the other constructed sculptures. They stare out at us, confronting us, but with these works, we stare into them, we are pulled into them, drawn into their captured dramas where there is no beginning and no end, only a game of waiting and watching, where all sounds are silenced, the distant plane, the water, the air, and all movement is stilled forever.

Without doubt, George was ahead of his time, and he is much needed in an art world that lacks authentic individuality. There is a space where George should be, a space devoid of his kind of restlessness and precision, his criticism and originality, his iconoclasm and imagination, but whose absence as a poet and a visionary is compensated by the presence of his work, work that speaks for itself, speaks for him, and speaks for all of us.

I am forever indebted to George, and I am sure I am speaking on behalf of many artists whom he enlightened and inspired and changed.

An edited version was published as 'My Teacher, George Fullard', in *Tate Etc.* 38 (autumn 2016): 24–7; https://www.tate.org.uk/tate-etc/issue-38-autumn-2016/my-teacher-phyllida-barlow-on-george-fullard.

'At Sea: A Conversation by Fax between Phyllida Barlow and Alison Wilding, 22.08.98–02.09.98' was first published in 1998 in the catalogue *Alison Wilding: Grounded* and subsequently included in *Phyllida Barlow: Objects for … and Other Things*. In this written correspondence Barlow exchanges views with her fellow sculptor and old friend, the British artist Alison Wilding (born 1948). They cover topics that include working processes, privacy and the reception of the work, elitist spaces, and truth and lies. They consider not being able to work and 'hard-workingness', edges, drawing, appropriators and readymakers, and Conceptual Art.

At Sea: Conversation by Fax with Alison Wilding

1998

You talked about 'this time'. Is there something different or changed about the way you are working and thinking about your work now, 'this time'?

Your fax really spooked me – until I realised it was from you … ! I think it is only now, three months after returning from Rome, that I am back in the studio and working. OK, there is *Ambit*, and the new work in Skipton Castle fig. 153), and the two sculptures I made in Rome. So this time is about starting again, now – doing it, getting it right, but finding it slipping through my fingers ('it', what is it?). 'This time' has a sense of urgency. There is also a sense of repetition, if 'this time' then what was 'last time'? Last time was here – working in the studio – it went well, slowly, but well. This time it didn't do that – but I think I worked through a lot of stuff that I do not want in order to get where I am now (i.e., today and doing it, and it's fine). A bit like you and I talking rubbish into the tape when we tried to record an interview. You have to do a lot of what you know is no good in order to get rid of it, to get it out of the system.
Love, Alison

'Getting it right' and 'talking rubbish': control is important – is it? (School ma'am.) How do you know when you are getting it right? How experimental are your processes – or are they more reactive than experimental? Even if you 'get rid' of a lot of what you think is no good, do you remember it, store it in some way for future use? Is the process of 'doing a lot of what is no good' part of some kind of ritual courtship to familiarise yourself with something that takes time (more than anything else), to make itself known to you? Why do you need to be familiar with what you do? Is the feeling of urgency because there is a dread of the time this courtship process consumes?

Could you do without it – this courtship?
Phyllida

P.S.: Essential listening: Sunday, Radio 3, *St Matthew Passion* (plus weather like November in August).

'Getting it right' or 'finding it' is dependent upon a loss of control. I don't want to be in control in those evolutionary beginnings to making something – I want to catch up with it – or catch it. I do not know if the processes can be described as 'experimental' – probably something must be either experimental or proactive, as a way of kick-starting it, and the rest follows. 'Getting rid' of stuff means that it's not for now – maybe it will be there, ready, waiting for the future; it seems to be important to make those decisions early on – before anything becomes really concrete. I do not want an elephants' graveyard in my studio! It is a necessary ritual – or 'courtship', as you called it – it means I hold on to something I want to do and the rest can wait and, if necessary, it is there waiting for later – if by that time it has not been superseded by something else. I don't think about needing a familiarity with something – more a rush of excitement that is perhaps the opposite of that – the unknown factor. Urgency is a fear of it disappearing – of time passing so fast anyway these days, and maybe that the 'ritual courtship' will not go anywhere. Is there another expression for 'ritual courtship'? Ritual implies that I know it's not for real, but it is. I used to think that it was a struggle being acted out or rather a conflict. And sometimes it is.

If *St Matthew Passion* was last night I missed it, but I watched a bit of *Drugstore Cowboy*.
Love, Alison

Yes, 'courtship' is probably not the right word – too prudish … I was thinking of restraint and self-control, not surrendering to the first thing that comes along – leaping into bed with anyone, so to speak – instead the ability to eliminate and edit before, rather than after the event.

I have been sorting slides of the work I am showing at the Chapter Art Gallery in Cardiff, *Time and time again* – and sorting out my doubts about it (fig. 154). The objects overfill the space as I wanted – but I do not know if it works or not. Should there be more objects, to really crush the space, or fewer objects doing more with the space? The work has been greeted with silence, except for those ambiguous comments such as 'Are you pleased with it?' or 'I must come back for a longer look.' Suspicious statements inferring dissatisfied viewers! Mental focus is enviable; the determination to seek out. And the urgency rather than desperation, my equivalent, which is a recipe for mistakes that later will need correcting. It takes time, 'it' being a kind of recognition of ease between myself and the proposed work, or the debris of try-outs, results of the desperate need to engage with physical stuff, without any clear idea of what to do. Boredom and disappointment – how do you respond?
Phyllida

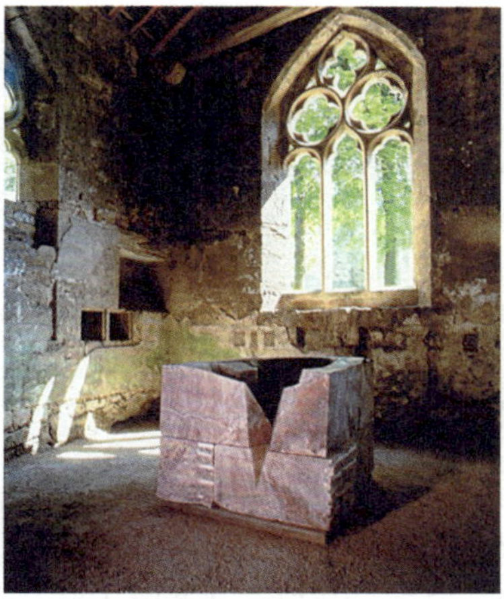

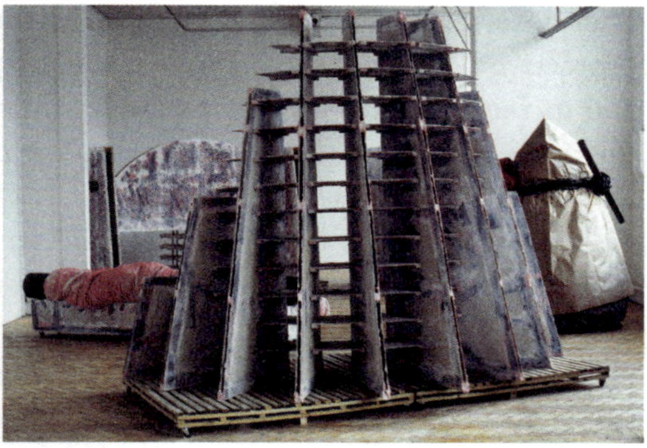

LEFT TO RIGHT:
fig. 153 **Alison Wilding**
Harbour, 1994–6
fig. 154 *Time and time again*, 1998

Do you think that your frustration with what you have just done is because there can be no dress rehearsals – like life, actually? And there is rarely enough time or favourable conditions to do it in – it is a very tough thing to take on, you know, partly because it is a very public act. Well, fuck the dissatisfied viewers. They have got it all wrong – they want a map, and they do not realise that they have to throw all this away. 'My way' seems inevitably more cautious, yes, more edited out, in private; but the confrontation with the public is the same. Lots of people in Skipton saying 'What is it?', 'Excuse me for asking but what is the point?', and at the same time they are grabbing hold of that frail piece of alabaster as if it was a handle. Boredom and disappointment: where does the boredom fit in? Perhaps with the same dull responses. Is it possible to excite people, or are there always only going to be a minority who are open and brave enough to confront this kind of unknown? I am bored when I need a buzz from what I am doing and not getting it. Perhaps this accounts for the popularity of the YBAs, their ability for instant gratification.
Love from Alison

Is boredom more static than disappointment? I can recover, sort of, from disappointment because it is more organic, and its anger creates a kind of hope for the next excitement.

I love the title (and what I can see of the work from the slides you showed me): ***In Shadow*****. It sums up 'privacy'. The sculpture appears rooted in its place, almost hidden, recalling those sleeping tomb figures. Is privacy to do with nakedness? Being naked, not just undressed, but stripped down bare. Different from that dismal quest for 'truth'. Because, as a compulsive liar, being stripped is terrifying when things are uncovered.**

Therefore, showing work is fearful. It is being scrutinised when the protective lies have been removed. The maps, like symptoms of tourism and its fantasies, are protective, and the thrill of showing work is because the maps have been thrown away, leaving the work isolated for the full scrutiny of the public eye.

Is privacy central to art-making? And especially non-making? Is stalking something within one, which has this thrilling possibility of revelation, only to be done in private? Is art-making a kind of birth, pain and pleasure precipitating a dread of the death of the new-born thing? Are we, am I, perversely savouring pain in order to experience pleasure?

Increasingly I long for elitist places to show work, very protected but not exclusive. Also, in the present climate, the object, more particularly sculpture, is in the doldrums. The non-visual qualities of sculpture need acknowledging as do its lineage and its history, in order for it to be considered as a serious contender to the quick-fix-approach of so much contemporary art.
Love, P

All my life I have been an obsessive truth-teller and envied those who lived according to their version of events, but like you I think that the search for truth in art is utterly pointless. (I didn't know you were a compulsive liar!) The more stripping, exposing I can do in privacy, the easier it is in public. Though of course, it is never that easy, but neither, to be fair to the observer, is the act of looking: it can be like swimming for land in the middle of an ocean with nothing in sight – for me, that is the most physically terrifying thing I can think of. Looking at art is – or perhaps should be – that scary.

The thing about elitist places – though we all hate them (well, not all of us) – is that they do the difficult work for the artist. They may not be the best places to show work but at least the viewer knows they are not on a building site, in a hardware shop, or a waiting room.

I remember conversations, in the 1980s, about whether making sculpture was analogous with having children (for women, that is). Obviously I only understand half the equation, but there is undeniably something very fierce and strong about producing a new thing. I have never felt that it was a surrogate. Has having children also gone out of fashion?

Tell me about the non-visual qualities of sculpture – Eric Peskett used to talk about the presence of objects in the dark. I have always liked this idea …

PRIVACY IS NOT ALWAYS THE CORE OF MAKING, but making must be born out of that condition at least at some point. Hermaphroditic.
Love, Alison

P.S.: I agree with you about boredom and disappointment. Boredom is like low pressure; disappointment is a keen physical thing, it hurts. It is not fatal but can linger if not watched. xxx, A

It is not knowing that makes me a compulsive liar. I do not know where my work comes from. I can only guess that it is some sort of play with something out there; visible and in there; invisible. Whether this is true or not I do not know and I do not care. The new thing (certainly not a surrogate child) is neither one or the other; it gets revealed like talking to myself, rather secretly, and as such, might be only half-heard and therefore misunderstood.

But what of understanding, of being understood? Understanding what? Does it matter? Why should art be 'understood' (and what does 'understanding' mean in this context)? That overused word 'experience' is a catch-all, and too limp and pathetic. Yet it is the significant word because it allows for imagination and speculation, which I believe the non-visual qualities of sculpture depend upon – anything, that is, other than what is literally visible: weight, density, unseen surfaces, what do they do? What are they in contact with? The interior – where is it? The time it takes to walk around it, and its space/location, the place/placing, next to, on, by, with, from, away, near, far, here, there; size: the space it owns; does the work claim more or less space than its dimensions? What if touched? Cold, damp, warm, scratchy …

Absolutely, experiencing sculpture in the dark – and as an imagined state for the work. Darkness reveals the sound and movement inherent to sculpture: not literally so, but as locked into the substance as a memory of its making. All such qualities get obliterated by the scramble to justify and explain through verbal language.

The viewer: my guilt. I never consider the viewer. When swimming without sight of land are you the maker or the viewer? Or both? Is that what is so terrifying? Yes, terror, dread, fear – they are familiar as ongoing states, but I am never sure why they are there. In fact, letting go of the work is comparatively painless; I relish it, and once gone, in its place, I no longer feel vulnerable on its behalf. It is me who becomes vulnerable. A kind of longing to forget it. Instead there is accountability, which is where all the feelings of privacy and intimacy come in, and an embarrassment of having to speak about things which should remain contained in the work. But speaking and writing is a rich resource – everything which is not 'it' can be written and spoken.

'The New Thing': I have never equated my work with my children as such, but touching the work has reminded me at times of touching them – especially when they were little. It is another thing now – not easy to talk

about. My reference to giving birth was to do with bringing into the world a new thing, nameless, a different thing; but different from what? Then placing it, finding a place for it. You said once that you did not think about the placing. I cannot believe that!

Honesty and truth – they seem different – are they? Longer and longer. Love, Phyllida

Yes, truth and honesty are not the same thing, are they? I should have said that I have been obsessively honest (or straightforward) in my life, whilst the 'truth' is out there somewhere.

Don't we all make work for ourselves? The best experience with the work is when it is in the right place and we are alone with it and it is not exactly alive, but sentient, open to speculation, responding to daylight then darkness and somehow breathing. A good way, I think, to measure the presence (or not) of a piece of work. Meaning, understanding, total immersion is locked into that situation. Which is why for me, nipping into the National Gallery, say, to look at Titian's *Portrait of a Young Man* for two minutes will always be satisfying. I want to see it when I wake up, when the lights are out, when I am having a drink. Is this why people buy art?

More on truth, lies, and inconsistencies: a student has sent me a list of questions to answer. Most of them are either unanswerable, e.g., 'Do you have an overriding aim in your work?', or so complicated that it would take days to think about them. I have suggested that she go to Skipton to see *Desormais*, but apparently that is not possible. Why should it matter what I have to say, when there is a chance to see what I do? She obviously does not know (but I will tell her) that I am so inconsistent and contradictory in what I say as to be downright untruthful at times. (Did I really say that thing about not caring about the placing of work? I did not mean it!) The sculpture is not inconsistent. But at the same time I do not think that the artists should be so arrogant and removed as to let the work exclusively speak for them at all times, hiding behind its myth or theory. First of all though it must be seen at first hand. I suppose I am just annoyed at having to answer her questions.

Swimming: out of depth without sight of land is my own personal nightmare, and there is nothing exhilarating in it. Whereas being out of my depth in my work is. Is this the flipside of boredom? Being the viewer need never be that bad, even after having thrown away the map. I think that is what Adrian Searle is very good at doing – he throws himself at the mercy of the art he is looking at and describes his experience.
Love, Alison

I want to discuss that not-being-able-to-work place you have referred to in the past. It seems linked to the 'horror of being out of depth without sight

of land' … (I remember you telling me that your father threw you into the swimming pool to teach you to swim. Is that correct?) But can one's personal horror be a touchstone? Is it somehow, incomprehensibly, reassuring to know what one's personal terror is? What is it like to be terrified and not know, to have no image which mirrors the paralysis of fear? From your description, which is exhilarating and sensual, your personal nightmare has a metaphorical energy. It is alive and vividly represents the state of absolute isolation, where survival depends on summoning unknown sources of energy, intuition, and improvisation, all with the full knowledge that these might be of no help. But not-being-able-to-work is like that, isn't it?

Can retrieving deeply buried responses and resources trigger creative survival?

To somehow carry on working through that time – but then when-you-cannot-work, you cannot!

How to rediscover land: very biblical – I keep thinking of the dove with the olive branch in the Old Testament. Not-being-able-to-work seems to me a place of no security: the awful, awesome weight of water beneath your barely floating body, not you but the sea in control.

Words and lying. Writing about places makes me think about the gap between myself and the work, and the descriptions I attach to my work which seem to fill this gap ambiguously. The feeling I get from these descriptions is like lying. Telling what the work is about, or what it refers to, creates a separate, rival object, which does not equate with what is there, and can become enhanced with glamour and expectation, something words are so capable of doing, and which the task of looking and remembering, is not.

I so agree with you about looking at the Titian. There is a real need to allow one's act of looking to carry on, like a kind of storytelling which has no beginning, middle, or end, just a continuous state of arousal. Looking, I think is a slow burn, a gathering up of curiosity, into which fall, gradually, those qualities of expectation, glamour, excitement, etc. Words are quicker.

Yes, being alone with the work when it is in its place is like meeting with it for the first time. A brief encounter which can go either way – love or hate. It is a relationship, however brief, but the meeting in that place is always a surprise: something I thought I knew well becomes something I do not know at all and which I cannot recognise. Again, like stalking – from the making to the place: stalking something that is not there, or something that is there, but is unknown, and then, when it is there, still not knowing.

Is not-knowing like not-being-able-to-work?

I have a recurring dream about drowning: dark blue sea, brilliant sky, people drowning – my children – no hope of rescue – all to do with having witnessed a drowning, aged eight.

xxx, Phyllida

Not-being-able-to-work continued: there is a dull dread which feels a bit like being a child with something unpleasant to look forward to; a foreboding; and being at sea, treading water – more apt than the personal nightmare of swimming without horizons – put perhaps a watered-down version of it. (Yes, my father did throw me into the swimming pool, and I could not swim until I was fourteen – my recurring sea dream is being caught between huge, towering, frozen waves.)

I think you have put your finger on it exactly with the question 'How to rediscover land?', by digging deeper into your hidden resources, yourself. There is another option, which is to stop looking inwards, close the system down, get out, see, do, and go. Do you ever do that? I don't. It is like an itch I must scratch, I cannot leave it alone (digging deeper). Like a dog that follows a smell, I return to the studio. That's the fear, I think, that the smell will go away, taking it with it.

So there is the water (the fear) and the earth, we are uncovering the elements at last. I loved your image of the dove – which makes the connection between the sea and the land – which are of course in a kind of conflict. For me, the sea is fear, dread, but also movement, potential, weightlessness, sensuality, CREATIVITY. Where land and sea meet is forever-shifting territory – the ultimate edge.

The image of the bird/dove makes this connection between sea and land look like an act of faith, but it is of course in the genes: migrating across oceans (no precedent, no horizons). It is not in our genes, but we have to develop an instinct, a technique which enables us to cross land and sea at will. The land is where the territory is staked out, what we know – the sea is where it happens, where we drown or not.

I like the slow burn, it is the missing element.

Doesn't the glamour of words seem like top dressing?

Love, Alison

My equivalent to your straightforwardness could be hard-workingness. I do not see this as any great virtue because it can blind and mask what is really there and the essentials to be done. I have worked hard, overworked, when standing back, waiting, and watching would have been infinitely more productive.

My hard-workingness is not as ordered as a Protestant work ethic, it is, unfortunately, more hysterical, panic-stricken, as if driven to exorcise something. So yes, I do keep going, and, like you, I cannot close the system down. With this drive to work comes the desire to push the work, to work something through, however inadequately. It is connected to the malleability of certain materials, like clay, where there can be a quick response from the material to a change of thought. Though I no

longer work with clay, that particular attitude towards materials remains: a relationship which assumes that materials can be easily changed, even at the eleventh hour, into something else, better, right. Working at it, being unable to leave it alone, seems very deep-rooted within me and, at times, something I long to shake off, in order to find another, easier way, which allows for shortcuts. Hence my fascination with appropriations and readymades. They exemplify for me the divorce between thinking and doing and between hands on and hands off. The appropriators and the readymakers, seem to have translators who do their work for them whilst I have to slog it out word by word, getting things wrong, not knowing the pronunciation, spelling, etc. etc. Theirs is a seamless process, where the thinking is the creative act and where the results appear cleaner, more sensible, and more shrewd, with fewer mistakes and less abuse of material. Their struggle is done away from the work; they can stand back and wait; altogether a more reliable activity. But in the end, I am not fully convinced, envious yes, but the clinical nature and the coldness of what they are doing is more often than not repelling. I want hard evidence of who is saying what and not be fobbed off with the messenger, a kind of servant to the hidden artist. Appropriation and readymades have changed into something else – Duchamp's *Why Not Sneeze, Rose Sélavy?* is so scuffed and worn, full of muffled noises, unlike the new army of shiny and glossy appropriations and readymades. Do readymakers and appropriators make mistakes? How do they try things out? How do they 'push' the work? Maybe the answer to this is Duchamp's long, self-imposed silence. Still, I do envy them. I feel I have to rely on the flukes that emerge from physical making, endless, often frustrating revision and the perpetual turmoil in the studio – all this is so far removed from the intellectual neatness of the readymade.
xxx, Phyllida

Words and readymades, re: top dressing. Verbal language and written language are so close to the readymade and complement it so well. By comparison, sculpture is essentially wordless – that is part of its vulnerability. Is this why readymades score so effortlessly in comparison to sculpture? As if displacing an object with verbal/written language is a plus – much easier than the complicated act of looking.

Let's get back to water, swimming, and places beyond the horizon!
Love, Phyllida
Next: 'acts of faith', 'edges', 'digging deeper' – lots more to talk about.

Overworking: I do it with drawings, especially when at the moment it feels as if I am chasing a chimera. I think I deliberately push them over the edge to see if there is anything at all I can salvage. Inevitably, they all go into the bin. I know when to stop, but until then I cannot leave them alone. They make me very angry. It reminds me of shooting a take for a film – you can do it a hundred times in the hope that the 101st time will be it. (How do I know?) I think that's similar to working with clay?

Readymades and appropriations: I think you should relax about them. They are here to stay. On one level you can displace an object with language and as you said, it's seductive, glamorising, mythologising, and very persuasive, but I think that deep down we both find it not totally nourishing. Sculpture is that oddball thing that can side-step language – this is why it frustrates writers. The more I think about it the more anachronistic I could make it sound. When I think about how baffling sculpture is to many people I think of those time machines in SF books and films which are always seamless monoliths made of unknown materials with no obvious way in, (and when they open there is usually a gremlin-thing inside which is not so interesting).

Yes, let's return to 'acts of faith', 'edges', etc.
Love, Alison

On Edges; another anachronism; the longing to make edges without structure and physical materiality, knowing full well that the character of sculpture's physicality makes this an impossibility: therefore light, distance, fogging, fracturing become essential aesthetics as a means for diffusing edges and challenging the solidity of material. Heroic attempts to blur and dissolve the rigidity of sheet materials and the density of solid materials. I try to do this by using paint on surfaces while you seem to do it by choosing particular materials: polypropylene, rubber, metal, or alabaster. They all seem to react with or to light, but for what?

Someone described to me their visit to Donald Judd's emporium at Marfa. He went into one of the large spaces, a converted barn, and there appeared to be nothing there. In fact the shininess of the metallic surfaces of the objects had fused with the intense brilliance of the desert light, dissolving the objects into invisibility. The edges and the space had magically become one. Is this a sculptor's ultimate ambition, or desire for edges? To push them to the edge of their existence and to liberate the edge of its edginess?

Drawing and Drawbacks
I never know what to draw = dull
I end up drawing the things I am going to make = boring
I think of other artists' drawings = confusing
I become self-conscious, I draw my feelings = ugh!
I must begin with the materials and get rid of images = incompetent

Discover that I am back to 1 = hopeless
A rush of indifference = hope

Yes, I get angry with drawing, and paranoid and defensive. A nagging voice taunts me with the whisper 'Drawing is the epitome of being an artist. If you cannot do it then you are not an artist'. So, if I am not an artist what am I? Our daughter Tabby recently asked a little boy what he wanted to be when he grew up. 'A person', he replied. I feel like that with drawing. If I am not an artist because I cannot draw then I will make do with being a person.

Violence and Edges: making edges by cutting, slicing, stitching, pinning, pinching, filing, sawing, nailing, breaking, tearing, etc., etc. These acts, like touch, can go either way, gentle or violent, mending or wrecking, the surgeon or the murderer, the lover or the abuser. I know Madame Bourgeois has gone through all this in depth, but it does seem apposite. Who are we when we cut, slice, nail, hit? Which character are we assuming? And does that character become part of the work as much as the formal aesthetic-conscious decisions? I am sure that my acts of making are a series of sublimated double-sided acts. Dionysian and Apollonian, split between the repairer and the destroyer, between the caress and the hit (another horror of mine besides drowning: hitting children), but brought together like a dissonance. Do you think of your acts of making as purely functional, as a means to an end or as loaded with insignificance well beyond this?

Last word on appropriation and readymades: here to stay and very much (for me) about here and now. It is my conflict of wanting to be here and now, but recognising that I could be a member of a tribe on the verge of extinction, which has not yet invented the wheel, always making, making, making, with no noticeable results. Meanwhile, the neighbouring tribe picks up what is lying around and produces innovative and progressive objects … with ease, simplicity, and elegance. Yet there remain doubts …
Lots of love, P

Edges: if you wanted to make edges without structure then I have wanted to make objects without edges – rather to achieve dissolution between solid and liquid. Like you I admit to difficulties with this one. I can see (although I have not been there) how Judd succeeds with this in Marfa – in those carefully controlled conditions – and it makes me realise that I have probably never really seen a Donald Judd! Which of us would not like that ultimate control? But – inconsistent again – I like the mutability of certain materials and how they react in unheated spaces – like a concrete floor sweating or a wall dripping; alabaster sweats, changes colour. As volatile as changing light conditions. A material like polypropylene helps in distancing, dissolving, but inherently it traps a dangerous aesthetic (as I see it), and I am afraid of it and alabaster can do a similar thing. You asked if these materials react with or to light, but for what? I think it is a question of velocity. Some materials are dense and matt and deadening and stop you like black rubber (unless the intention is otherwise), others slow down or suspend light. And then of course they also reveal something inside, beyond, expanding, opening out. You used to talk a lot about cutting through things. This is a way of revealing without cutting (more stroking than whipping).

Edges again: twice, as a student, and at different times, I made a work specifically without edges. Both of them were installed outside in fog, which solved the problem for a photograph. But it was The Emperor's New Clothes when the sun came out. Conceptual Art has no edges. Discuss.

I have always been obsessed with how much space my sculpture can hold – and maybe this is an indication of its true edge, an invisible field around it. What you have headed 'Violence and Edges' refers to what I mean by the work coming about through conflict. We are all the things you describe when we make the work (cutting and stroking). Nowadays I have more distance on it, perhaps I am more knowing and I need to do less physically, but that makes it sound like a bag of tricks with a load of special effects – which is not true either.

The conflict is very much there in drawing where a need to find a subject or a meaning fights with a desire to explode things in a rather infantile way. I feel an awful pressure to make the same or similar drawings, which I resist. But the breakthrough to the next series is rare. I am also embarrassed by the activity – it seems so private – why is that? (Not the finished thing but the doing of it.)

I went for years not drawing without being troubled by it. Now I draw more regularly, I worry much more about it. Your work seems so direct and immediate which is what drawing should be.

Sometimes I have a physical urge to draw, usually when the studio is least set up for it. I have always equated drawing with discipline, and felt the lack of it.

All for now, Alison

I want to return to fear and fright in order to respond to the edgelessness of Conceptual Art. As the camera becomes the most convenient, desirable, and fashionable means through which the object and its physicality can be dissolved, fractured, and then captured, it seems to have become more and more questionable (and dangerous, not to say risky) to make physical objects – a sculpture – as an end in itself which has all those qualities of

light, movement, sound, temperature locked within it, which are revealed imaginatively rather than literally. And instead of it being a passive engagement to unlock those qualities, it demands an active engagement. You have a walk around, stand back, approach, stalk the space the sculpture occupies in order to extract, step by step, the information it contains, its non-visual qualities. Not so with camera art. Therefore the affrontery of sculpture, its inherent obstructiveness, that it exists at all generates hostility from the viewer who can expect to be rewarded only by a prescribed system of looking. And to complicate matters further, sculpture does not conform to an ordered process of looking: look, then think, then understand: 1 + 1 = 2. Sculpture is a 1 + 1 = 3 experience.

Conceptual Art has been devoured by advertising; think, for example of the ongoing Silk Cut campaign in the 1980s which has generated an endemic style. The public now knows how to 'solve' the conceptual element of an artwork. It has become fun, like working through a puzzle book, or doing a crossword.

1970s Conceptual Art did not have edges, and would not be trapped, and the camera and text became vital props to substantiate it, and probably initiated its demise as 'radical' art at the same time. And since the 1980s and the rise and rise of the pictorial object (vitrines, framed objects, and objects on plinths), Conceptual Art has become subsumed within the image. The edgeless nature of much Conceptual Art has been replaced – probably because of a lack of economic value – with actual objects – which have glamour and commercial value. It is as though that vital curiosity to find ways of fracturing form has become extinct. Your experiment of photographing sculpture in the fog when you were a student is such a vivid description of the crucial ambivalence which makes making such an uncertain, but alive activity. The very thing that gets made is the very thing that is desired to be dissolved: life and death. What is form?

You don't have to answer. Sometimes I feel as though the forms I use have been reduced to '101 ways of using an 8 by 4 sheet' or wrapping, where the inevitable 'bundle' results. What is the use of innovation and invention? And where does invented form fit in – i.e., a form which is not just the result of bending sheet materials, or scrunching fabric, etc.?

Is geometry a way of giving the amorphic form a familiar order, disciplining it? To remove it from its sculptural inheritance and from nature? Habitually I return to plaster – great bursts of energy, mixing up buckets of the stuff with absolute conviction, and, two days on, exhausted by the physical slog involved, there is nothing there other than overworked, laborious 'forms': dead things, which tell me to go and get a life somewhere else. You have found a very precise way of using the liquidity of plaster – poured very directly, then into bronze, its essence of wet to dry held tight.

I want to be up to my neck in the stuff with a miraculous result forthcoming. But it is not like that. Fabrics, etc. have fulfilled something of that desire, but it is a kind of mimicry, and very clean. What is the longing for filth, mess, and spillage?
Phyllida

The longing for dirt: does it go back to a time or evoke a feeling of sheer pleasure that has nothing to do with meaning or process (is this what they call a precognitive experience? but let's not get into that!): getting your hands dirty or like a good shit. It's also a beginning, a state of flux, a formlessness – pre-form, pre-anxiety. And a reaction against the clean, the hard, mechanical edge; but it doesn't preclude a transformation into that latter state. My favourite stuff, although it's not dirt, is sand; either as the tide has gone out leaving it packed hard, silvery, and ridged, or sand as the tide comes in and is undergoing a transformation, a total collapse. Very, very sexy.

Fears and forebodings: Yes, I think geometry is a way of circumventing invention – disciplining amorphic form – very severe discipline.

I remember Jon Callan repeating one of Michael Craig-Martin's mantras that art is about observation not innovation. How annoyingly right that turned out to be! Yes, it's all one: advertising, fashion, music, Conceptual Art. Personally I like going against the grain. Your description of being part of a tribe on the verge of extinction (I nearly wrote 'distinction') was brilliant but neighbouring tribes also get wiped out by the common cold …

If, as seems likely, we are about to go into world recession or worse, it will be interesting to see how this affects the next big thing in art – or not. But I sense a hiatus, not stasis: hold on – anything might happen!
Love, Alison

Is the tragedy of sculpture (its doom), the fact that it can never be that pre-form, pre-anxiety state, and when it tries to be, it ends us being that surrogate that you referred to earlier; a paltry illustration and imitation, and altogether an unfulfilling second-hand experience? And is sculpture's closeness, materially and physically, to that territory of the basic reflexes and urges of animals (including humans) and nature which makes it feared and scorned – in a lot of cases understandably so – as an art form? As though its next of kin is all those functions of animals, humans, and nature which are without thought: raw, basic, uncontrollable.

But I don't trust or respond to those acts of making which have been forced to elevate themselves to the supposed integrity of craft as a bid to civilise sculpture. I'm sure the viewers who latched on to the alabaster as a 'handle' to an understanding of the work were ever hopeful that it was 'crafted', and then it – the work – would have a use, and would be

civilised, removed from its primeval state. In those terms *Harbour* (1994–6) fails magnificently! Is the ambivalence of where and how sculpture exists because of its anarchic rejection of fulfilling the expectation of its materials? It thwarts rational resolution, always destabilising expectation.

(Digression, ref. MC-M: I don't see observation and innovation as mutually exclusive. Surely observation requires innovation to translate it, doesn't it?)

More about making: isn't the desperation and urgency something to do with finding the shortest route for an act of making: to be economic with craft, if not with time or labour?

Sand, Sea, and Edges: your consistent return to the sea's edge is fascinating. Is the sand, as evidence of the mutability of edges because of its state of flux, also an ultimate object, because it can't be edged? The fact that it drinks up its other edge, the sea, affirms the fallibility of edges as always rigid, which they are not; they are capricious and the sand's reaction to the tide is an ideal example of why there is a compulsion to argue with the fixity of materials and how they become sculpture, and where the edges should, could be.

Sculpture!: sculpture's verticality and horizontality is something I have succumbed to over the last few years, and increasingly with enthusiasm. I have used structure as a strength, and support, on to which I can fling all kinds of slippery things – mess – and see if it sticks. The cool, calm, upright, and horizontal posture of structure is, for me, an equivalent to geometry: it permits autonomy, isolation, independence, and as a strength, it can take all kinds of assaults and remain standing, or lying, refusing to die, unless murdered in cold blood.

I love that strength, which I interpret as masculine and sexy. The assault I understand as myself, and I'm not clear what that is, but it is all the stuff that gets flung at, smeared, and hung on these structures. What ends up on the floor is a rich potential, nagging for attention, and possibly threatens to be more interesting than the object it has escaped from. Removing the work from the evidence of its making, from the surrounding mess, is always a relief, and enables me to know whether these structures have been able to survive the assaults inflicted on them. Like the ridged sand being the evidence of the force of the tide. I like the idea of a structure being a restraint (what you call a discipline?) to emotive gestures: both the labour intensiveness of making the structures (tedious, rational, organised), combined with their resulting strength – which can control and restrain what can be done to them, and the limits to which they can be pushed. For me, the structures are like the land, and the stuff that gets flung on them is anything that isn't land: weather, emotions, mess, memories …
Love, Phyllida

Craft: is well-made the same as crafted? I don't think so. I hate the crafty. I think there's a balance, rough edges are OK. I hate craft processes – like the interminable fifty stages of making a beautiful mould. I love shortcuts even though sometimes they don't work.

Your voice: I'm glad you have found it – you sounded very positive and optimistic about what you do, and you make a great case for making sculpture and the need for it. It's not cool, is it! Too much passion? Not enough irony?

Dazed and confused: this morning I've done two things.

Flicked through the pages of the above magazine which I take to be a microcosm of hard-edged cultural high spots. Couldn't tell what I was looking at – art, advertising. A batch of photos of disabled people wearing amazing clothes superficially no different from the models in other articles. I thought it was a totally hermetic magazine 'noir', glamorous, dangerous, a textbook for today.

Spent the rest of the morning losing control of bowls of plaster and pieces of thin alabaster. What I thought I saw coming towards me, an eventual resolution of seeing bulk through transparent stone which also formed part of it – has come to nothing. I feel like a spider being dropped from its web and then laboriously climbing up it again, except that's a totally inept analogy – the spider must climb its web, but I'm stalking something which has no edges or guidelines and each time I find myself in this place it's as though it were for the first time instead of for the thousandth.

What a pity this is the last fax.
Love, Alison

First published in *Alison Wilding: Grounded* (Sunderland: Northern Gallery for Contemporary Art, 1998), unpaginated; reprinted in *Objects for ... and Other Things: Phyllida Barlow* (London: Black Dog Publishing, 2004), 81–96.

Included in *Slade Magazine* in 2002, Barlow writes in '... from the mouth to the tail ... che el morro al rabo' about her former student, the Spanish artist Angela de la Cruz (born 1965). She describes de la Cruz's studio and writes about the process of making – of de la Cruz and more generally – with particular reference to control and timing.

Angela de la Cruz: From the Mouth to the Tail

2002

HYSTERIA
Rammed and jammed. Angela's studio is full. A small clearing is the working space, whilst on all sides the paintings, these painted structures, bulge, flop, and elbow their way into each other, and jostle for a place. Many are stashed unceremoniously behind a temporary screen, into which a glimpse reveals the extent of the energy and demonstrative restlessness of this work. A large shelved structure is host to myriad cans, pots, and jars, brimming and seeping with colour: it dominates the right-hand wall. Crowded studio, cramped working space, spilling shelves seem utterly private. It is revelatory and confessional. You feel compelled to avert your eyes, as if confronted with the shock contents of a bathroom cabinet, which have been mistakenly revealed, or with the nether regions of a dirty clothes basket, which have accidentally overflowed in front of an unsuspecting visitor.

WORK
This initial encounter triggers the usual response to such a working environment: glorious chaos, struggle, more witch's kitchen than studio, painful, orgiastic, violent. Why does the tactile use of paint elicit such responses, when, in fact, the control and the need for timing, and the sense of moment, is so much the order of the day? To lash out with paint, and to use the gestures of destruction – breaking, damaging, cutting, ripping, tearing – don't these belong to the realms of bad behaviour and are nothing more than hysterical outbursts, temper tantrums, and attention-seeking? But isn't this just simplistic projection, this equating of seemingly messy actions with out-of-control emotions? In fact, there is the urgency of the highly tuned athlete and musician to reckon with, and their exacting needs for precision. To strike when the moment is right. And how to know this 'moment'? No doubt that experience is the essence. And lots of it. Finding out and knowing when that gut feeling says it is right. Again, isn't this all too arbitrary? Shouldn't such a runaway commentary be substantiated? But how? Anyone can claim something is 'right', especially when it comes to sloshing around in an ooze of paint. Yes, lots of paint has a bad reputation. In the final analysis, isn't it just an excuse for some kind of deficiency and lack? And such a manipulative way of disguising that lack. However, is

this always so? What about the long calculations of waiting for the right moment, and the anxiety of not knowing, never having anything completely reliable, doubting the moment of action, mistrusting that it will ever be possible to do 'it' again: there are the dark mementos of this expression, and the background rumblings to the so-called outbursts. Such ruminations plumb the depths and are proof enough.

CONTROL

The two large canvasses are drying: they have been painted deep red and laid horizontally, thereby occupying the entire working space. They are uprighted and stacked together. They have to wait. No further action planned. But already a richness emanates: the colour such a particular red, and the surface worked to a shine. But now the excitement has to be put on hold. A kind of restraint must be exercised: waiting and watching. So what to do with this extra time? Make some sculptures. Join two upright pianos together, and a chair to a stool. Back to structures. To manipulate their rigidity and make them as malleable as the paint. Somehow that is always present, that need to manipulate and alter, evidenced by the join, where one part of a structure meets another, and how that structure can be remade, as with the surgical interventions on canvas stretchers, which might appear to be snapped or broken, but which are so very calculatedly 'operated' upon: the inferred damage a singular creative gesture, essential for the production of a new object. No brutal, unconsidered outburst. Cool, calm, incisive action. A one-off hit. And then the reckoning: is it OK? Does it work? The anxiety returns: the price is paid for that moment of delight.

HOT

Exhaustion. Paint is dormant. It is not only surface. It is the inside, the other side, the side which is usually unseen. Then it is awake. Every time it is different. Sometimes it seems as if it is the same, these surfaces, which are not surfaces but constructions, constructions which happen to be paint. Building is so physical, and with a substance that resists structure, and is semi-liquid, it makes for an impossible task. All the more reason to lie in wait, and to have everything prepared. The stacked and stashed works also wait. There is an uncanny symbiosis and reciprocation. Who needs who most? Huntress and hunted, the painter and the painted, coexist in a precarious relationship. The newly painted red canvasses are at ease. They are, as yet, still unknown. The others, not so. They have been around, and have been watched for some time. Nothing is certain, nothing is secure. Changes are always imminent. Yesterday's finished works could be today's subjects for remakes to be worked over, cut into, altered, manipulated, rebuilt, reinvented. There are no ultimates, and there are relationships to be renewed and the next possibilities to be tested. The heat is always on.

PASSION

There is only the present. No nostalgia. The doing is living, being alive within the painting and outside of it. Death is not a subject. Making is the evidence. Waiting is the staunching of the spillage, damming up expectation in order to release it when there are no other options. But that is not despair: emptiness is a signal to act, to pounce. The heat has cooled and clarity prevails, however briefly. Then familiarity resumes the confrontation with the consequence. And the heat returns: this is the exterior beneath which complexity resides, hidden and predatory: a cold menace masquerading as criticism, which can demoralise and destroy, clouding self-belief, leaving doubt and lack of confidence in its wake. But this chill can also be a philanthropic accomplice: it can assuage impatience, quench that restless anxiety which seeks mindless action for relief, allow time to mature the burgeoning sense of urgency. Play for time, get to know the demons: tame them, and then let them loose. The passion has its biology: it can flourish and decay, and its cycle leaves nothing unused: it can devour what it ejects, and vice versa, and through such an ecosystem, there is an economy: excess is the resource, not as an end in itself, but as the provider of the energy for an action. Canvas, paint, frames, structures, all compete, and no single component wins over any other: what remains survives, lives, and is a new entity. Everything has been used: 'from the mouth to the tail', *che el morro al rabo.*

First published as '… from the mouth to the tail … che el morro al rabo', *Slade Magazine* 4 (2002), unpaginated.

First given as a paper at the 'Encountering Eva Hesse' conference at Tate Modern in London on 15 November 2002, this talk was subsequently included in both *Phyllida Barlow: Objects for … and Other Things* and the 2006 publication *Encountering Eva Hesse*. In 'Lost for Words' Barlow discusses the contradictory nature of the work of German-born American artist Eva Hesse (1936–1970) and the way it defies verbal language. She considers Hesse's distinct sculptural language, her use of materials and processes, and the reductive way in which her work is labelled as emotional. Barlow describes her encounter with Hesse's *Sans II* (1968) at SFMOMA in San Francisco. She identifies the misleading and paradoxical nature of works that appear to be hot – highly handled – and those that appear to be cool.

Eva Hesse: Lost for Words

2002

Description and the thing described. A long-standing relationship which works well enough. Or does it? With sculpture rooted in process and touch which evidence themselves as the essential experiences of the object itself, it can be difficult to translate such qualities into verbal language. The difficulty belongs to an expectation that what is said, what the words are, will have an absolute integrity when matched against the object itself. My contention is that the work of Eva Hesse repudiates verbal language, and particularly a language initiated by the process of naming.

The currency of sculpture which can use the language of naming becomes easily empowered by critical backup, and the more the work can be named, the more such naming renders the work's physicality and materiality redundant. The network of meanings which can be constructed from the associations with the sculpture's naming eventually displace its physical and material qualities with an image, and the more pictorial the object, the more easily achieved is its physical and material displacement.

Non-image-based qualities, such as tactility, weight, texture, depth, height, width, darkness, light, smell, temperature, emptiness, fullness, and qualities inherent to materiality, physicality, and process use descriptions such as stretchiness, fallingness, droopiness, rigidness, fatness, thinness ... Although apt enough, the problem is how to substantiate such descriptiveness, give it clout, equivalent to, but different from, the rich discourse which can be constructed around work which lends itself to being named. The semiotic chain generated from naming can also spawn numerous meanings to which equally numerous critical theories can be attached. Inevitably, I believe, such work acquires an intellectually superior identity than work which cannot invite such tactics.

Whilst in the US, I sought out Eva Hesse's work. They were few and far between, but in the end I saw three. All were memorable. But how I came upon a section of *Sans II* (in the San Francisco Museum of Modern Art) has interested me: perhaps I was not concentrating, or at saturation point, but I did not notice it, when it was there in front of me (fig. 155). As it and I stood locked in a blank stare, I knew that to come across this work, as if by stealth, was the experience: there was, in fact, nothing surprising. Like many sculptors experiencing the work of Hesse, everything is absolutely clear: the materials, their processes, how the gridlike form and structure could have been made, and the variegated discolouration of the ageing, resin-impregnated fibreglass.

The fragility of the work, its light-saturated surfaces, its combined strict formalism with the undulating, slightly sagging edges, are Hesse's signature; these are hers, and to such an extent that whenever such results reveal themselves within an artist's process, and alarmingly the work begins to look Hesse-ish, he or she can have the knee-jerk reaction to back off, because the sense of pastiche can be overwhelming. Hesse has invented a sculptural language which is so completely hers that it can be impossible to appropriate some of the processes, even though they are generic and available to anyone, for fear of stumbling upon an almost, but definitely not, Eva Hesse.

This near copyright on materials and their processes creates a dilemma. Numerous experiments within art schools, usually at foundation course level, encourage using materials such as plaster, latex, cement, wax, resin, all liquid-to-solid materials. The point of these experiments is to get young artists to test out and experience the nature of materials, to find out what they do, to witness their time-based properties, and to experience the hands-on, the mess, and all.

Once these processes have been discovered, what next? To make a series of near-miss Eva Hesses, because by this time, art students, new to such processes, will have been introduced to Hesse, and, like an author condemned to an exam syllabus, these processes become identified with Hesse and with a coded message that this is 'emotional art' because it is wordless; it is primal: so, quite literally, it is as if nothing more can be said. But the narrative continues. Because such processes come packaged as emotional, the resulting work is delivered as 'personal', about 'feelings', as if no other art can claim such sanctity. And, as if things cannot get much worse, because of these claims, the resulting work, by default, refutes questioning or criticism. And a protected species is born.

This scenario explains something of the lack of a robust critical language which can compliment these processes, materials, and resulting works. The claims that 'emotion' is evidenced through an appearance of tactility, materiality, and process is dubious, but there is probably some truth in it as well. More importantly, there is this difficulty with making a critical and descriptive language work for the work itself, rather than avoid the work by jumping to critiques and theories culled from existing canons which substitute for the actuality of what is there.

So the work of Eva Hesse, as a generalisation, is not promoted in art schools beyond the most primary stages of an experience of sculpture, relegated, as I believe she is, to introduce and induct a sculptural language at a basic level, rather than to manifest a profound relationship to making, which reveals extraordinary depths of intellect, emotion, and psychology.

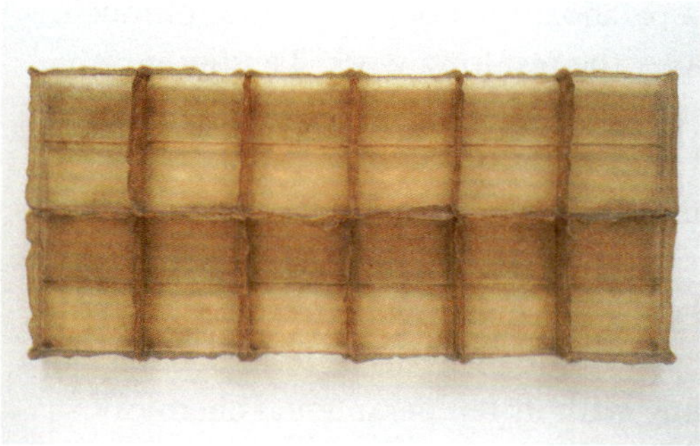

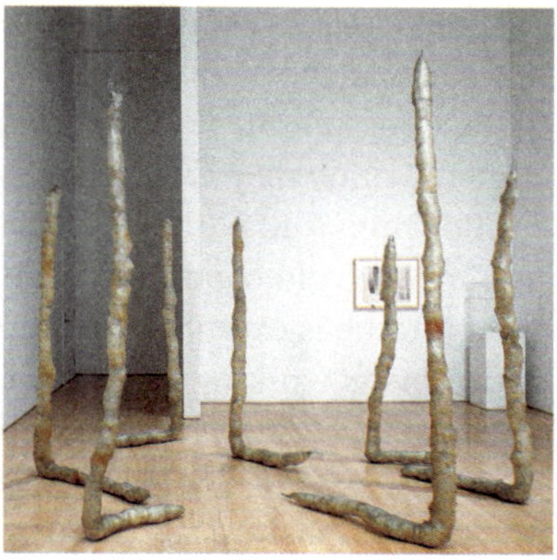

LEFT TO RIGHT:
fig. 155 Eva Hesse
Sans II, 1968
fig. 156 Eva Hesse
No title, 1970

Her work, at worst, can be reduced to art-school exercises to impress upon wary students the virtues of making: as a teaching aid to informality, the fun of playing with stuff, the emotiveness of spillages, splashes, and mess, and the transformatory mysteries of processes. And having clocked these, it's then on to the real stuff, the stuff with meaning, as if meaning is somehow oppositional to emotion, and the processes of making.

My initial blankness on meeting *Sans II* diffused slowly. Restlessness, anticipation, and an anxiety about missing a wonderful opportunity were dissolved by the act of moving and looking. Dark and light, a rhythm, from one blurred, boxed form to the next, everything a repetition, but everything different, and the open-ended emptying out into the space beneath, which became full and supportive like an invisible plinth holding every side of the work, sealing interior, exterior, and surrounding space into a symbiotic dependency.

By now I am as close to the work as I can be. A different mood prevails, a fear of disturbance: close up the work demands stillness and silence. There is a pulling inwards, as into long-frozen ice, an odd response, when the material itself has warmth. The chill is bewildering, at odds with the embedded hairs of the fibreglass, and the softly caramelised edges, and the aged, yellowing resin. It doesn't make sense, but then this is all in my mind, isn't it? And not really anything to do with the work.

But of course it is. Objects are emotive, because of their formalism, their structure, their place and time in relationship to ours. Upright and suspended things are different to collapsed and recumbent things, obvious enough, but being there with objects in these conditions influences our own condition, the way we look, move, and behave. The memory of the work is not the same, however powerful, just as a text is not the work.

My description is identifying a paradox: the hotter the sense of touch, and the evidence of process, the cooler the resulting work. Tactility is duplicitous and misleading. Liquid-to-solid materials only have so much time in which they can be handled whilst they are setting: it is a one-hit relationship. And with a material like resin, if it has not set, due to a faulty mix, or too cold conditions, the process of restoring the surface to how you want it to be is excruciating. And there were such nightmares encountered with Hesse's working methods. To get dripping lengths of resin-sodden cloth to hang, drop, fall exactly so, working with its temperamental chemical reactions, as in *No title* (1970) would have only permitted minimum contact of tactile, hands-on, activity (fig. 156). Resin's carcinogenic potential is now notorious ... Therefore, *No title*'s tactile heat is in stark contrast to the reality of its making where the resin impregnated fibreglass would have been as deftly, and as quickly manipulated as possible, in fact, as hands-off as possible.

Meanwhile, those supposedly coolest of cool objects of Donald Judd or John McCracken, of Jeff Koons or Damien Hirst, have every inch of them handled, touched, manipulated, not necessarily by the artist but certainly by their fabricator.

The work of Eva Hesse is contradictory. If its materiality and process are the work, then these belie their pragmatism, offering paradoxes instead: where hot is cold, touched is untouched, anti-form is precision, and place is time. The work could not be more different and complex than its simplified interpretations within art schools, or its reputations which have mythologised its sensitivity, confusing it with sentimentality and nostalgia.

My conundrum is how to evidence through language what is there and the being there, a language which can have a critical status unencumbered by an over-emotive rhetoric on one hand and an overladen theoretical position on the other. The work of Eva Hesse is gloriously nameless. But an Eva Hesse is unequivocally an Eva Hesse. For me, it cannot yield to a worded, semiotic process. Its paradoxes are its meanings. The work exists as if it has always been in the world. And, paradoxically, despite its unequivocal signature, it exists as if it could have been made by you.

First published as 'Lost for Words' in *Phyllida Barlow: Objects for ... and Other Things* (London: Black Dog Publishing, 2004), 210–18, and in Griselda Pollock and Vanessa Corby, eds., *Encountering Eva Hesse* (Munich and New York: Prestel, 2006), 217–21.

Barlow writes about Welsh artist Sean Edwards (born 1980), on the occasion of his residency and exhibition, an off-site project for Chapter Arts Centre, Cardiff, in 2006. She begins her essay with some notes on the work of the German artist Imi Knoebel (born 1940), in particular his piece *Raum 19* (1968), which she saw during her visit to the exhibition *Imi Knoebel: Primary Structures* 1966/2006 at the Henry Moore Institute, Leeds (2006). This show was a catalyst for her thoughts about the work of her former student Edwards. She considers perfection, appropriation, and eBay as a resource and reflects on the sense of effortlessness, edginess, and open-endedness that she perceives in Edwards's work. She addresses questions of authorship and the role of the viewer.

Sean Edwards: Finders Keepers

2007

INTRODUCTION

Imi Knoebel's *Raum 19* occupies the back gallery at the Henry Moore Institute (fig. 157). The work is made of hardboard and consists of stacks of familiar studio paraphernalia, which have been remade with sanitised precision. It is pristine, and exudes a tension particular to the material's fragility, uniformity, hard-edged finish, and weight. The hardboard fossilises the painting stretchers, boxes, canvasses, cupboards, shelving units into blanks where their former identities of what they once were are not required and have been erased. It is what they have become which captivates. I am looking at a memory of a studio, paralysed and stunned into stillness and silence – comatose. Where there were once noises and movements generated by the artist's activities of doing, making, thinking, and testing out, there are now only empty carcasses. The experience is unsentimental and unnostalgic: it is entirely sensual and sentient of the present without any haunting encumbrances of the past to influence this stark reality of now. Like the detective's clichéd white outline of the victim's body, these anaesthetised, mnemonic stacks have their imprint of time embedded within them. The captured state of these objects is more photographic than sculptural. It is photography without the photograph.

THE PERFECT BAG

Imi Knoebel's exhibition at the Henry Moore Institute became a relevant trigger for the discussion between Sean Edwards and myself. Perhaps it was Knoebel's use of precision and Edwards's reference to perfection which initiated the comparison. Edwards is clear about what attracts him to the objects he deploys within his work. One object in particular summarises the long-standing relationship he can establish with things, and the processes he engages with to identify their use within his work. The object in question is a 1970s Tesco bag. The familiar Tesco blue-and-white striped logo, from the 1970s, is what Edwards describes as perfect. The perfection is the aesthetic spacing of the stripes, the space they occupy on the bag, and the number of stripes, their width, and height. Such exactness underpins Edwards's activity, his process of making and discarding, and his need to wait and watch the work with hawklike attention. The 1970s blue-and-white striped Tesco bag lies on the floor held in place by an upturned glass (fig. 158).

The glass has been swilled in orange paint. It seems to have caught the bag in a half-twisted turn which has slightly lifted the handles, like a passing gust of wind.

WORKPLACE/SHOWING SPACE

The images of Edwards's residency and exhibition show nostalgic schoolrooms where the work is secreted into the different spaces. An installation shot offers an undemonstrative use of the space with objects placed here and there. At first glance, the image is more like a working studio than an exhibition. The objects are raw, scant, effortless, even impoverished, more like remnants than fully formed things. Some placings are more logical than others. Some objects are more appropriated than others. And some are double acts, where appropriated objects and materials are combined. Being able to name the objects keeps them in check, containing their process of making and their temporality. As such, the naming is deceptive, offering a grasp of the objects too quickly as if the work is simply a list of dictionary definitions: look, there's a paint can with a stick attached; or, there's a firework on black bubble wrap; and over there, there's a bag with an orange glass on it. This speedy assimilation is the lure to Edwards's irrepressible need to engage with a twilight world of salvaged, half-used, and discarded ephemera. And it is anything but a speedy encounter. The relationship Edwards establishes with his chosen things is for the long term. There are no shortcuts, no quick fixes. But what is the attraction of these chosen things, and how does the work get made? Is placing the work its final act of making? The images I am being

LEFT TO RIGHT:
fig. 157 Installation view, *Imi Knoebel: Primary Structures 1966/2006*, Henry Moore Institute, Leeds, 2006
fig. 158 Sean Edwards
Untitled, 2006

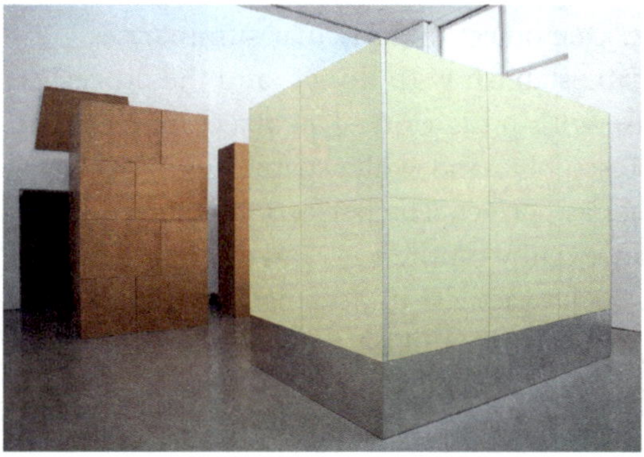
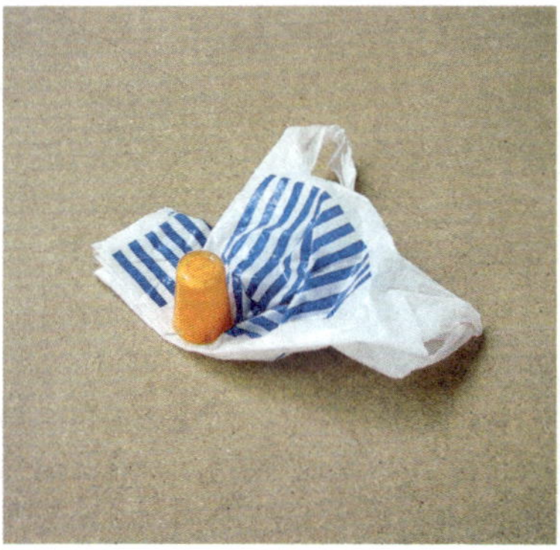

shown are evidence of an event. Here is a place where something happened, and this is what is left behind. Edwards summarises his approach to making and exhibiting work with characteristic straightforwardness: 'I have a suitcase which I will take to Amsterdam as part of a group exhibition. It will not contain work, but it will contain ways of making. Making is an event.'

EBAY

I ask if there are categories for different groups of work. However, Edwards's ideal is that each work is a separate category, that all objects (in the world) have a separate category, that there are no groupings. But what about differences between, for example, the decision to remake, as a copy, a set of discarded shelves, but to use, as is, a salvaged set of rolling pins. Why not copy the rolling pins as well? No, it is all about the separate functions of the work, and it is arbitrary as to which objects get copied and which can be salvaged and used as found objects. Maybe rolling pins are more difficult to copy than shelving units. Maybe the function the shelving units have in the space, forming a corridor, make them more architecture than object and therefore more generic, like a wall, which can be built anywhere. How does Edwards use appropriation? For him, there is the all-important attraction to things. Without that initial spark, the creative catalyst fails to ignite. What is important is the discovery of an object which 'doesn't need anything more doing to it'. Back to the Tesco bag, which, as Edwards states, is 'a perfect example' of appropriation. This particular 1970s bag was bought off eBay. Interestingly, the eBay resource must be revising the canonised and historicised views of the readymade, hastening its demise, where it now seems nothing more than a twentieth-century relic. Meanwhile, eBay makes anything and everything available at the click of a button, as does the internet per se. Searching for the work is now a process in itself – in Edwards's case, an eBay process. Somewhere out there on eBay is the work ready to be tracked down, ready to go. eBay has become a category in itself, a shopping category, as yet without an art history or morality to control it. It provides a democratic service to artists where buying their work on eBay places them on a par with all other shoppers. Making art from eBay becomes about shopping. It is just another way of doing, and another way of passing time.

HARD WORK WITHOUT LABOUR

Edwards's apparent effortless making is beguiling. It masks any struggle and doubt which may have been encountered in the process of production. But easiness is not necessarily easy to achieve and not an end in itself. Edginess is crucial as a foil to easiness. It may all look effortless and easy, but the objects do not behave in an easy and effortless way. Questions are provoked. How can such slights of hand, such fragile interventions and such barely existing things be judged? Can one work be better than another? And if so, how? Edwards has robust criteria to contend with such questions. He quotes his experience of curating a recent exhibition as demonstrating his fascination for objects and how his responses to the work exhibited by the different artists provoked envy of their creative relationships to objects so different from his own. This enabled him to grasp his own fascination more clearly. Incompleteness is central and offers the potential for the objects Edwards engages with and manipulates to continue beyond their final moment of being made. Edwards is generous to his viewers: they are offered the work as theirs, to continue it imaginatively beyond his control. And the work plays with accidents, inviting anticipation: the role of wrapping paper on the floor, the spent firework lying on the black bubble wrap, the scattered, abandoned hockey sticks. What are all these disparate objects doing? How did they come to be there? Are they meant to be just lying around? What happens next? The precision inherent to the objects themselves is persistently contradicted by the ambiguity of their placing and arrangement, thus offering an open-ended, restless experience of the work and its occupation of the space it inhabits, with more questions than answers forthcoming. However, Edwards's most important criterion for a work's success resides within its physical intensity. The physicality can be disguised and as such, it can be unrecognisable as being physical. As with the white spray-painted carrier bag which contains the rolling pins and the wetted newsprint, which left to dry over a radiator, has taken its form, like a crisp, shell-like cast. These barely visible evidences of actions question the preconceived notions of physicality, defying its orthodox identity of weight, texture, conspicuous materiality, and laboriousness. Edwards's preference is to recognise the physical intensity of less ponderous manifestations: the forensic trace of a hidden mark, the breath on the windowpane, the accretions of dust on books. The challenge for Edwards is to capture for real these effortless acts through his equally, seemingly, effortless making process. Paradoxically, such subtlety takes effort, hard work, and time.

FREEBIES

The residency has been a seminal experience for Edwards. A month's uninterrupted interrogation of his activity has affirmed his creative focus. He is confident about how the work can be placed in the world and relate to an audience. His desire for the work to be 'continued' by its audience gives intensity to the moment Edwards finishes the work and hands it over, not literally but conceptually, when it no longer is his work but everyone's. This brings me back to Imi Knoebel. This artist's work could be made by anyone. Its ownership, although inherent to what is there and how it has come to be, is rooted in his thinking and not necessarily in the objects themselves.

As in Edwards's work, there are paradoxes in Knoebel's work as well. Such seemingly cold work is initially remote and depersonalised. In fact its blankness can belong to anyone and can be representative of anyone's home, workshop, kitchen, garage, etc. The generosity is to the viewer. The work becomes theirs to elaborate upon. The only problem is whether the viewer responds. Similarly, Edwards offers his work, equally generously, for anyone 'to continue and to complete'. Edwards abdicates from having the final say for this mental and imaginative process. But the catch is whether there is anyone there to fulfil such an ambition, to take advantage of such a freebie. Edwards is philosophical. He celebrates his defiance of needing too many specifics to justify the work's existence. He can do for himself what he wants others to do; he can 'continue' the work regardless of exhibition space, studio space, or audience.

The residency has enabled the work to claim its edgy identity, where it hovers deceptively between life and art. This is a tough and uncompromising place to inhabit, both for the work itself and for the artist. Edwards is uncompromising in making this place his own.

With ‘A Must-Have for Everyhome’ Barlow has created a fictional dialogue between herself and the British artist Eric Bainbridge (born 1955). It was included in *Eric Bainbridge: Forward Thinking 1976–2008*, the catalogue to accompany his exhibition at Middlesbrough Institute of Art, Middlesbrough, UK, in 2008. It is based around their conversations since meeting and teaching together in the mid-1980s. In this playful exchange ‘they’ discuss Bainbridge’s work and in particular his chosen materials.

A Must-Have for Everyhome: Conversation with Eric Bainbridge

2008

Phyllida Barlow: What is it?

Eric Bainbridge: What do you think it is?

PB: Natural or man-made?

EB: What's the difference?

PB: It's got to be from somewhere.

EB: In the earth.

PB: Or laboratory.

EB: Could be both, man-made and natural.

PB: And it's heavy. Rounded and lumpy, blistered, like acne, or like spotted dick – a pudding – plum pudding.

EB: That's ridiculous.

PB: No – it's delicious.

EB: Well, taste it then – or put it in the oven and cook it … could be good.

PB: It's irrefutably itself like your sofa.

EB: Fake leather and fake stone; couldn't be better.

PB: And opposite to each other. What else? Teacups … they're Pyrex – such a 1950s material – and a stepladder.

EB: They're not so opposite.

PB: Stepladders can be shelves, that's why.

EB: But it's not a stepladder – it's a slide projector stand, from the 1960s (fig. 159).

PB: Of course! It's too fragile for a stepladder. But it, whatever it is, and the cups are related hereditarily – Pyrex and Formica must be the same family. At the RA Summer Exhibition a furious couple stood beside this projector stand/cups sculpture and declared it the worst work in the exhibition, then paused and declared, no, the worst work ever.

EB: Probably right!

PB: Because it looked like something left behind during installation – forgotten, out of place – that's its perfection. And, like so much of your work, it is a succinct declaration of sculpture, but under cover of being something else. It fulfils everything a sculpture can fulfil. It is both free-standing and a plinth. Formally dynamic, balanced, without function, different from every point of view. 'Too small to be a monument, and too big to be an object' (that famous Tony Smith quote misquoted), and it has air flowing all around it and through it, so it references the hole in sculpture without actually using that device … the list is endless.

EB: And to think Marcel Duchamp was doing this ninety years ago, with the same response.

PB: An object is always objectionable.

EB: Unwanted.

PB: But may have been, once.

EB: Once what?

PB: Wanted – like teacups, stepladders – no, projector stands and urinals – and like the bubblegum you told that Brighton student to use to join together her sculpture.

EB: That's more about surprise and banality, things being in the right and wrong place at the same time.

PB: Like the craze for fixing upturned polystyrene cups to the hubcaps of London buses – that delight in the perfect fit of such a chance discovery.

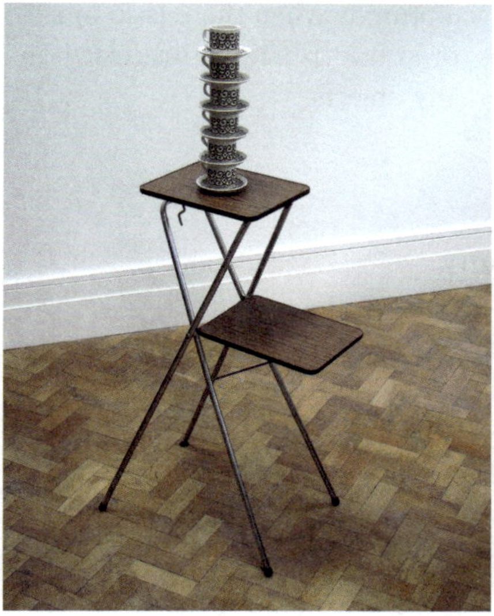

LEFT TO RIGHT:
fig. 159 **Eric Bainbridge**
Untitled (Stepladder), 2006
fig. 160 **Eric Bainbridge**
Untitled, 2006

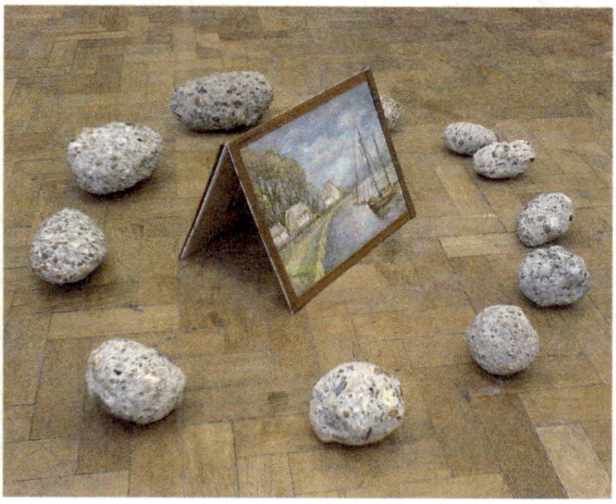

Or finding chewing gum stuck to the underneath of a canteen table, or a lost glove fitted on to the spikes of railings …

EB: It's necessary to hold on to banality but reverse its expectations.

PB: You did that literally with the fur fabric, turning it inside out.

EB: No – that was more to do with formalism – to soften the plywood structure beneath the upholstered surface so that its Minimalist style became kitsch. Making the corners rounded and the surface spongy – Minimalism with a soft touch, literally, yet seamless and tight.

PB: Is upholstery always kitsch, whatever the fabric or material … ?

EB: 1950s, 1960s, and 1970s designers were concerned with the formalism of pattern. Bold acts of theft from high art became translated into mass-market devices for the household – curtains, crockery, furniture, carpets, wallpaper …

PB: But you have fused something of those surfaces and decorative qualities from mid-twentieth-century design with 'real' kitsch – cheap fairground pottery figures, which used to be given as prizes. The hole in the base of those cheap pottery figures, required for firing the clay, fascinated you as a parallel to the 'hole in the sculpture' you identified with so much modernist, twentieth-century sculpture – Henry Moore, for example.

EB: Maybe there's a need to find out what sculpture is when there is so much of it about, but unclaimed, in pound shops, or as bric-a-brac, or discarded on streets. So much stuff, so many things, so many objects.

PB: Back to Duchamp's *Fountain*.

EB: Yes and no, that's all so twentieth century.

PB: Old school?

EB: Old school and academic – appropriation, or whatever you want to call it, is material. It's only stuff. It's that simple and is not a moral issue or an art issue.

PB: Using some materials could become a moral issue, like wood, stone, paint … using up valuable resources.

EB: Let's not go down that route. Choosing this and that from car boot sales, Oxfam shops, eBay, or the internet is anything but using valuable resources. It's taking chances, salvaging, and recycling. It's about making choices and exerting particularity, being exact and precise, even if you don't know what for or why.

PB: It could all be very nostalgic. Why isn't it? Your work, I mean …

EB: It might be, but exchange is a straightforward way of getting a job done. Exchange means adapting – finding the shortest route for getting that job done and making necessity be inventive. Nostalgia, even aesthetics, are not my priorities.

PB: Is it like this – must have a flat surface; OK, inspect that lot of Formica kitchen worktops dumped on the street; choose the best one. That'll do the job … ?

EB: But they would not be Formica – that's far too classy. It would be, and is, some cheaper equivalent.

PB: From kitchen units to high sculptural form, with a twist.

EB: Sounds like an exotic cocktail.

PB: The Bangkok glowing light is a bit of a cocktail, pastel shades merging one into another. It completely disarms the formalist rigour of the structure it inhabits.

EB: That's the second time you've used the word 'inhabit'.

PB: It's because the work uses a series of inhabitations, one within another: there's the relationship which the components have with each other within the work, and then the relationship the work as a whole has with the space it is in. It is all crucial and demanding and uncomfortable. It makes the space very restless, and the work, i.e., the sculpture, does become an obstacle, something to be avoided … that's the beauty and the thrill.

EB: The glowing light bulbs are so smug.

PB: More than smug … they're a *coup d'art*.

EB: What does that mean?

PB: It means that they are an unbeatable found or readymade or appropriated object for the use of making an art object … it will be in the Oxford Dictionary as a new twenty-first-century art phrase. Everybody's using it.

EB: Not in Sunderland.

PB: It began in Sunderland. Back to these lumps. Where did they come from … they're perfectly moulded, a kind of ultimate lump … they're also a *coup d'art*. They are hybrids, things between a useful and a useless object/thing (fig. 160).

EB: The sea washes them up. They're concrete and aggregate pieces broken off from the sea walls, which have been rolled around by the sea to become smoothed out lumps. The salt water must be a perfect abrasive.

PB: They taste good, especially uncooked … Lumps and light bulbs, Pyrex and tangerines. This particular but disparate set of objects, materials, things lie around and seem to be lost, or not to have a place. They, and you, seem content to let things bide their time. Piles of paperwork, catalogues, administrative stuff all coexist with a huge stored sculpture as well as images, prints, drawings, stacks of fake Formica surfaces, tacky 1970s crockery – all seemingly indifferent to not having the right place such as a desk, filing cabinet, or table. This room – both your office and studio – allows anything to happen in a way which a proper studio might not. A studio screams out 'Make art!' whilst an office is the last place where art might be made.

EB: Things just happen. That's a very upright structure there, a work in progress … I don't know yet how to finish it. I come in here to do one thing and end up looking at it. I will not be thinking about it, but it will be at the periphery of my vision and then I might know what to do. It's having it around and being able to look at it casually that helps me make decisions.

PB: There are so many paradoxes: place and non-place, formalism and kitsch, structure and casualness, decoration and solidity. There is something of the circus – spinning plates, juggling with fire – within the work. There is the integrity of 'revealing all' – truth to materials – combined with a sleight of hand – the con artist and his 'Find the Lady' three-card trick …

EB: Are you saying my art is a con?

PB: Sort of … but that's its triumph. The tangerines are captured on the Formica surfaces as if caught as they fell. The sculpture is performing a sleight of hand. Its serious, Minimalist, Caro-esque stance and Picasso-like posture (like his 1950s *Bathers* series) are spoofed by these three tangerines. They are the jokers in the pack. There's this bravado and flare to play with sculpture as a very formal inheritance from the twentieth century, yet there is also the trump card. Playing around with very familiar, often domestic stuff and re-presenting it with a designer's precision, as if these sculptures could be functional. A must-have for every home.

EB: Not in Sunderland.

PB: But I told you, it all began in Sunderland.

First published as 'A Must-Have for Everyhome,' in *Eric Bainbridge: Forward Thinking 1976–2008* (Middlesbrough: Middlesbrough Institute of Art, 2008), 41–5.

This short text, 'Was It or Wasn't It?' was written for *Beuys Is Here*, the publication accompanying the eponymous exhibition held at the De La Warr Pavilion in Bexhill-on-Sea, UK, in 2009. Barlow recalls attending an event at Tate in 1972 involving the German artist Joseph Beuys (1921–1986) and her feelings of hostility at the time. Remembered by Barlow as a conversation or interview involving Richard Hamilton, it appears, in fact, to have been the performance *Information Action* by Beuys staged at the Tate on 26 February 1972. This lecture and discussion were held in the Duveen Galleries as part of the group show *Seven Exhibitions* (and Richard Hamilton was a member of the audience). Barlow goes on to describe her encounter with Beuys's work *Earth Telephone* approximately twenty years later, in the 1993 exhibition *Gravity & Grace* at the Hayward Gallery, London, and the re-evaluation of Beuys's work this prompted her to make.

Joseph Beuys: Was It or Wasn't It?

2009

It was 1972, and the venue was the Tate Gallery. I was late. The crowd was dense and impenetrable.

The sense of awe was oppressive and authoritarian. I could not see him, Joseph Beuys, or hear what was being said. I knew it was an interview, or a conversation, and Richard Hamilton was involved. I was hostile to the occasion because of the adulation and sycophancy. It seemed Masonic and closed, as if some special membership was required.

Also, at that time, I had been to performances of other artists where a sheep had been slaughtered (Roundhouse), and a man had defecated on a glass table (Arts Lab), and a young woman had slashed her arms with razor blades (in a basement space on the Charing Cross Road). Long gone was the sublime gentility of Gilbert & George's *Singing Sculpture*. It was now considered a necessity to parody political intent, and to be all too eager to adopt cruelty and self-loathing as tools to provoke shock and disgust. I had categorised Beuys's actions in amongst this frenzied troupe.

I walked away from that evening at the Tate disconsolate, feeling excluded. But looking back at that time and scrutinising the black-and-white documentation of Beuys's interview with Richard Hamilton, there is a reflection in those images, and my memory of that era, that is captured. It was a time desperate for change. There was no confidence in how the Cold War, Vietnam, the economic deadlock, and the injustices in Northern Ireland and throughout the UK would lift.

And so to *Gravity and Grace*, the seminal exhibition at the Hayward in 1993, curated by Jon Thompson, which revisited Arte Povera, identifying that movement's legacy for sculpture. Somewhere between Giovanni Anselmo's *Invisible*, Mario Merz's *610 Function of 15*, Eva Hesse's untitled work with three nets, Marcel Broodthaers's *Brick Ladder*, and his *Sculpture*, Gilberto Zorio's *Chair*, and Bruce Nauman's *Double Steel Cage Piece*, I wandered uncaringly past Joseph Beuys's *Earth Telephone* (fig. 161). I was probably thinking dismissive thoughts: an arrogant knowingness where I assumed I had been there and done that. But the two objects, the double act which constitutes *Earth Telephone*, initiated half-remembered thoughts about Beuys's reflections on sculpture from twenty years earlier: expansion and contraction and their relationship to vacuum and mass. When I had read this in the 1970s, I was excited by Beuys identifying sculpture with a presence of impenetrable emptiness, the vacuum, which

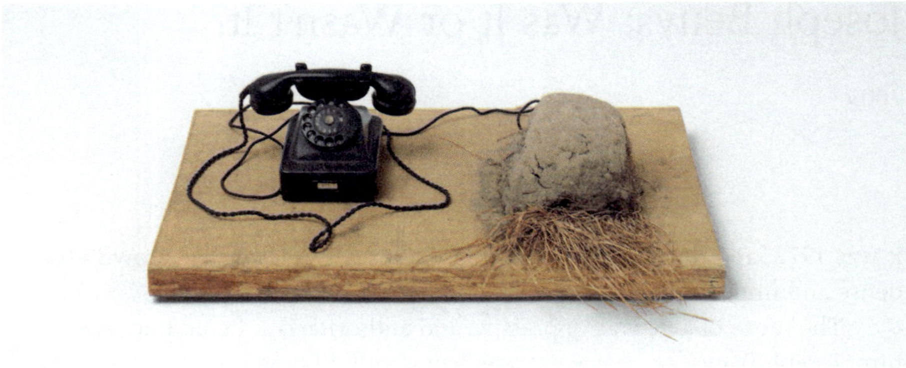

fig. 161 **Joseph Beuys**
Earth Telephone, 1968

could implode in on itself to become dense substance, the mass. Somehow my initial, and dismissive, glance at *Earth Telephone* was enough to prompt this memory, a prompt which made me retrace my steps and stop in front of the wood block in thrall of the paired-up objects upon it – the black Bakelite telephone and the grey-brown lump of earth and straw.

In that moment of being captured by this doppelgänger object, I did not see an image. The objects as named things had vanished. Instead I saw an exterior and an interior: a black, lustrous exoskeleton for the dense brown nodule next to it. They existed in antithesis to one another but with complete symbiosis. They begged the question of whether a ball of mud is the opposite of a black plastic shell. Or is the telephone the mould for its cast innards of earth and straw? And whilst watching them, for that was what I was doing, why did I have this compulsion to make one fit into the other, over and over again? It was a mental game, full of anxiety, which refused to be resolved, but one which evidenced hands pressing earth into the telephone casing, shaping it quickly and expediently, and then briskly turning it out.

Beuys's identification of sculpture with expansion and contraction and vacuum and mass was there before me. The lustrous, black telephone, a metaphor of expanding airless space, had contracted into this imploded mass of earth. The vanishing act had trounced my complacency transforming it into enchantment.

First published as 'Was It or Wasn't It?', in *Beuys Is Here* (Bexhill-on-Sea: De La Warr Pavilion, 2009), 16–18.

In 2011 Barlow was invited to select a work from Tate's collection and write a response for *Tate Etc.* She chose *Modulation of Space I* (1963) by Spanish artist Eduardo Chillida (1924–2002). She describes the piece vividly, explaining the fascination it holds for her and relating it to her own work and that of German-born American artist Eva Hesse (1936–1970).

Eduardo Chillida: In the Heat of the Moment

2011

Rising up or collapsing? Folding or unfolding? Exhaling or inhaling? Crouching or cringing? It seems larger and more voluminous than before. Is this because of its different location? Previously it was in Tate Britain. Then, I could walk around it and view it from the back, as well as from the sides and front. I'm now confused. I'm seeing it at Tate Modern. Is it the same Chillida? Yes, the iron bars forged into contorted loops are there as before – but the size and volume seem to have doubled.

Twisted shapes and structures have a capricious history within sculpture. The invented forms that emerge from materials being pulled, pushed, stretched, poured, piled, compressed, and coiled have been frequently usurped by a preference for the appropriated and readymade. Eduardo Chillida's *Modulation of Space I* (fig. 162) is a hybrid fusing both the readymade and invented form. The solid iron bars from which it is forged are themselves readymades. It is a heavy, recalcitrant, unyielding material which requires great heat to make it malleable, and great strength and skill to twist and turn it into something other than its original prepared lengths.

The transformation of the dead weight of the bars into the interlocking series of raised loops, angular sections trapped beneath and awkward protuberances which constitute *Modulation of Space I* has to be achieved so quickly in the forging that a moment in time is forever captured within the folds and coils of the sculpture. Similarly, the heat is somehow retained. It is as if it is still darkly smouldering, emanating an inherent sense of danger.

Modulation of Space I is delicately balanced on three points at the edges of its structure. Air circulates through its loops, counteracting its heaviness and making it seem both light in weight and absorbent to the light within the space in which it is located. The pressure of the forging process has caused raised creases to expand on the tight curves. Splits have been cut into the metal when hot to assist its moulding and modelling. The contrast between the bold structure, the thickness and darkness of the materials, and the ease of the flow of the iron can also displace its sculptural qualities: it becomes a drawing seemingly scrawled into space at speed with gestural confidence.

Gravity, as well as time, heat, and forged iron, are its materials. The effortless loops, arching upwards as well as folding on top of each other, defy their own weight. The visceral piling-up of these apparently weightless

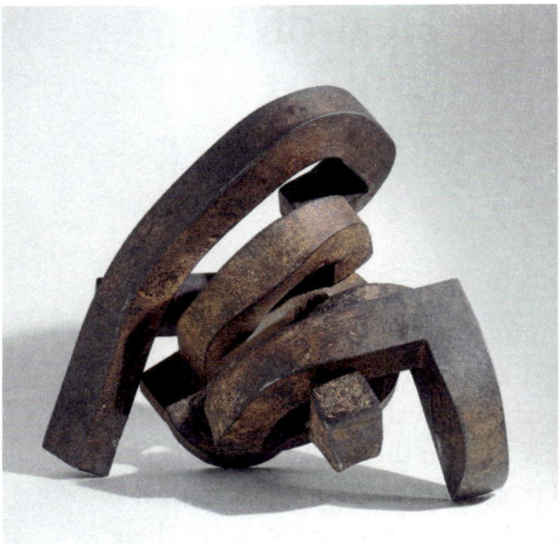

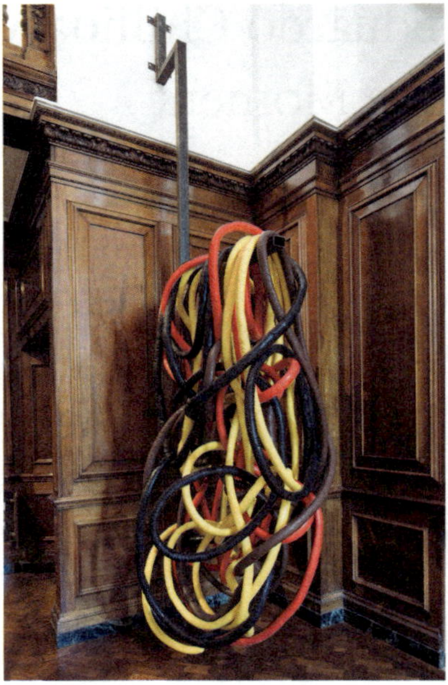

LEFT TO RIGHT:
fig. 162 **Eduardo Chillida**
Modulation of Space I, 1963
fig. 163 *RIG: untitled; coils*, 2011, installation view, *Phyllida Barlow: RIG*, Hauser & Wirth Piccadilly London, 2011

curves begins to beg questions. How did Chillida know when to stop wrestling with the hot iron, to not add another curve or angle? When was enough enough?

The immediacy of action retained within the coiling metal is alive in its now static form. But it is anything but still. As I walk around it, I provide the movement which reveals the restlessness of this work. It is different from every point of view. It is impossible to hold it as a single image. No wonder I could not fully remember it.

Now, I begin to think of another work whose use of gravity is physical, material, and anarchic. How would Chillida's *Modulation of Space I* respond to sharing a space with Eva Hesse's *Contingent* (1969; fig. 44)? Her eight suspended sheets of resin and latex-soaked muslin are about as opposite as is possible to the predatory, forged-iron object. Suspended from fixtures overhead, the fragile sheets are openly vulnerable. Their armatureless bodies refute sculptural language, instead behaving more as painterly surfaces. But they are as sculptural as *Modulation of Space I*. And both pieces represent the physical and material manipulation of space, time, and gravity which sculpture can exert. They are not concerned with pictorial images in three-dimensional form, but with sculpture which is rooted in actions applied to materials and processes to evidence – what? Perhaps these actions transform themselves into emotions, and that is what we are left to fathom.

For me, Chillida's contorted forms wrestled from white-hot metal end up evoking power and fear – they are coiled ready to pounce. But when I walk around to the back of the sculpture, the perilously leaning forged metal bars seem both defensive and threatening in their awkwardly balanced stance. I turn to have a final look at Chillida's piece. Its dramatic hold on me retreats. It is in its place, cordoned off and plinthed close to the gallery wall. I retain the sense of its coiled tension, its captured movement, and its dangerous balance. Now, as I write this, what I am remembering isn't visual. It is the actions of heat on iron and their enduring effects of fear, stealth, and defiance. I want danger, awkwardness, a sense of perilous balance, and the evidence of time through the materials and their processes to be evident in my work. I am continuously taunted by guessing when enough is enough. *Modulation of Space I* is inspirational as it keeps me guessing: I cannot work it out. I cannot resolve it. It is always different.

Back in my studio, paper rope coils are being bound in glossy tapes (fig. 163). The paper rope is rigid and recalcitrant. It is difficult to manipulate, and the added tape is making it even more unyielding. These coils will be slung over a wall fitting. I want them to be a loose, unformed, and unravelling kind of object. But embedded within their process of making is a deep envy for forged, white-hot metal.

First published as 'In the Heat of the Moment', *Tate Etc.* 23 (autumn 2011), 84–5; https://www.tate.org.uk/tate-etc/issue-23-autumn-2011/heat-moment.

On 30 March 2011 Barlow gave a lecture at Leeds Art Gallery as part of a series of talks relating to the British artist Henry Moore (1898–1986) to accompany the exhibition *Henry Moore: Prints and Portfolios* at the Henry Moore Institute, Leeds. In this slide talk Barlow discusses artists that have interested her and speaks about some of her own exhibitions and works. She states at the outset that she is unclear of her views on Henry Moore. Included here is the part of the lecture in which she focuses her attention on him.

Henry Moore

2011

[...]

So Henry Moore, where does he fit in? [...] The reason I've shown the masks and this work (fig. 164) is that I think his early work done in the 1930s has this kind of modesty about it and simplicity about it, which maybe says something about the evolutionary cycles of artists. The more successful their work becomes, what happens to it? Does it become grandiose? And therefore loses some of that kind of simplicity or directness of approach that I think Moore's early work has. It's as though he really was trying to find these figures within the forms, within the materials that he was so captivated by and yet he belonged to that British craft tradition of figuration meets landscape meets craft that I think has been such an absolutely huge influence. I would say it's a huge influence on Anish Kapoor and Antony Gormley. It's like the island race of the British Isles, it's trapped within this world of idealism about where the landscape, an idyllic notion of the English landscape, meets this highly romanticised version of the figure, which I think a lot of future generations, after Moore, just had to challenge and take apart.

The other thing about Moore I find very, very strange is the plinth, but also the way so much of his work takes on a kind of ceramic pot look. I find it really worrying, the way the works hit the plinth (fig. 165). [...]

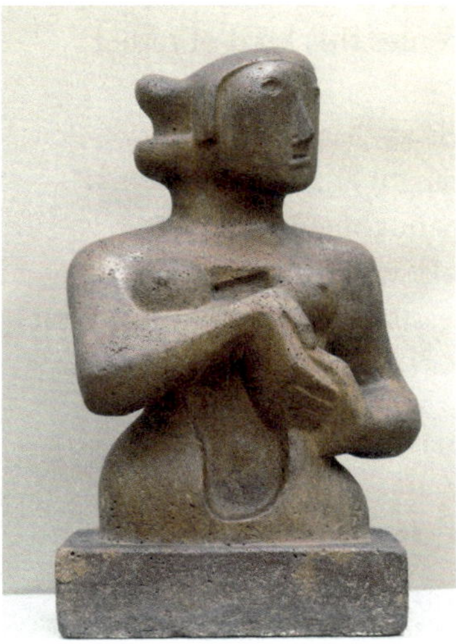

fig. 164 **Henry Moore**
Half-Figure, 1929

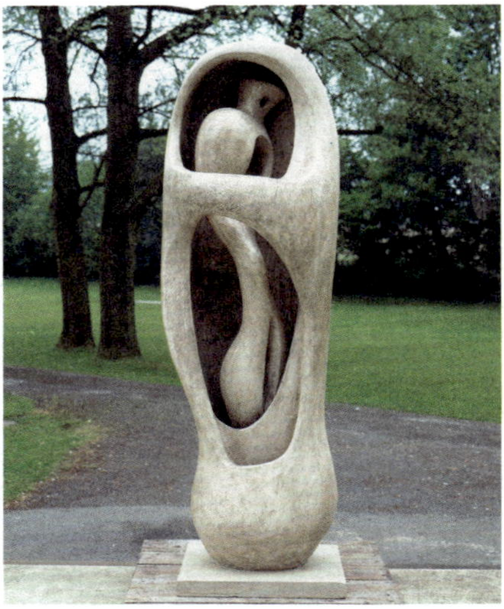

fig. 165 **Henry Moore**
Upright Internal/External Form,
1952–3

Maybe again, that for me is where he seems to be so immersed in something that's to do with craft, and it's almost as though there's another work within these works that's sort of ready to leap out, that throws caution to the wind and allows gravity to take over and maybe knock these things over or allow them to fall about and roll about on the surface, rather than having to be in this very strict upright ceramic-pot-type role. These works I think I find quite difficult. I think with all his work there's again, like the earlier work I've shown, this tremendous belief in sculpture and what that belief is, is that the plinth becomes a stage and the world within the plinth is this very, very unique frozen moment of the object that we're looking at and using bronze to do that. Of course now, for a lot of sculptors, it becomes enormously problematic because it's like this artifice where there is this big, black hole inside the bronze, which I think a lot of us just want to get inside there and see what that is. And so the bronze itself just becomes this kind of rather fake surface.

But, you know, having said all that, it sounds as though I am very mistrustful of him. I'm not, I just think he was caught at a very particular time between a kind of Victorian age and a rampant contemporary age, or an age that was changing the whole relationship with materials through a post-industrial society and all sorts of social pressures that made this heroic form of sculpture making, in a way, questionable.

[...]

An audio recording of this talk is held at the Henry Moore Institute Research Library, Leeds.

This is an edited version of the conversation that took place between Frances Morris, director of Tate Modern, and Barlow as part of the conference 'Through the Writings of Louise Bourgeois: New Perspectives on Art and Psychoanalysis' that was organised by the Freud Museum, London, and held at the Courtauld Institute of Art, London, on 17 March 2012. Barlow selected six sculptures by the French-American artist Louise Bourgeois (1911–2010) that are key for her: a series of wood *Personages* (c.1946–54), *Avenza Revisited II* (1968–9), *Nature Study* (1984), *Articulated Lair* (1986), *No Exit* (1989), and *Cell (Eyes and Mirrors)* (1989–93). With particular focus on these works, Barlow and Morris exchange views on Bourgeois's oeuvre. Barlow identifies her first encounter with the work, and they consider Bourgeois's processes, materials, and subject matter. They discuss a number of works by Barlow, and in so doing they forge connections between the two sculptors' work.

Louise Bourgeois: Conversation with Frances Morris

2012

[...]

Frances Morris: Phyllida, when did you discover Louise Bourgeois's work, and was she part of your finding your voice as an artist?

Phyllida Barlow: [...] The first time I saw Bourgeois's work was when I was at Chelsea Art School when it was in the old building just on the top floor of what was then the Polytechnic. There was an incredibly inspired set of teachers there headed by Lawrence Gowing and George Fullard, who probably no one here will have ever heard of, but somebody who emerged from the war thoroughly damaged physically when a hand grenade went down the barrel of the tank he was in at Monte Cassino and blew up and he was the only survivor. His work was all about the kind of disaster of war. And he happened to have this small catalogue from the Peridot Gallery (fig. 166).

FM: Which brings us to your first choice.

PB: Yes, and he said, 'You will like these.' I remember him just giving it to me and I think that there wasn't a library at Chelsea Art School then, but Norbert Lynton, who was a very distinguished art historian, began the library at Chelsea then, and I think he was just collecting everything he could get his hands on. So, I had the opportunity to see this work and I just remember thinking, 'This is fantastic, this isn't like Henry Moore, Barbara Hepworth', and then the whole string, the sort of barrage of British sculpture that was what we were meant to be looking at then.

FM: It wasn't like that, but did you think it was like other things?

PB: No.

FM: Or did it feel completely fresh and new and –

PB: I thought it was like the eroded driftwood that you might find off the sea coast. And also importantly for me, George Fullard was a tremendous fan of Louise Nevelson, and it actually seemed to link very closely with Nevelson's accumulations of objects that she made. And I think it's important to try and see Louise Bourgeois fit in the context of these other artists who were actually doing quite similar things in a way. Not in any way as a put-down to Bourgeois, but perhaps it actually strengthens her work.

FM: So there is a kind of aspect of bricolage about the work, isn't there?

PB: Yes.

FM: These were made, principally, from bits of discarded wood that Louise found on the rooftop of her home. Which would have been the old planks from the water towers. So they're sculpted but they're also sort of collaged aren't they?

PB: Yes, and whittled. They have a sense of being, again, that incredibly powerful thing of feeling that her hand has been over the entire … almost like a blind act, where the works have been explored, not so much visually but physically. And the original image of these *Personages* is of these very square, and I think you write about that, kind of square chunks of wood, which she has obviously whittled and worn down through various carving, and maybe even other processes.

FM: What I think is interesting about them, is not just the making of the objects themselves, but it's the way that they were installed that was so incredibly important. Looking isn't just about looking at a sort of static thing on a plinth or on a pedestal, but it's about actually engaging with the space that they occupy.

PB: And enjoying a kind of confrontation of a moving, sentient, a live being, against something that is supposedly still. But as you walk round them, they themselves, in a different kind of way, offer themselves up for a sort of movement, because the other sides of these works are often surprisingly different. Some of the orifices and openings don't actually go the whole way through. They're like small niches that have sort of burrowed out of the surface of the wood.

FM: And they do feel very handmade.

PB: Incredibly.

FM: Is that important?

PB: Yes, they're like … in some ways, they're almost amateur. I mean, if you don't know the size of them they could almost be kitsch. Perhaps they are a bit kitsch, actually.

FM: But also perhaps they are a bit amateur.

PB: Yes.

FM: I mean Bourgeois hadn't trained as a sculptor.

PB: No, exactly.

FM: It's one of the things that's always struck me as rather extraordinary about her. She trained as a painter, but then in the course of a long career she seemed undaunted by taking on, almost driven by a need to take on any number of sculptural challenges, different tools, different media, different techniques.

PB: I think sculpture is very divided in that respect. I think when I was at Chelsea and then the Slade, you were actually taught in a very disciplinarian way, the five disciplines of sculpture. And if you couldn't do them you were berated and abused and I couldn't do them, I was hopeless.

FM: OK, so this is something you did do (fig. 167)?

PB: Oh yes. This –

FM: 1963?

PB: Yes, and this shows the sort of influence of Bourgeois on me. But it also shows the influence of loads of male sculptors. I mean, I absolutely love the phallocentric object and I … in the face of this audience, I think one of the problems I had with the first onslaught of feminism was this desire to kind of demolish the phallus. […] But my relationship with sculpture was the love of this thing, of trying to make something that wouldn't stand up, stand up. That just seemed to me an incredible challenge, I suppose. And I didn't succeed most of the time.

FM: You're still working on it, aren't you?!

PB: Yes, still working on it! But just to go back to this, this whole relationship with something like plaster, which I still have and still love. I think for me

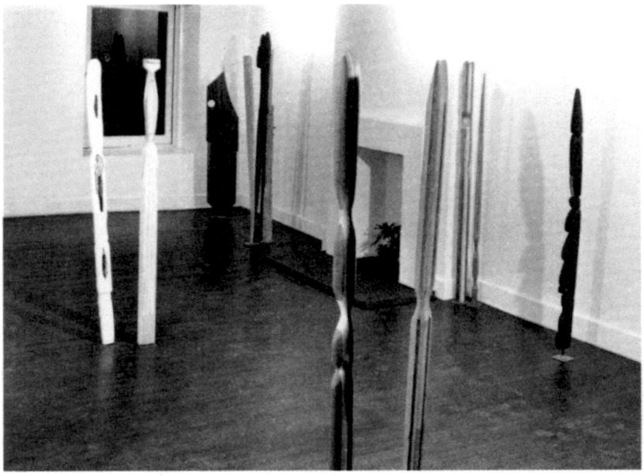

LEFT:
fig. 166
Installation view, *Louise Bourgeois: Sculptures*, Peridot Gallery, New York, 1950

BELOW:
fig. 167 *Untitled 1963*, 1963

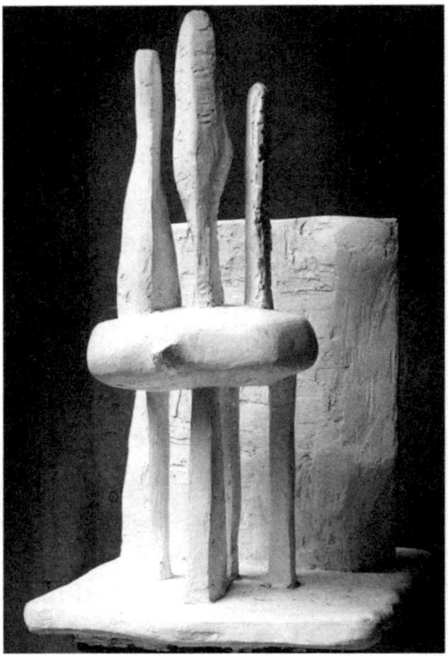

RIGHT:
fig. 168
Boxes, 1968

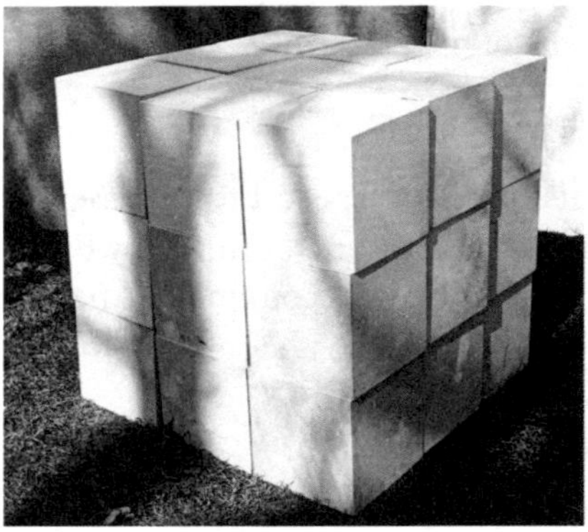

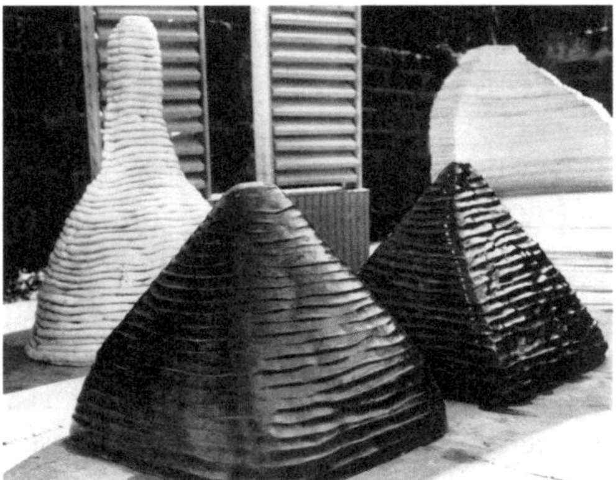

LEFT:
fig. 169 *Eleven Pieces* (detail), 1968–9

the whole act of modelling from clay, building something up from clay, was the one thing that I could develop a relationship with sculpture from. The other things – welding, wood construction – were all a disaster and I think … when Bourgeois made that shift that you so cleverly diagnosed, from the *Personages*, which are these whittled, wooden upright objects, to these things with orifices, I think my sort of crude interpretation was to get the wooden things and stab them into the … They're like a vagina and a penis. Those two conditions of being a human being, I think for sculptors are absolutely fundamentally fascinating. One that makes itself through an absent space and the other, which announces itself through various states of 'erectitude,' if you want to call it that.

FM: Bourgeois's *Personages* date from the late 1940s and early 1950s, and she began to be known then. An early work from that period was bought by the Museum of Modern Art […]. So, she wasn't unknown, in the extremely male-centred, American-dominated environment of New York of that period. She did extraordinarily well. She had a prominence and a respect. But then there was a decade, I think it's the decade of psychoanalysis, where her work recedes from the public scene, but it's in that decade that Minimalism happens, and during that decade, Minimalism and the beginnings of Postminimalism. Now you were working through that era, and I've just got two examples here, *Boxes*, from 1968 (fig. 168), and *Eleven Pieces*, from 1968–9 (fig. 169). You were in a way, I think, responding to that moment in time when artists were beginning to explore materials and the stuff of art outside of the five disciplines that you were taught.

PB: Yes. Yes, I suppose the -isms were coming in thick and fast throughout the 1960s and in the 1970s and it was an incredibly vibrant time. But when I talk to my husband about it he always says, 'I hated the 1960s.' I think there is another voice that can say that the 1960s was also an uncomfortable time, oddly enough. We were terribly unfashionable because we were married. We got married in 1966, and I think at that point we lost half our so-called friends. We didn't smoke marijuana, I mean, we were terribly conventional. I think the idea of trying to make in this whole environment of these -isms coming in one after another, was actually an incredibly enlivening challenge because my eyes took me to Europe more than to … or to certain aspects of America.

FM: So, you might have been looking at the Italians, Arte Povera?

PB: Absolutely. When I became aware of them it was like … why was this kept such a secret?

FM: And what was it about their work that was liberating for you?

PB: It was its fracture. It was allowing the work to embrace both the fallen and the collapsed, as well as something that was possibly, extremely thoroughly made. Mario Merz using chewing gum to hold the glass frames of those domes together. The gesture of making being something absolutely in the moment and also permitting the collapse to happen at the same time.

FM: Which might bring us to our next choice of work by Louise, which is *Avenza Revisited II* from 1968–9 (fig. 24). The 'Revisited' refers to the fact that Bourgeois had made a work entitled *Avenza*, which was a floor-based sculpture, which appears as a series of tumescent mounds in latex. Mounds that might be breasts or phalluses. And then she seems to have taken on your challenge, to lift the sculpture in an almost impossible way.

PB: With a hole. With a gaping hole. With a cave.

FM: So, underneath this sculpture is this extraordinary lair.

PB: Yes, the empty space is the thing that seems to be holding the work up, which is something that Bruce Nauman does in a very different kind of way. But I just think, my question is, with the latex *Avenza*, what was that taken off? Because, in order to use latex, as we know from Eva Hesse's work, you have to … latex is a wonderful medium for making a mould, so I feel there must have been something for the original *Avenza* that was plaster or something that she poured the latex over and then removed that to make all sorts of variations on that theme of these breasted, phallic forms, which seemed to endure throughout her work. And maybe one of the things I wanted to raise about her work is, I think she is an incredibly innovative artist, but I think she's innovative around quite a few themes. And I think that's what is really, for me, inspirational. That these breasted, phallic forms is one theme. The *Personages*, which then reoccur as hanging shapes and then in *Articulated Lair* (fig. 150), which we'll come to, they're hanging downwards, but it's still basically the same form, the same shape.

FM: One of the things that I think is extremely interesting about this work, is just the process of its making, or the process of its germination. She began with a sculpture that was grounded, and I think Louise, referred to this type of work as sort of anthropological landscapes. So there's very much a feeling of it being a grounded terrain and obviously melded with the body, but the impossibility of it, skied in this way. You can't really see it in this image, but it's raised up and supported on this great sort of outpouring. Almost as if the mould had somehow opened in the pour and the material has swept down from the table and landed in this sort of growth of a head of hair, isn't it?

PB: Absolutely. It's a spillage.

FM: A spillage. And is it the result of an accidental spillage or is it something that Bourgeois intended to make?

PB: That's what I find so unendingly magnificent about this work, is that we don't know. I'm not aware, maybe other people are, if there are any descriptions of how this actually came about. But what you feel in its presence is that she is still there, because, with this liquid-to-solid material she has engraved in it, what seem to be fingermarks, and I assume, maybe it's an assumption, that those are her fingermarks. So the thing sort of contains her presence in the most vibrant way. You feel as though the work, when you're in front of it, and I've only seen it twice – I saw it at the Palais de Tokyo, and then at the Tate.

FM: We had it at Tate Modern, yes.

PB: Yes. You do feel that it is living, it's in the present tense, it's now. It's not in the past tense, and that's because of how she's actually allowed the material, this wet plaster, to accommodate her, to have her imprint in it. But it is highly modelled and the spillage at the back, which is this great swirling whirlpool of plaster that's on the floor is very, very contrived as well, isn't it, as a modelled form. As is the whole thing. But you do feel it comes from some out-of-control moment that she's then taken control of. I think plaster has its own rigidity, so it wouldn't be that difficult to raise it up, the original *Avenza* form.

FM: And what is so interesting, is just at the time that she's dealing with the uncontrollable or going with the uncontrollable, she's almost, I think, in the same year making very, very similar works in a highly controlled way through marble carving and using master carvers.

PB: Yes. Perhaps I have a slight problem with some of the carvings, where I feel there is a kind of loss. I mean if we look at *Cumul I* (fig. 151), which I don't know if you know it, which is the white, floor-based work. I mean it's an incredibly erotic, sensual piece with these lidded forms, which look half asleep. I always think of her comments that, what does she say, 'Horizontality is a desire to give up'. The vertical is I think 'being alert', and the suspended form is 'ambivalent'. I think for me, that is such a wonderful way of 'emotivising,' if that's the right word, very, very rigid formal language that has sort of often dogged sculpture, I think. I can't imagine an American Minimalist sculptor using that kind of language to describe their work.

FM: This work and work like it came out of a period where Bourgeois was, as I said, not exhibiting very much. Her family moved to the house in Chelsea, where Louise then continued to live until her death. And she moved from a situation where she had a rooftop studio, and the light of New York, with the city growing around her, to working in a basement, in a very dark subterranean place. And I think it's interesting that this very sort of visceral, organic, handmade work came out of a dark, dank, lowly place.

PB: On the other hand, how much does sculpture need to be seen when it's being made? The sense of her stalking this work and being in its presence as it, as she put it, 'Did its own thing,' as the plaster solidified. The moment when a sculptor, who's using these materials, has to hand over their entire desire for what they want to achieve, to the material itself, and whether that's a kind of blind moment, I find fascinating.

FM: Have you had your blind moments?

PB: Yes.

FM: I slipped in two works here from the 1980s (figs. 170–1). You spoke at Tate Britain a few weeks ago about your own work, and you mentioned that during the 1980s you were at home and you were bringing up an impossible number of children, and also trying to work, and your working life was conducted late at night.

PB: Yes.

FM: I think at home and I think you said in the dark, I'm not quite sure. I'm sure it wasn't in the complete dark.

PB: No, it was when they had supposedly all gone to bed [...]. Then, we sort of shared it, my husband and I shared this peculiar routine, so I would then go into the studio. And I was interested in trying to make sculpture without image. Trying to see where an edgeless object ... I mean it's an impossible thing to demand ... So I would set up materials in quite a random way and not have the studio lights on and work without looking at what I was doing in a very intentional kind of way.

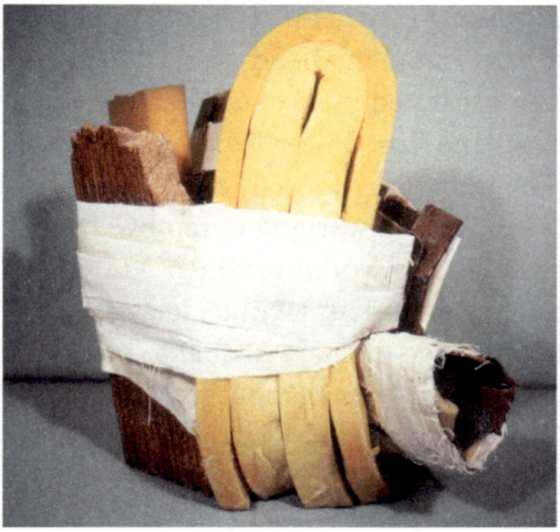

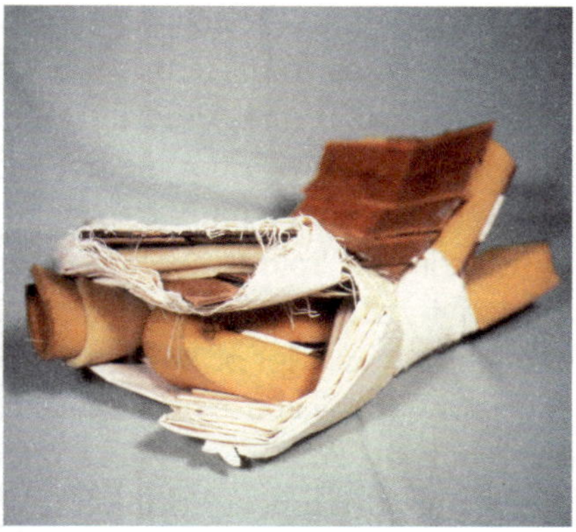

LEFT TO RIGHT:
fig. 170 *Touchpiece*, from the *Nightworks* series, 1982–3
fig. 171 *Touchpiece*, from the *Nightworks* series, 1984

FM: Yes, it's so interesting because the very first time I went to visit Bourgeois in the early 1990s, she was sitting in her day room at a table and throughout our conversation, which went on for about three hours, apart from the moments where she got up and walked away because she didn't want to talk to me any longer, she was working on something in her hands, as if she was working in the dark. And I think maybe it's something absolutely fundamental to the sculptor's art, or the kind of sculptor, the relationship with your hands, which isn't something to do with your eye or even your brain necessarily.

PB: I think, for me, to discover clay was like a release from prison. It meant also that there was less chance of being right or wrong, which I think, that then was the life room ... and for painters was a very crucial thing. It was as though you had kind of transgressed a critical framework. And I think that is something that's incredibly vital to a certain sculptural language. It's not everybody's idea of sculpture at all, but it is about a kind of non-visual, visceral, physical experience that is hopeful, it's hoping to reveal. Maybe it doesn't always, maybe it's closer to failure than success, whatever those two words mean.

FM: Your choice of material here is so interesting because this is tape, isn't it (fig. 172)?

PB: It's Sellotape [...] which was wrapped round my hand, which is why your description of *Rondeau for L* fascinates me, because I can't help seeing it (fig. 173). Almost as though, the way the plaster is on that, is almost like somebody making a mould. It's expedient rather than expressive. I think I was interested, in the Sellotape one, of thinking of what if sculpture is just a job? I'm going to make this Sellotape wrap round my hand until I can no longer do it anymore, and I did, and then excavated it out. And then the other one made with boiling hot bitumen, and I used these wooden tongs to just wind it round a bit like spaghetti, I'm embarrassed to say, on these tongs until I couldn't hold it any longer (fig. 174). So almost trying to remove from the activity, a kind of emotional expressive way of working, which oddly enough I see in a lot of Bourgeois. Despite its enormous tactility, I see a very expedient practical use of the material, which we then are invited to get our hands on. And it's at that moment, I think there is a language, which is the language of touch. I think if at that moment you do touch, the magic or whatever you want to call it, is gone. I think the fact you can't touch is quite a remarkable sculptural privilege in a way.

FM: What about the role of metaphor in relation to a work like this? Is there any opening for metaphor? Or is it all about the materiality and the process?

PB: I think it is and I think I can't control how people will see these or interpret them or use metaphor. I think what I dread most is the symbol. And I think that's my problem often with Bourgeois being appropriated as a symbolic language, that it symbolises trauma, or it symbolises this. Actually I suppose that's why I want to get back to, as you've described with *Avenza Revisited II*, how was it done? [...] Can I just ask you what would the metaphor be for you?

FM: Well, I suppose they feel amoeba-like. They feel very emergent, they feel pregnant with sort of becoming. I don't know that they're a metaphor for anything, but they're very, sort of sensual.

PB: I would call that more ... my hope would be that that was about a process that doesn't know when to stop. That, to me, the wrapping, my relationship with binding and wrapping, I think, is the striving to find something which doesn't quite know when its ending is. Whether that's a metaphor –

FM: Or where it begins. The Sellotape one, the Sellotape is translucent, and so there's a sense of a kind of interior space, that is actually maybe something that's quite hidden, but interior/exterior is important in Bourgeois and something that I think comes through in so much of your work. And often a concealed interior.

PB: Exactly.

FM: But you talked about marble and your reservations.

PB: Well, the one I love of this, the version I love of this [*Nature Study*], is the red wax one, and I did actually speak to the person who's collected this work, and it requires enormous care (fig. 175). But the red wax one is just so visceral and so alarming because you do sense this soapy surface as being incredibly fragile in contrast with this, I think, alive but dead creature. Stuart Morgan, if any of you know his writing, he's written brilliantly on this work where he describes what creature can be supposed to be covered in hair but is hairless, is headless but is absolutely alive ready to leap into action.

FM: And of course this is a work that Bourgeois, like many, described as a self-portrait. So –

PB: Really?

FM: Extraordinary.

PB: Yes … Well, no. Is it extraordinary? Because, as a parent you are sort of headless.

FM: And multibreasted!

PB: Yes! I thought you hadn't noticed!

FM: I think I meant the collective Mother, not just you, Phyllida!

PB: But I think the idea of the feminine as being quiet and docile, I mean, I don't have to tell this audience, but the sort of rampant anger and rage that's inherent to this work and the surgical precision with which the head has been removed. I think it does speak about, not just maternal relationships, but relationships in general – ambivalence and –

FM: You've said two things that are really interesting in the context of Bourgeois's work. One is the absence of a head. Something that I've been more and more troubled by is the complete absence of the head in Bourgeois's work, apart from one or two very early self-portrait drawings until the very late fabric work, where she really takes on the head.

PB: But they're the head of the sex-toy dummy, aren't they?

FM: The recent?

LEFT TO RIGHT:
fig. 172 TORSO, 1986–9
fig. 173 **Louise Bourgeois**
Rondeau for L, 1963

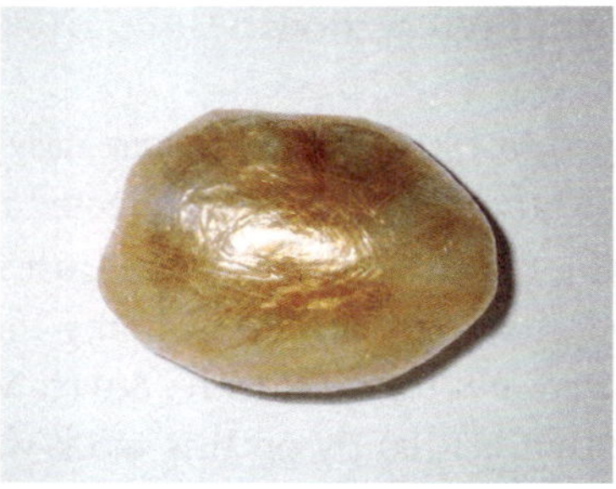

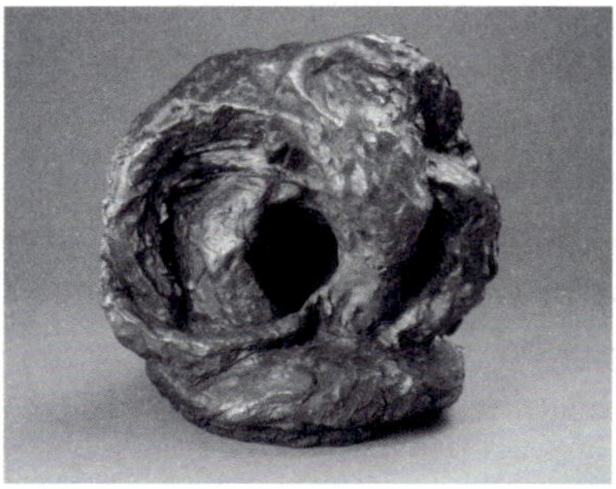

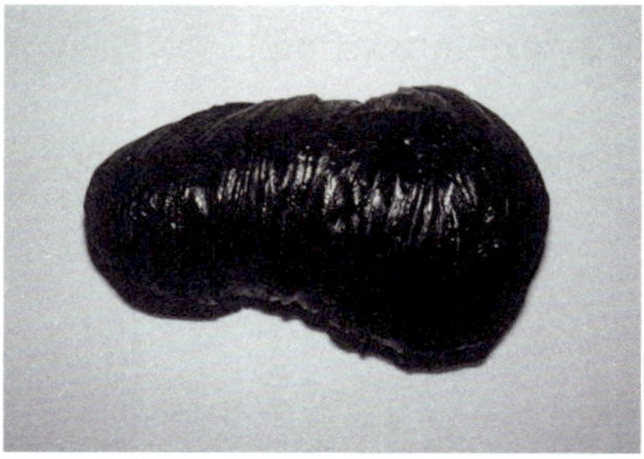

ABOVE:
fig. 174 Clench, 1989

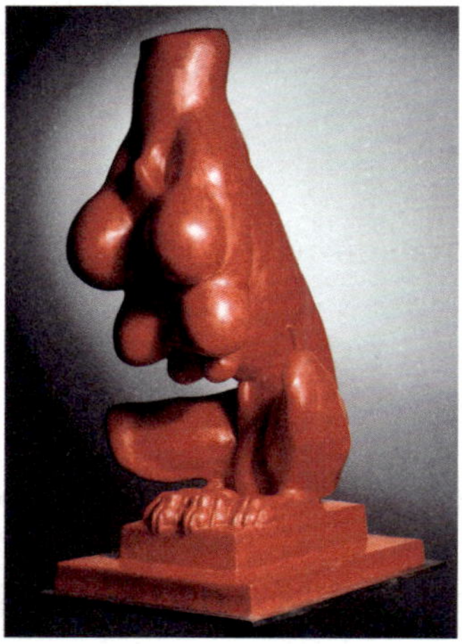

RIGHT:
fig. 175 **Louise Bourgeois**
Nature Study, 1984

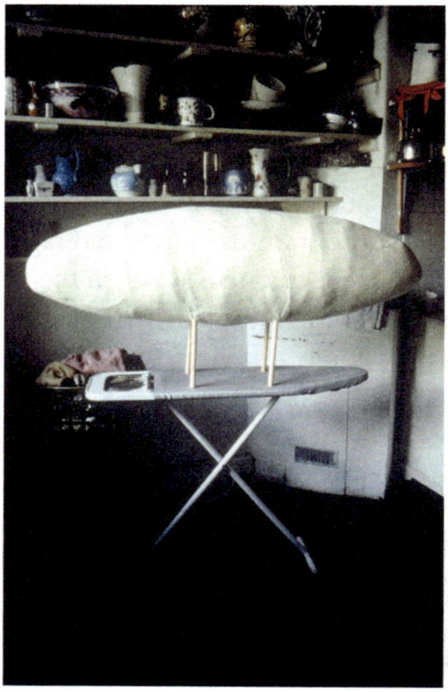

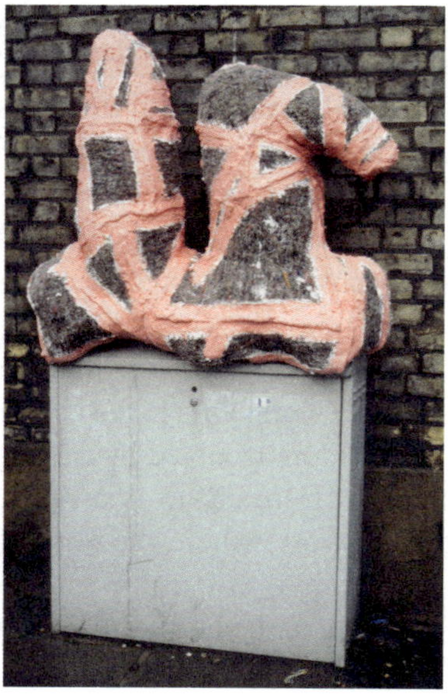

LEFT TO RIGHT:
fig. 176 Object for an ironing board, 1994
fig. 177 Object for street furniture, 1999

PB: Yes.

FM: Yes.

PB: That's a very displaced kind of head, isn't it?

FM: Well it's decapitated. The head and the body very rarely come together in Bourgeois's art.

PB: Incredible, isn't it?

FM: And the other interesting thing, is that we talk about materiality and the very close relationship between form and materials and process in Bourgeois's work, and yet, by the middle of the 1980s, she's making work like this. That then she makes, or has made in many different materials, and I am always slightly troubled by the divorce between the process and the –

PB: By the different materials –

FM: Well, because this exists in marble and in plaster and in red wax, but also cast rubber. And then there's that very highly polished version as well.

PB: Yes. I'm sympathetic to that. This sounds strange, but maybe you don't need many so-called ideas to be an artist. Maybe a limited repertoire of so-called ideas. I mean what is an idea? Is it a thought, or is it an instruction that has then got to be carried out? I don't think it is with Bourgeois. I think it's a fleeting, sentient desire that then finds its language through these works. But how you then relate to that when it's done, and the possibilities for its afterlife, might mean that these things require different ways of being produced through the template. The rubber version of this is pretty incredible as well, I think.

FM: Yes, extraordinary. Speaking of unfolding series, returning to the same idea through a number of iterations, this is a series, your *Objects for*, that I really completely adore. I don't know why, I thought the juxtaposition of this after *Nature Study* somehow worked rather well (fig. 176). [...] Is this your own self-portrait?

PB: I'm sure! Yes! I'm certainly not going to try and find out!

FM: But this is an extended series that you made in the 1990s.

PB: And continue to make.

FM: Can you say something about the need to return to the same, it's like sort of itching a spot or picking a scab.

PB: I think, it perhaps goes back to what do artists do? Where are they? Where are all these artists? What happens when you don't have exhibitions? Well, you get on with it, you just do it. You signed up for life, and maybe you don't know where to put things when you've done them, and I suppose one of the questions was where does art end up? On people's walls or … but what if it's an inappropriate object that ends up in an inappropriate place (figs. 22, 113)? What are the rules of the game? So I began to make things that would be kind of uninvited guests to both domestic spaces and then spaces on the street, where I just left the works and some of them lasted an hour, some of them are oddly enough, still there (figs. 21, 114, 177). It's quite extraordinary. So for myself maybe, when a work is done, I really don't want it hanging around anymore. I'm quite glad to see it go. But also, questioning for me about the destination for artworks when you possibly don't have one.

FM: But also I suppose the space for the audience. Putting these out on the street is outside the gallery, but it's turning the street into a –

PB: Yes.

FM: … and the passerby –

PB: I have never thought of that, I'm very bad at the audience. I hardly dare finish this sentence because it sounds so utterly selfish, but I dislike the audience intensely in relationship to the work.

FM: OK, so let's move swiftly on!

PB: But, I was thinking of the object's life, if you know what I mean, but it's an interesting thought.

FM: I thought you were taking control of the space of art in some way.

PB: Yes, I am taking control of the space of art but from the object's point of view, not from my favourite people, who are the Haringey rubbish collectors!

FM: Thinking about Bourgeois's work, there is, I think, from the 1980s onwards this insistent desire to control the space in which the art is shown

[…] so the space becomes the work and the work is the space and the things that are in it are part of the space and the work. And this really is the kind of underlying drive of so much of her work from the 1980s onwards. And this is a work, *Articulated Lair*, from 1986, that I know you were very keen to have as part of your six (fig. 150).

PB: This wasn't in the Tate show, was it? […]. This was in the Pompidou show. I think it overwhelmed me because there is one of my favourite things, a wonderful possession of size. The size of these articulated screens is probably about five metres high, I would say. Again, the cavernous space that we've seen in *Avenza Revisited II*, the excavated hole has suddenly become a space to inhabit, to actually walk into, or this is my narrative of the work. The *Personages* are now strung up like trophies, hanging upside down, and are rubber and so they're incredibly potentially violent but hang in this very dormant way. And then there's this sinister little stool, which is clearly a child's stool. So, there is this daunting change in size from what is almost like a kneeling, crouching position, looking up at these things, and then the things themselves. Everything is in a state of abeyance. It's as though it's waiting and perhaps it's very filmic, perhaps it's very literal. But actually being in that space is uncanny. You are in something that to me is essentially incredibly sculptural because you have to keep on turning around. You become a kind of vigilante in that room, surveying it in the way that the work is surveying you.

FM: It is incredibly sculptural, but it is also an experience that then draws you to other experiences, whether it's of the concert, through association, whether it's the concertina of screens around a hospital bed or some kind of restraining device. It's laden with emotion.

PB: But also the point that you made, that it also refers to the *Red Rooms* (figs. 181–2), because the articulated panels you can look through. So, there is this sort of voyeuristic peering into the space, which is powerful.

FM: Peering in and of course peering out.

PB: Yes, exactly.

FM: So, thinking about interior/exterior, I just wanted to show this work from 1975 of yours, which no longer exists, I think (fig. 178). Is that right?

PB: No, none of the works we've seen so far exist. Yes, this was 1975. Two hundred or maybe more old stretcher frames from paintings that had been

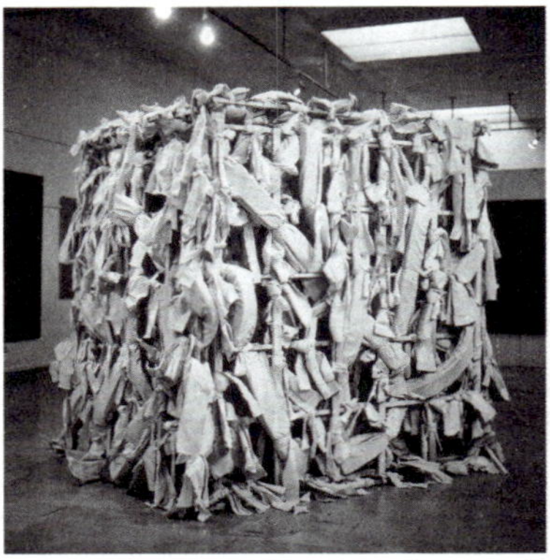

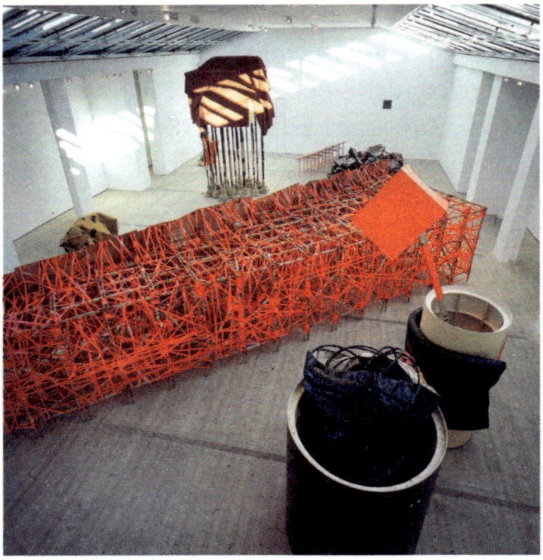

LEFT TO RIGHT:
fig. 178 *Shedmesh*, 1975
fig. 179 Installation view, *Peninsula*, BALTIC Centre for Contemporary Art, Gateshead, UK, 2004–5

abandoned that I was able to get hold of, and the inside one is quite small, and it's made from the canvas being removed from the stretchers, and then used as a kind of padding to hold the stretchers together. So, it's built out from a very small core right out to this exterior, which is the bit you see. But then when you were able to go up closer, you look out into this dense sort of thicket of stuff that seems to not have a very clear interior. But, it also suggests to me, something that I find very remarkable about sculpture is, when do you stop? Could it have just gone on and on? Perhaps that's the very something that I love about making, is not knowing when to stop.

FM: Well, you made an exhibition, at the BALTIC in 2004–5, called *Peninsula* (figs. 92, 179). Which is a very big space, so you didn't really ever have to stop. This is one of the largest objects in that exhibition, which I think, were there five or six discreet sculptures?

PB: Yes.

FM: Again there's no point in the installation where you can ever see the whole thing.

PB: No.

FM: And is that important?

PB: Yes. I think, again, it's about challenging the image. Trying to escape the image and make the act of looking become a kind of subject of the work.

The fact that this meets you full on as you went into the space, it was perhaps more important to me than holding a single image of it. And then it meant going round either end of it. I mean, to me, this work wasn't tall enough. The space is remarkable at the BALTIC, and one of the remarkable things is that you can get above it and look down on it, and I think this should have been another section higher. I think it wasn't the right –

FM: Not quite high enough.

PB: – scale and that's something that I think I was able to maybe address with the recent Hauser & Wirth show.

FM: In relation to that, *No Exit* (fig. 145) was a work that you felt very strongly you wanted to be part of your selection. That too is a work that you can't encompass in a look, it has to be negotiated and you're always blind to certain aspects of it.

PB: Yes, the surprise is the little door at the back with the rubber heart in it.

FM: In that conversation, the one you did at Tate Britain, I think you said that you really wanted people to have to crawl into your work. And this is a work by Bourgeois you have to crawl into in order really to access it.

PB: Yes. Also I think, perhaps there was something about this work, which is an inherent sense of sound that sculpture may have. The creaking stairs, the sort of fear, I think this is a work full of fear and again, to me, it brings into play her recurrent theme of the phallic objects. This is very phallic with the two spheres on either side, and then this need to circumnavigate the work. To discover exactly what it is. Her language is obsessively persistent, but takes many variations around single forms, single formal statements in a way.

[...]

FM: Which brings us to your most recent work at Hauser & Wirth last year. And this is again, a work that was literally impossible to see from any particular point.

PB: That's right, yes.

FM: You walked in and I felt immediately diminished, physically diminished to a sort of child's eye view (fig. 98). It felt like walking into the legs of a table and only when you went upstairs that you were able to look down on it and then it became something completely different. Is that something that has always been in your work or something that's particularly –

PB: It's something I long for. And the space allowed this to happen. You're not always as an artist in such a fortunate position to be able to give several viewings of the same work and to me that's an absolute sculptural gift, where the height of the space is then something you can actually experience as you go up the stairs. I think Bourgeois talks about vertigo, and I think the vertiginous in sculpture is a fascinating material in its own right, because it addresses for me the idea of gravity as a material. Not as something that is just a natural occurrence, which of course it is. But in sculpture it's something you have to almost physically work with as the silent material that's resisting everything you do.

FM: And what about the element of time? Thinking about this work in relation to Bourgeois, I'm struck by the many parallels between this installation on three floors, with staircases linking them and different perspectives, and the three towers that Bourgeois made for the opening of Tate Modern. Where there were experiences of gravity and high and low and looking in and out and expansive space and cramped space and yet all unfolding through time. You're very, very aware of time in that. And in this too.

PB: Yes, I think what the twentieth century did for sculpture was to bring time into it through film. And I think Bourgeois, actually her work is very filmic, and I think particularly European film, from the 1960s and 1970s, I see as very … I was thinking of the film *Un chien andalou*. And thinking how close that film is to a lot of her *Cells* and earlier *Lair* works. The sort of juxtaposition of completely unlikely things. And I think film invites this, obviously this duration and sculpture requires duration for it to be experienced, and that again can be a material.

FM: So this is, for those of you who didn't see the show, the view from the balcony of these sort of boxlike finials covered in fabric, tables or canvasses or tents, lots of different readings (figs. 54, 103). And then this extraordinary basement installation, this wedgelike structure and stuff (fig. 100). I mean … it's stuff, what is it?

PB: Yes, it's cement and fabric mixed together and just rolled around cardboard tubes. It's not very glamorous in how it's been made. And various other things all enmeshed and crushed.

FM: And then, this is the upper floor (figs. 104–5), and in fact this installation took place on four floors because there hanging from the ceiling in the attic are those extraordinary, what would you call them (fig. 106)?

PB: Pompoms!

[...]

FM: Bringing us to your final selection from Louise [*Cell (Eyes and Mirrors)*] (fig. 143).

[...]

PB: I think the way this work keeps you out and takes you in, is the contrast to the early *Articulated Lair* where you do enter it. But this one, that brings you these seven mirrors when you never escape yourself actually being in the centre there. And in contrast with these ephemeral fleeting images are these absolutely rock-solid granite eyes, breasts, whatever they are, in the middle. That contrast between different physicalities is just one of her absolutely amazing qualities.

FM: But also, I think, one of the striking things about this, and it speaks to an aspect of much of her work, is the way she very deliberately engages with the audience. Unlike you Phyllida, who wants just to ignore the audience! Bourgeois very, very deliberately draws you into the work –

PB: Do you think she is, or do you think she's addressing herself primarily in these works?

FM: I think it's both. When you think about the *Red Room* and the way that the mirror is installed, the concave mirror, it's so positioned, very specifically to capture you, as you walk in. And it is about entrapping you.

PB: Entrapping, and also it's her who is writing the script.

FM: Absolutely. She's writing the script, but she's writing you into it.

PB: Yes, that's true.

FM: I think the work wouldn't exist without that.

PB: I think what I revere about her, is that I see her as the first audience.

Absolutely. It's ingrained in the work. And I think that's all I'm meaning about the audience. If you make the work for an audience, I'm dubious about how you as an artist can permanently carry that load. Whereas, in a way I would say, if you have the resilience to say what is my relationship with this? Am I getting this relationship? Is it unfolding for me? Then I think there's a chance that maybe another person might get what you're doing as well, maybe not.

FM: Before Louise got very elderly, she had a habit in conversation with people at a point where she didn't like the direction it was taking, she had two strategies. One was to get up and walk out of the room, which was extremely alarming, because when was she going to come back? And the other was she would pick up a mirror and hold it at you.

PB: Do you want to leave the room, Frances?!

FM: I wish I had a mirror! But I think what she was doing with the mirrors was setting you up for your own… to take responsibility.

PB: But what's going on in her head at that moment?

FM: I'm not sure but it's at that moment that she wants you to take it into you, to deal with it. And one of the interesting things about the towers in the Turbine Hall, they were all set up at the top for encounters. Either encounters with the self, there was one that had a single chair and a mirror. There was another that had two chairs and mirrors. And I think it was about throwing it back at you.

PB: But from her own very clear identity with how to do that. I mean, at what point is Bourgeois just an outrageous playground bully? And completely able to manipulate and control because that is a whole other subject of her work. That's what I meant if you hold a mirror up to somebody to silence them, it's an extremely aggressive –

FM: Yes, I think the work is very aggressive.

PB: So do I. And that intrigues me more than anything else. And that's why I see her first audience as being very much herself. And I agree with you, they're generous in how they allow an audience in.

FM: That feels like a very good moment to end, on what intrigues us most.

In the first part of this text written in response to the work of Swiss sculptor Hans Josephsohn (1920–2012), Barlow describes a life class in 1961 at Chelsea College of Art, London, where she worked from a female model to sculpt a reclining figure. She describes working with plaster, a material that was a revelation to Barlow and a pivotal discovery in the evolution of her work. In the second part she describes her visit to Kesselhaus, Sankt Gallen, Switzerland, and her encounter with the work of Josephsohn, in particular the plaster versions of his sculptures.

Josephsohn: From Memory

2012

1961. September. Chelsea School of Art. London. Sculpture Studio.
We are told to come prepared: bring a role of chicken wire, scrim, a plastic bowl, short lengths of wood, a trowel, a scraper, an axe, an adze,
a broad chisel …
Plaster will be supplied.
Wear old clothes.
We wait.
Today's life model, Christine, lolls idly against the studio wall. She is wearing a black dressing gown.
She smokes slowly, inhaling in long breaths.
The studio doors are pushed open.
Bob Clatworthy and Liz Frink enter. They are laughing between themselves.
They are oblivious of the group awaiting their arrival.
Christine is being placed on the life model's dais. It is a reclining pose.
We are making a reclining figure.
Get a large wooden base.
You don't need an armature.
Cut a large piece of the chicken wire.
Roll it up and lie it on the board.
Cut lengths of scrim.
Mix the plaster.
Dip the scrim in the plaster and fold it over the wire netting.
Let the plastered scrim set.
Mix more plaster. Let it thicken.
Look at the life model. Now turn away. You are not copying her.
Trowel on the plaster. Work quickly.
Hit the setting plaster with wood to mould and shape the reclining form.
Be quick.
Don't use your hands.
Mix more plaster.
Quick.
Look quickly. Act quickly.
Plaster won't wait for you.
Stop fussing. Keep moving backwards and forwards. Keep the whole form alive.
Now turn your plaster shape upside down.

I am working on the parts which are hidden. The underneath.
I attack with wood, axe, and trowel.
I slab and stretch the plaster. It slops and slurps.
Gravity is more in control than me. But I let the plaster slap and splash in large folds.
Trowel, timber lengths, and scraper scour and push.
The plaster is alive. I drag it. It is larva.
Then it freezes.

I am building. Strata upon strata of beaten, slurped plaster – alive, dead, go, stop.
I turn my plaster block over.
It is better the other way round
– then turn it back – it will still be a figure …
I am on this side and then that side.
I use the plaster when it is almost set.
I pull the wet, thick plaster across the existing set layers with a short length of timber.
It is an oozing crust. The plaster is setting; the ooze is caught.
The curving, slumped back of Christine is there and not there – a surging mass, approximate, exuberant –
it is vestigial evidence and a memory of the life model's back, trapped in a sweep of barely controlled plaster:
a monstrous form – luscious and inchoate.
I am finding out and beginning. Nothing will ever be the same.

*

2012. Kesselhaus, Sankt Gallen, Switzerland.
We have toured the foundry.
It is the end of the day.
And now there is another room to show us.
It is the last of the maze of rooms.
There are large doors foretelling a large space.

The large room is high ceilinged and lit by windows along the wall to our right.
Occupying the floor space are plinths.
The sculptures hug the plinths – a close fit.
The bulk is alarming.

It is an inchoate form.
It is loaded on to the plinth.
Weight and gravity are locked in.
The surfaces, plaster, must be newly rendered – but they are fifty years old.
The figurative form is a phantom buried within the lumpen mass –
more human than a human.
This is the poured, pushed, slabbed, scraped stuff of fifty years ago.
It is now. The plaster is held – the folds and furrows, the drags and pulls remain.
Time stands still.

Heads: stacked one on the other.
Remember Chardin's still lifes: domestic objects lined up, their raw tactility
unadorned but monumentalised and immortalised.
What is a still life? – life stilled?
These stacked and shelved heads, how long have they waited?
Row upon row of raw plaster lumps.
Touched – only just. How, and with what?
Plaster sets – liquid to solid – bodily – it doesn't wait.
These stacked heads are caught. Heavy and solid in their moment of
entrapment – their liquid origins transformed into white, now dusty, permanence.
Snatched from becoming anything more – abandoned, solitary ...
Eyeless? – No. Smudged, squashed, small holes squint outwards.
The rounded mounds watch and wait. A crowd. Witnesses of
their own production.
Solid, immovable, lump upon lump.
How are they 'heads'?
Their skinless skin contains all it has to – nothing is surplus.
Yes, again, the now murky whiteness of the aged plaster holds enough:
The hardly touched, once wet and hardening stuff, is gestured into shape – as
much rock-like as heads.
Every action revealed. Expedient. Necessary.
Every crevasse and crease of the hardened plaster exact.
It is present and now. Not then.
Speed and time are complicit; both become as material as the plaster.
Silent, motionless.
Feral, emergent – entirely us.

Both participants in the 2013 Carnegie International, Barlow and American artist Vincent Fecteau (born 1969) embarked on an email correspondence in which they exchanged views on their own and each other's work. The interview was published in *BOMB Magazine* and excerpts were included in the catalogue for the International. Both artists were also included in the group exhibition *Sculptural Acts* at Haus der Kunst, Munich, in 2011–12, and in the very brief excerpt included here Barlow describes her encounter with Fecteau's work on that occasion, with reference to David Lynch's film *Blue Velvet*.

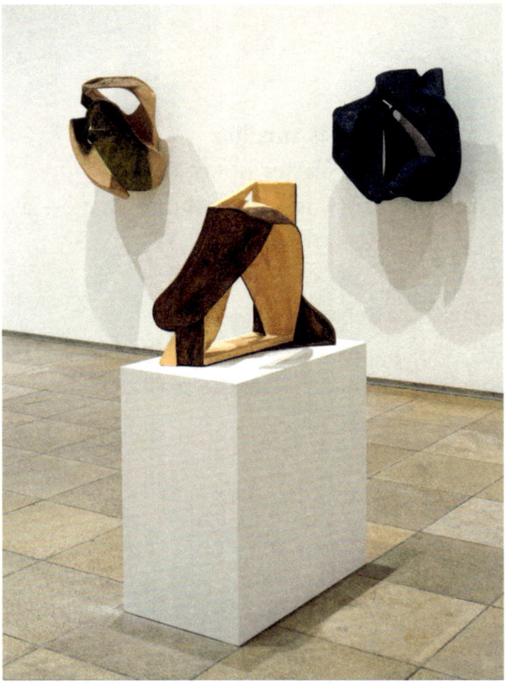

fig. 180 Installation view of work by Vincent Fecteau, *Sculptural Acts*, Haus der Kunst, Munich, 2011

Conversation with Vincent Fecteau

2013

[...]

Phyllida Barlow: At the beginning of David Lynch's *Blue Velvet* (I haven't seen it for years), Kyle MacLachlan comes across a severed ear lying amongst the litter of leaves. An extraordinary filmic sequence follows which caught my imagination completely: the camera peruses the ear as a sculptural phenomenon. The mixture of the dead leaves and the fleshy severed ear was so materially compelling, so sculptural. Your two wall works in the exhibition at Haus der Kunst reminded me of this (fig. 180). I write from memory: one of them opened itself up with hybrid curved forms arching out from the top and bottom, with gaping cavities through which a heaving interior could be seen – very bodily but also the opposite. This work was a strange yellow-brown on its outside and dark inside – a half-remembered, redundant mechanical part, salvaged, but remaindered. The other wall work was dark in all respects. Its interior and exterior were fused as one, as if turned inside out. It was truly painful and uncomfortable, and unforgiving too. Slits and openings seemed arbitrary, as if this object were manifesting something in a state of reparation or recovery, but in the knowledge that it might not make it. An object in a state of limbo – its fragility a reminder that I was looking at myself. These amazing works exemplify my fascination for folded forms. By keeping themselves half-hidden they invite curiosity but refuse to yield up their secret interiors. They are erotic in their curling in on themselves, and innately visceral. They prompt the desire to touch and probe. But the only person who touches the sculpture is the artist – everyone else has to imagine those tactile encounters rather than fulfilling them, and this is such a vital part of the sculptural experience.

[...]

Published in BOMB 126 (Winter 2013–14), 48–57; https://bombmagazine.org/articles/phyllida-barlow-vincent-fecteau/. Included in part in 2013 *Carnegie International* (Pittsburgh: Carnegie Museum of Art, 2013), 31–2.

These edited excerpts are taken from a public exhibition tour of *Louise Bourgeois: Structures of Existence; The Cells* led by curator Julienne Lorz and Barlow at Haus der Kunst, Munich, on 10 March 2015. They discuss in detail a number of key works in the show by the French-American artist Louise Bourgeois (1911–2010), including *Articulated Lair* (1986), *Red Room (Child)* and *Red Room (Parents)* (both 1994), *Passage Dangereux* (1997), *Precious Liquids* (1992), and *In and Out* (1995). They consider the manipulation of the audience, Bourgeois's use of colour, materials, and forms, the filmic quality of some works, her use of the grid, and the language of arrangement. Barlow speaks of the tendency towards symbolic interpretations and the desire to find meaning and articulates her own wish to avoid biographical readings of the work.

Louise Bourgeois: Exhibition Tour with Julienne Lorz

2015

Julienne Lorz: So the piece we're going to talk about is behind us: *Articulated Lair* from 1986 (fig. 150). It's the first work that Louise Bourgeois considered a 'Cell.' She didn't name it at that point yet; it's not in the title. But *Articulated Lair* is for her the first *Cell*. And interestingly, from 1980, at the age of seventy, she starts to work in a really big, old sewing factory, in Brooklyn. Before that she'd been working in her little brownstone house – in New York – five metres wide at the most or something like that. So very small-scale. But suddenly she has this huge amount of space, and she has this studio and increasingly starts to work on a larger scale.

Phyllida Barlow: Yes. So, Julienne raised a very interesting point about whether she started work on the *Cells* to make a private space for herself within the bigger space? And I thought of it in sculptural terms, which is really my relationship with Louise Bourgeois. I know there's a huge psychoanalytic narrative about Bourgeois's work. And I think that's fascinating in itself. But I'm interested in the sculptural language, how form and materiality are as expressive as the verbal language of a psychoanalytic narrative that can be placed all over that. So I saw the *Cell* almost as a kind of plinth, of a way of being able to put together disparate forms to create a very specific mood or atmosphere. My wonder about Bourgeois is, what is that mood? What is that atmosphere that we are so either, quite honestly maybe a bit repelled by, but also hugely attracted to? So she's playing, the work is kind of playing with our emotional polarities. And I feel that she does that through a very, very traditional formal language. The *Cells* all use uprightness as a statement to both keep us out and lure us in. Also, they make us need to go round them, which is in itself the language that sculpture seems to own over, say, painting or works that go on the wall. The fact is the sculptural form blocks our way, takes up the space that we might want to be in, and forces us to do a negotiation, a kind of choreographic dance around the work whether we like it or not. And I think Bourgeois, with these *Cell* works, is extremely clever and very knowing in how she psychologically plays with us through her formal language –

JL: And through the physicality of that. It's not just an object you're walking round, but it's actually architecture to a certain extent.

PB: Yes. It makes you look in a certain way. You have to look in all directions. Then I think what I find so compelling about these works is the spaces in between, which, you become a voyeur, you become a spy to the scene within. And immediately, I think your emotions are sort of aroused. 'What is this inside space doing to us? Why am I looking at it? Or am I just looking? Or am I watching?' I was asking Julienne whether in German you have many different words for the act of seeing, because I think in the English language we have 'looking', 'observing', 'regarding', 'scrutinising', 'peering', 'watching'.

JL: 'Spying'.

PB: I think there are about twelve words for the act of looking. And we can sort of choose which one we're doing when we look at her work, because I think the work really forces you almost to take on one of those –

JL: Those roles.

PB: Those roles or one of those verbs, if you will.

JL: Exactly, which then puts you into a very particular frame of mind, to a certain extent, as well.

PB: Exactly. Yes.

JL: So in a way, you have to [...] put yourself in relation to the work.

PB: And even if you want to reject being emotionally manipulated by the work, it's still a response. It's still a frame of mind, isn't it?

[...]

JL: Let's head inside. [...] For conservational reasons [...] very few works today can actually be entered physically, but some of the *Cells* that Bourgeois did were never meant to be entered either. So she's played with both. But this one, we're allowed to go in, and one is also meant to go in. [...] What's interesting is we've seen the outside, which is sort of this very forbidding black. But then you come inside, and there's actually quite a lot of lightness to it, in the sense that you have colours appearing. The blue, and this creamy white, which I was told was never really properly bright white. So it's not just the age of the piece, but it's always this slightly off-white.

PB: They're very institutional colours, aren't they? Are they the colours of a hospital or school, something like that? So, they're powerful in my opinion, in that respect. And we were talking earlier about Bourgeois 'The Great Inventor', but inventor with, I think, a very limited vocabulary. If we look at these fabulous shapes, and you turn them round the other way in your head, they're not unlike the works that she was doing in the 1940s and the 1950s. So she sustains this language of these sort of phallic forms right through to a few years ago. And I think that, to me, is possibly one of the greatest things about her work, that her vocabulary isn't about endless experimentation with form in the sense of having to bang her head against a wall and think up newer and newer and newer shapes and forms. She's actually using quite a limited vocabulary, but in this endlessly innovative way. Also materially. And I think this work actually encapsulates all those different ways of approaching the thing. I think the hanging shape was something she ascribed to a state of ambivalence and ambiguity. If things are hanging, they don't know quite where they are in the world, whether they've fallen and collapsed or whether they're upright and alert. And to me, it's that that gives this space this atmosphere that I think is so intriguing about her work, that it is so powerful in its atmospheric content. [...] Also, in the best sense, Bourgeois's ability to manipulate us – we're meant to sit on the stool, we're meant to be a protagonist in her drama, in her theatre – and I think there can be a lot of moral ideas. Certainly in the UK there's a kind of morality against theatrical art. Well, I actually love theatrical art. That way in which you know you're being manipulated by an artwork. You think of Gian Lorenzo Bernini's extraordinary *Ecstasy of Saint Teresa* in Rome (fig. 29), I mean, you can't be more manipulated emotionally than that. And I think it is something about the physicality of sculpture that can actually sort of invade your private space and allow you to succumb, like going to the opera. You know, I went to Munich Opera in 1962, actually. I just fell in love with Wagner at that point. I love that huge emotional wave that you know you can resist. All you've got to do is walk out of the theatre, or walk out of the sculpture. But I think it is part of a creative language. It is part of how an experience can be, in a way, both deeply confusing and perplexing but utterly beguiling as well.

[...]

JL: [...] There are only two *Cells* that belong together in the whole of the series, namely the red rooms: *Red Room (Child)* (fig. 181) [...] and *Red Room (Parents)* (fig. 182) [...].

PB: I think, for me, the most significant thing about these parent and child works, when I first saw them in 1995, was it just struck me that her work has an incredible relationship with a filmic language, with the idea of capturing and giving you the glimpse, or the short look at something, which you then, because that short look is made into a physical materiality as sculpture, you can go back and revisit it. But with a film it's more… it's no longer difficult to do that, you just rewind. But it's a very different sensory experience. I think this idea of film having a language which can become sculptural is an extraordinary phenomenon about her work. It's also this idea of making the gaps between the doors actually be a very, very coherent physical presence that the viewer – that's us – that we can actually participate in, so that we are being given these snatches of the work. Then when you eventually find the opening, you're given the *mise en scène*, the actual vignette of this work. And in some ways, maybe that sculptural language goes from being sculptural in the sense of having to walk round to becoming pictorial. It's like a magical trick almost, you know? You go from one kind of physical state to another. And I think that's something that I feel happened to Bourgeois as she grew older, and she was no longer perhaps in absolute one hundred percent control of the production of the work, of physically making the work. It went from the intimacy of handling plaster and wax and even stone herself, to perhaps working collaboratively with people. So from having been making work in a very sentient way, perhaps not even a particularly visual way, as we see in the earlier works through there, these become visionary works. They become absolutely heightened visual, almost hallucinogenic experiences, that somehow record her memories. But they no longer have that absolutely, traditional sculptural language of working directly with a material like plaster or clay or wax, materials that are going to, as she put it, 'Plaster does its own thing.' You can't be in complete control of it. You mix it and it will go off. You can't stop that. And stone resists you. She's got all these very wonderful, simple maxims about these different materials. But these works, I think, are a kind of shift, an imaginative shift, that we see.

JL: Yes, and exactly what we were talking about at lunchtime in terms of the material kind of taking off on its own and taking its own path such as plaster or even latex or other kinds of materials. But it seems like with these *Cells*, she's trying to capture them, gather a sense of control again. And this is where we were wondering, maybe it has to do with the fact that she's suddenly confronted with this massive studio and what do you do? 'Well, I need my domestic space again,' the space she feels the safest in, in a way.

PB: And we get a new language which, to me, is the language of arrangement and placement, rather than a formal language of shape, where the shapes are autonomously secreted within a lump of stone, or within plaster or wax. It becomes about placing, and possibly there are a whole range of people who are involved in making the glassworks or casting things or even carving things. But her final sort of *coup de théâtre* is to do the arranging. And I think there's nothing wrong about being a superb arranger as an artist.

JL: No, and I think especially, as you go around the *Cells*, what's so extraordinary is that there are some elements that will recur, but they're in a different context, and they're in a different arrangement. Each *Cell* has its very own atmosphere, and so it doesn't matter that some of these elements are recurring because they are suddenly in a totally different context. So they appear differently and give a different sense, or they kind of emanate a different sense.

PB: Yes. But I think there is a shared language between these *Cells*, which is that of fragmentation, of how you deal with broken-up thoughts, a broken-up fragmented dream state or thinking and –

JL: Memories, as well.

PB: Yes, and things that are half-formed and how you turn that into something as physically real as these works. And I think the walls are, to me, plinth-like. They're a way of actually displaying and controlling, not only us, but controlling the sheer spread of work and the amount of work. That you can bring things like an arm or a hand or a collection of glass things. It can all somehow be absorbed, and it works. It makes sense because of the control of this outside. I mean, it is very stage-like as well, isn't it?

JL: Absolutely. But also what you were saying about this fragmentation and fragmentation of, well, memories, emotion. Because with regards to her first *Cells* from 1991, she speaks about the fact that these *Cells* are all about pain and the past that she's relived, or reliving through these different things in her childhood and so forth. It's almost as if *Cells* become like little nutshells or something, almost as if a huge trauma, can only be dealt with in little parts. So it becomes like little individual parts. 'OK, now I can only bear to deal with that much.' And 'I can only bear to deal with this much on this occasion.'

PB: Do you think we need … I mean, does the work speak that enough so that we don't have to, in a way, pry into that biography of hers? How much do we need the phenomenal Bourgeois biography? I mean, personally, I'll come clean. I don't want it. Because I want to find or make this language work for me, which sounds very arrogant and selfish. But I don't want the overlay of narratives that have been enhanced by psychoanalytic theory and goodness knows what else, to sort of bully me into a way of, in a way, seeing this purely as symbolic, as a collection of symbols. I think they're more than that. I think

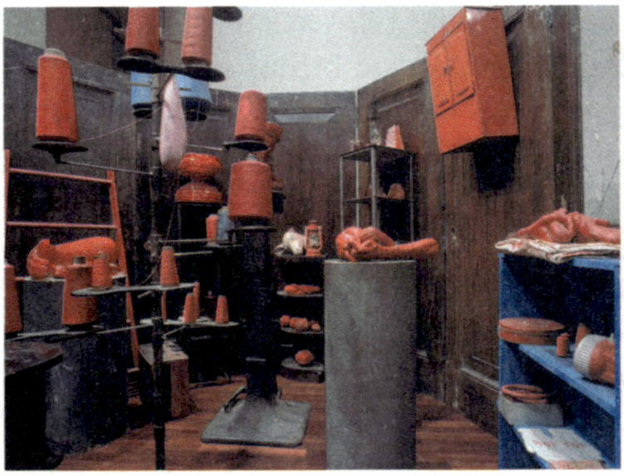

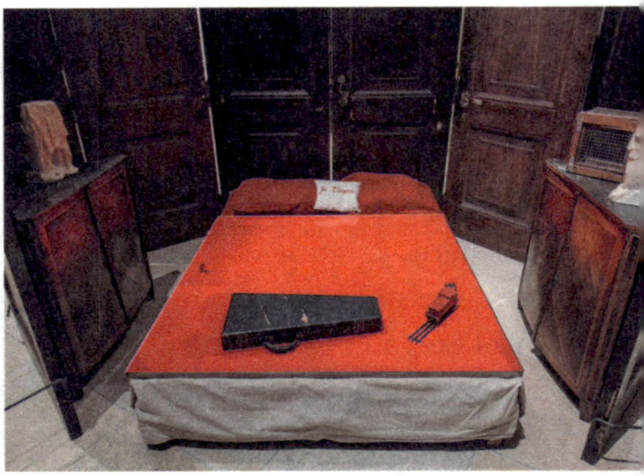

ABOVE LEFT TO RIGHT:

fig. 181 **Louise Bourgeois**
Red Room (Child), 1994

fig. 182 **Louise Bourgeois**
Red Room (Parents), 1994

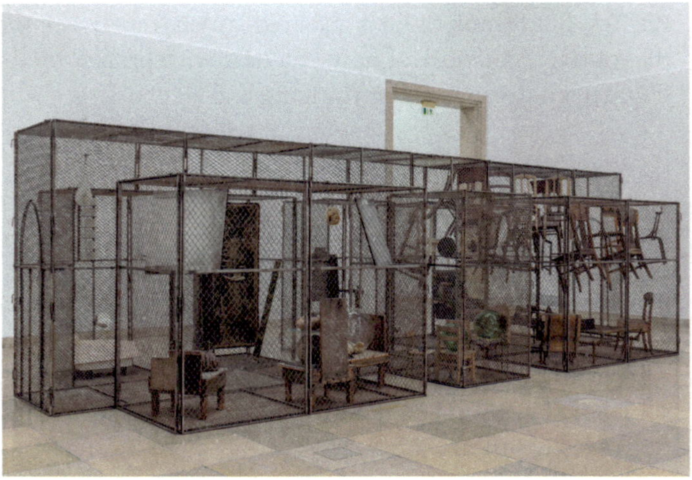

RIGHT:

fig. 183 **Louise Bourgeois**
Passage Dangereux, 1997

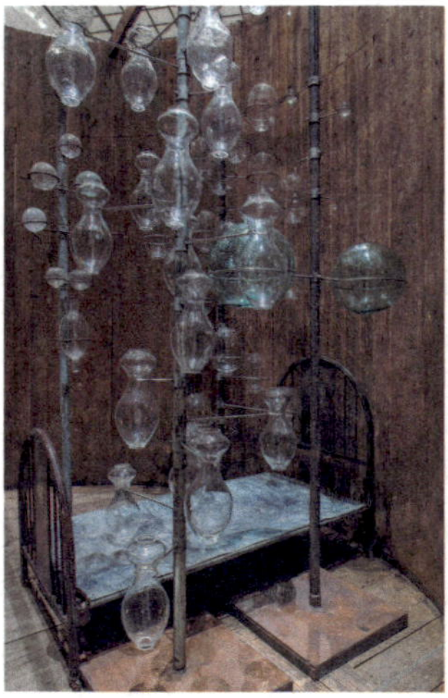

LEFT:

fig. 184 **Louise Bourgeois**
Precious Liquids (interior detail), 1992

BELOW:

fig. 185 **Louise Bourgeois**
In and Out, 1995

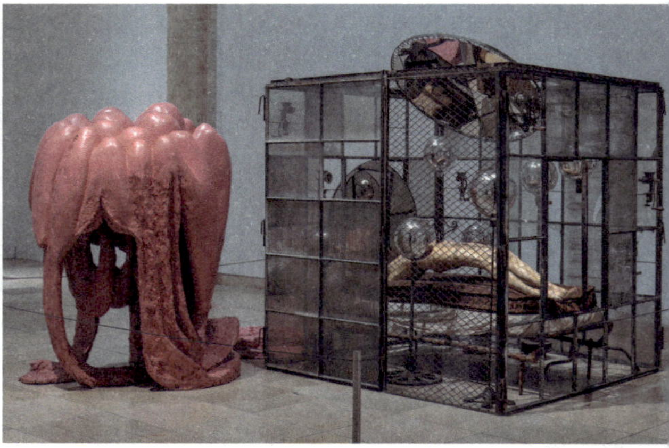

they're about compulsive, obsessive human behaviour, about accumulating, about breaking huge emotional actions. That is what makes us human.

JL: No, absolutely. This biographical aspect is something we talked about today as well. Where do we bring this in? Because it's a very important aspect that Bourgeois herself has kind of brought into existence for people to know about. When she had the show in 1982 at MoMA, at the same time, she worked with *Artforum*, and suddenly there was this photo story of her childhood and it was called 'Child Abuse'. The curator of the show had no idea this was happening. So suddenly, this exhibition took on a whole new slant because she'd sort of –

PB: Co-opted into that.

JL: Yes, exactly. And I think this is the crux of it to a certain extent because over years, over decades, her work has been looked at with this kind of colouring, with this kind of idea about it. But I also think it's too short. You have to think beyond that, also because her work is absolutely universal as well.

PB: Yes, absolutely. I'm not denying that there isn't a huge personal archive which she plunders continuously and very resourcefully. But I think once it becomes its own reality as an artwork, it sort of relinquishes that. And that's what I'm curious about. That a bed is a flat, horizontal form in a rounded space, to me, becomes its own very, very powerful language. And I can't explain anything more than that. But if you do that, and you're looking down, and you've got this, there's a collection of conflicting, quite abstract processes going on there, which have their own emotional content, which overrides, I think, having to explain it in very literal, symbolic terms.

JL: Absolutely. Also the materiality in this sense: What does fragile glass convey? What does that give off?

PB: Potential to break. There's that sort of sense of imminence that something might happen. One knock and this whole kind of *Alice Through the Looking Glass* world is going to just disintegrate. And there's a fragility there, which I think is also an emotional state.

JL: Exactly. So, she uses a language that is actually, even if you don't know anything about Bourgeois's personal trauma, it's a language that I think you can still understand.

PB: Can I just ask everyone what they, I mean, you don't have to answer me, but I wonder what your view is of the use of red? Is it warning? Or is it warm? The red is so powerful in these *Red Rooms*, and it seems to make the work have a very distinctive quality, which is quite different from a lot of the other works, I think. Again, I feel it's very theatrical and very filmic. It's actually saying, 'Look at me in a certain way.' You know, 'I want you to stand there, and I want you to watch.' And even though we may watch and watch and watch, nothing will quite happen. The only thing that will happen is what it does to us. We become the main player. And actually she moves sideways, and we take on a kind of role in that watching and that looking. We're performing. And I think the red is a very, very powerful tool in that respect.

JL: And the mirror, particularly in *Red Room (Parents)*, this is where you get a whole different view. In most *Cells* there are the mirrors that give you a different view. Also distort a view, give you a different sense of what you're actually seeing, different sense of reality, different sense of time.

PB: Well that's the extraordinary time factor, which I think, again, is a filmic thing. That one minute you're in the work, because the mirror captures you and you become part of the work, next minute you're out of it. You're spat out. Not wanted anymore. And in a way, the film has moved on. It's on to the next thing. But what's so extraordinary in this work is the way it will enable you to see parts of the room that you can't see. And I was telling Julienne that I went to a lecture at the university where I taught, and it was on seventeenth-century pornography. It was a very academic lecture. It was about seventeenth-century etchings and how, in their sort of erotic form, the male protagonist in these etchings looks into a mirror so we as viewers can't see the naughty things that are going on. We can only speculate. And there's something of that in her use of mirrors in the way that we're left to speculate about what these … almost as if these are stages set for something and we have to –

JL: Imagine the rest or –

PB: Or abandon it. Just walk away from it. And that's also something I think is very powerful, is the way, as a viewer or protagonist or somebody who's being manipulated to be an actor in her drama, the nothing-happening-ness of them makes the only choice be that you've got to turn your back and walk away –

JL: Yes, there is a sort of stillness or frozenness as well.

PB: Yes, exactly. It's very powerful.

[…]

JL: So, this is the biggest *Cell*. And it's also one of the early ones that are very transparent, from 1997: *Passage Dangereux* (fig. 183).

[…]

PB: I'm curious. You mentioned that she moved from using these very solid walls to these mesh walls. Bourgeois, in her drawings and in her sculpture, had a real affinity with grids. She saw grids as a means for organising chaos. I think she said, 'With a grid, everything has its place.' And I think there's a kind of quest with Bourgeois to bring disparateness, to give it order, give it sense in a way, that there's no need to censor that chaos or that fragmentation. […] I suppose what I love is the grid, these kind of art tropes, which are being taken over by, say, the Minimalists or other huge movements. But someone like Bourgeois uses it in an almost opposite kind of way. She uses it to play with life and place the elements of life within that. So it's almost like a score, a musical score […]. But when you look at the people caught in it, in a way the grid also performs. Or the cagelike thing begins to form like a mirror as well, almost as though we're seeing ourselves across with … it's very nice seeing it with lots of people, actually. […]

JL: Well, the general trajectory of this piece is this sort of sexual awakening, the beginning of things like the breast, birth, and little elements that belonged to her father, the cuffs. Then other elements appearing, like the perfume Shalimar that turns up in a lot of the *Cells*. Then you have bones, bones that may suggest death, and a chair that looks like an electric chair. Again, this idea of maybe …

PB: Punishment.

JL: Punishment, that's the word, exactly. And then the little child's swing in front of a tapestry. And you sort of move alongside the *Cell* and you wonder, 'Why the hanging chairs?' Here you can then think about Bourgeois's father, who collected chairs, which he hung from the ceiling in the attic. All of these, partly little elements, create a fragmented whole.

PB: It's interesting because when I look at this piece, because this was in the Tate as well, I immediately thought of Bruce Nauman's chairs. Does anyone know the works where he hung chairs from the ceilings at all? I think in a way those works of Bruce Nauman are incredibly un-American. I think they're very European. And Julienne and I were saying that Bourgeois –

who's worked in New York since 1938, was it? – that she's still so much a European artist, I think. I think it doesn't carry that American sense of the open wilderness and the wide, open spaces. It's got a European kind of claustrophobia about it that I think one can see in a lot of Parisian artists of the 1940s.

JL: Absolutely, yes. Well, and also maybe, much more traditional, because she was educated in Paris. [...] In a way, she's bringing this European tradition with her to the US ... she was certainly very knowledgeable of art history.

PB: Oh hugely so, yes.

JL: Her husband was also an art historian, of course. But she had a traditional kind of education before she then studied also at other places in New York.

PB: Yes, exactly. And I think that the evolution of her language, when she first started using these circular, spherical forms, they were very much eyes. And I think it's interesting even with her highly charged language, which always seems to connect to quite specific memories, it's funny how they begin to take on a life of their own. They become containers, or they become almost formal prompts throughout some of these works, just as a circular, spherical thing that argues maybe with other kinds of objects that are around. You see that language gradually kind of liberating itself, because I think of this very, very powerful visionary world she's entered from the age of seventy onwards. Also the way that you can sort of half enter it. So again, she's kind of frustrating us in some way about how we use this work, I suppose. But again, the one thing that moves in this work is us. We are the moving component, and everything else is frozen in time. And I think this element of time in her work is absolutely extraordinary. It is a material. I was saying to Julienne, what is the syntax of her work? Is it always in the past? Do you all feel that we're looking at the work as though it's past, you know, it's happened? Or is it happening now? Or is it about to happen? I think it's very interesting about where we place the grammar of the work, you know, past, present, or future.

JL: And I think this is exactly where the mirrors are so important. Because you're immediately in the present. You have to be in the sense that you're looking at yourself or –

PB: And that kind of contradicts the possible overegged nostalgia that might be associated with the work. It's a sharp reminder that we're in the now.

[...]

JL: So, you can look in on both sides [of *Precious Liquids*] (fig. 184). Just to give a bit of context for this work: it was actually a water tower like you would see on the rooftops of New York. And this was actually on the top of her studio and she asked Jerry Gorovoy, her assistant, she said, 'Jerry, I want that water tower.' So they got it for her. It didn't quite fit into the studio, so they had to cut the top off. The piece was created in 1992 for the Fridericianum, for Documenta IX in 1992. And it was incredible. Most of you will have been, I'm sure, Fridericianum has this rotunda, this kind of round space, and they were super nervous. They just got it in by, like, that much on either side. So it was really squeezed into the space and at the time, 1992, meant to be walked through, which we can't do anymore today, unfortunately. The title, *Precious Liquids*, relates to liquids that are, well, worthwhile gathering, or making sure that they don't escape, so this is where the glass vessels come in that sort of filter the liquid. Liquid could be anything, anything bodily. It could be tears, it could be sweat, it could be blood. And then on the bed, there's a little puddle of water. Inside you have these two pairs of huge spheres. One of them, now I'm trying to remember, I think they're rubber. She's made other ones in stone, but I think those black ones are in rubber and those ones in wood. And then you have the sculpture again, which again, this is what's so fascinating –

PB: From the 1960s.

JL: From the 1960s. There is this huge, black coat hanging inside, underneath which is a little child's white vest, which on one side has the word 'mercy' and on the other 'merci' – as in 'thank you' in French – stitched. And then of course, also very important, there's this big metal banner and on it is welded, 'Art is the guarantee of sanity.' Do you believe in that?

PB: Yes, I do!

JL: So this idea of keeping herself sane through making art. [...] This is also a very phallic shape that is then next to these kind of drooping breasts. And so you have in an abstract form quite often, also this sort of physicality in there, or the body keeps turning up in different guises.

PB: Again, nothing happens. And I mean that in a –

JL: In a good way.

PB: Great way, yes. Nothing happens. And all this symbolism that we can ascribe to this, it's like we need to be reassured that there is a meaning in this. Like it's the biggest dread that this actually doesn't have any meaning. It's, in a way, about a kind of imaginative gesture, and things are brought together because of their beauty, because of their awkwardness, because of their recalcitrance to behave properly. And that's what the work is for me, in a way. And these glass things are just amazingly beautiful, but I also find them sort of worrying because they have this slightly medical quality about them. You think of things being dripped into people's bodies. There's one where she used those glass *ventouses*. [...] But nothing is being used. The bed is empty. Has something been removed? Or is something going to come? Is the hideous black coat, is that about to be worn? Has it been worn? Is it the image of a nightmare? On and on we can go. And we actually never get anywhere, you know?

JL: No, it's true. Because also the bed is not a restful place, it looks, well, hideous as well in a sense, you know? Uncomfortable and kind of not something you –

PB: Hostile.

JL: Hostile, yes. Exactly.

PB: I think the characteristic of her work can be often assembled in one's mind through verbs of action. Aggression, fear, all those things, and they can actually take on a life of their own, rather than having to be ascribed to specific stories.

[...]

JL: So this is *In and Out* from 1995 (fig. 185). In a way, this is a good work to see in relation to the *Spider (Cell)* because *Spider*, along with *In and Out*, is one of the few *Cells* where Bourgeois is actually leaving the *Cell*.

PB: But the spider is used as a spatial control, isn't it? It launches itself over us, to make us behave in a certain way. I think this work, for me, was an absolute total shock and surprise. I didn't know anything about this work. So it was absolutely wonderful to see it because I felt that the monster within, the monster contained within these *Cells* and *Lairs*, had suddenly escaped. It produces a complete antithesis to the containered state of the things within the *Cells*. It is like a feral creature that, in a way, is almost the nightmare that's emerged from within the highly controlled environments of these *Cells*. Suddenly, here it is, competing with that order. Because I think the *Cells* are very ordered. They aspire to a kind of chaos, but they never quite get there.

But I think this wonderful, wonderful sort of luscious, bulbous, overflowing, half-man, half-woman creature, combines every sort of erotic aspect of the human. It's prowling, it's almost waiting on the outside of this very, very tight world within.

JL: Which goes with the title, of course, *In and Out*, she's called it. And interestingly, again, this pink shape looks like nothing you've ever dreamed of, but it's actually derived from an earlier sculpture that she made in the 1960s, *Avenza*, which was latex, I think?

PB: It was plaster that was then cast (fig. 24). But the top shapes that have now become much more formalised, much more rounded and ordered, in the first version of this, they're actually quite tentative. They only just emerge above the huge mass of plaster. And, again, this is Bourgeois's extraordinary ability to take from her archive of shapes and forms, and reuse them and redeploy them and give them a totally new life and a new subject, in a way. This is no longer the kind of extraordinary sort of sexual thing of the 1960s. I mean this is highly sexual, but it's become a different sort of sexual. It's very organic, almost bursting at the seams. You don't quite know whether it's at full growth, or whether it's subsiding in form, or whether it's withering and perhaps even dying, or whether it's got another stage to go to. It's at a very interesting point in its development, I think.

JL: But, OK, we're totally fascinated by the pink thing. But what happens if we were to think of them separately? I mean, in a sense they kind of function on their own. But bringing them together, what effect does this have? Is Bourgeois contrasting chaos with orderliness?

PB: In a sort of absurd way, I wonder whether the pink thing is us. You know, this is what we've all been doing round the *Cells*. And is this the protagonist that spies and peeps and peers and –

JL: Watches.

PB: Watches, yes, into these private worlds.

[…]

Invited to write for the catalogue for an exhibition of early wood reliefs by American artist Joel Shapiro (born 1941) at Dominique Lévy, New York, in 2016, Barlow contributed an imaginary dialogue around the work of Shapiro, entitled 'Act'. The nameless fictional interlocutors talk about balance, stillness, gravity, colour, shadows, and edges. They reference Shapiro's exhibition at the Musée d'Orsay, Paris, in 2005, which was part of the Correspondences series, for which Shapiro paired his *20 Elements* (2004–5) with *La Danse* (1863) by the French artist Jean-Baptiste Carpeaux (1827–1875). The conversation incorporates an exposé of Barlow's thoughts on syntax and sculpture with reference to Constantin Brâncuşi, Eva Hesse, and Bruce Nauman.

Joel Shapiro: Act

2016

STILL

'did you say "balance"?'
'I didn't mention balance; it seemed too obvious …
as if that is a solution to what it is;'
'I'm not trying to solve it – I like its balance'
'… it's defiant; we don't have to find a solution …'
'its balance is beautiful'
'it's more a portrayal of balance … everything is discretely fixed …'
'even so, balance is what it is …'
'is balance its subject?'
'it doesn't matter … maybe its subject is us – its difference from us but how we appear – our stance, our physicality …'
'is it perfect? could it shift another inch or two? would it then be a completely different work?'
'it's perfect as it is, but, yes, it could shift but it would be a different work …'
'… of course it would be a different work – it is as it is, not an inch more and not an inch less …
and its stillness?'
'stillness is a condition'
'of what?'
'of things'
'of things that are not us?'
'that reflect us – that make us aware of our flesh and blood, our mess …'
'but some things which are not us can move – mechanical things, and organic things'
'they have a kind of still movement – maybe it's to do with sentience – knowing that certain things, which even though they move, are not sentient'
'is something which is "still" a symptom of being dead?'
'no – absolutely not'
'*Untitled* (1986; fig. 186) has stillness as a condition of what it is – it is a moment of focus'
'… a moment that endures'
'a captured movement'
'movement and moment … it's a movement caught in a moment'

'... but much more than that'
'precision?'
'a precise moment'
'... we are moving around it'
'... it becomes restless – restless but still'
'the blue colour holds it all together'
'... for me, it's the legs perched on the floor, only just making contact, that freezes it ... '
'... I'm holding my breath ...'
'it's sentient ...'
'because the blue crate is an orifice ... it shifts the space around it'
'it owns stillness, but everything else moves'
'... a reptile is still, so still, as it waits to strike its prey – it's a terrifying stillness ...'

QUIET

'sci-fi ... silent objects gliding unanchored – it's always there, ever since *Star Wars* ...'
'... long before that ... 1950s B movies ... why are we talking about sci-fi? – and what's always there?'
'... something about constructing an illusion – believing that something is real ...'
' – these coloured shapes are playing at floating, rather than actually floating (fig. 187) ... ?'
'thank goodness they're not actually floating ... the guy ropes, or tension wire, is another kind of plinth – a way of fixing, a way of giving stasis to an object's inevitable state of succumbing to gravity'
'... gravity is always in control ... pulling and pushing'
'gravity is a material in its own right ...'
'– the blue sculpture has either fallen or is about to rise up – it's such a dynamic anchor in the space – is that a tautology? whatever ...
... it is irrefutable –
and its reality is that it is neither fallen or about to rise up, it is what it is – it's blue – ultramarine blue –'
'what do you see or experience first, the blueness or the shape? or are both perfectly synchronised?'
'it's all so quiet, as well as still ... and the anticipation, but of what ... ?'
'perhaps that's what the atmosphere of sci-fi is ...
anticipation, premonition ...'
'and quiet, or do I mean silent ... is outer space silent? – they say it contains all the sounds ever made, and those recordings of the sound of the big bang are like the worst kind of radio interference ...'

'… but those sound geeks, or noise geeks, find that beautiful …'
'… it is …'
'why are we thinking of all this when we are surrounded by these suspended forms?'
'otherworldly – detached?'
'from what?'
'… expectation – of modernism?'
' – that's absurd … what is the expectation of modernism, and when did modernism begin? was it with Édouard Manet? it could have been St Thomas Aquinas for all I know …'
'oh my God … (literally) … how could St Thomas Aquinas possibly be a modernist … ?'
'… all his discussion about light, and the different meanings of light … I've just taken what I wanted from his writings, so it's all inaccurate – but light as revelation, as in revealing what is actually there, as well as revealing knowledge, and light as enlightenment, and light as understanding, and light as weight, and light as infusion, a blurring of space …'
'… that is an accurate description of what is here … and the quietness of silence, which has its own weight … '
'… tautology …'
'and is colour always an absolute – defying description – yellow is yellow, orange is orange, red is red?'
'… but it can be likened to something … using similes …'
'… doesn't actually tell you what the colour is …'
'but words never tell you what something actually is …'
'… this yellow, this red, this orange, this blue, they all show you what they are …'
'unnameable'
'quiet'
'no – silent'

ALONE
'ancient …'
'yes'
'… are we talking about the same thing?'
'… what are you thinking … ?'
'… form'
'as in shape? and where, what and how, and turning things upside down, doing the unexpected, trying to find out what is there, or here … ?'
'… are form and concerns with form out of fashion?'
'they can never be irrelevant – even anti-form has form … chaos has form'

LEFT TO RIGHT:

fig. 186 **Joel Shapiro**
Untitled, 1986

fig. 187 Installation view, *Joel Shapiro*, Nasher Sculpture Center, Dallas, 2016

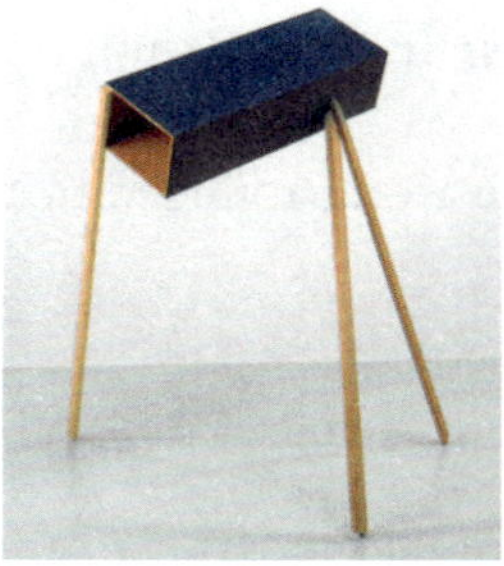

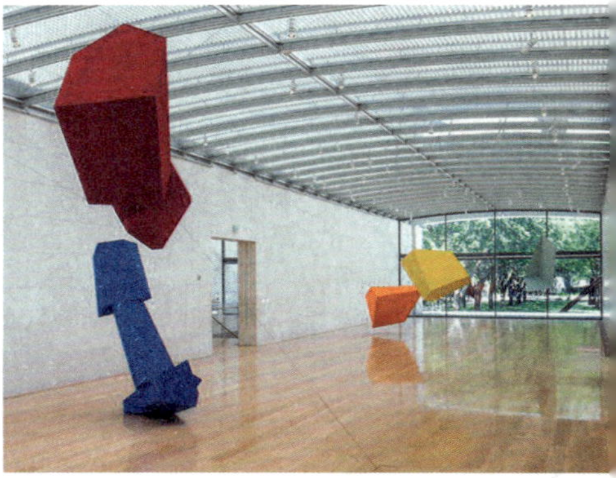

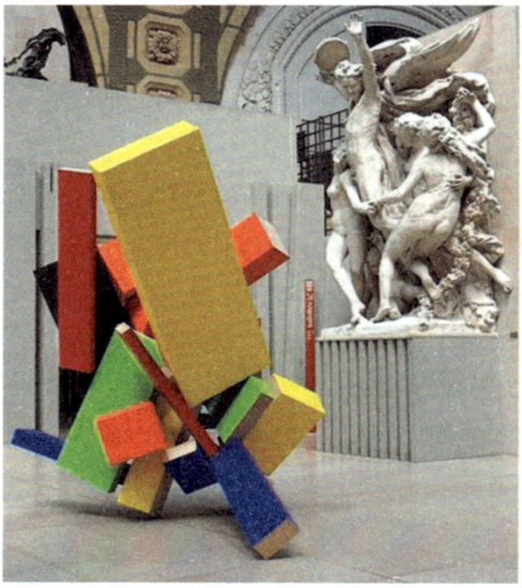

LEFT:

fig. 188 **Joel Shapiro**
Installation view, *Correspondences 03. Jean-Baptiste Carpeaux/Joel Shapiro*, Musée d'Orsay, Paris, 2005

BELOW:

fig. 189 **Joel Shapiro**
Untitled, 1980

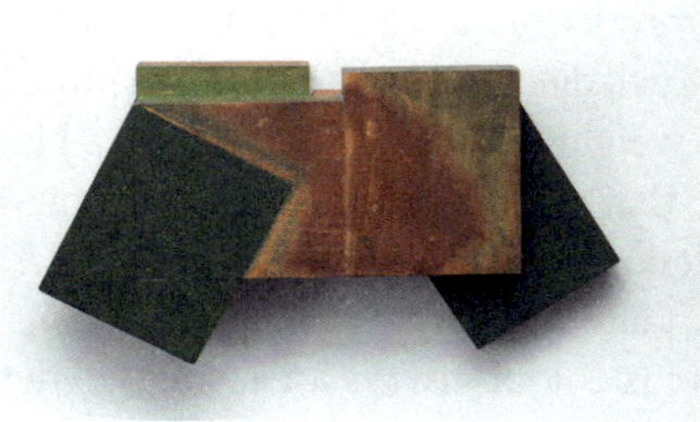

BELOW:

fig. 190 Installation view, *Joel Shapiro: Works in Wood and Works on Paper*, Texas Gallery, Houston, 2008

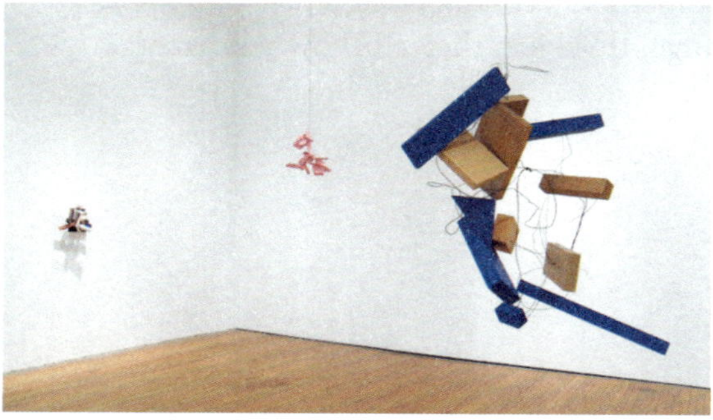

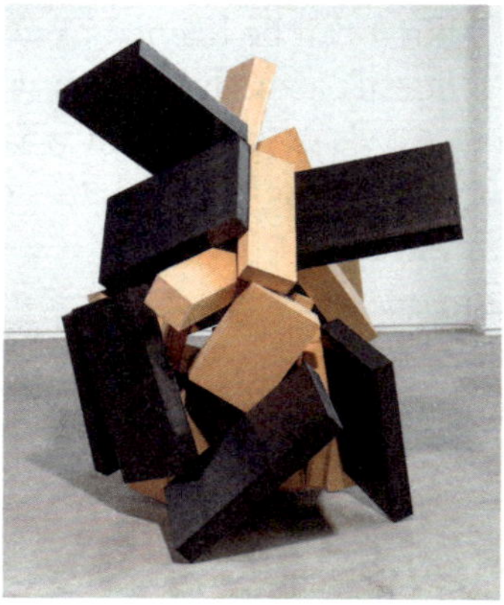

ABOVE:

fig. 191 **Joel Shapiro**
Twenty-Six, 2005–8

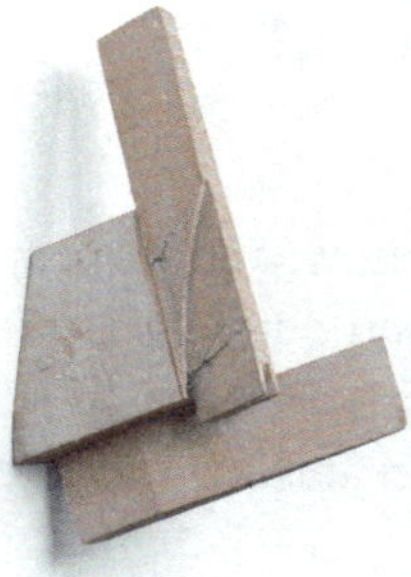

LEFT:

fig. 192 **Joel Shapiro**
Untitled, 1979

'… we're being boring …'
'… too much about art history'
'the two works, *20 Elements* and the Jean-Baptiste Carpeaux, challenge all that (fig. 188)?'
'… *20 Elements* … so which was the last one to be added … ?
'… it might have been the blue extended oblong, or the red, or the yellow … but the excitement is that it all seems to have happened at the same time, like a clap of the hands … it's immediate'
'the yellow is slammed in – it's aggressive and accurate – it stops anything else'
'the Carpeaux is congealed but writhing – *20 Elements* is broken but held'
'they both have rhythm …
20 Elements is alone, unafraid to be solitary, and independent, yet capable of responding to a presence different from itself – unforced'
'… not imitative –'
'… or pastiche'
'is it piling up, or tumbling down?'
'accumulating, one way or the other …'
'… what is buried beneath, what supports what … ?'
'… a clutter of …'
'colour … ?'
'it's a riddle'
'it makes you look and look and search …'
'like the Carpeaux … looking for a centre, watching all the folding and unfolding – allowing the tangle of curves
to make a confusion which can be unravelled … it's luscious'
'… more luscious than *20 Elements* … ?'
'maybe – but more familiar –'
'like the familiarity of nature, or fabric … a more clichéd lusciousness than the lusciousness of the piled up, uncompromising colours of *20 Elements*?'
'… would we look so hard if one or the other of them was not there?'
'… *20 Elements* is a samurai to Carpeaux's twisting and turning tableau … the samurai stands firm, steadfast … and alone'
'being alone can be luscious – in the moment,
no expectations, just at one with whatever is there …'
'but *20 Elements* is not passive …'
'being alone is not passive – it's different from being lonely …'
'resolute'
'expectant'
'anything might happen'
'it will survive'

SHADOWS

'… painting …'
'what about it?'
'… the wall … ?'
'it could be an upright floor'
'does the wall demand uprightness from us – we have to stand, unlike the floor space where we can bend, stretch, crouch, wander, stalk … and look at the same time, as if we are searching'
'you can do that with the wall'
'but there is no other side'
'… is the wall more confrontational, where nothing can hide?'
'full frontal exposure'
'not entirely – the back and sides are concealed – usually'
'not always …'
'… squinting sideways to see how wall works are hung, etc. …'
'looking into the shadows'
'deceiving shadows'
'they dramatise'
'and solidify …'
'… a paradox-to offer such an uncompromising viewpoint, but show only half the object …'
'the one viewpoint is stark – the floor space is different: continuously undoing whatever is there; uncompromising in its lack of resolution … it's a quest to find what we are given … that's a paradox as well …'
'and the shadows … walls are good for shadows; a wall displays shadows as much as it displays the work … and shadows have to be culled, quenched, or else they take over, literally overshadowing the work …'
'but the shadows in the works themselves … the wall works … are they mimicking the forms within the works? … a brown square becomes a square shadow, imprinted on the shape beneath … it invites curiosity where simplicity becomes complex (fig. 189)'
'dark spaces hidden under and within the structure as a whole …'
'unreachable, dissolving the pictorial into solidity – the dark spaces, the shadowed spaces, become substance as much as the substance of the works themselves'
'shadows as material …'

NOW

'syntax – I'm always going on about it … the 'when' of a work – is it then, now or will be …'
'… do you mean when we are actually looking at this work, or the time it has within itself?'

'an inherent quality of its time – its sense of being in the present, now, or in the past, or in the future ...'
'examples ... ?'
'it's a projection, an interpretation, a fallacy ...
but sculpture has a cumbersome inheritance – for permanence, longevity, for solemnity, monumentality ... all open to abuse ...'
'... again, examples of how you experience this syntax quality in sculpture ... ?'
'Constantin Brâncuşi, Eva Hesse, Bruce Nauman ...'
'who, what – is occupying which time frame?'
'Brâncuşi *Blond Negress* = present, Hesse *Contingent* = past, Nauman *Suspended Chair* = future ...'
'explain ...'
' ... it's a question to the work, not about the work we're engaging with, and they are not literal questions, they are questions where guesswork is more pertinent than accuracy; they are questions about the temporal qualities of what we are experiencing from the thing in front of us – what is happening, what has happened and what will happen? what's the work doing, and how is it doing it? the Brâncuşi head is a polished bronze ovoid shape with prominent mouth but eyeless, which holds a constant state of watchfulness; the polished, reflective surface absorbs all around it; it is always in the present; Hesse's *Contingent* is suspended in rows: they're hung out; their fragility and ephemerality equivocates with so many loose, hung-out things, whether that is domestic washing on lines or the public display of flags; *Contingent* is holding on to its moment of making; it retains that as a gesture completed and finished rather than ongoing; it holds on to its past ... '
'and this suspended work of Shapiro (fig. 190) ... ?'
'it's in the future tense ... it will happen, or it's about to happen ... like Nauman's *Chair* is about to fall, and, when gravity has its way, will fall ... '

EDGE

'... so difficult ...'
'what?'
'... the edge to edge – to build, construct, like this'
'... where the joins don't show ... '
'yes, where the joins don't show ... and where it's not just about craft ...'
'... it needs craft and skill to be this seamless –'
'but I'm in the work, absorbed by it ... I'm caught up in it ... the skill and craft aren't showing as such ...I'm beguiled ... and I want to be beguiled ... it's the black – it's like some cruel embrace – squeezing the pale sand – '
'– and the shapes, the different oblongs, rectangles, squares?'

'*Twenty-Six* (2005–8), its title, but information rather than a cryptic message – an alphabet, open to all (fig. 191)'

'– an alphabet?'

'… the twenty-six in the title could refer to the twenty-six letters of the alphabet … and alphabets have a democracy: they can be used in any way anyone wants to use them –'

'it's a fallen angel – outstretched …'

'that's very literal … '

'– I mean it in an abstract sense – another paradox – where something as sublimely perfect as those abutting edges, so razor sharp and incisive, become transformed into a threatening presence –'

'– it has surgical precision – it's chilling – it emanates a cold touch – a remote, hands-off touch …'

'I don't think so – every inch has been touched, but it's a touch that isn't conspicuous or out to emotionally blackmail; it's a touch that is economic and expedient – it's generous in that the process of production doesn't wear the toil and struggle of its labour; it offers ease and a simplicity – that is hard to achieve; yet it has a familiarity in that its surfaces can be associated with the matter-of-factness of simple, off-the-shelf furniture, but the detail is refined and anything but furniture … I can't possibly predict what's on the other side and how these shapes, and the formal juggling of their totality, play out …

it's not didactic'

'… because?'

'… it's up to us, the audience, the viewer, to initiate their experience – we are given the bare essentials: twenty-six blocks, edge to edge, no visual interference, like with some steel sculpture where the welding globules interfere with the joins – it is assertively poised, inviting us to prowl around it, and, at our peril, to imaginatively climb into it, to sense those knife-like, surgical edges … it's an awkward, confrontational exploration … '

'*Untitled* (1979; fig. 192), wood and white primer – a favourite?'

'because it combines so much which is inherent to so many of the works … recent works and past works … '

'… more paradoxes?'

'maybe not'

'– I am in its thrall; maybe I'm jealous of it … maybe I am overconfident in how I read it –

its aesthetic, its immediacy, its transformation from wood to ghostly thing …'

'… is it made from offcuts?'

'I'm assuming so – reassembled almost as they would have fallen from being cut – I can visualise the pieces on the floor and the excitement of the work being there, ready to go, and the impromptu act of collecting the pieces and

the delight of finding how to put them together … and it being as much a drawing as an object'
'… and the wall, and the seamless joins, the blanched wood, the raw, cut surfaces …'
'– it's all there, the surgical precision, the untouched but hotly handled assemblage, the captured moment …'
'edge to edge –'
'explicit, silent, complete'

First published as 'Act', in *Joel Shapiro* (New York: Dominique Lévy Gallery, 2016), 21–7.

This brief excerpt, taken from an unpublished text titled 'Observing', focuses on the sculpture of the Italian artist Medardo Rosso (1858–1928).

Medardo Rosso: Observing

2018

[...]

I return to Medardo Rosso;
tomorrow is the study day at the Courtauld;
in preparation, I am making notes –
what am I thinking about his sculpture:
I am concentrating
fixing my mind on *Child at the Breast*, *Conversation in a Garden*, *Woman with a Veil* ...
eliminating everything else,
letting the work in ...

it's the edges –
how he finds the edges to the work
without succumbing to a fixed outline –
the works invade the space that surrounds them
but with stealth, nudging themselves into the territory we occupy,
seeming to be alarmingly alive ...
and yet these beings are suffocated by their processes of making –
so many paradoxes ...
living death;

watching the sculptures,
waiting for them to awaken,
is slow ...
I take my time and they take theirs;
it is an impasse,
full of frustration
where beauty is sacrificed to diffidence
and a rebuttal to the 'object' as a finished, definable thing;

[...]

‘In Her Own Time’ was Barlow’s contribution to the monograph *Olga Jevrić*, the first in English on the Serbian sculptor, published to mark two solo exhibitions at PEER and Handel Street Projects in London in 2019. Barlow describes the sculpture of Olga Jevrić (1922–2014) in some detail, observing it to be like flesh and bone. She writes of Jevrić’s focussed sculptural vocabulary and the works’ sense of enormity despite their smallness, the way in which the sculptures marry simplicity with complexity, and the works’ sense of dynamism. Barlow recounts her first significant encounter with Jevrić’s sculptures in storage in Belgrade and how it triggered memories of the influences from the 1960s that informed her own practice. She concludes by describing seeing the exhibitions of Jevrić’s work in the two galleries.

Olga Jevrić: In Her Own Time

2019

... like eating something that is not often on the menu ...
– Melanie Counsell, after seeing the Olga Jevrić exhibition at PEER, July 2019

night and day
cold and hot
hard and soft
open and shut
full and empty
still and moving –
rough and smooth
silence and noise
fast and slow

the list is endless, and banal –
but despite their banality, opposites can be pertinent;
and there is always the well-known maxim that opposites attract;
and they can become complicated:

what are the 'opposites' to such everyday things
as a tree, the sky, a chair or a tennis racket –
which 'opposites' do these singular things attract?
and even more subtle is whether there can be opposites for such conditions
as a reverie, the sound of humming, or the emotion of hurt feelings –
do these require descriptions to identify what their exact qualities are
in order to discover their opposites?
or do these conditions not have opposites?

but everything has an opposite, doesn't it?
so maybe associations and comparisons become significant
in capturing the sense of what the opposites might be
of emotional, psychological, or physical conditions:
is the opposite of 'pain' simply 'pain-free', or 'painless'?
but these are 'opposites' that only emphasise the condition of 'pain',

offering nothing about what the state of being 'pain-free'
or 'painlessness' might be;
and can the conditions of being 'pain-free' and 'painless'
only be experienced when there has been pain?

describing the particularities of pain therefore
becomes essential in order to discover its opposite –
those who suffer from persistent pain
talk about being imprisoned by it,
its unrelenting presence,
a phantom state, but all too real and grotesque;
pain is monotonous, cruel, devouring, incapacitating, menacing,
and all of these can play with similes:
pain is like being imprisoned, and being devoured,
like a menace from an unknown source, as is its cruelty –
always a threat, which incapacitates;
and being imprisoned by pain implies an unjust incarceration
without reason

but why this perusal of 'opposites'
when the subject of this writing is the sculpture of Olga Jevrić?

the simple answer is that Jevrić's work
is construed around the most beguiling,
but potentially brutal, of opposites:
flesh and bone;
and why would flesh and bone be considered opposites?
each needs the other:
the bone requires the flesh to make movement possible
while the flesh needs the bone for support;
one is hard, rigid, and structural, the other soft, flexible, mutable;
the attraction between these opposites is harmonic,
and each becomes dysfunctional without the other;

Olga Jevrić was a sculptor, born in 1922 in Belgrade, Serbia,
where she died in 2014;
an artist who has been a well-kept secret;
the brutal cultural gagging by political regimes, the strife of civil wars,
destabilised economies, and numerous other Eurocentric complexities
have hidden so many artists across Europe,
and Olga Jevrić is one such artist;
however, thanks to the dedicated collaboration of

Fedja Klikovac of Handel Street Projects, Richard Deacon,
the Olga Jevrić Estate in Serbia, and Ingrid Swenson of PEER,
this extraordinary artist's work is now seeing the light of day;

Jevrić has a focussed sculptural vocabulary,
obsessively and repetitively fusing structure and mass;
the materials are consistent –
steel rods are welded, brazed, and bound at intersections
to construct basic, upright, and horizontal structures;
the steel rods are interrupted by forms modelled
from a compound of cement and ferric oxide,
and these modelled lumps and shapes carry the touch of the maker herself,
as if emerging from the stroke and grasp of a cupped hand,
forms that could be being impaled by the rods
or could be hugging and clinging to these structural elements (fig. 193);
there is both certainty and uncertainty
here is the powerful combination of flesh and bone,
but with none of the literal connotations that such naming implies:
there is no flesh and no bone
but these works reverberate with the fragility of the exposed flayed body,
whether that be as metaphor or as memory,
whether that be rooted in war-damaged and devastated buildings and
humanity or in the dreadful state of aftermath,
all of which is redeemed in the raw beauty of these works
where deep, dark pain is given compelling new life through
simple acts of making,
through the bone of steel and the flesh of rust-impregnated cement;

the works in the exhibitions
at PEER and Handel Street Projects
are all small in size,
the largest work measuring approximately 120 centimetres high,
but their size belies their potential scale:
although complete and succinct as they are,
these works harbour a sense of enormity,
particularly with the small block sculptures
where the scratched, rugged cement and ferric oxide slabs
are perilously balanced, or forcefully erect, or lie casually recumbent,
as if fallen randomly;
and although performing as models
the block sculptures beg to be experienced as structures and forms
that interact with our own physical size –

to rise above us, prompting us to reconsider
our relationship to them and the world around, natural and human-made;

but the small size of these works emphasises
the intensity of the acts of making
that have brought them into existence

the various elements
that comprise many of the sculptures in both exhibition venues
are hand-sized and evidence the squeeze of fingers and palm;
the immediacy of how the materials have been handled is urgent
and very much in the present:
these works could have been made today;

the compression inherent to the forms
in both the rod and lump works and the block works
provokes an unease,
and, as mentioned,
questions arise as to whether
the skeletal steel rods and long nail structures,
which protrude erratically from the pressed shapes
of the rod and lump sculptures,
are stabbed into the cement and ferric oxide lumps, trapping them,
or whether these lumps are squeezed around the rods, clinging on,
as if about to slip –
are these forms, which are so fixed by the rods and nails, in fact on the move,
about to escape and break out of their incarceration?
or are they protected by their steel framework
and therefore settled where they are?
this uncertainty is at the heart of the work
and is its invisible centre –
an emotion rather than a subject;

the larger works, which extend beyond the hand-held
and are between 30 and 120 centimetres in height,
also carry this hot immediacy,
and the larger size enables the mechanics of the works to be fully appreciated;
empty spaces, opened up by the fretwork of steel rods
and accompanying cement and ferric oxide lumps,
are danced around by the pushing, pulling, balancing, protruding, tumbling,
catching of the forms as they embrace or are impaled
on the lethal rods and nails;

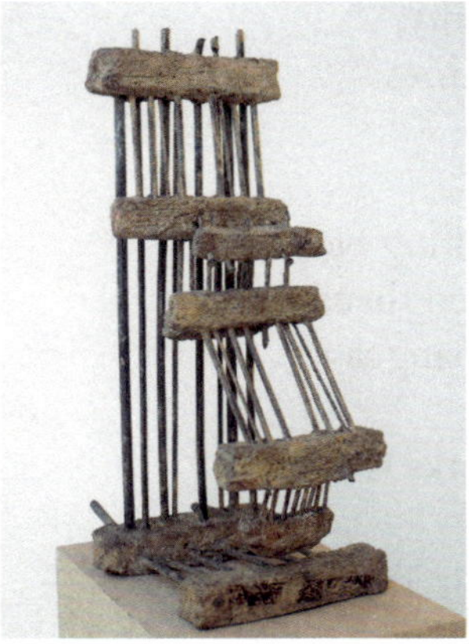

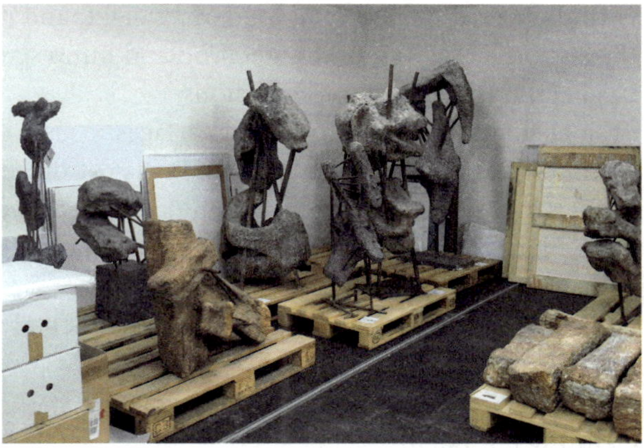

LEFT TO RIGHT:
fig. 193 **Olga Jevrić**
Weaving through Space, 1969/1978
fig. 194 **Olga Jevrić**
Sculpture by Olga Jevrić at Heritage House art storage, basement of the Svetozar Marković University Library, Belgrade, 2019

the daylight that punctures these works deceives:
lumps become thrown, landing as if by chance,
emphasising spontaneity, improvisation, and anti-form characteristics
with an effortless ease,
and the bright, gaping, empty spaces
become as substantial as the lumps themselves;

there is a simplicity in the language
but a subtle complexity in how the works achieve contradictions:
the rhythmic tossing and turning of the mass of the lumps is bewitching;
flames of an open fire command the same restless fascination:
no sooner is a pattern discerned in the flames than it disappears …
an Olga Jevrić work mesmerises in a similar way –
searching for where the centre of a work might be
leads us into a flickering world of visceral surfaces
folding inwards, outwards, around, and through,
and although trapped into the stillness of sculpture,
these works seduce and lure their viewers into an uncanny quest of looking,
an act that has no final resting place

our physical act of looking and searching
is given a different focus with the block works –
majestic arrangements of chunks of the cement and ferric oxide compound;
if these are sedentary objects then their stillness competes

with their relationship to light, dark, weight, and gravity;
the airborne juggling of the steel rod and lump sculptures
has been transformed into collisions
of light-filled and dark-shadowed surfaces,
manipulating the innate solidity and mass of the resulting blocks;
upright and stern, recumbent and indolent, leaning and thrusting,
these blocks also have a simplicity in their sculptural language,
and a complexity:
their obvious desire to become huge monumental works is clear,
but as small nameless objects
they are defiant in their obstinate ambiguity,
claiming an indefinable identity,
refuting both the natural and the human-made world;

May 2019, Belgrade, Serbia,
a civic building,
a typical institutional building,
columned, with a flight of steps
up and down which students are coming and going –
maybe a university building, a library perhaps

inside, it's down four flights of stairs,
past closed doors concealing corridors and rooms,
then arriving in a basement,
and another corridor, disappearing into darkness,
lined on both sides with stacks of books,
paperbacks, dust covered, dormant;
an occasional title or name fleetingly appears:
Freud and His Masters … , Derrida: Reconsidering His … , … Aristotelian …'
the corridor narrows and opens up into a room, brightly lit,
with a low ceiling bisected by large, galvanised air vents;
it is a room that functions as a storage space;
stashed at one end, expediently and unprotected, huddled together,
some thirty sculptures by the deceased artist Olga Jevrić (fig. 194);

at first, it is a heap, squatted on palettes on the floor –
the uniformity of colour is bewildering: muted greys, pinks, and rust reds;
each work merges into the next,
an organic mass, abandoned and almost akin to debris;
gradually the works reveal themselves as entities …
a folded form, suspended but pierced by a steel rod, attracts my attention;
it conceals other lumps and bumps, also pierced by steel rods;

it is beguiling in its directness and simple construction;
I am intrigued by these qualities – they are familiar,
I know I have seen something like this before …
and another work distinguishes itself,
a barely touched, but modelled, cement carapace, hollowed out,
shielding a regiment of nails, sharp ends upwards –
a brutal, raw, and protecting object;

other works offer themselves,
and soon I am thoroughly engrossed;

I am back in the early 1960s
introducing myself to the contemporary sculpture of that time;
I am deeply involved and intrigued;
it is a steep but compelling learning curve
as I look at Germaine Richier and discover Louise Nevelson
and, of course, Pablo Picasso's sculpture;
Jean Arp, Naum Gabo, Henri Laurens;
there are many others,
and a lot of cumbersome European sculpture,
and Americans,
in particular David Smith, whose work is a difficult inspiration;
I look further afield
and stumble upon the Gutai group, Meret Oppenheim,
César, Ossip Zadkine, Fritz Wotruba …

the diversity is both thrilling and disconcerting –
where do I fit in? where are the women? are all acts of making the same,
from fixing together a bicycle wheel and a stool,
to modelling swollen female forms?
how to choose, and how not to choose?

at that time, I browse my books on sculpture,
black-and-white photographs, numerous images,
many male sculptors,
a range of materials but mostly bronze and stone;
the solid and massive and the open-framed and elegant…

but by 1963 the sculptureness of what I was feeding upon begins to pall;

the mid-1960s come to the rescue
Arte Povera emerges in the UK, along with Land Art, and art made beyond

the studio, from the US and Europe, and numerous interpretations of those movements that eschewed the previous sculptural beliefs of the 1940s, 1950s, and early 1960s;
in the basement with the stored Jevrić works
I reminisce to myself about the sculptural language
I so vehemently rejected in the early 1960s,
having been so enamoured by it when I first began to make sculpture;
and now, laid out before me, was all that that language espoused,
and I was again profoundly moved by it and what it stands for:
its wordlessness, its intense formalism
where different postures claim such different emotional motives –
vertical versus folded, horizontal versus vertical, diagonal versus suspended …
and the traces of making are revealed, the fragility of incompleteness,
the timing of when to stop, the rawness of the materiality and physicality,
the provisional acts of fixing and joining, the economy of touch,
the unstoppable improvisations …

back to May 2019, and back in London,
I get out my old books on sculpture:
Michel Seuphor's *The Sculpture of this Century*,
Jean Selz's *Modern Sculpture: Origins and Evolution*,
and
Carola Giedion-Welcker's *Contemporary Sculpture: An Evolution in Volume and Space* –
they all date back to the late 1950s and early 1960s;

although astounded and moved by seeing and experiencing Olga Jevrić's work
in the basement storage space,
and shocked by its powerful presence and distinctive identity,
I am also bewildered by how comfortable I am with it
because it is so familiar to me;
it is as if I had always known the work
and am able to experience it with clarity and total empathy;

on the cover of Giedion-Welcker's book
is an image that resonates:
a black-and-white image showing an elongated modelled form, cast in bronze,
suspended in the centre of a cage, densely constructed from thin rods welded
to form overlapping triangular frames;
the apexes of the triangles thrust upwards, pleadingly,
while the recumbent form trapped in the centre
is both imprisoned and protected;
the work is titled *Model for the Monument to the Unknown Political Prisoner*,

1955, bronze, by Luciano Minguzzi
for me, Jevrić's work is contextualised by the remarkable sculpture
that emerged before, during, and after World War II,
reflecting the violence, destruction, and cruelty
that the world was being plunged into;

the formal, intellectual, aesthetic, and conceptual concerns
that ranged from the impact of Duchamp and the readymade,
through to the highly skilled, compressed masses of dense carvings
that reveal imaginative adventures into invented form,
and on to the spatial experiments with transparency, frames, and grids
that opened up sculpture to gravity, light, and time –
these provide the background to Jevrić's extraordinary body of work,
lying dormant in the library basement in Belgrade;

Jevrić is referenced in Seuphor's book –
the work illustrated is *Project for a Monument* from 1956,
utilising both an open framework of steel rods and
the mass of modelled cement,
and even though it is a small work it somehow
embraces sculpture's then concerns;

now, visiting the exhibitions at PEER and Handel Street Projects,
this relationship with a history of sculpture
in which I was so immersed in the early 1960s disappears

released from its basement store
and installed in the two exhibition venues,
Jevrić's sculpture takes on its true powerful significance:

Olga Jevrić's space-hungry works now have the space to stand alone,
and the demands that each work makes for the space it requires are fulfilled;
light and air flow through these works
revealing their visceral potency, their deeply personal singularity
and, above all, their opposing forces:
their uncanny relevance to the troubled times we live in now,
reciprocated by their awkward beauty and enlightening physical presence;
an embodiment of hope and despair, and despair and hope;
a timeless affirmation that opposites do attract.

First published in *Olga Jevrić* (London: Ridinghouse and PEER, 2019), 23–35.

In 'A Soliloquy' Barlow offers a personal response to the work of American sculptor David Smith (1906–1965). She focuses on her encounters at different points in her life with three particular works, *The Letter* (1950), *Wagon II* (1964), and *The Sitting Printer* (1954–5).

David Smith: A Soliloquy

2019

I am writing about David Smith's sculpture.
I write about what I remember –
Not about facts, figures, dates, history, why, when,
where, what, how –
I will speculate,
I will adapt what I remember,
Seeking the experience,
Trying to nail it,
To what it was that has remained –
Sentient, visceral, luscious, nostalgic;
Full of longing,
As if there is a death.

Maybe 1963? Maybe the Tate?
I am standing on one side of *The Letter* (fig. 195) …
I am looking through the rows of hieroglyphic shapes;
I try to make it solid, filling in the gaps between the shapes;
I am uncomfortable;
I cannot make it become a whole;
It escapes, becoming transparent;
The room beyond devours:
The hieroglyphics are dancing unevenly into the space beyond;
Passers-by are colliding and interrupting the steel boundary and the horizontal bars;
The hieroglyphics flicker with balletic grace – captured and stilled;
I don't yet know that sculpture can defy its own language;
That this is both solid and full of air;
That the space it owns is endless:
That this isn't an image – fixed –
But it is an image which constantly unfixes;
I am walking around it;
It becomes a slice, edge on:
Nodules and lumps and bumps bulge out of the frame;
It is another work;
A conjuring trick;

A flattened, upright, gridlike structure has compressed itself into a column;
Then round to the other side and the flattened grid with its dancing hieroglyphics reclaims its place –
Sieving the space; letting the world beyond itself come and go –
Its transparency controlling all within its realm.

(1963: I am in my (art-school) space outside but in the basement;
I build a timber frame. Then another one;
I join them together with horizontal timber strips about ten inches long;
I cover the structure with chicken wire;
I smother the chicken wire with plaster-soaked scrim;
It is a white, solid wall.
I make a series of turret shapes;
I have been looking at Indian sculpture and architecture;
I like the decoration that enhances and defies the curvaceous forms;
I am decorating the plaster walls with swirls and circles and 'S'-shaped reliefs;
I am told that proper sculpture has nothing to do with decoration;
But I am remaking *The Letter*, which I stood beside yesterday;
I am remaking it as it should be;
I am solidifying the air;
I add the turrets on to the top edge of the wall;
I have made a two-sided sculpture (fig. 196);
I am intrigued by what I have done
But it has nothing to do with *The Letter*;
I have not made air solid;
I have not made transparency;
I have not made flickering movement become stilled;
I have not made space active and vibrant and devouring;
I have not made the world around enter and collide with the structure;
I have not let anything in, and then witness its escape;
I am in thrall of *The Letter*;
I am discovering the anomalies and contradictions,
the paradoxes and oxymora
Which sculpture so defiantly uses,
And as such, repudiates definition,
Embracing so much which is not sculpture into its realm;
Sculpture is sculpture's worst enemy;
There is a vast territory, a no man's land,
Where sculpture is as much about painting, theatre, film, performance, as it is about sculpture.)

I am returning to stand beside *The Letter*;
The air, the transparency, the weight, the soft flex, the edge,
This osmosis between its space within and its space beyond –
How can that ever be emulated?
I want it to be mine;
I want to be the only person who knows it;
I am jealous of it;
I am duped and tricked;
I have been thinking that sculpture was this
But now it is that …
And I know nothing.

Much later, maybe it's the 1980s or early 1990s – and I don't know where. Maybe a gallery or a museum, but the place has dissolved. Only the object, the sculpture, remains, locked into my mind.

Is it a sculpture? Only as much as the word 'sculpture' distinguishes one kind of object from other objects – those other objects in the world around us that can be defined by their use … domestic, functional, everyday, public, expedient.

This sculpture is a hybrid: neither useful nor useless. The initial encounter announces an object that is a trolley: familiar, heavy, and purposeful. It is an object parked more than displayed, waiting to move on. Its familiarity is deceptive because it is anything but familiar; if it is a trolley, then how can its skeletal structure serve any purpose? And, as its title claims, how can it be a wagon? Is it some abandoned rail-track equipment, now defunct and stripped down to its bare elements? The curved armature, an axle, is expedient in how it joins the front and rear, grabbing the arched wheel axles with functional simplicity, the front part wrapping itself around the steel bar with a tight grip, the rear bolted on uncompromisingly to the arched wheel support. The wheels themselves are solid discs. Toylike in design but anything but in their weight and form; in fact more like weightlifters' dumb-bells. There is a freak wheel at the rear left, it being three or four times the size of the others; as such it translates as having a specific purpose. But what? Its idiosyncrasy begs questions but none that can be answered.

And so it stands its ground: its four wheels unyielding, steadfast on their spot; but the double-kinked forged steel stump, heavily welded to the axle, hewn and fettled, a raw deadweight, stands erect and phallic, pert and awake in the middle of the horizontal axle; there is a determination that this is its place; this is not cargo to be carried by this wheeled structure; and it's not a balancing act, although it could seem like that, but a contradiction: its posture is alert and expectant, ready to move despite its perpetual stillness;

LEFT:
fig. 195 **David Smith**
The Letter, 1950
BELOW:
fig. 196 *No Title*, 1963–4

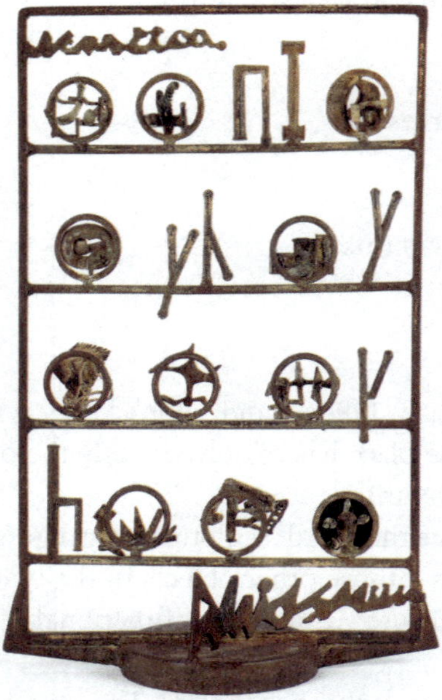

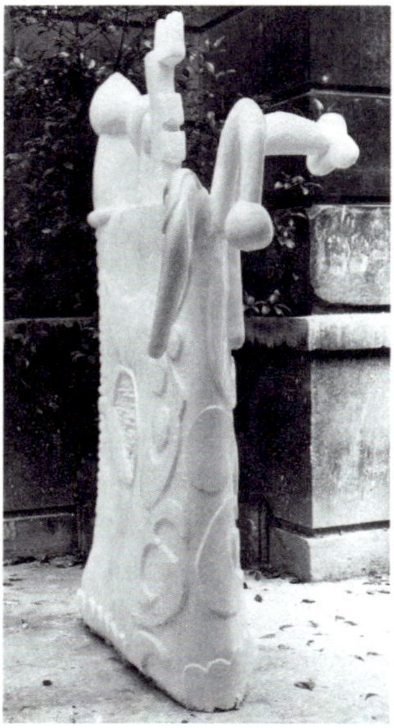

RIGHT:
fig. 197 **David Smith**
The Sitting Printer, 1954–5

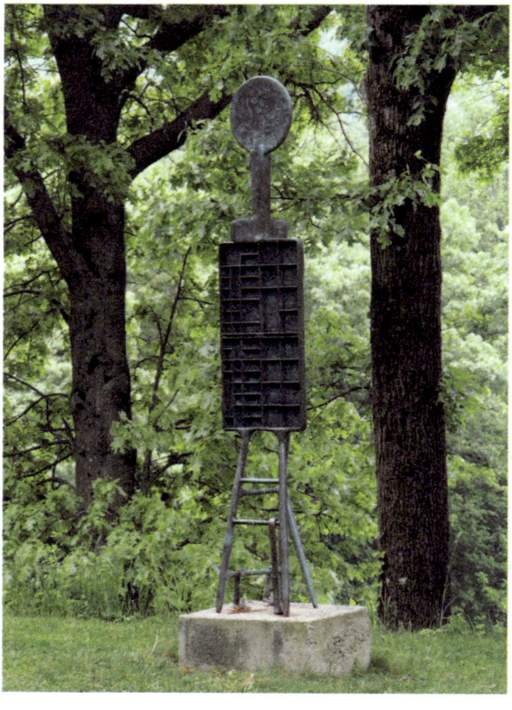

it pins the object to where it is but speaks of an unpredictable and urgent force that could release movement at any time. As such, it is the compass needle to why and what this indefinable object is, and where it might be going.

Despite its title – *Wagon II* (fig. 37) – it is potently unnameable.

But this nameless, indefinable object is bespoke – irrefutable, stubborn, and perfect, refusing to answer to what it is; it cannot be argued with; and it waits with a dangerous patience. Its magnificent authority could survive anywhere – it is self-sufficient, confident in its oddness and its enigma. Every act of production is exposed; nothing is hidden; the lean, fleshless structure commands the space it holds. Who would dare to typecast it, or compare it to something we might think it is like? Yes, it is a sculpture, and as such it has the freedom to be singular, different, awkward, beautiful, and gloriously without explanation.

It's November 2018. And a cold day, contradicted by the bright autumn yellows and reds. We've come to Storm King.

At the brow of a tree-lined hill is a group of David Smith sculptures. Momentarily, they are camouflaged – their muted greys, blacks, and patinated greens indistinguishable from their autumnal environment.

The Sitting Printer is the first to emerge (fig. 197). I think of Marcel Duchamp – the bicycle wheel on the stool, and the stool appropriated as a plinth by both artists. And how much I dislike the word 'appropriation'. And how Duchamp has claimed the intellectual high ground because of the readymade, the *objet trouvé*, the found object … and its current legacy, which has morphed into eBay as the readymade resource for anything and everything. And the impact this is having on 'making'. No doubt, it is positive, but not necessarily so. Arrangement as display can be a dull replacement to the awkwardness which fixing disparate elements together demands. I marvel at the awkwardness of *The Sitting Printer* – the blatant contradictions of its stacked-up bronze-cast found objects – stool supporting the printer's type case, itself supporting the top components of circular dish attached to a deceiving neck and shoulders – deceptive because from the side these uppermost parts are robust and broad, but from the front they become slender and fragile, whilst the rectangular printer's tray is a mere slice from the side and broad from the front and back. The forms twist counter to each other. For me, it shares similar formal inventions as *The Letter* and *Wagon II*. And with that I have this sense of how deeply rooted a sculptural language can be initiated. I think about Louise Nevelson and her obsessive hoarding and stacking, the thunderous presence of *Black Wall*, where her tireless 'appropriating' and use of readymades, or found objects, transcends what Duchamp achieved, mutating her materials into malleable stuff which buries the origins of these found objects into energetic formal concerns, pushing the work into dangerous territories of courting ugliness and clumsiness, and an abuse and reinvention of craft, all delivered with an urgency to bring into the world a new entity, fearless and brave. And how this fearlessness, this commitment to the object as different, maybe at the expense of a conventional idea of beauty, is what I have connected to through my fifty-year relationship with the sculpture of David Smith.

But the Smith sculptures are beautiful, elegant, and superbly crafted. Looking at Pablo Picasso's sculpture, at Julio González and Ossip Zadkine, and Germaine Richier, at Fritz Wotruba and Barbara Hepworth, and François Stahly and Étienne Martin, and Isamu Noguchi and Jacques Lipchitz … what is it about these mid-twentieth-century artists (sculptors)? Although a lot of my experience at art school was inspired by and promoted adventurous approaches to making sculpture, it was also disciplined: sculpture was taught through learning specific techniques – casting, welding, carving, construction – and with these techniques came many other processes with materials – clay, plaster, wax, Ciment Fondu, sheet materials of ply and metal, which in turn led to the use of fabric, paper, papier-mâché, sand, resin, earth, and much more besides. However, I was not good at most of the techniques that were expected to be learnt and to which great importance was attached. It was humiliating to be incompetent at acquiring these skills, but it instilled in me a defiance and a determination. It also encouraged awe for the works of the aforementioned artists, not least the sculpture of David Smith. Inevitably, during the early 1960s, I turned against these artists, but not Smith, Richier, Nevelson, and Picasso. They have remained consistent reminders of the courage that the contentious, difficult art form of sculpture demands, where the quest for a sculptural language is more demanding than a belief in sculpture as a definable art form.

And now I browse the works of those artists I rejected so vehemently in the 1960s, marvelling at the brutal formal language, the excessive emotion, the contrary forms, restless and unresolved, the lumpen qualities, the solidity, and the open, fretwork structures … each claiming this hope for a sculptural language which transcends the great skills, crafts, knowledge, and experimentations of making, presenting instead the remarkable conviction of new forms, distinct and separated from the world around, but reflecting everything about that world – an unknown form, resilient, defiant, and contentious, to reciprocate all that is known. The sculpture of David Smith will always fulfil that promise – always surprising us with endless contradictions, embracing ugliness and courting beauty, manipulating labour into a lightness of touch, surprising us with dangerous alchemies of weight and weightlessness, partnering with painting and drawing to solidify line and mass, and persistently refuting sculpture only then to reclaim it.

First published in Clare Lilley, ed., *David Smith: Sculpture 1932–1965* (Wakefield: Yorkshire Sculpture Park, 2019), 55–7.

Invited to contribute to the catalogue for *The EY Exhibition: The Making of Rodin* at Tate Modern, London (2021), Barlow visited the museum dedicated to the French artist Auguste Rodin (1840–1917) in Meudon, France, in September 2019. She recounts her experience of the plaster gallery, its extreme whiteness, and the impact of light on the sculptures. Barlow writes of the use of whiteness in sculpture and considers the relative qualities of marble, plaster, and clay, the working processes they require, and the meaning each material carries. She references Rodin's *The Walking Man* and *The Call to Arms* (also called *The Defence*) and considers the sense of violence and use of sexualised imagery in his work, as well as the way in which it resists finality.

In Between: Speculations on a Visit to Rodin's Studio at Meudon

2019

GETTING THERE
Paris is rammed –
there is a public transport strike.
impatience and frustration are rife;
there are blaring horns, crowded pavements, arguments,
frantic gesticulations;

the thirty-five-minute journey to Meudon takes two hours.

HESITATION
unexpected, and unprepared for the monochrome environment,
the plaster gallery at the Musée Rodin in Meudon is a world unto itself
and, on initial encounter, almost indecipherable;
the plaster and its whiteness cause the sculptures to fuse.
the light falling on this parade of figures is filmic,
performing like a developing black-and-white photograph:
the sculptures begin to unfold,
the play of light and dark forcing the whiteness of the plaster to reveal the substance of these forms,
separating one sculpture from another.

WHITENESS
whiteness is familiar as an aesthetic quality within sculpture;
the whiteness of marble is a signature of skilful endeavour,
from Hellenic statuary through to the Renaissance
and on to the present day:
artists as disparate as Barbara Hepworth, Eva Hesse, Louise Bourgeois,
Germaine Richier, Alberto Giacometti, Jean Arp, Ai Weiwei, Marc Quinn,
Franz West, Rachel Whiteread
have all used the inherent whiteness of marble and plaster,
played with the absorption and reflection of light, enhancing shadows
so that darkness becomes an inherent part of how a form is sensed.

TRICKS OF THE LIGHT

paradoxically, in this gallery filled with Rodin's plaster casts in various shades of white – both of his most renowned works, more raw and exposed than the bronze versions, and of smaller works, treasures which even now carry the heat of the moment – it is the darkened hollows and unlit curves that generate a sense of movement.

but it is a movement that has just happened, like in the game 'grandmother's footsteps', where the 'grandmother', back turned, tries to catch out the movement of the advancing children to send them back to the starting line, producing a queue of stock-still children caught in various frozen moves – arms outstretched, a leg in the air, a body bending forward, only just able to balance …

I am looking at *The Gates of Hell.*
I turn around and look back at the central platform
with its crowd of sculptures
and catch *The Walking Man* unawares.

the sculpture shifts, as if about to transfer its weight.
but it's the trickery of the deceiving light,
coming and going as the sun dips behind clouds,
only to emerge with a bright ferocity,
that changes all that is caught in its glare.

and so, on this particular autumnal day,
the assembled works are performing,
manipulated by the sun's capricious dance.
their restless but frozen actions are uncannily teased into animation.

the matt surface of the plaster
enables this play of light and dark to enhance every subtlety of touch:
the ridges of pressed and pushed clay,
half-finished actions revealing the material's malleability,
but now imprinted in cast plaster;
these small events on the torso of *The Walking Man* are pressure points,
punctuation marks, loci of tension,
revealing its surface as a manuscript of incidents,
something that can be traced, a landscape to be traversed, to be lost in,
forcing the figure itself to dissolve.
the image is displaced; this expanse becomes the work.

white marble carries the self-importance of the monument,
committing the sculpture to an inescapable longevity –
a quality that demands respect, even if that respect is not deserved.
similarly, there can be the domination of the skill and craft of the carving
process, evoking wonder and awe, sometimes at the expense of the object itself.

plaster is a humbler material.
it begins its cycle of use as an earthbound substance pulverised to a powder;
it is then combined with water to become liquid, followed by a solidifying
process – one that cannot be halted.
Louise Bourgeois referred to plaster as having a life of its own,
and having to let it do what it has to do.

an artist has to collaborate
with the time element of the setting process,
work with this behaviour:
thinking and doing have to be speedily combined;
but although plaster solidifies
it can then be broken, smashed, carved, hammered, brutalised.

it was Eva Hesse, in her correspondence with Sol LeWitt, who wrote:
'plaster! I have always loved the material. it is flexible, pliable, easy to handle
in that it is light, fast working. its whiteness is right.'
so the whiteness of the plaster sculptures at Meudon should not surprise.

plaster, and its whiteness, is a sculptural convention.
if the whiteness of marble provides the signature for a work
destined to be finished,
then the whiteness of plaster is the signature of a work in progress:
the clay original can be reproduced to become an enduring manifestation,
and every stage, from modelling the clay to mould-making, to retrieving the
cast from the mould, provides departures for further experimentation
and investigation;
the beauty of the plaster mould can compete with the cast,
with its solidity, encasing the clay, framing and trapping it,
which enhances the clay's contrasting softness.
the clinical act of mould-making reveals the sensuous qualities of clay
and provocatively questions whether the intended object is hierarchically
better than the process which is to give that object longevity and permanence.

the behaviour of plaster, both its unstoppable movement from liquid to solid
and the flexibility of how it can be applied, mean there can be risks at stake,

and mistakes become part of the processes of making.
as such, plaster belies its solidity, offering a material that performs both
for the exacting procedures of mould-making and casting
and the impulsive, spontaneous actions of rapid decisions;
resilient and adaptable, it allows changes and reworkings,
encouraging immediacy, gesture, the courage to make mistakes.

AN ASSAULT ON EMPTY SPACE
halfway along the Meudon plaster gallery, on the left side, there is an extravagant work –
it is *The Call to Arms*, or *The Defence*.

it doesn't appeal in the way that many of the works do,
and I am curious about its cumbersome composition:
the powerful physique of the male figure,
taught, upright, but in a state of imminent collapse,
spreading diagonally across, close to death,
contrasts with the heroic winged figure that erupts behind him.

walking behind the sculpture, which sits about a metre from the wall,
I am close to it and it towers above me. the figurative images disappear
and I am now immersed in a succession of folding and unfolding surfaces.
the folds are substantial, protruding from the main mass of the work, and
as I walk round it, the back of the body of the winged figure emerges
with seeming randomness.
limbs appear and disappear, emerge and are swallowed.

the ferocious dynamic of the writhing environment that embraces both figures contrasts brutally with the aggressive v-shape of the winged figure's outstretched arms – fierce and enraged female strength at its most unrestrained – and the zig-zag diagonal structure of the male figure, his inevitable frailty exposed, who straddles the whole composition, fusing opposing energies.

the torrents of cloth and nature are a single entity complementing both the ferocious winged figure and the collapsing man: humanity and nature consume each other. whatever the subject of this work might be, its identity of force, strength, collapse, chaos, power, and eruption speak of today's catastrophes. the more detached this work becomes from its original narrative, the more powerful it is as a metaphor for our contemporary chaos – political, environmental, social.

The Call to Arms claims the void that was once where it now is – the void that sculpture inevitably takes on, activating it. but in this work the void also remains present: the writhing mass that embraces both figures only emphasises emptiness. it is an unfamiliar, dark place that must be physically negotiated, summoning up horrors of every kind, horrors with a force of their own, even if only figments of the imagination.

clay appeals to direct action as plaster does.
plaster is quick,
it demands acknowledgement of its time.
clay, if kept damp, offers a longer duration,
and unlike plaster, the actions on clay can be revealed in minute detail,
every impression transferred to the plaster cast.
but Rodin's small works, and particular passages in his larger works,
refuse the overmethodical use of detail that often emerges from academic
convention and its requirement of verisimilitude.
in Rodin's hands, clay is a material to be burrowed into,
pressed, pushed, opened up, excavated, explored
– despite the stability and control provided by the armature within –
so that the filling of an empty space with clay is an attack,
an assault on that empty space.

VIOLENCE
what kind of energy did Rodin exploit? is it aggressive? is it perverse? is there a chaotic confusion between desire and power? is there sexual naivety? is there a compulsive sexual craving driven by unsatiated desire? is there a schoolboy fascination for female anatomy, for opening up and splaying the female body, as if satisfying some extreme fantasy? is there a confusion about female desire as being inherently wrong, so that it is portrayed as an abject state?

Rodin has an obsession with penetration, particularly in the small sculptures;
hot with the immediacy of touch, the female body is stretched and opened up,
capturing the dancer's and gymnast's flexibility to a torturous extreme,
revealing all that the body can expose;
genitalia become orifices that are as much a focus
and entry point as an open wound.
there is excruciating vulnerability in the squeezed immediacy of these splayed, stretched figures – specimens pinned to the most fleeting moment of a movement, caught and trapped in positions that render the body at its physical limit.

inherent to the casting process is the act of disappearance:
a brutal sacrifice of the clay original,
wrenched from the mould, and discarded;
this clay original, as Robert Morris inferred,
bears the hand's touch as an autobiographical and performative inscription,
and is a powerful signature registering both time and authorship;
theatricality erupts from the intimacy of surface
and the drama of vivid composition,
tendering a self-conscious sensitivity for a very public exposure
from a very private endeavour.

HAUNTINGS
not robust enough to withstand prolonged exposure
to changes in temperature, moisture, or dryness,
plaster is inherently impermanent;
it is thus not appropriate for outside, thereby escaping a role for monuments,
memorials, and other solemnising identities;
it is a material for the studio and
for the more protected domains of interior spaces.
its fragility, combined with its whiteness, evokes a sense of ephemerality,
of displacement, as if the work has not arrived –
it possesses a poetic strength:
like snow, plaster has irrefutable materiality,
but one contradicted by its transience.

here at Meudon, the sculptures are in waiting, in limbo,
removed from their clay-bound originals,
and transposed to the provisional state of the plaster form,
proudly incomplete, caught in between their authentic moist,
pliable clay versions
and their future rigid, monumental, bronze-cast identities.

momentarily, the plaster gallery at Meudon is ghostly:
familiar works, usually experienced through the dark gloss of bronze,
now appear as pallid phantom echoes of those other selves.

the silence and stillness of the place, the lambent light,
randomly spotlighting the sculptures, and the numerous small works,
some of which are in the original terracotta clay,
conspire to distil an experience of Rodin's sculpture as ephemeral,
where there is a threat of disappearance, and where the actions of making are
more theatrical, more visceral, more restless, more aggressive, more urgent

than anything the finalising gleam of bronze or the skilful smoothness of carved marble can achieve.

here, in this twilight world of the plaster gallery at Meudon,
the paradoxes of making are laid bare evidencing the constant shifts,
conflicts, and tensions between the fluid unpredictability of surface
and the solid mass of form, between the actions of the touch of handling
and structural rigidity, between the complete and the unfinished,
between monumentality and abject reality;
the violence inherent to the acts of making compete with the sensuous
interpretations of human frailty and vulnerability which in turn compete
with the conventional expectation of sculpture to be finished and resolved;
this state of flux turns confrontation into aspiration:
now there is uncompromising celebration of form as subservient to surface,
reflecting and absorbing light, of violent acts of making to reveal
the here and now
as a continuous present tense capturing the guises of human behaviour
which offer the sculptural object as resisting resolution and finality,
to revel in the *non finito*, and the beauty of the potential and of the unknown.

First published as 'in between', in Nabila Abdel-Nabi, Chloé Ariot, and Achim Borchardt-Hume, eds., *The EY Exhibition: The Making of Rodin* (London: Tate Publishing, 2021), 70–81.

POSTSCRIPT

In 'Glimpse', Barlow shares a recollection of a moment from her childhood. This memory is the starting point for a new outdoor work at Hauser & Wirth Los Angeles.

Glimpse

2020

OUTSIDE
it was a long time ago –
an enclosure, on heathland, an outcrop in the heather and gorse;
a circle of rusted railings, decrepit, close to collapse, ominous –
we ran wildly round this broken construction,
revelling in its anonymity and ambiguity,
but aware of the notice boards fixed to the railings,
eroded into blank façades, but emanating warnings, and threats of danger.

it was our discovery, and it would be our place.

we squeezed into the empty space enclosed by these disintegrated posts;
we hurled ourselves around the inside perimeter –
stumbling on the coarse grass tussocks,
landowners of somewhere unknown to the rest of the world,
blissful, ecstatic, and full of excited fear of what this place might be,
this dissolving steel ring syncopating earth and sky …

INSIDE
the staircase splits into two, left and right –
on the left, a small door into the attic beneath the eaves of the roof,
a small window, half-moon horizontal, at the far end;
this dark space seems detached from the rest of the house;
the water tanks gurgle, the pipes groan and grumble;
on a grey blanket, shells, stones, dried plants are laid out in rows;
a secret museum has found its place …
it's high up, remote,
an adventure where the tops of trees are framed by the half-moon window,
and the life below is miniature.

UPSTAIRS
one staircase looks at another –
above, air;

so much empty, gaping, intangible space;
out of reach,
but that is where the adventure is,
to climb into the empty space, to look up, hoping for the sky;
to sense the weight and light and time of empty space
intruded upon by the reach and stretch of unnameable things –
plaster, cement, colour, clumsy, elegant, surprise, hang, lean, stretch …
the excitement of perilous moments, the sentient fear of vertigo …

and here, these big shapes, anthropomorphic, stare and wait,
dumb, curvaceous, still, biding time …

LIST OF WORKS

Unless otherwise noted, all works by Phyllida Barlow.

fig. 1: Waste disposal centre, North London

fig. 2: Cormorant in oil slick, Scotland

fig. 3: Ruined modernist building

fig. 4: Netting, King's Cross, London

fig. 5: *Depot* (detail), 1995, painted wood, upholstery foam, canvas, industrial PVC tubing, hardboard, red tape, rubber tubing, and painted shuttering plywood, overall dimensions: 600 × 240 × 1800 cm / 236¼ × 94½ × 708⅝ in.; installation view, Museum of Installation, London, 1995

figs. 6–7: *untitled (four)* (detail), 1977, timber, upholstery foam, paint, hardboard, canvas, steel frame, twine, sugar, and varnish, dimensions variable

fig. 8: *Strangers* (detail), 1985, rags, rubber, tarpaulin, tape, upholstery foam, street debris, plaster, rubbish, paper, and paper rope, each part approx.: 210 × 210 × 240 cm / 82⅝ × 82⅝ × 94½ in.

fig. 9: *Fill* (detail), 1983, Formica, canvas, timber lengths, string, studio debris, hardboard, chipboard, and upholstery foam, overall dimensions: 450 × 900 × 1200 cm / 177⅛ × 354⅜ × 472½ in.

fig. 10: *Touchpiece III*, 1982, paper, cardboard, plaster, and scrim

fig. 11: *Landscape*, 1968, plywood and car-body filler, 100 × 100 × 100 cm / 39⅜ × 39⅜ × 39⅜ in.

fig. 12: *Truce* (detail), 1997, painted hardboard, painted wood, fabric, industrial PVC tubing, felt, tubing, casters, polystyrene, rubber tubing, timber lengths, and upholstery foam, overall dimensions: 1200 × 240 × 1200 cm / 472½ × 94½ × 472½ in.

fig. 13: *Shedmesh*, 1975, stretchers, canvas, and upholstery foam, 200 × 200 × 200 cm / 78¾ × 78¾ × 78¾ in.

fig. 14: *Expanse* (detail), 1987, polythene, PVC, carpet felt, paper, and upholstery foam, overall dimensions: 305 × 1220 × 457 cm / 120⅛ × 480⅜ × 179⅞ in.

fig. 15: see **fig. 12**

fig. 16: *untitled: metropole* (detail), 2003, paint, timber boards, canvas, satin, wool, hessian, and cord, overall dimensions: 180 × 150 × 300 cm / 70⅞ × 59 × 118⅛ in.

fig. 17: *HOST I*, 1986–9, glass, polythene, and Sellotape, 22.5 × 35 × 17 cm / 8⅞ × 13¾ × 6¾ in.

fig. 18: *smallwallwork: 3*, 2010, wire netting, scrim, cement, dust, spray paint, and cardboard, 29 × 29 × 25 cm / 11⅜ × 11⅜ × 9⅞ in.

fig. 19: see **fig. 12**

fig. 20: *Dawn till Dusk* (detail), 1999, carpet felt, painted wood, painted hardboard, paint stripper, bitumen, canvas, cardboard, casters, brown paper, parcel tape, and casters, overall dimensions: 600 × 540 × 540 cm / 236¼ × 212⅝ × 212⅝ in.; installation view, Sculpture Triennial, Royal Western Academy, Bristol, 1999

fig. 21: *Object for a lamp post*, 1999, blanket, paint, and wood, 90 × 200 × 200 cm / 35⅜ × 78¾ × 78¾ in.; installation view, York Way, London, 1999

fig. 22: *Object for the television*, 1994, plaster, television, and television stand, 150.8 × 103.5 × 51.5 cm / 59⅜ × 40¾ × 20¼ in.

fig. 23: Installation view, *Phyllida Barlow: Bad Copies*, Henry Moore Institute, Leeds, 2012

fig. 24: Louise Bourgeois, *Avenza Revisited II*, 1968–9, plaster, plastic, and wire on wood base, 149.9 × 141.9 × 240 cm / 59 × 55⅞ × 94½ in.

fig. 25: Étienne Martin, *The Nina Night*, 1950, bronze, 136 × 80 × 80 cm / 53½ × 31½ × 31½ in.; and *Large Couple*, 1946, alder wood, 215 × 60 × 50 cm / 84⅝ × 23⅝ × 19⅝ in.

fig. 26: Gilbert & George, *Singing Sculpture*, 1970, performance

fig. 27: Franz West, *3 or 17*, 1992–3, consisting of an *Adaptive*, c.100 × 45 × 40 cm / 39⅜ × 17¾ × 15¾ in., 17 pedestals, various measurements

fig. 28: Michelangelo Pistoletto, *Venus of the Rags*, 1967/1974, marble and textiles, 212 × 340 × 110 cm / 83½ × 133⅞ × 43¼ in.

fig. 29: Gian Lorenzo Bernini, *Ecstasy of Saint Teresa*, 1647–52, Santa Maria della Vittoria, Rome

fig. 30: Bruce Nauman, *Collection of Various Flexible Materials Separated by Layers of Grease with Holes the Size of My Waist and Wrists*, 1966, aluminium foil, plastic sheet, foam rubber, felt, and grease, 7.6 × 229.2 × 48.5 cm / 3 × 90 × 19⅛ in.

fig. 31: Walter De Maria, *The Vertical Earth Kilometer*, 1977, sandstone plate (200 × 200 cm / 78¾ × 78¾ in.), and brass rod

fig. 32: Bruce Nauman, *Model for Tunnel*, 1978, fibreglass, polyester resin, and wood, 70 × 410 × 410 cm / 27½ × 161½ × 161½ in.

fig. 33: Lucio Fontana, *Nature*, 1959–60, bronze, 61 × 73 cm / 24 × 28¾ in.

fig. 34: Barbara Hepworth, *Pelagos*, 1946, elm and strings on oak base, 43 × 46 × 38.5 cm / 16⅞ × 18⅛ × 15⅛ in.

fig. 35: Jean Fautrier, *Large Tragic Head*, 1942, bronze on marble base, 38.5 × 21 × 21.5 cm / 15 ⅛ × 8 ¼ × 8 ½ in.

fig. 36: Germaine Richier, *Water*, 1953–4, bronze, 144.1 × 64 × 98.3 cm / 56¾ × 25¼ × 38¾ in.

fig. 37: David Smith, *Wagon II*, 1964, steel, 214 × 117.5 × 287.5 cm / 84¼ × 46¼ × 113¼ in.

fig. 38: Claes Oldenburg, *Model for a Mahogany Plug, Scale B*, 1969, plywood and Masonite, painted with latex, 149.9 × 99.1 × 72.4 cm / 59 × 39 × 28½ in.

fig. 39: Marcel Duchamp, *Why Not Sneeze, Rose Sélavy?*, 1921, wood, metal, marble, cuttlefish bone, thermometer, and glass, 11.4 × 22 × 10 cm / 4½ × 8⅝ × 4 in.

fig. 40: Alberto Giacometti, *Disagreeable Object*, 1931, wood, 15.6 × 49.1 × 11 cm / 6 ⅛ × 19⅜ × 4⅜ in.

fig. 41: Lynda Benglis, *Quartered Meteor*, 1969, cast 1975, 150 × 168 × 158 cm / 59 × 66⅛ × 62¼ in.

fig. 42: Robert Morris, *Untitled (Steam Work for Bellingham)*, 1974, rock and steam, dimensions variable

fig. 43: Stencilled hand, cave painting

fig. 44: Eva Hesse, *Contingent*, 1969, fibreglass, polyester resin, latex, and cheesecloth, 350 × 630 × 109 cm / 138 × 248 × 43 in. (variable), 8 units

fig. 45: Pablo Picasso, *Glass of Absinthe*, 1914, painted bronze with absinthe spoon, 21.6 × 16.4 × 8.5 cm, diameter at base 6.4 cm / 8½ × 6½ × 3⅜ in., diameter at base 2½ in.

fig. 46: Gordon Matta-Clark, *Day's End (Pier 52)*, 1975

fig. 47: Louise Bourgeois, *The Blind Leading the Blind*, 1947–9, wood, painted red and black, 170.4 × 163.5 × 41.2 cm / 67⅛ × 64⅜ × 16¼ in.

fig. 48: Installation view, *Nairy Baghramian and Phyllida Barlow*, Serpentine Gallery, London, 2010

fig. 49: *SWAMP; untitled: barrier*, 2010, wallboard and paint, 120 × 650 × 650 cm / 47¼ × 255⅞ × 255⅞ in.; installation view, *Displaced Fractures – On the Break Lines of Architecture and Its Bodies*, Migros Museum für Gegenwartskunst, Zurich, 2010

fig. 50: *STREET untitled: banners*, 2010, fabric, timber, polystyrene, cement, scrim, overall dimensions: 900 × 500 × 400 cm / 354⅜ × 196⅞ × 157½ in.; installation view, *Phyllida Barlow: STREET*, BAWAG P.S.K. Contemporary, Vienna, 2010

fig. 51: *STREET untitled: heap 4*, 2010, polystyrene, plywood, paper, plastic, paint, and tape, 400 × 400 × 120 cm / 157½ × 157½ × 47¼ in.; installation view, *Phyllida Barlow: STREET*, BAWAG P.S.K. Contemporary, Vienna, 2010

fig. 52: *untitled: structure*, 2011, wood, paint, plaster, and screws, dimensions variable; installation view, *Phyllida Barlow: Cast*, Kunstverein Nürnberg, Nuremberg, 2011

figs. 53–4: *RIG: untitled; blocks* (detail), 2011, polystyrene, fabric, timber, and cement, overall dimensions: 720 × 1190 × 1040 cm / 283½ × 468½ × 409½ in.; installation views, *Phyllida Barlow: RIG*, Hauser & Wirth Piccadilly, London, 2011

fig. 55: *RIG: untitled; containers; leaningcoveredholed*, 2011, MDF, cement, casters, pegboard, polystyrene, wire netting, fabric, hardboard, plaster, and paper bag, overall dimensions: 215 × 340 × 360 cm / 84⅝ × 133⅞ × 141¾ in.; installation view, *Phyllida Barlow: RIG*, Hauser & Wirth Piccadilly, London, 2011

fig. 56: *untitled: 21 arches*, 2012, polystyrene, cement, scrim, paint, and varnish, overall dimensions: 600 × 787 × 533 cm / 236¼ × 309⅞ × 209⅞ in.; installation view, *Phyllida Barlow: siege*, New Museum, New York, 2012

fig. 57: *untitled: tyresplacards*, 2012, wadding, paper, tape, fabric, plywood, and paint, dimensions variable; installation view, *Phyllida Barlow: BRINK*, Ludwig Forum für Internationale Kunst, Aachen, Germany, 2012

fig. 58: *untitled: tarpaulinsrockssticks*, 2012, polystyrene, scrim, cement, paint, and tarpaulin, dimensions variable; installation view, *Phyllida Barlow: BRINK*, Ludwig Forum für Internationale Kunst, Aachen, Germany, 2012

figs. 59–61: Installation views, *Phyllida Barlow: … later*, Hauser & Wirth New York, 2012

fig. 62: *untitled: holedwall*, 2012, wire netting, polyurethane expanding foam, cement, scrim, and paint, 149.9 × 119.4 × 208.3 cm / 59 × 47 × 82 in.

fig. 63: *untitled: stage* (detail), 2011, timber, polystyrene, paint; 330 × 1350 × 500 cm / 129⅞ × 531½ × 196⅞ in.; installation view, *Sculptural Acts*, Haus der Kunst, Munich, 2011–12

figs. 64–6: Installation views, *Phyllida Barlow: scree*, Des Moines Art Center, Des Moines, US, 2013

fig. 67: Phyllida Barlow, *TIP*, 2013, timber, steel, spray paint, paint, steel mesh, scrim, cement, fabric, and varnish, 701 × 914.4 × 2728 cm / 276 × 360 × 1074 in.; Richard Serra, *Carnegie*, 1985, Cor-Ten steel, 1183.6 × 579.1 × 647.7 cm / 466 × 228 × 255 in.; installation view, 2013 Carnegie International, Carnegie Museum of Art, Pittsburgh, US, 2013–14

fig. 68: *untitled: brokenupturnedhouse*, 2013, steel armature, polystyrene, filler, papier mâché, paint, PVA, sand, plywood, timber, and varnish, 360 × 480 × 330 cm / 141¾ × 189 × 129⅞ in.; installation view, *Phyllida Barlow: HOARD*, Norton Museum of Art, West Palm Beach, US, 2013–14

fig. 69: Installation view, *Phyllida Barlow: dock*, Tate Britain Commission, London, 2014

fig. 70: *untitled: 100 drawings*, 2013, acrylic on watercolour paper, 325.6 × 414 × 3 cm / 128¼ × 163 × 1⅛ in.

fig. 71: *untitled: GIG*, 2014, fabric, paper, cord, timber, and paint, overall dimensions: 300 × 500 × 1400 cm / 118⅛ × 196⅞ × 551⅛ in.

fig. 72: *untitled: postscorral*, 2014, timber, paint, cement, scrim, plywood, wire netting, PVA, and sand, overall dimensions: 346 × 745 × 1647 cm / 136¼ × 293¼ × 648⅜ in.

fig. 73: *untitled: stackedchairs*, 2014, timber, plywood, cement, paint, sand, PVA, and varnish, overall dimensions; 150 × 640 × 455 cm /59 × 252 × 179⅛ in.

fig. 74: Installation view, *Phyllida Barlow: tryst*, Nasher Sculpture Center, Dallas, 2015

figs. 75–6: Installation views, *Phyllida Barlow: set*, The Fruitmarket Gallery, Edinburgh, 2015

figs. 77–8: Installation views, *Phyllida Barlow: demo*, Kunsthalle Zürich, 2016

figs. 79–80: Installation views, *Phyllida Barlow: folly*, British Pavilion, 57th Venice Biennale, 2017

fig. 81: *quarry*, 2018, cement, fibreglass, waterproofing agent, paint, polystyrene board, polyurethane foam, PVA, sand, steel, and wire mesh; overall dimensions: 120 × 120 × 120 cm / 47¼ × 47¼ × 47¼ in.

fig. 82: *prop*, 2018, cement, fibreglass, paint, steel, timber, waterproofing agent, plywood, polyurethane board, polyurethane foam, sand, PVA, and polystyrene, 600 × 400 × 60 cm / 23¼ × 157½ × 23⅝ in.; installation view, High Line, New York, 2018–19

fig. 83: Installation view, *Phyllida Barlow: tilt*, Hauser & Wirth New York, 2018

fig. 84: *untitled: lintelshadow; 2018–2019*, 2018–19, cement, hessian scrim, PVA, paint, pigment, plywood, polyurethane board, polystyrene, polyurethane foam, spray paint, steel, and timber, 600 × 720 × 650 cm / 236¼ × 283½ × 255⅞ in.; installation view, *cul-de-sac*, Royal Academy of Arts, London, 2019

fig. 85: Installation view, *cul-de-sac*, Royal Academy of Arts, London, 2019

fig. 86: Susan Hiller, *Witness*, 2000, audio-sculptural installation, c.400 speakers, 10 audio tracks, each with multiple recordings, wires, and lights, dimensions variable (installed size approx. 700 × 900 cm / 27½ × 35⅜ in.); installation view, Artangel commission, The Chapel on Golborne Road, London, 2000

fig. 87: Mirosław Bałka, *Dawn*, 1995; installation view, *Between Cinema and a Hard Place*, Tate Modern, London, 2000

fig. 88: Carl Andre, *Karlsplatz*, 1992; installation view, Whitechapel Gallery, London, 2000

fig. 89: Lee Hassall, installation view, *Skylark Fashions*, Fordham Gallery, London, 2000

fig. 90: *untitled: riff, 3, 2015–16*, cement, plaster, paper, cardboard, polystyrene, polyfoam board, wire, string, tape, plywood, fabric, carpet felt, wadding, upholstery foam, scrim, wire netting, steel mesh, wool, timber, paint, spray paint, filler, and polyurethane foam, 155 × 164 × 29 cm / 61 × 64⅝ × 11⅜ in.

fig. 91: *Threat (detail)*, 1986, timber stakes, carpet felt, refuse sacks, bitumen, paper, and polythene, overall dimensions: 1200 × 270 × 1500 cm / 472½ × 106¼ × 590½ in.

fig. 92: Installation view, *Peninsula*, BALTIC Centre for Contemporary Art, Gateshead, UK, 2004–5

figs. 93–6: see **fig. 48**

fig. 97: Installation view, *Phyllida Barlow/ Jess Flood-Paddock*, The Russian Club Gallery, London, 2009

fig. 98: see **figs. 53–4**

fig. 99: *RIG: untitled; hoops*, 2011, plywood, timber, cement, paint, scrim, wire mesh, and varnish, overall dimensions: 124 × 360 × 280 cm / 48⅞ × 141¾ × 110¼ in.; installation view, *Phyllida Barlow: RIG*, Hauser & Wirth Piccadilly, London, 2011

fig. 100: *RIG: untitled; stagechairs*, 2011, timber, cement, and paint, 230 × 429 × 350 cm / 90½ × 168⅞ × 137¾ in.; and *RIG: untitled; tubes*, 2011, polystyrene, wire netting, fabric, and cement, overall dimensions: 51 × 280 × 80 cm / 20⅛ × 110¼ × 31½ in.; installation view, *Phyllida Barlow: RIG*, Hauser & Wirth Piccadilly, London, 2011

fig. 101: *RIG: untitled; crushedboxfeud*, 2011, timber, cardboard, cement, and fabric, 140 × 230 × 150 cm / 55⅛ × 90½ × 59 in.; installation view, *Phyllida Barlow: RIG*, Hauser & Wirth Piccadilly, London, 2011

fig. 102: *RIG: untitled; broken shelf 3*, 2011, steel bracket, timber lengths, fabric, plaster, scrim, and tape, 119 × 360 × 90 cm / 46⅞ × 141¾ × 35⅜ in.; installation view, *Phyllida Barlow: RIG*, Hauser & Wirth Piccadilly, London, 2011

fig. 103: see **figs. 53–4** and **102**

fig. 104: *RIG: untitled; hive 2*, 2011, plywood, polystyrene, felt, foam, plasterboard, linoleum, cardboard, chipboard, and wadding, 98 × 125 × 70 cm / 38⅝ × 49¼ × 27½ in.; *RIG: untitled; hive 3*, 2011, plywood, polystyrene, felt, foam, plasterboard, linoleum, cardboard, chipboard, and wadding, 100 × 120 × 66 cm / 39⅜ × 47¼ × 26 in.; and *RIG: untitled; twist*, 2011, plaster, cement, paint, and wire, 41 × 66 × 45 cm / 16⅛ × 26 × 17¾ in.; installation views, *Phyllida Barlow: RIG*,Hauser & Wirth Piccadilly, London, 2011

fig. 105: *RIG: untitled; emptyunits*, 2011, plywood, plaster, and paint, overall dimensions: 300 × 1140 × 750 cm / 118⅛ × 448⅞ × 295¼ in.; installation view, *Phyllida Barlow: RIG*, Hauser & Wirth Piccadilly, London, 2011

fig. 106: *RIG: untitled; pompoms*, 2011, fabric and paper, 16 balls, overall dimensions: 277 × 866 × 805 cm / 109 × 341 × 316⅞ in.; installation view, *Phyllida Barlow: RIG*, Hauser & Wirth Piccadilly, London, 2011

figs. 107–8: Installation views, *Phyllida Barlow: siege*, New Museum, New York, 2012

fig. 109: *Sofa, floor & drawings*, 1970–1, canvas, paint, wooden frame, hardboard, plywood, drawing, fibreglass, resin, pigment, and clay, overall dimensions: 240 × 500 × 360 cm / 94½ × 196⅞ × 141¾ in.

fig. 110: *untitled: arches*, 2012, acrylic on watercolour paper, 56.4 × 75.9 cm / 22¼ × 29⅞ in.

fig. 111: Installation view, *Phyllida Barlow: BRINK*, Ludwig Forum für Internationale Kunst, Aachen, Germany, 2012

fig. 112: Phyllida Barlow, *untitled: upturnedhouse*, 2012, and Willem de Kooning, *Woman VI*, 1953; installation view, 2013 Carnegie International, Carnegie Museum of Art, Pittsburgh, US, 2013–14

fig. 113: *Object for the sitting room*, 1994, blue tarpaulin, rubber hose, and sitting room, 100 × 150 cm / 39⅜ × 59 in.

fig. 114: *Object for a street grit bin*, 1995, tinfoil and loaf of bread, 90 × 200 × 200 cm / 35⅜ × 78¾ × 78¾ in.

figs. 115–19: see **fig. 69**

fig. 120: see **figs. 77–8**

figs. 121–3: see **figs. 79–80**

fig. 124: *untitled: leaningfence*, 2012, wood, cement, scrim, paint, and varnish, 430 × 460 × 1420 cm / 169¼ × 181⅛ × 559 in.; *untitled: stackedobjectsonapiano*, 2012, polystyrene, scrim, cement, paint, varnish, and fabric, 330 × 360 × 500 cm / 129⅞ × 141¾ × 196⅞ in.; installation view, *Phyllida Barlow: BRINK*, Ludwig Forum für Internationale Kunst, Aachen, Germany, 2012

fig. 125: *untitled: bottle rack*, 2007, bottle rack, wood, paint, plaster, and fabric, 150 × 140 × 130 cm / 59 × 55 × 51⅛ in.

fig. 126: *untitled: folly; pianostack/anvil; 2016/2017*, 2016–17, plywood, timber, paint, spray paint, cardboard, polyurethane board, polystyrene, polyurethane foam, PVA, cement, and scrim, 205 × 278 × 340 cm / 80¾ × 109½ × 133⅞ in.

fig. 127: see **figs. 79–80**

fig. 128: *untitled: sadmonument*, 2012, insulation foam, polystyrene, scrim, cement, paint, fabric; 800 × 200 × 180 cm / 315 × 78¾ × 70⅞ in.; installation view, *Phyllida Barlow: BRINK*, Ludwig Forum für Internationale Kunst, Aachen, Germany, 2012

fig. 129: *after dark into black*, 2000–1, hardboard, paint, felt, black mattress, plastic pipe, rubber tubing, painted fabric, paper, tape, roofing batons, stitched hessian, casters, and plaster/concrete, overall dimensions: 750 × 330 × 900 cm / 295¼ × 129⅞ × 354⅜ in.

fig. 130: *untitled*, 2001, acrylic on paper, 56 × 76.3 cm / 22 × 30 in.

fig. 131: *untitled*, 1965–6, coloured pencil on paper, 30.5 × 31.8 cm / 12 × 12½ in.

fig. 132: *untitled*, 1967–70, pencil and coloured pencil on paper, 59 × 73.7 cm / 23¼ × 29 in.

fig. 133: *untitled*, 1968, coloured pencil and pastel on paper; 45 × 53.8 cm / 17¾ × 21⅛ in.

fig. 134: *untitled: looking down on enclosed space*, 1977–80, compressed charcoal on paper, 56 × 76 cm / 22 × 29⅞ in.

fig. 135: *untitled*, 1975, pencil on paper, 55.8 × 76.2 cm / 22 × 30 in.

fig. 136: *untitled*, mid-1980s–early 1990s, pencil on paper, 42 × 29.6 cm / 16½ × 11⅝ in.

fig. 137: *untitled*, 1980s–90s, acrylic on paper, 38.2 × 56 cm / 15 × 22 in.

fig. 138: *untitled*, late 1990s, acrylic on paper, 42.1 × 58.8 cm / 16⅝ × 23⅛ in.

fig. 139: *untitled*, 2001, acrylic on paper, 56 × 76.3 cm / 22 × 30 in.

fig. 140: *untitled*, 2009–10, acrylic on paper, 42.5 × 59.8 cm / 16¾ × 23½ in.

fig. 141: *untitled: stack; 2008*, 2008, painted timber, plaster, painted ply, and stack, 600 × 250 cm / 236¼ × 98⅜ in.

fig. 142: Marcel Duchamp, *Why Not Sneeze, Rose Sélavy?*, 1921/1964, wood, metal, marble, cuttlefish bone, thermometer, and glass, 11.4 × 22 × 10 cm / 4½ × 8⅝ × 4 in.

fig. 143: Louise Bourgeois, *Cell (Eyes and Mirrors)*, 1989–93, marble, mirrors, steel, and glass, 236.2 × 210.8 × 218.4 cm / 93 × 83 × 86 in.

fig. 144: Man Ray, *Indestructible Object* (originally titled *Object to Be Destroyed*), 1923/1933/1965, wooden metronome and black-and-white photograph on paper, 21.5 × 11 × 11.5 cm / 8½ × 4⅜ × 4½ in.

fig. 145: Louise Bourgeois, *No Exit*, 1989, wood, painted metal, and rubber, 209.5 × 213.3 × 243.8 cm / 82½ × 84 × 96 in.

fig. 146: Étienne Martin, *Large Couple*, 1947, bronze with brown patina, 175 × 73 × 73 cm / 68⅞ × 28¾ × 28¾ in.

fig. 147: Louise Bourgeois, *Spiral Woman*, 1951–2, painted wood and stainless steel, 127 × 30.5 × 30.5 cm / 50 × 12 × 12 in.

fig. 148: Louise Bourgeois, *Lair*, 1986, rubber, 109.2 × 53.3 × 53.3 cm / 43 × 21 × 21 in.

fig. 149: Louise Bourgeois, *Maisons Fragiles*, 1978, steel (two elements), 213.4 × 68.6 × 35.6 cm and 182.8 × 68.5 × 35.5 cm / 84 × 27 × 14 in. and 72 × 27 × 14 in.

fig. 150: Louise Bourgeois, *Articulated Lair*, 1986, painted steel, rubber, and stool, 281.9 × 655.3 × 490.2 cm. / 111 × 258 × 193 in. (variable)

fig. 151: Louise Bourgeois, *Cumul I*, 1969, marble, 56.8 × 127 × 121.9 cm / 22⅜ × 50 × 48 in.

fig. 152: George Fullard, *Infant with Flower*, 1958, cast 1960, bronze, 76.2 × 41.9 × 38.1 cm / 30 × 16½ × 15 in.

fig. 153: Alison Wilding, *Harbour*, 1994–6, cast silicone, rubber, and alabaster, 130.5 × 152 × 158 cm / 51⅜ × 59⅞ × 62¼ in.

fig. 154: *Time and time again*, 1998, painted wood, painted fabrics, felt, industrial PVC tubing, brown paper, painted hardboard, pallets, and casters, overall dimensions: 600 × 420 × 600 cm / 236¼ × 165⅜ × 236¼ in.

fig. 155: Eva Hesse, *Sans II*, 1968, fibreglass and polyester resin, 96.5 × 218.4 × 15.6 cm / 38 × 86 × 6⅛ in.

fig. 156: Eva Hesse, *No title*, 1970, fibreglass, polyester resin, polyethylene, and aluminium wire, installation variable, 7 units, 300 × 300 cm / 120 × 120 in.

fig. 157: Installation view, *Imi Knoebel: Primary Structures 1966/2006*, Henry Moore Institute, Leeds, 2006

fig. 158: Sean Edwards, *Untitled*, 2006, 1970s Tesco carrier bag, glass, and household gloss paint, dimensions variable

fig. 159: Eric Bainbridge, *Untitled (Stepladder)*, 2006, teacups, saucers, and projector stand, 158 × 43 × 64 cm / 62¼ × 16⅞ × 25¼ in.

fig. 160: Eric Bainbridge, *Untitled*, 2006, concrete and found paintings, 30 × 60 × 60 cm / 11¾ × 23⅝ × 23⅝ in.

fig. 161: Joseph Beuys, *Earth Telephone*, 1968, telephone, cords, earth, and grass on wood board, 20 × 76 × 69 cm / 8 × 29⅞ × 27 in.

fig. 162: Eduardo Chillida, *Modulation of Space I*, 1963, iron, 54.6 × 69.8 × 40 cm / 21½ × 27½ × 15¾ in.

fig. 163: *RIG: untitled; coils*, 2011, steel bracket and tape, 480 × 230 × 200 cm / 189 × 90½ × 78¾ in. 2011; installation view, *Phyllida Barlow: RIG*, Hauser & Wirth Piccadilly London, 2011

fig. 164: Henry Moore, *Half-Figure*, 1929, cast concrete, 42 × 27 × 19.5 cm / 16½ × 10⅝ × 7⅝ in.

fig. 165: Henry Moore, *Upright Internal/External Form*, 1952–3, plaster cast with surface colour, 201.5 × 68 × 75 cm / 79⅜ × 26¾ × 29½ in.

fig. 166: Installation view, *Louise Bourgeois: Sculptures*, Peridot Gallery, New York, 1950

fig. 167: *untitled*, 1963, modelled plaster, 122 × 91 × 61 cm / 48 × 35⅞ × 24 in.

fig. 168: *Boxes*, 1968, 27 plywood boxes, each 30 × 30 × 30 cm / 11¾ × 11¾ × 11¾ in.

fig. 169: *Eleven Pieces* (detail), 1968–9, pigmented resin, fibreglass, plywood, and hardboard, dimensions variable

fig. 170: *Touchpiece*, from the *Nightworks* series, 1982–3, upholstery foam, paint, paper, canvas, wood, rope, and rubber, 40 × 30 × 30 cm / 15¾ × 11¾ × 11¾ in.

fig. 171: *Touchpiece*, from the *Nightworks* series, 1984, upholstery foam, paper, canvas, wood, rope, rubber, and paint, 20 × 50 × 30 cm / 7⅞ × 19⅝ × 11¾ in.

fig. 172: *TORSO*, 1986–9, glass, polythene, and Sellotape, 30 × 42.5 × 20 cm / 11¾ × 16¾ × 7⅞ in.

fig. 173: Louise Bourgeois, *Rondeau for L*, 1963, bronze, 27.9 × 27.9 × 26.7 cm / 11 × 11 × 10½ in.

fig. 174: *Clench*, 1989, bitumen and canvas, 20 × 30 × 50 cm / 7⅞ × 11¾ × 19⅝ in.

fig. 175: Louise Bourgeois, *Nature Study*, 1984, red wax over fibreglass with aluminium, 76.2 × 48.3 × 38.1 cm / 30 × 19 × 15 in.

fig. 176: *Object for an ironing board*, 1994, blanket wood frame, wool, mixed threads, and ironing board, 60 × 170 × 150 cm / 23 ⅝ × 66 ⅞ × 59 in.

fig. 177: *Object for street furniture*, 1999, blanket, and paint, 90 × 200 × 200 cm / 35⅜ × 78¾ × 78¾ in.

fig. 178: see **fig. 13**

fig. 179: see **fig. 92**

fig. 180: Installation view of work by Vincent Fecteau, *Sculptural Acts*, Haus der Kunst, Munich, 2011

fig. 181: Louise Bourgeois, *Red Room (Child)*, 1994, mixed media, 210.8 × 353 × 274.3 cm / 83 × 139 × 108 in.

fig. 182: Louise Bourgeois, *Red Room (Parents)*, 1994, mixed media, 247.6 × 426.7 × 424.1 cm / 97½ × 168 × 167 in.

fig. 183: Louise Bourgeois, *Passage Dangereux*, 1997, mixed media, 264.1 × 355.6 × 876.3 cm / 104 × 140 × 345 in.

fig. 184: Louise Bourgeois, *Precious Liquids* (interior detail), 1992, wood, metal, glass, alabaster, rubber, fabric, embroidery, water, and electric light, 425.4 × 445.1 × 445.1 cm / 167½ × 175¼ × 175¼ in.

fig. 185: Louise Bourgeois, *In and Out*, 1995, metal, glass, plaster, fabric, and plastic; cell: 205.7 × 210.8 × 210.8 cm / 81 × 83 × 83 in., plastic: 195 × 170 × 290 cm / 77 × 67 × 114 in.

fig. 186: Joel Shapiro, *Untitled*, 1986, plywood, cherry, maple, and oil paint, 165.1 × 139.7 × 157.5 cm / 65 × 55 × 62 in.

fig. 187: Installation view, *Joel Shapiro*, Nasher Sculpture Center, Dallas, 2016

fig. 188: Joel Shapiro, *20 Elements*, 2004–5, wood and casein, 307 × 3 × 335.3 × 215.9 cm / 121 × 132 × 85 in.; installation view, *Correspondences 03. Jean-Baptiste Carpeaux/Joel Shapiro*, Musée d'Orsay, Paris, 2005

fig. 189: Joel Shapiro, *Untitled*, 1980, wood and oil paint, 21.6 × 43.2 × 9.2 cm / 8½ × 17 × 3⅝ in.

fig. 190: Installation view, *Joel Shapiro: Works in Wood and Works on Paper*, Texas Gallery, Houston, 2008

fig. 191: Joel Shapiro, *Twenty-Six*, 2005–8, wood and casein, 172.1 × 152.4 × 137.2 cm / 67¾ × 60 × 54 in.

fig. 192: Joel Shapiro, *Untitled*, 1979, wood and white primer, 24.1 × 7.6 × 17.8 cm / 9½ × 3 × 7 in.

fig. 193: Olga Jevrić, *Weaving through Space*, 1969/1978, ferric oxide, iron, 41.5 × 18 × 21 cm / 16⅜ x 7⅛ x 8¼ in.

fig. 194: Sculptures by Olga Jevrić at Heritage House art storage, basement of the Svetozar Marković University Library, Belgrade, 2019

fig. 195: David Smith, *The Letter*, 1950, welded steel, 95.3 × 63.5 × 30.5 cm / 37½ × 25 × 12 in.

fig. 196: *No Title*, 1963–4, timber frames, wire netting, and plaster

fig. 197: David Smith, *The Sitting Printer*, 1954–5, bronze, 221 × 40 × 43.2 cm / 87 × 15¾ × 17 in.

Editor: Sara Harrison
Publisher: Michaela Unterdörfer
Managing editors: Jennifer Magee and Stefan Zebrowski-Rubin
Editorial support: Rosa Bacile, Elly Hawley, and Sophie Treharne Nurse
Project assistants: Mélanie Letoré, Courtney Meier-Neal, Nicolas Ochart, and Charlotte Riedel

Book design and typography: Elizabeth McLean
Copy-editing and proof-reading: Tas Skorupa
Image assets: Rosa Bacile
Pre-press: LUP AG, Cologne
Production coordination: Christine Stäcker
Printing: Offsetdruckerei Grammlich GmbH, Pliezhausen
Binding: Idupa Schübelin GmbH, Owen

Cover Paper: Munken Polar Rough, 300 g/m^2
Paper: Munken Polar Rough, 90 g/m^2
Typeface: Joanna

Additional courtesy credit is also due to the following institutions and photographers:
figs. 23, 157: Henry Moore Institute (photo: fig. 23, Jerry Hardman-Jones); figs. 33–7, 41, 87, 142, 144, 152, 162: © Tate; fig. 46: The Estate of Gordon Matta-Clark and David Zwirner; figs. 48, 93–6: Serpentine Gallery (photos: Andy Keate); fig. 49: Migros Museum für Gegenwartskunst (photo: FBM Studio); figs. 50–1: BAWAG P.S.K. Contemporary (photos: Oliver Ottenschläger); fig. 52: Kunstverein Nürnberg – Albrecht Dürer Gesellschaft (photo: Stephan Minx); figs. 56, 107–8: New Museum (photos: Benoit Pailley); figs. 57–8, 111, 124, 128: Ludwig Forum für Internationale Kunst (photos: Carl Brunn); figs. 63, 182–5: Haus der Kunst (photos: fig. 63, Wilfried Petzi; figs. 182–5, Maximilian Geuter); figs. 64–6: Des Moines Art Center, Des Moines, Iowa (photos: Paul Crosby); figs. 67, 112: Carnegie Museum of Art, Pittsburgh, Pennsylvania (photos: fig. 67, Melissa MacRobert; fig. 112: Greenhouse Media); fig. 68: Norton Museum of Art, West Palm Beach, Florida (photo: Lila Photo); figs. 74, 187: Nasher Sculpture Center, Dallas, Texas (photos: Kevin Todora); figs. 75–6: The Fruitmarket Gallery, Edinburgh, UK, 2015 © The Fruitmarket Gallery

(photos: figs. 75–6, Ruth Clark); figs. 77–8, 120: Kunsthalle Zürich (photos: Annik Wetter Photographie); figs. 79–80, 121–3, 126–7: British Council (photos: Ruth Clark); fig. 81, Jupiter Artland, Edinburgh (photo: Allan Pollok-Morris); fig. 82: © Friends of the High Line, courtesy the High Line (photo: Timothy Schenck); figs. 84–5: Royal Academy of Arts (photos: Simon Neal); fig. 86: Artangel (photo: Parisa Taghizadeh); fig. 88: Whitechapel Gallery Archive © Whitechapel Gallery; fig. 92, 179: BALTIC Centre for Contemporary Art (photo: fig. 92, Colin Davidson); fig. 97: The Russian Club Gallery; fig. 125: New Art Centre, Wiltshire; fig. 129: John Hansard Gallery; figs. 47, 143, 145, 147, 150–1, 166, 175: the Louise Bourgeois Studio (photos: figs. 47, 147, Christopher Burke; fig. 143, Marcus Leith; fig. 145, Rafael Lobato; figs. 150, 175, Allan Finkelman; fig. 151: Peter Moore; fig. 166, Aaron Siskind © The Easton Foundation); fig. 153: Karsten Schubert, London (photo: Peter White); fig. 154: Chapter Gallery; figs. 155–6: San Francisco Museum of Modern Art (fig. 155, purchase through a gift of Phyllis C. Wattis, photo: Ben Blackwell; fig. 166, photo: Ian Reeves); fig. 158: Tanya Leighton, Berlin; fig. 161: Glenstone Museum, Potomac, Maryland (photo: Tim Nighswander / Imaging4Art.com); figs. 164–5: Henry Moore Foundation; fig. 180: Galerie Daniel Buchholz Cologne/Berlin (photo: Wilfried Petzi); fig. 186: Paula Cooper Gallery (photo: James Dee); fig. 188: Musée d'Orsay (photo: Sophie Boegly); figs. 189, 192: Lévy Gorvy (photos: John Berens); fig. 190: Texas Gallery; fig. 191: Pace Gallery (photo: G. R. Christmas); figs. 193–4: Courtesy of PEER (photos: fig. 193, Rosa Harvest; fig. 194, © Ingrid Swenson); fig. 195, Munson-Williams-Proctor Arts Institute © bpk / Munson-Williams-Proctor Arts Institute / ProLitteris; fig. 197, Storm King Art Center, Mountainville, NY (gift of the Ralph E. Ogden Foundation, photo: Jerry L. Thompson)

Additional photography:
figs. 6–9, 13, 109, 178: Martin Orpen; figs. 17, 38, 69–73, 90, 110, 115–19, 130–40: © Alex Delfanne, all rights reserved; fig. 18: Mike Bruce; fig. 24: Stefan Altenburger Photography Zürich; figs. 53–5, 98–106, 163: Peter Mallet; figs. 59–62, 83: Genevieve Hanson; figs. 148, 173: Christopher Burke; fig. 159: Cavendish; fig. 160: Miles Thurlow; fig. 181: Marcus Schneider

Cover Art: Film still from *PHYLLIDA*, directed by Cosima Spender, produced by Hauser & Wirth in association with Third Channel and Peacock Pictures

Library of Congress Control Number:
2021932799

Distribution:
Europe and the UK
Buchhandlung Walther König
Ehrenstrasse 4
50672 Cologne
Germany
Tel +49 221 20 59 6-53
Fax +49 221 20 59 6-60

All other territories
ARTBOOK | D.A.P.
75 Broad Street, Suite 630
New York, NY 10004
US
Tel +1 212 627 1999
Fax +1 212 627 9484

ISBN 978-3-906915-48-7
Printed and bound in Germany

Hauser & Wirth Publishers